Praise for *Think Like an Entrepreneur, Act Like a CEO*:

"Bev is the ideal ca[...]piration. She encourages and educates peop[...]udge and sometimes with a firm hand. But, either way, she gets people to where THEY want to go. She motivates them to be the best they can be at whatever career they choose. She also guides people seeking second and third careers in life. She works under the philosophy that it is NEVER too late."

— Thomas Hodson, Joe Berman Professor of Communication, Scripps College of Communication, Ohio University and General Manager of WOUB Public Media

"This phenomenal woman has blessed me with her knowledge and expertise to become a better manager and a better person. With this book she can do the same for you."

— Arlean Leland, Associate General Counsel, Civil Rights, Labor and Employment Law, U.S. Department of Agriculture

"Reading a career tip chapter by Bev Jones is like having a wise counselor with a gently authoritative voice sitting next to you offering the best advice that money can buy and that you can realistically follow. A pure pleasure."

—Ira Chaleff, author of *The Courageous Follower* and *Intelligent Disobedience*

"Bev is an amazing coach who reaches beyond promoting leadership and excellent management skills to help her clients understand that it's not just about success at work. She demonstrates that if you take care of yourself and your health and your family, and you work on bringing other people up along the way, it makes you a fuller, richer, better person. With this wonderful book, Bev brings her insightful coaching to a wide community, including you."

—Sherry Little, former Acting Administrator of the Federal Transit Administration, now Partner and Co-founder, Spartan Solutions LLC

"Career coach Beverly Jones will show you how to handle tricky challenges at work, make change your friend and, most of all, have the career you want and deserve."

— Richard Eisenberg, Work & Purpose Editor, Nextavenue.org

"Bev is an expert coach and a fine teacher who can turn academic research into sound, practical advice. She is amazing, and we are excited about her book."

—Dr. Mark Weinberg, Founding Dean, The Voinovich School of Leadership and Public Affairs at Ohio University

"Bev is a great coach, and every page of her book is teeming with insight drawn from her path breaking career in industry as well as her steadfast support of hundreds of clients as a leadership, executive, and career coach. Whether you're a client or a coach, read this book and prepare to drink from a bubbling stream of sound advice and inspiration."

— Coach Dave Goldberg, President of ThreeJoy.com and coauthor of *A Whole New Engineer*

"Beverly's book offers practical insights and tips grounded in decades of experience. Her pragmatic, thoughtful observations and commentary will prove invaluable to young legal practitioners, government and corporate lawyers starting to step into leadership decision-making. Her sage counsel and coaching will help make them better stewards of the future."

— Michael J. Zimmer, senior attorney and ABA Energy and Environment Section Committee past chairman of two committees

50 Indispensable Tips to Help You Stay Afloat,
Bounce Back, and Get Ahead at Work

THINK

LIKE AN

ENTREPRENEUR,

ACT

LIKE A

CEO

BEVERLY E. JONES

Foreword by Kerry Hannon, author of *Great Jobs for Everyone 50+*

THINK LIKE AN ENTREPRENEUR, ACT LIKE A CEO
EDITED BY ROGER SHEETY
TYPESET BY KRISTIN GOBLE
Cover design by Rob Johnson
Printed in the U.S.A.

To order this title, please call toll-free 1-800-CAREER-1 (NJ and Canada: 201-848-0310) to order using VISA or MasterCard, or for further information on books from Career Press.

The Career Press, Inc.
12 Parish Drive
Wayne, NJ 07470
www.careerpress.com

Library of Congress Cataloging-in-Publication Data

CIP Data Available Upon Request.

To my mother, Lorna Jones, who continues to reinvent her career
as an artist at age 95.

ACKNOWLEDGMENTS

I am so grateful to my husband, Andy Alexander, for his support. Of course, it is wonderful to have a resident expert editor. Knowing that he has read every word of the book and given me a thumbs-up is great for my confidence level. More than that, the two of us always approach careers as a team effort, and I appreciate his years of patience and support for this project.

I'm also indebted to my friend and frequent brainstorming partner Kerry Hannon, who wrote the Foreword and shared "Love Your Job" tips. Kerry convinced me that writing a book can be fun and manageable, and then she taught me how to do it. Kerry also introduced me to freelance editor Debra Englander, who helped me find my agent and then did a preliminary edit of the book. As a first-time author, I needed a lot of guidance, and Kerry and Debby helped me stay on track.

I love the feeling of being supported by talented professionals. And it has been such a pleasure to work with an assured, straightforward, competent pro like my agent Cynthia Zigman at Second City Publishing Services. Thanks for sticking with me and getting the deal done, Cindy. I already have thoughts about the next project.

I might not have kept going on the book were it not for the years of encouragement—sometimes even the kindest possible nagging—from a long list of family, friends, and colleagues. Special thanks to Ira Chaleff, Bob Deans, Emily Emmett, and Merry Foresta, who were kind enough to read early versions of the proposal and encouraged me to keep going. Thanks, too, to Sherry Little, Andrea Wilkinson, Gayle Williams-Byers, Bruce Jones, and Libby Vick for being my faithful cheering squad.

Ohio University is my home town and a center of my still continuing education. I so appreciate the support and enthusiasm of many friends there, including: Jan and Tom Hodson and many of Tom's colleagues and fellow alumni of the Scripps College of Communication; Mark Weinberg and his team at the Voinovich School of Leadership and Public Affairs; and JR Blackburn, Ann Brown, Sue Chiki, and the rest of the OHIOWomen crew.

Many of my clients have been part of this process. I won't mention their names, and the book's anecdotes have been substantially changed to hide personal details. But you know who you are. I'm very grateful for all the suggestions for e-zines, blog posts, and book chapters. Thanks for your interest through the years and for so much enthusiastic support for this and other writing projects.

Finally, thank you Career Press, for your confidence and professionalism.

CONTENTS

FOREWORD

When I hear people grousing about their jobs or their boss, I want to holler: Suck it up! Do something about it. Stop being a victim.

In my books, columns, and speeches that I deliver around the country, I dole out job advice for all workers from 22 to 82 and beyond. It's about finding meaning and joy in the work you do every day. It's about feeling like you're relevant and making a difference.

My career advice runs the gamut from helping people make the most of where they are right now, to finding strategic ways to pivot to a successful career change, or developing a strategy to reenter the workforce after a job loss, or perhaps to land a part-time job to earn income in retirement to shore up financial security.

Sometimes, all it takes is making small changes to how we work or view our work to get our mojo going.

Regardless of our career stage, we all run up against difficult bosses, feeling stuck with no signs of promotion, and feeling like we have no work-life balance, bored, and burned out.

For nearly a decade, one of *my* trusted experts, who I have consulted for several of my books and columns, is Clearways Consulting career coach Beverly Jones. She's my sounding board and my guiding light on many career and workplace issues, particularly as they relate to workers over 50.

I've found Jones' advice to be practical, straightforward, and frankly, doable. It ranges from big-picture soul searching to seemingly simple moves someone can make to get unstuck, such as uncluttering his or her office.

One keystone of Beverly Jones' motivational and knowledgeable counsel to her clients is to know that you "own your career." And in her superb and enlightening book, *Think Like an Entrepreneur, Act Like a CEO*, she has woven her concise advice together to offer hope and help to all of us.

When you change your attitude to Me Inc. and think like an entrepreneur, instead of feeling like a cog in the wheel, you're the driver. You run your career like a one-person business. You accept that no one else is going to do it for you. "Most of our workplace blues comes from a sense of powerlessness," Jones says.

Not only can this shifting of your internal thinking help you navigate your current workscape, if you're job-hunting, it can also ramp up your chances of getting hired.

Here's why: An entrepreneurial outlook gives you confidence, swagger, autonomy, and choice.

It works. Having grown up in a household where my father ran his own business, I was encouraged to think like an entrepreneur and to always have freelance projects outside of my main job. As a result, I've always been nimble and not entirely dependent—even psychologically—on one boss.

I learned to view my primary employer as my "client." It's liberating, and it has helped me navigate my career path and remain resilient during rocky patches.

By addressing the tangible challenges workers face, Jones' compelling book proves that by squarely tackling these internal and external shifts, it's possible to find happiness and success in not only our working lives, but in our personal lives, too.

"Do something every day to work toward your goal," she urges. "Once you have some picture of where you want to go, get things moving by taking small steps toward that vision."

Jones' mantra: What really matters is that you do a little something on a regular basis.

As the saying goes, a journey of a thousand miles begins with a single step.

Think Like an Entrepreneur, Act Like a CEO starts your personal passage to a better working life. Read this book for the inspiration, guidance, and tools to help you discover smart ways to take control and get your career in gear.

Kerry Hannon, author of *Great Jobs for Everyone 50+* and *Love Your Job: The New Rules for Career Happiness.*

INTRODUCTION

As an executive coach, I know the path to professional success isn't what it used to be. In many ways that's good. Today, there are more professional opportunities available than ever before. But in order to reap the rewards and enjoyment from a successful career, you must know how to acquire the skills you'll need for your journey, how to manage yourself in unexpected circumstances, and how to roll with the punches.

For decades I've worked closely with high-achieving professionals and I've learned that you can't predict where your career path will take you. But you *can* prepare for it. You can learn smart workplace tactics and, at the same time, gradually build qualities that will bring you success.

For much of the 20th century, success seemed to be a matter of climbing onto the right organizational ladder and hanging on. Professionals were expected to be loyal and conform to institutional values. In exchange for loyalty, big organizations offered the promise of lifetime employment.

Now, the idea of spending your whole career in one place, keeping your head down, and continuing to do pretty much the same type of work seems quaint. Careers flow through many phases, involving numerous relationships, shifting skill sets, and startling change.

Your career is likely to include many jobs. Perhaps some will be full time and long lasting, whereas others could be short-term, freelance gigs. There may be times when you juggle several jobs or businesses at once. Sometimes your career may not involve paid work, but your professional growth will continue as you go back to school, volunteer, or take on a fellowship as a way to explore new directions. You'll be in charge of your career. Nobody else will guide it.

And as you move from place to place, you may find that workplace cultures vary widely, making navigating on the job more confusing than ever. For example, you may find yourself in a situation where dress is casual, hours are flexible, and the hierarchy is loose. But although things look informal at first glance, you soon have to decipher complex relationships and meet productivity expectations that are extraordinarily high but never actually defined.

The whole concept of "career" is different than it was in the last century. When I talk about your "career," I'm not just thinking of what you do at the office. Your career is no longer distinct from the rest of your life. It includes everything you do to stay in shape—physically, emotionally, spiritually, socially—in order to do your best work. Your career encompasses your learning experiences, from the books you read to your circle of friends, vacation pursuits, and community activity.

"Professional" is another word that has shifted meaning. The traditional professions included doctors, lawyers, architects, and other specially educated, licensed, and relatively well-paid experts. But now the definition includes anybody who is seriously engaged in meaningful, challenging work. Today's professionals are committed to building their skills and expertise, and maintaining quality and ethical standards, in myriad fields from IT to the culinary arts.

And whereas modern professionals still want to be compensated, they expect more from their work—they want to find meaning and fun on the job, and at the same time enjoy a richer, broader life.

To get what they wanted from their professional life, your parents needed to demonstrate loyalty. But what you'll need for *your* varied career is to be adaptable and resilient.

Professionals who are "adaptable" are able to put aside assumptions about their tasks, bosses, or clients, and try new strategies to achieve what they want. They are willing to be flexible, sometimes experimenting a bit as they tweak their performance or build stronger relationships with colleagues.

Career resilience means being able to anticipate risks and feel comfortable with change. Resilience involves limiting damage during turbulent times. It means knowing how to absorb hard knocks, to regroup, and to bounce back when the worst happens. It's the ability to start feeling better and bolster your confidence after a setback. It's remaining engaged in the midst of shifting challenges. Resilience brings security in a constantly changing world.

My observation from watching hundreds of adaptable, resilient careerists is that, regardless of where they work, most tend to be entrepreneurial thinkers. They are curious, open-minded, and skilled at spotting trends and turning them into opportunities. They resist the urge to be defensive or get bogged down in the past. Instead, they handle each challenge as it comes along and then quickly refocus on the future. They keep learning and building their social networks. And they are open to new ideas, agile in tumultuous situations, and willing to keep building social, technical, and managerial skills.

In addition, over the long haul, the most successful professionals act like savvy chief executive officers. They are quick to take responsibility and are always planning ahead. They share the praise and turn quickly to problem solving when things go wrong. They know their own value system and they organize themselves to live within it. And they listen to other people and are typically eager to support their success.

Adaptable, resilient people may not start out that way

Resilient people aren't necessarily born with a unique ability to be flexible, bounce back, or forge ahead. Often, they are ordinary folks who gradually learn behaviors, attitudes, and work patterns that allow them to adapt as needed.

I'm a good example of someone who started out as a risk-averse worrier, but through the years became more flexible. At the age of 20 I was looking for a secure job track. But as it's turned out, I've reinvented my career again and again.

As an undergraduate at Ohio University, I studied journalism and planned to become a reporter. Then I was sidetracked by student activism to promote equality for women. That led to work in the university's administration and, at the same time, I became the first woman in Ohio University's MBA program. Eventually, I was called upon to take a fresh look at the university's employment practices and create its first affirmative action program.

From there I went to Georgetown University Law Center, thinking I'd settle down on a secure career track as an attorney. After a brief stint at the Securities and Exchange Commission, I went to a series of Washington law firms where I discovered that, in private practice, lawyers must be entrepreneurs. It was particularly tough for women to develop a client base and step into firm leadership, and during my years as a young lawyer I had some tough lessons about bouncing back and forging ahead.

Eventually, I was hired by my biggest client, Consolidated Natural Gas Company, to take charge of public affairs and policy. The leaders of that Fortune 500 Company had great integrity and were good managers. I enjoyed my work and found satisfaction in fighting for issues like the development of alternative power projects.

I thought I was at CNG for life, but then a corporate merger changed my plans. My job suddenly disappeared. But I was fine. As a corporate officer I was well compensated with a severance package and I discovered that I'd finally outgrown the need for a job that seemed secure. I decided to create a new career built around the activities I enjoy the most.

I realized that throughout my various jobs I was always fascinated by mentoring younger colleagues and helping guide them into leadership. So I went back to school, including to Georgetown University's wonderful Leadership Coaching program. And now for more than a dozen years I've been working as an executive coach, consultant, and speaker. I've worked with thousands of people, ranging from graduate students and young professionals to leaders at the highest levels of government, academia, and corporate life.

I've had an opportunity to help clients become more adept careerists without having to learn all their lessons the hard way. I can watch close up as they practice thinking like entrepreneurs and acting like effective CEOs. And I've seen how it is possible for people to become increasingly comfortable with change while mastering strategies for a flourishing work life and professional success.

What would it take for *you* to think like an entrepreneur and act like a CEO?

You may think you don't have the power, direction, or energy to create your dream career. And maybe you've never found change to be easy. But when, challenge by challenge, you learn how to deploy a broader range of workplace strategies, you'll get better at entrepreneurial thinking and acting like a leader. As you maneuver and succeed in surprising circumstances, your confidence will grow, and so will your resilience.

This book is a practical guide to help you become more nimble in the workplace. It will teach you how to build career resilience by overcoming common predicaments and by capturing opportunities, one by one. Though it draws on recent research and the advice of experts, the book isn't a theoretical treatise or an academic study. And although I talk about my experiences and those of friends and clients, the book is really about *you*.

Every chapter offers you simple, actionable tactics for tackling a career question that may be keeping you awake at night. The detailed strategies will show you how to:

→ **Handle specific workplace challenges.** One by one, the 50 chapters will show you how to navigate tricky career situations. You'll find practical answers for questions such as how to respond gracefully to praise from the boss, how to get over it when you don't get that promotion, and how to soften the letdown that comes after you finish a big project. As you master challenges like these, one puzzle at a time, you'll expand your set of career survival skills. You'll become more skillful at shifting gears and forging ahead. And with time, your resilience will grow.

→ **Create your own go-to change process.** A key to being more adaptable is having a comfortable way to get started when it's time to make a career shift, particularly if you find change to be difficult. The chapters will also help you to develop your own approach for analyzing work-related questions and finding ways to move forward. They will encourage you to think about how success might look in the future. And they'll show you how to create an action plan that can move you toward that vision of success. When you have mastered simple and reliable approaches to sorting out problems and making a change, you can face almost any career challenge.

Through the years I've shared these strategies with countless clients, so I know they work. Each chapter will help you coach yourself through an immediate quandary while creating the skills and awareness that will make you unstoppable. My hope is that—whether you read the book from cover to cover, or pick and choose chapters as you need them—you'll find lessons for a career that takes you where you want to go.

Throughout the book you'll find true stories about real people. Sometimes, particularly when I talk about a client, I have changed personal details to preserve confidentiality. In that case, the person will be given just a first name, with an asterisk to serve as a reminder that the name and personal facts have been changed.

I know from long experience that you *can* create the kind of career you want, and I've written this book to help you succeed in the kind of work that you enjoy and find satisfying.

To Launch Something
New, You Need
a Good Plan

Your long and varied career is likely to include a series of new jobs and other fresh starts. In 2014, the median time workers had been with their current employer was 4.6 years, according to the U.S. Bureau of Labor Statistics. And even if you defy the odds and stay with the same employer for much of your work life, your positions will change; you'll take on new projects, clients, or assignments; and your entire organization could be repeatedly transformed.

What I learned from my worst first day at work

My worst first day was 30 years ago, but it remains a vivid memory. I was a few years out of law school and shifting to a new firm in the nation's capital. The title on my business card read "partner" instead of "associate," in recognition of the clients I was able to bring along with me.

On my first day, I arrived in a new suit, with an empty briefcase, eager to make a good impression in the Washington office of this Virginia firm. But the attorneys who had interviewed me were all out of the office that day, and nobody else seemed pleased to meet me.

I found my way to the most senior Washington partner and introduced myself. He was curt: "At the interviews they all thought you were so great, but frankly I don't see it. You're going to have to prove yourself before anybody here gives you work."

The first friendly word was from the kind firm administrator who took me to lunch and warned me about a few things. She told me that there had been controversy over my title. And she hinted that in this male-dominated firm, both attorneys and support staff would need some time to get used to the idea of working with a woman lawyer.

The cool welcome was a challenge, but the most uncomfortable part of the day was that I had absolutely nothing to do. Well in advance, I had caught up with work for the clients I was bringing with me. This was back before there was a Web to surf, and I struggled to look busy. Instead of hustling over the weekend to finish my client work, I should have prepared a long list of things to do.

That night, I called my father, holding back tears. To cheer me up, he described his experience with new jobs: "The first day is always the worst day. The first week is always the worst week. The first month is the worst month. And the first year is the worst year."

I don't buy into the pessimism embedded in Dad's view of new jobs. But in that case he was prophetic. Within days the partners who had hired me returned to the office and greeted me with enthusiasm. And in successive weeks, months, and years I found my niche in the firm and eventually felt fully accepted.

My immediate anxieties were eased when I connected with colleagues who were more welcoming than the ones I encountered on that first day. But my time at the firm improved largely because I learned a critical lesson on Day One: nobody else was in charge of making me successful. That was my job. I went to work on my second day with the beginnings of a plan for how I would keep busy, take care of my clients, find new ones, and market my services to other lawyers in the firm. I never again assumed that the leadership would carry the responsibility for my success.

How to get off to a great start

These days it's hard to imagine that any established business would make so little effort on employee orientation. Often, in a process human resource experts call "onboarding," organizations develop elaborate plans to ensure that a new hire can quickly get to know key insiders and stakeholders, learn about performance expectations, and become familiar with the internal culture. Leaders may work hard to help recruits get a feel for the environment and develop realistic expectations about their roles.

But even when you're supported by onboarding pros and a welcoming boss, you're wise to have your own plan for starting your new job or assignment. *Whether you are joining a different company, changing slots in the same outfit, or launching a new project, consider these tips as you lay out your plan:*

→ **Learn what your boss wants.** Initially, your manager may be vague about what she wants you to do. Of course, you should ask about your expected deliverables and the best way to report on your progress. But don't count on clear, complete answers. Be prepared to do some detective work. Observe how your boss interacts with her other direct reports, what she typically wants to know, and how she sends information up the line. Notice her schedule, like when she seems to catch up on e-mail or which days she tends to work late. Get a sense of what *she* must do in order to be successful, and look for ways to help. Study the organization's mission and consider how your contribution— and hers—fit within the big picture.

→ **Get to know people.** When managers and professionals run into trouble with new positions or projects, it's typically not because they don't have the technical skills. Rather, they are more likely to fail because they misunderstand the culture or don't establish working relationships with the right people. During your first months, be methodical as you reach out to teammates and others who seem to have information to share. E-mail them, saying, "Since I'm new to this role, I'd like to set up a little time to hear your perspective and learn more about your projects and background."

→ **Listen and learn.** When you meet your new colleagues, ask questions and really listen to what everyone says. Resist the urge to talk about yourself and your successes in the old job. Keep an open mind, avoid offering criticism before you understand the history, and be cautious about choosing sides among warring factions.

→ **Set short-term goals.** As you start to feel that your feet are on the ground, create realistic objectives for your first few months, then for the first year. Reconfirm your understanding of your boss's expectations, focus on areas that seem to be high priority, and identify some relatively easy near-term achievements. Don't try to do everything at once, but identify specific preliminary steps—like introductory meetings—to move you in the right direction.

→ **Do what you say you will.** One of the worst ways to start out is to create a trail of broken promises. Deliver on every commitment you make, no matter how small. For example, if you offer to make a phone call or send along information, do so immediately.

→ **Be on time.** A simple way to demonstrate respect and enthusiasm is to meet all deadlines and show up on time for every meeting and appointment. This can be more challenging than usual if you're following a different schedule and you're operating in an unfamiliar environment, but it's worth the extra effort.

→ **Adjust your attitude.** It's not unusual to experience a letdown soon after you start your job. Once you're beyond the excitement of the move, you may realize that not everything is meeting your expectations. If you start to feel that the honeymoon is over, it will be time to make an important choice. You can give in to your disappointment and become preoccupied with how they've let you down. Or you can choose to focus on the positive aspects of your situation and commit yourself to doing what it takes to reach your goals. This is a good time to remember that you're the CEO of your career, and it's your job to navigate the bumps and barriers.

→ **Give yourself four to six weeks to work like crazy.** There's no way around the intense upfront investment required to kick off something new. This can be exhausting and isn't the best way to live for the long haul. But be super focused and consider working at an unsustainable pace for a month or so. For this brief time, you'll keep your weekends pretty clear, postpone social obligations, and skimp on household chores. At the same time, set a deadline, clearly marked on your calendar, for when you'll pause and reassess your work style. Consciously add back the things you temporarily cut from your life, and tweak your goals from this point on.

→ **Manage stress.** Adjusting to your new assignment will undoubtedly produce moments of uncertainty that can lead to a high level of stress. Select a strategy for managing anxiety and include a fitness program. You may feel like you have no time to work out, but that's shortsighted. The time you spend on keeping your cool and boosting your energy is an investment in your success.

Even if you're a person who enjoys change, starting something new can be unnerving. But once you are comfortable with your approach for planning and launching a new gig, your transition will feel less daunting.

Start your plan here

To create a quick and easy plan for launching a new job, answer these five questions:

1) What is my job description?

2) What are my most important objectives for the first year, including the things my boss wants most from me?

3) Who are the people who will be impacted by my work, who can help me to be successful, or who have information that I need, and when can I meet with them for 30 minutes?

4) What are quick and easy wins, including meeting people and learning about the job, that I can deliver during the first three months?

5) What organizational, fitness, or other habits will help me to perform at my best during the first three months?

2

Think Like an Entrepreneur, Wherever You Are

When I was in my 20s, it never crossed my mind that I would run my own business like I'm doing today. Back then, I wanted job security. And I felt secure at big organizations with clear and enduring missions like the Securities and Exchange Commission, where I worked right after law school.

It was flattering to be recruited from the SEC to my first law firm. But when I first arrived, I missed the roadmap to promotion that had been so clear in a government job. Then when I watched more closely, I began to understand the "rules." At the law firm, the partners with power were the ones with their own loyal clients. So, I began recruiting clients, not at first realizing that I was in effect creating my own little enterprise.

When I saw the chance to quickly become a partner, I took my clients to another firm, the one I wrote about in Chapter 1. On that first day, I still was thinking of the law firm just as I would any other employer. But I was immediately forced to see how my arrival appeared from the firm's perspective. The partners didn't view me as an employee so much as a very small business to integrate into their operations. As a partner I was obligated to market my services, produce billable work, and bring in more money than the firm had to spend in order to pay me and cover my overhead.

I gradually realized that every organization of any significant size is a collection of smaller operations, all of which have to produce products or services that somehow support a shared mission. Years later, when I joined my largest corporate client as the public affairs executive, I understood that I had to think like an entrepreneur in order to find success and real security.

At Consolidated Natural Gas Company, a Fortune 500 utility conglomerate, I was brought in as a change agent. I had to reorganize or invent costly outreach services, like lobbying on national issues and helping communities through our foundation. In every budget cycle I had to sell the CEO and the board on my expensive programs, always explaining how they would support both the company's service mission and its bottom line.

By the time CNG disappeared years later through a merger, I had developed a sense of what it's like to invent a business. And I was ready to try on my own.

How to think like an entrepreneur

Before law school, I earned an MBA. I came away from business school with the impression that some folks are born with an entrepreneurial gene, but the rest of us just aren't cut out for creating our own thing. However, today's view is that entrepreneurship *can* be taught. And entrepreneurial literacy will contribute to your success, regardless of your field.

In recent years, countless universities have created programs dedicated to the new interdisciplinary academic field of entrepreneurship. They draw students, from engineering to the arts, who understand that they'll always need the knowledge, skills, and flexibility to easily redefine their jobs or even create their own enterprises.

The fascination with entrepreneurship isn't limited to undergraduate students. Journalist and career guru Kerry Hannon, who penned the foreword to this book, has written extensively about how entrepreneurial activity could be the next act for millions of Baby Boomers. She reports that a rising tide of people ages 55 or older want to keep working on their own terms, and at times that requires starting a new business.

But even if you don't expect to ever create a business, developing a more entrepreneurial *attitude* could bring new vitality to your existing job. You might start your mental shift by imagining how it would be possible to reinvent your current job, change career gears, or launch a business or nonprofit at some point in the future. When my clients try to envision a different path, it often changes the way they look at their current environment. They may develop a more adventuresome spirit, experience fresh insights about their work, or connect with people in new ways.

"Intrapreneur" is the newish term that some use to describe the employee of a large organization who acts like an entrepreneur. That might mean inventing something new without being asked, or accepting the task of turning a rough idea into a profitable, finished product.

However we label them, I particularly enjoy working with clients who start thinking more like entrepreneurs. Even during the roughest economic times they keep bouncing back, whether by renegotiating their job to meet a new need or heading out on their own.

You can start immediately to develop a more entrepreneurial approach to your work. *If you want to act like an intrapreneur, start here:*

→ **Know the mission.** Entrepreneurs tend to be passionate about their work. They set goals and they plan activities to support those goals. To be truly goal-minded, it's not enough that you understand your own objectives. You also should understand your organization's mission, the challenges it faces, and the way your contribution supports the collective strategy.

→ **Focus on the customer.** If you start a business, your customers will ultimately determine whether you succeed. Everything you do in a business must be focused on your customers. It's your job to know what they need, what they want, and what they think. And it's the same if you work in a large organization. Your success depends on the products and services you deliver to your bosses, your colleagues, and other "customers" as well. Ask yourself how you might better serve your current customers and look for ways to broaden your customer base.

→ **Understand business basics.** As a professional, you should be familiar with all the functions that make up a simple business. You need to be comfortable with commercial lingo and clear about how various businesslike activities are embodied in your organization, even if it's a government agency. Ask yourself: Do I have a mental picture of the operations that bring this outfit to life—everything from product development to budgeting, marketing, and sales? Do I understand the roles of support services like human resources and public affairs?

→ **Practice failure.** Successful entrepreneurs know that everyone has, and can learn from, false starts. When they experience a failure, they analyze what went wrong and apply the lesson to the next opportunity. There's a saying that "entrepreneurs fail their way to the top." But if you're used to success, you may become so afraid of failing that you won't take chances. This can stifle your inventiveness and limit your ability to collaborate and innovate. To mitigate your fear of failure, take up some activities where your success is *not* assured. For example, if you have no talent for dancing but your spouse loves it, sign up for a class. So what if you don't excel? The two of you will still have fun and you'll discover that it can be okay to not excel.

→ **Choose to be positive.** As we'll discuss in later chapters, the research is clear: you *can* learn to be more optimistic. Begin by noticing your own language, including the way you talk inside your head. If you are given to complaints, regrets, and self-deprecation, learn to let that negativity go.

→ **Build your brand.** Your "brand" is what you stand for, including your values, your personal characteristics, and the quality of your work. We'll describe in Chapters 4 and 5 how you already have a brand, but it may not be the one you want.

3

Listening Is Your Sure Fire, Go-to Career Strategy

In Chapter 1, we talked about how one of your most important strategies for launching a new job or assignment is to meet as many key people as possible and listen carefully when they're speaking. In fact, if I could magically give you one super career skill, it would be listening.

By "listening" I mean you not only shut your mouth long enough for the other person to talk, but you also shut down the voice in your head when it tries to tell you what to say next. You concentrate on the speakers, and you hear what they say even if it means you have to fight the urge to be defensive or interrupt.

Neuroscience and philosophers suggest that people go through life aching to have their concerns acknowledged and their presence felt. When you truly listen, you meet that need and connect with the speaker in a special way, even though it might not seem like it at the time.

Listening is so fundamental to human interaction that you can usually tell if a person is actually hearing you, or is just pretending. Research on "mindful listening" shows that speakers can sense whether the audience is paying attention or just waiting for their turn to talk. When you're really listening without passing judgment, you're more likely to be seen as genuine, charismatic, and even attractive.

Becoming a stronger listener is like building your physical strength. You build your listening "muscle" by noticing your reactions to a speaker and then putting them aside. For example, let's imagine your friend says, "You let me down." You instantly think, "That's not true!" But rather than butting in, you put that defensive thought aside and hear what else your friend has to say.

Then you could go further and encourage the friend by asking positively worded, open-ended questions. Instead of arguing, you might ask, "How might I have handled this in a more supportive way?"

You can sharpen your skill by practicing throughout the day in low-stress situations, such as conversations with a barista or sales clerk. For just a minute or two, give your normal concerns a rest and shift your focus to the needs and interests of someone else.

Great listening goes beyond hearing someone's words; it means noticing body language, facial expressions, and signs of emotion. It helps to be relaxed, so you might want to take a few deep breaths before starting a challenging conversation. A good way to begin a listening session is to summon up compassion for the speaker by imagining what it's like to see things from his or her perspective.

Times when exercising your best listening skill is a good strategy

If you want one essential ability to help you become more resilient, work on the habit of genuinely listening to other people. *Here are six situations where active listening is a particularly smart way to go:*

1) **When you're starting something new.** If you're joining a different team or meeting new people, it's tempting to talk a lot, to show off your expertise. Often, the better approach is to ask questions and demonstrate your strength by paying close attention to the answers.

2) **When you're a leader.** Listening is a core competency of leadership. You'll grow as a leader if you practice the discipline of letting others talk before you do. As your team members speak,

show that you're listening by nodding or restating a speaker's points. And find ways to let them know that you care about what they think, even though you may not always agree.

3) **When you're trying to make your case.** When we fall into debate mode during a meeting, we may ignore others' comments and obsess about the points we want to get across. Instead, it's more effective to understand our colleagues' goals and concerns so well that we can frame our suggestions with a minimum of conflict. Collaboration is a vital career skill, and it starts with appreciating the viewpoints of all the players.

4) **When you're in the middle.** Have you ever found yourself caught between two warring parties? You know it would be a mistake to take sides, but it can be a challenge to participate in meetings without seeming to align with one faction or another. The best approach here is to consistently present yourself as an open-minded listener. Let everybody know you're always willing to be fair and hear what folks want to communicate.

5) **When they're hard to get along with.** Once we start thinking of people as difficult, we may stop really hearing them. As they speak, we feel defensive and start working on our rebuttals. At some level they know we're ignoring them, so their obnoxious behavior gets worse. You can often defuse a tense situation by putting aside your resistance and concentrating on what is being said. By quieting your negative inner commentary, you may launch a new era of healthy communications.

6) **When you want to look confident.** When people feel insecure, they may chatter about nothing, brag too much, or insist their opinions are correct despite the weight of the evidence. Genuinely confident people aren't afraid to stay quiet. They already know what they think and now they want to know what you think. If you want to come across as self-assured, look for opportunities to shine the spotlight on others. Ask questions and be respectful of the answers.

Listening is a powerful strategy. It can help you understand what's happening, show that you care, and contribute to the growth of a supportive community.

4

Tweak Your Brand to Send Clear Messages

Do you feel squeamish when people start talking about "personal branding"? Maybe you think it means pretending to be something that you're not.

If that's your view of branding, get over it. There's the real you, the essential person that you are. And related, but not exactly the same, there's the professional. Your professional persona should be deeply rooted in your true values. But the person you are on the job is just a piece of your whole package.

Also, in your professional life—whether or not you know it—there's your personal brand. Your brand might be quite different from the essential you, and even the on-the-job you. Even if you don't want it or like it, you *do* have a brand. It's already out there, alive, and influencing the way people react to you.

Understand and shape your personal brand

Your brand distinguishes you from everybody else.

Originally, the word "brand" simply meant a name or symbol indicating the owner or producer of a product. For example, ranchers used hot irons to brand cattle so they could spot their own steers among the free-roaming herds. And back when soap was usually just called "soap," Pears Soap was named after the barber who invented a new kind of gentle cleaning bar.

Today, the term "brand" isn't the same as a brand name. In a "branding" effort, marketers try to distinguish a product, highlighting how it differs from its competitors. But the modern concept of "brand" is even broader than that, because it encompasses not just the qualities of products but also how customers *feel* about those products.

When we refer to a "brand," we're getting at something that reaches way beyond the actual product to include a full range of customer reactions. For example, the Coca-Cola brand reflects not just soft drink attributes and whether people like the taste, but also the emotional reactions customers might have to the happy messages in Coke commercials.

Your personal brand isn't the same as the real you, because it's defined partly by what people *think* about you. It's based on *their* assessments of your expertise, your work, and your character. Your brand is powerful enough to open—or close—career doors. But it might be quite different from either who you are or the high achiever you try to be when you're on the job.

In other words, even if you are a good person and you work hard, there's no guarantee that your brand reflects your best qualities and will bring you the career success you deserve.

This is a lesson that Sally* had to learn. She's a smart, tech-savvy, and collaborative project manager, but she'd been turned down for promotions. Beth, her manager, asked me to help Sally understand why she wasn't being taken seriously.

With Sally's permission, I spoke with some of her colleagues. Several described her as "a flake." Part of Sally's reputation was based on her appearance. She loves fantasy events and science fiction conventions, and sometimes she allowed weird fictional characters to influence her fashion style at work. Even worse, she bored colleagues by talking endlessly about the weekends she spent at shows related to her interests.

People liked Sally and found her amusing, but they thought her hobbies were silly. Sally's eccentric personal tastes had become such a big part of her brand that coworkers overlooked her strengths.

As we talked, Sally concluded that she didn't have to give up the things she loved to do in her free time. But she didn't want her passion for them to hold her back at work. ***So she launched a three-pronged plan to rebuild her brand within the company:***

1) **Manage appearances.** Sally aimed for a more mainstream personal style, so that her coworkers' reaction to her clothes and grooming wouldn't blind them to her competence. She began dressing more like her boss and she tucked her long hair into a neat French braid. She also stopped trying to interest work friends in her weekend activities.

2) **Build expertise and let it shine.** Understanding that it's not good enough to appear more like everybody else, Sally wrote a "brand statement" that described ways she wanted to be seen as unique. In particular, she hoped to be recognized for her technical abilities. She set the goals of becoming expert in a hot new technology and having her expertise recognized. She took an online course, kept studying and experimenting on her own, and published an article in an industry journal. As she learned more, Sally prepared a "how-to" guide for her colleagues and, with her characteristic enthusiasm, she said "yes" when they needed help.

3) **Show up like a leader.** Sally took a course that required her to start a leadership journal. As she wrote about the leaders she admired, she became more conscious of how she wanted to appear. She wrote a list of the leadership characteristics she most admired, looked at it frequently, and thought about it as she planned her participation in routine meetings. Visualizing the kind of leader she wanted to be helped her become more confident about her contributions and decisions.

Rather quickly, Sally changed her brand. Beth said other managers were talking about how Sally had "finally grown up." With her new, well-chosen expertise, Sally became known as an innovative thinker. Soon, she was assigned to a key project.

Try these strategies to manage your brand

To gain control of your brand, start with an honest assessment of how you come across. If you're creating impressions that don't serve you well, then it's your job to change them. ***If you're ready to do some rebranding, start here:***

→ **Research your current brand.** When marketers want to enhance a product brand, they may start with customer surveys. If you want a better sense of your brand, gather feedback from other people. On the job, this might take the form of a "360 review" in which your bosses, direct reports, and other colleagues are quizzed by a third party about your performance. A simpler approach is to ask colleagues how you might be even more helpful.

→ **Look in the mirror.** As Sally found, people are more likely to regard you as successful if you fit in with the crowd and look professional. Even in dress-casual offices, your aura of success is impacted by your personal style. People are influenced not only by how you put your look together, but also by the way you speak and carry yourself. If you feel that it's time for a make-over, find inspiration by looking around for people who appear energetic, polished, positive, and powerful.

→ **Promote your work.** It is not enough to build expertise and do good work. You need to share news about what you've been doing and learning. You could give speeches, write articles, or send out progress reports. Or you can show what you know in more subtle ways, such as offering your services to someone who needs your help.

→ **Shape your online presence.** The way you show up in an online search has become vital to your broader professional brand. When you meet someone for the first time, the person may have already Googled your name. You can't get around this by doing nothing. Your name is out there somewhere. An easy starting point for your online strategy is to create your profile on LinkedIn.com. If you can't bear to share, you don't have to complete the entire form. You can project your brand to the world simply by typing in a few sentences in the "Summary" section of LinkedIn's profile template.

Building your brand is the antithesis of being fake or manipulative. It's about becoming better attuned to how your work impacts other people, more aware of relationships, and more adept at understanding and displaying your inner self.

5

Start Now to Build Leadership into Your Brand

Lodged within your broader image is your brand as a leader. Your reputation as a potential leader may take years to fully develop, but it begins long before you manage a team or have a lofty title. Even when you're just starting out, your leadership reputation influences how much people trust you and whether they want to work with you.

It starts in small ways. You look like a leader any time you spot a problem, create a plan to solve it, and then execute your plan. You act like a leader when you treat other people with respect and you leave them feeling a bit more positive. And you can become known as a leader when you accept responsibility and follow through on what you promise.

As we discussed in Chapter 4, the full scope of your personal brand includes the impression other people have about you, from your clothes to your technical skills. The leadership component of your brand is particularly important because it's close to your core values. If you have a strong leadership brand, other people will have faith in your ability to deliver at a high level. Beyond that, when you're clear about the kind of leader you want to be, your own standards will help you to make decisions. And once you decide how you want to be known, it will be easier to focus on your highest priorities.

How to make leadership part of your brand

How people regard your potential to lead is a significant part of what makes you distinctive. Your particular aura as a leader may have a huge impact on the kinds of opportunities that come your way. *This four-part exercise can help you define and project a leadership brand that will serve you well:*

1) **Create your vision of leadership.** A simple way to create your vision of the leader you will become is to compile a list of personal qualities that you want to develop, and that you want others to see in you. Begin your vision by coming up with the names of leaders whom you admire; they could be teachers, bosses, or historic figures. When you've named three to five leaders, start your target list of personal qualities by asking yourself:

   ◆ What characteristics set these people apart?

   ◆ Which of these characteristics do I want people to use when they describe me?

   ◆ Which of these qualities sounds most like me when I'm at my best?

2) **Expand your vision list.** Review the following words and phrases that many people have used to describe effective leaders, and add to your own list any qualities that strike you as important:

   ◆ **Always growing.** The best leaders are constantly learning something new. It doesn't have to be job related. Your development as a leader is tied to your development as a person, and the growth areas you pursue in your free time can impact the way you show up on the job.

   ◆ **Self-aware and good at building relationships.** Research by leadership expert Daniel Goleman suggests that strong leaders are distinguished from the mediocre ones by their level of "emotional intelligence." And that means you have self-awareness, like noticing when you're too angry or distracted to handle a delicate matter. In his book *Social Intelligence*, Goleman says "we are wired to connect" with one another and by becoming more *self*-aware we get better at managing our interactions with others.

◆ **Positive.** A leader's attitude has an enormous impact on the team, and most people are more productive when they are around positive people.

◆ **Engaged.** To lead we must be actually focused on the people and activities around us. Other people can sense whether we tend to stay present in the moment, which can influence whether they see us as genuine and charismatic leaders.

◆ **Service oriented.** Leadership may begin with the feeling that you want to help others, perhaps by delivering what they need or helping them to succeed. The concept of "servant leadership" emphasizes attributes like kindness, trust, empathy, and the ethical use of power.

◆ **Well organized.** Good intentions aren't enough to deliver results. To achieve their goals, effective leaders develop work habits and systems associated with productivity.

◆ **Collaborative.** There's a big demand for people who can work well with others to achieve shared goals. One reason for this is that innovation is so often the outgrowth of a collaboration involving people with different views and skill sets.

◆ **Energetic.** To be at their best, leaders must manage not just their time but also their energy. This includes physical energy, which is linked to exercise, nutrition, and stress management.

3) **Study your vision list.** Now that you have a list of the leadership qualities you intend to develop, post it in a conspicuous place and look at it frequently, including each morning. Because we tend to remember pictures more easily than words, some people like to create an icon to represent the characteristics they're working on. Bill*, a client, came up with five attributes to define his

style of leadership. For each one he created a symbol—a simple picture—to capture a quality he wanted to develop. Because he's an avid biker and was training for a mountainous 100-mile ride, his symbol for "perseverance" was a triangle, representing a challenging mountain. Bill could glance at his sketch of those five icons and instantly recall the characteristics he hoped to develop as a leader. Eventually, to thank his wife for supporting his efforts, he had a jeweler find or create each of the icons in a charm. Then he was reminded of his growth path each time he looked at the lovely gold bracelet that his wife wore.

4) **Act this way.** A key to projecting your brand is identifying the attitudes and behaviors that will earn the reputation you want. Once your vision list is complete, a quick look will remind you of how to act. You might also consider a methodical way to practice the qualities on the list, one by one. If you're working on several characteristics, you might try a flavor-of-the month approach. Let's say you want colleagues to see you as reliable, creative, and positive. Go to your calendar and, for each of the next three months, choose one attribute to be your theme for the month. Now here is the most important part: If "be reliable" is your target for May, *commit to a specific type of behavior* to bolster your reputation for reliability. For example, you might plan to arrive right on time for every May meeting.

Your brand sets you apart from the competition. And your brand as a leader reflects and influences the way other people encounter your deepest values.

6

Power Up by Tweaking Your Personal Style

Did somebody tell you that if you work hard and do a great job, it won't matter what you wear to work? Sorry, that's just not the case.

The way you present yourself to other people has an impact on how they evaluate your accomplishments and potential. And your personal style—your clothes and grooming—makes a difference to the way you're perceived.

Obviously, your style is particularly important when you're job hunting or making presentations. Thinking about these occasions, I went to an expert, my sister, Libby Vick.

Libby spent 10 years in Washington politics and public relations, and for more than 20 years has been on the faculty at Northern Virginia Community College. In her business and professional communications classes, students of all ages and backgrounds explore how they come across on the job or in the job market.

Whether you're giving a speech or just trying to make a good impression, Libby says, "Your audience may focus less on your words than on your nonverbal message. In addition to things like posture and facial expressions, personal style is a part of that message."

Having a tasteful look doesn't require lots of money. Libby believes you can look smart whenever it's evident you thought carefully about how to put yourself together.

Women on a tight budget can still appear stylish. One approach that often works is to wear mostly black, or black and white. For men, dressing for success is both more flexible and more complicated than it used to be. A good tactic is to see how others dress and come up with a look that's a bit less casual than most guys in the group. But male or female, and whatever look you select, make sure your clothes are clean and pressed.

You'll feel better about yourself when you know you look good, and chances are you'll perform better as well. Libby says that in her early teaching days she didn't require students to dress up for presentations. Then she realized, "The speeches they give when they're wearing sweats to class are nothing like the speeches they give when they know they look good."

Libby says everything comes back to focusing on your audience and recognizing that all good communication is audience centered. So give some thought to messages you want to communicate and what your look will convey to the people you're trying to reach. If it's apparent that you made an effort, they may be more open to what you have to say.

Times to kick your style up a notch

Sometimes you feel too busy, tired, or disengaged to make an effort as you prepare for the workday. Losing interest in your appearance can be part of a downward spiral in your career. When that happens, a bit of a makeover might help you to break out of the funk.

Another time for a redo is when your career is on an upswing. A chic new look can be a subtle way to let the world know that you are on a roll. *And you may want to buff up your look when you:*

→ **Work with younger people.** If your wardrobe hasn't changed in years, they may assume that your mindset is back in the 90s, as well. Notice what your young colleagues are wearing and modify their choices to create a look that works for you. If you don't know where to begin, ask for advice from a fashionable friend, explore fashion blogs, or find a personal shopper.

→ **Work with older people.** It won't help your career if you look like a kid. Get rid of the flip-flops if your colleagues will think your informal dress suggests you don't mean business.

→ **Interact with clients or customers.** You won't make much of an impression if you're dressed like you don't really care. You'll be more credible if you look as if you considered all the details, including what to wear.

→ **Are giving a speech.** Libby says it's tougher than ever to make a presentation, what with audiences constantly yearning to check their phones. No matter how well you know your material, you'll lose your audience at the beginning if you look sloppy, uncertain, or unprepared. Dress up a bit in an ensemble that makes you look good, and you'll get off to a strong start.

→ **Hope to move up.** If you're eyeing a promotion, dress like you've already climbed the ladder. Instead of blending in with your peers, take a cue from your bosses, or their bosses, and dress as if you're one of them.

→ **Are seeking a new position.** In interviews, first impressions are critical. And people will register how nicely you've cleaned up, even before you open your mouth. Dressing conservatively is often the safest bet, but you'll also want to look like you fit in with the office culture. Being a little over-dressed is acceptable because it shows the interviewer how much you care.

→ **Want to avoid stereotypes.** My hip mother, Lorna Jones, passed her driving test at age 93. I asked if she'd been nervous about driving with a motor vehicle department official in her car, and she said it had been no problem because she was prepared. "I had my hair done and I dressed like a professional," she said. "After 80, if you dress casually or look untidy, people may assume you have dementia." When you look classy, folks are more likely to put their prejudices aside.

In a work setting, your personal image is part of your brand. It suggests something about how much you value the work, and how you expect others to treat you.

7

Talk Back to the Voice in Your Head

Throughout school there was a voice in my head saying, "If you don't study, you're gonna flunk." I've no idea where those words came from. My parents didn't pressure me about studying, but I heard the refrain every time I was tempted to skip my homework.

The voice seemed to fade away when I was an undergraduate, but it roared back when I entered Georgetown Law. I was excited to be in Washington and tempted by the leisure options, from museums to bars. That nagging warning, though, often kept me at my books. At times I even cranked up the volume, saying aloud to myself, "You're gonna flunk, you're gonna flunk."

After graduation, the message changed but the voice was more insistent than ever. During my early years in law, the message was often, "They aren't used to women here. You have to work harder than the men." The exhortations would wake me up in the middle of the night, and distract me in situations that should have been fun.

Eventually, however, I noticed that it wasn't the lawyers sitting longest at their desks who seemed to be getting clients. In a big "Aha!" moment, I saw that the tyrannical voice in my head could be wrong. Grinding out the written work mattered, but so did other activities, like building relationships. From then on, instead of always knuckling under, I practiced ignoring that voice, or even arguing back. When it told me to stay put, I might respond, "This dinner is a good opportunity and I'm going."

Then, as I summoned the courage to broaden my professional circle and pitch potential clients, I had to find ways to bounce back when people weren't responsive. I noticed that often, the worst part wasn't what *they* said—it was the scathing assessment from my inner voice. So I practiced ignoring messages like, "They'll never hire you," and told myself that disappointments are growth experiences. I would say to myself, "Okay, what did we learn here?"

Unlock new energy by managing your inner voice

Each of us has a repetitive voice in our head, commenting, warning, and judging. Sometimes the voice gets stuck in the past, perhaps returning us to moments that could have gone better. If the voice is preoccupied with things that could go wrong in the future, we call that "worrying."

Much Eastern philosophy explores ways to quiet the babble in your mind. Practices like meditation and prayer can help you stop listening to that tedious noise and become more in touch with a deeper, more connected you.

In the West, scientists have begun to understand the nature of our internal commentary, as well as the many ways it interacts with our physical health. It seems that the relentless voice in your head reflects not only your own past learning, but also the collective experience that you've soaked up from others. Some experts suggest that the voice evolved as a survival tool, and its incessant messages are rooted in ancient problems and dangers. At work, that voice can provide you with warnings and motivation.

When we're fully engaged in rewarding tasks, the voice may grow quiet. Too often, however, the whining monologue can become a nuisance, keeping us awake at night and subjecting us to needless worry. The voice can discourage us from taking risks, distract us from important work, and undercut our productivity.

The good news is that you don't have to let that negative self-talk exhaust you. **_Here are a few ways to break free from compulsive negative thought patterns:_**

→ **Just notice.** Simply observing _which_ thoughts tend to recur can help break their hold. Identify the niggling phrases that flow through your mind most frequently. Each time one returns, just observe it and try not to react. Remind yourself: It's just that old thought and I don't have to listen.

→ **Reframe them.** Make a list of your recurring negative thoughts. Draft a more positive alternative to each thought on your list. For example, if you keep thinking, "This job is boring," your rewrite might be: "Today, I will take one step to make this job more interesting." When the same old thought occurs, counter with the revised version. Repeat the reframed statement over and over. With enough repetitions, you can replace the old message with the more helpful new one.

→ **Name them.** You can get distance from recurring negative thoughts by putting a label on each thought pattern. For example, you might say to yourself, "That's just my Monday morning chatter," and let the babble go. Another technique is to visualize the narrator in your mind who is voicing the message. Then you may be able to dismiss your worries by saying, "Oh, that's just my Monday morning Grinch talking." I love Rick Carson's classic book, _Taming Your Gremlin_, which suggests that you imagine how your internal narrator may look. By picturing your nasty little gremlin, you weaken its power to badger you.

So much of building resilience and feeling more comfortable with manageable risk is a matter of getting out of your own way. A good starting point is simply becoming aware of the voice in your head and recognizing that you don't always have to listen.

8

How Do Other People Get Self-Discipline?

Do you know people who have so much self-discipline that it makes everything look easy? Does it sometimes feel like your career would take off if you had as much discipline as one of your colleagues?

That was the case with Doug*, an energetic communications and marketing consultant. He is an expert in his field and his charismatic personality helps him to attract more clients than he can easily serve. He has a strong team to share the work, but when we first spoke, Doug complained that he couldn't seem to get organized. He had so much going on that he couldn't keep track of the details. Opportunities would slip away when he failed to follow up, and he worried that his disorganization would result in a serious mistake.

Doug would invent reasonable processes for keeping track of prospects and client projects, and his team would adopt them. But then he'd create chaos by ignoring his own systems. He'd fail to report on his activity, forget about his promises, or reinvent a critical strategy without sharing the plans.

"The problem is I just wasn't born with enough self-discipline," Doug said. "It's easy for people like my assistant Jane, who's methodical but not so creative, but I'm a different kind of person. So how do I get more control?"

It is true that some people, like Jane, are naturally methodical planners, whereas others, like Doug, are more spontaneous. But, by definition, self-discipline isn't easy for anyone. A common definition is that self-discipline is "the ability to motivate oneself in spite of a negative emotional state." In other words, self-discipline is about making yourself do things you don't feel like doing.

And there's no single strategy for boosting your level of self-discipline. One reason is that this elusive quality can take many forms. Sometimes it's about avoiding immediate gratification in order to obtain a greater benefit, like when you quit smoking. Another type involves doing something you don't enjoy in order to achieve a goal, like running every morning so you can lose weight.

But you *can* develop more self-discipline if you want to. As I explained to Doug, building your self-discipline is rather like building your body. Even if you're very weak, you can start today to build the strength of your muscles, one by one, and with time you'll increase your level of fitness. In the same way, you can start now to strengthen your self-control "muscles." By working on them a little bit every day, you'll gradually develop more discipline.

You *can* increase *your* self-discipline

As a young professional, Doug loved deadline pressure and was proud of his ability to respond to client emergencies. But the cowboy style that worked when he was a sole practitioner wasn't effective when he was trying to lead a dozen people. He began to see how one of the most important qualities for career success, and for joy in life, is self-discipline. He stopped scoffing at research that suggests people with self-control are happier, better able to handle stress, and more likely to reach their goals.

More important, Doug discovered that self-discipline is a *learned* behavior. It is something you can work on, issue by issue, day by day, freeing you from considerable anxiety and wasted time.

Self-discipline looks different for different people. For Doug, it began with a new practice of writing things down. At first, he started writing for 10 minutes each morning, planning out his day. When that habit seemed firm, he began carrying around a notebook for capturing everything from phone messages to commitments he made to clients.

Try this plan for building your self-discipline

The people who stand out in a competitive environment show up on time, meet deadlines and commitments, take on the tough issues, and do everything they promise. To be that kind of person requires self-management. *If you're ready to build your discipline muscle, begin with this 10-point plan:*

1) **Start with a goal.** Is there something that you would like to do, if only you had the discipline to do it? Let's say, for example, that you think your job would flow more smoothly if you could get to work on time. Decide upon a manageable goal and express it in specific terms, like "I will arrive at work by eight o'clock every day for two weeks."

2) **Visualize what self-discipline would look like.** Identify the steps that could help you achieve your goal if you did, in fact, have the necessary discipline. To reach the office on time, would you turn off the TV and go to bed earlier? Lay out your clothes the night before? Fill up your gas tank during the weekend?

3) **Choose discipline.** Once you have a detailed vision of how you would act if you did have the discipline, start choosing to act like that. The opportunities to practice will take the form of a series of small decisions, like whether or not to turn off the TV at bedtime even if something good is on. Each time you meet the challenge of choosing self-discipline, you'll be exercising your self-control muscles.

4) **Write it down.** Keeping some form of log or diary is tremendously reinforcing and can help you to gradually build your self-control. Once you've identified the decisions that will help you get to work on time, keep track of how often you make the right choice.

5) **Reject excuses.** When you're trying to practice discipline, there's a danger you'll be defeated by the voices in your head. Notice when you're tempted by internal arguments such as, "I'm too tired to get organized tonight." Simply by becoming aware of how you rationalize will help you to grapple with temptation and keep you moving toward your goal.

6) **Encourage yourself.** Make a list of the excuses that typically prevent you from acting like a disciplined person. Then, for each one on your list design a positive phrase to help you get past that

excuse. For example, if your inner voice says "I don't have the energy," tell yourself, "I'll have more energy tomorrow if I get to work on time."

7) **Remove temptation.** It's so much easier to be disciplined when your temptations are out of sight. If late night TV is what's keeping you from getting a good night's sleep, can you move the screen out of your bedroom? Or hide the remote in another room?

8) **Acknowledge the difficulty.** Supervising your own behavior can be exhausting. In other words, we can exercise self-discipline only so much and for only so long, and then we're too tired to do more. So when you're trying to change, recognize the challenge and build your muscle in small increments.

9) **Reduce the pain by creating habits.** When you're working on a new behavior, the first few days are the toughest. But repetition quickly makes it easier. You start going to bed on time without having to agonize about it. As your new nighttime ritual becomes a habit, choosing it won't be so tiring. Soon you will free up your reserve of self-control for another challenge. So after you start getting to work on time, you might turn your attention to something else, like working on your "to-do" list.

10) **Reward yourself.** Positive reinforcement works. Support your change process by finding little ways to reward yourself when you do well.

As you move through the plan, play with the process. See what works for you. Treat setbacks as learning opportunities. Building self-discipline can become a game, with moments of fun and victory parties along the way.

9

How and Why to Keep Smiling

There still are scientists who claim that humans are the only animals who can smile. I don't believe that.

Daisy, our yellow lab, has a killer smile. As she establishes eye contact, her mouth drops open and the corners turn up, wider and wider. When she gives my husband, Andy Alexander, her love gaze, his big grin mimics hers. The two of them may briefly freeze like that, with locked eyes and happy faces. At other times, Daisy's smile overtakes her body and—still looking Andy straight in the eye—she gyrates with pleasure, from her wagging tail and wriggling butt to her vibrating shoulders.

I've noticed that simply by describing a Daisy smile, I can trigger an intense answering smile on Andy's face. Because he frequently travels, on occasion I'll describe her smile as we chat on the phone. In my mind's eye, I see his face light up at just the thought of Daisy's happy look.

Although there's disagreement about the validity of canine smiles, it's widely known that the human smile is contagious. Dale Carnegie wrote about that back in 1936 in his immensely popular book *How to Win Friends*

& Influence People. In its section on "Six Ways to Make People Like You," Principle 2 was just one word: "Smile."

Carnegie said, your smile "is a messenger of your goodwill" and a simple way to make a good impression. He advised readers to smile even when they don't feel like it, because action and feeling go together. If you smile you'll feel happier, and those around you may as well.

Reasons why smiling is still a good strategy

In the roughly 80 years since Carnegie drafted Principle 2, psychologists and other scientists have undertaken countless studies of the human smile. It seems that the phenomenon is more complicated than Carnegie suggested. For one thing, your smile and the message it carries are shaped partly by your culture. For example, in the American South people smile more often, and to stone-faced Northeasterners, their friendly demeanors may come across as fake. Also, immediate circumstances can shift the way your expression is interpreted. Normally your smile is positive for the person who receives it. But if you walk around with a big grin after you get the plum assignment, it might get under your office rival's skin.

Despite the complexities, however, modern research affirms that "Smile!" is often excellent career advice. ***Here are some why's and how's of smiling:***

→ **It's healthy and feels good.** Smiling can increase the release of endorphins and other mood-enhancing hormones. It can calm your heart rate and blood pressure, contribute to a heightened sense of well-being, and lead to improved health. Smiling can help you release tension and work-related stress with an impact so profound you may experience it at a cellular level.

→ **You'll look good.** When you smile, there's a better chance other people will perceive you as competent, attractive, likable, and memorable. They are also more likely to find you approachable and see you as trustworthy. And they'll think you look younger. On top of all that, the odds are better that they'll remember you the next time you meet.

→ **It's contagious.** We are hardwired to mirror each other's happy looks. When you smile at colleagues or clients, they may automatically return your expression. More importantly, as you exchange smiles with another person, the two of you connect in a more fundamental way. They actually experience the positivity underlying your smile and, as a result, could be more satisfied with your conversation.

→ **It spreads.** If your smile makes a team member feel good, his mood will improve and he'll be more likely to smile at the next face he sees. The wave of good feeling can become viral, moving from one person to another. The culture of your whole team can be improved by the addition of just one member who often smiles.

→ **Even fakes work.** The most powerful smiles are genuine, emanating from deep within you. But social smiles—those that require some effort on your part—are effective as well. And they can start a virtuous cycle. If you struggle to smile, but then I smile back, you will respond to my facial expression. Soon your tentative smile can become heartfelt.

→ **You can get better at it.** The more you practice a positive expression, the more likely it is that you'll experience spontaneous smiles. The trick is to start your smile from the inside, by thinking about something that makes you feel good. Simple techniques include summoning up the image of a loved one, or remembering a particularly happy event.

If you smile more regularly, your new habit can retrain your brain to see the world in optimistic ways. The more you smile, the more you'll escape the natural tendency of humans to focus on threats and other negativity. Your shift to thinking positively might boost your creativity and help you to be more productive.

An excellent way to support the habit of smiling more often is to consciously begin each morning with a smile. When you first wake up, summon up a happy thought and practice your best grin. Then your smiles may come more easily for the rest of the day.

10

The Real Meaning of "Networking" May Surprise You

While working with clients, I've often wished for another word for "networking." Too often, the term seems to suggest a disingenuous glad-hander, talking too much and passing out business cards to uninterested bystanders.

That's the image that seemed to hit Jack* when we spoke about ways he could lay the groundwork for a job transition. When I mentioned the benefits of expanding his network, Jack grimaced and said, "I don't believe in that kind of thing. I've already got some real friends, and I'm not going to go to boring industry events just so I can try to make some fake ones."

Your "network" is a vital, lifelong resource

Your "network" is a complex pattern of interconnecting relationships with other people. You might visualize it as a series of concentric circles, spreading out from you like a spider's web:

→ **Circle #1:** In this innermost ring are your best friends and closest family. Many people, particularly introverts, prefer to spend much of their time here. But even dear friends move away or change directions. So one reason to stay engaged with other circles is to recruit additional folks to join you here with your home tribe.

→ **Circle #2:** Beyond your core group are newer friends, as well as people you've known for a long time but don't see so regularly. Here you might include coworkers, neighbors, and friends of close friends. If you don't make an effort to stay in touch, it is all too easy for members of this crowd to drift out of your orbit.

→ **Circle #3:** This large group could include dozens, hundreds, or even thousands of acquaintances from through the years. Among them are kids you went to school with, coworkers whose faces look familiar in the corridors, the members of your yoga class, and neighbors you wave to when you're out walking. They might also include people you've never actually seen, like your social media buddies, or colleagues with offices on the other side of the world. When you start thinking about Circle #3, you might find it to be a rich source of professional contacts with whom you're seldom in touch, but could be.

→ **Circle #4:** Your network expands considerably when you include people with whom you simply share a community. Maybe you've never met them, but you certainly could, because you hang out in the same places, belong to the same organizations, went to the same college, or work in the same field. You have something in common with each of these people, regardless of whether you've met or not.

Each of your Circles has a special role to play. For example, when you're seeking clients or a new job, you might wish to focus your efforts on #3. That's because the folks in #1 and #2 hear much the same news you do. Even if you're not on a job hunt, Circle #3 can be a source of support. Leadership can be lonely, and approaching your work with a spirit of self-determination can be isolating, but you'll feel less alone if you connect with your professional peers.

It's hard to overestimate the value of all these various relationships in your career and your life. In all four of your Circles you can find people who will give you advice when you need it, and join the party when there's something to celebrate. They are a source of career intelligence and many will reach out to help, even though they don't yet know you well.

So networking is not about superficial glad-handing. It means expanding your web of connection, thinking about other people, and caring for human relationships with the potential to support you in every phase of your life. And it isn't something you do in a panic, when it's time to shift jobs. You can build networking into your normal life.

Don't wait until a crisis to care for your network

When Jack* asked me to coach him in preparation for a job change, I knew he needed to discover how his social network could help. As things turned out, it did take Jack a while to build the momentum for his search. And then, unexpectedly, he decided to stay where he was, because his employer restructured his role.

Although he no longer was working toward a career shift, Jack elected to keep building his Circles anyway. He had come to understand how hard it is to overcome a neglected network. And, to his surprise, he'd found networking to be fun. Jack became active in an industry organization and joined a hiking club. Most importantly, he made the effort to develop deeper relationships with a number of colleagues and neighbors.

On the other end of the spectrum was Paul*, who spoke fondly of his network and seemed to treat it like a living creature. I knew that, without my prompting, Paul would open his job hunt by working his expansive Circles. He was well prepared because he'd spent years not only meeting more people, but also building on the many relationships he already had in place. *As Paul understood, there are two important ways to tend to your network:*

1) **Keep it growing.** Collecting more contacts is what people often mean when they speak of "networking." To count, this requires forging a small connection with another person. It's not enough to just hand your business card to strangers. You have to look them in the eye, find something in common, and perhaps make it into their address book.

2) **Build on what you have**. Networking isn't just about encountering new people. Also important is staying connected with the ones you already know. Because my savvy client Paul understood this, he could rely upon a valuable resource for his career quest.

A naturally kind guy, Paul's routine style was to mentor young colleagues, reach out to people feeling left out, and set up lunches with old friends who acted too busy to plan for staying in touch. Paul was always willing to help, and so, when he needed help, he had a long list of professional contacts who were happy to return the favor.

Building and caring for relationships isn't something you can do in a rush. It's a gradual process that you can actually enjoy as you fold it into your regular life. And if you keep up the cadence of your networking, you're unlikely to find yourself alone in a crisis.

Try these ways to nurture your network

In a political, career-focused city like Washington, watching the many styles of successful networkers can be fascinating. Some of the more conspicuous are born extroverts, thriving in a crowd and always eager for the next party. And some of the more successful are people who have been described as introverts— like Barack Obama, Hillary Clinton, and Laura Bush—whose well-planned social outreach helps them create resilient support systems.

If you want to become a more adept networker, test a variety of techniques and find ones that are comfortable and effective for you. *To get started, try these strategies for developing new contacts and deepening existing relationships:*

1) **Be helpful.** The essence of networking is exchanging help and support with other people. In a brief meeting, you might simply offer a smile or a kind word to another person. A key principle is to remain alert to small, easy opportunities to add value. Try these ways of being helpful to the people you know:

   ◆ **Make matches.** Become known as a "connector" by matching needs and resources and making helpful introductions. Perhaps you meet someone who is moving to a new city and you have a friend who has lived there forever and is always looking for volunteers for his nonprofit. By making an e-mail introduction, you can help two people at once.

   ◆ **Show up.** If somebody you know is giving a speech or planning an event they regard as important, work hard to be there. They may always remember that you made the effort.

♦   **Cheer.** If an acquaintance does something well, let them know you noticed and offer congratulations. Don't be afraid to show your affection and be willing to share in the excitement.

♦   **Notice rough patches.** If you see that somebody has hit hard times, don't wait for them to call you. Assume that they would be around if you were in need and reach out.

♦   **Volunteer.** There is no better way to get to know people than to work with them. So to break into a group, look for a chance to help with their project. This might mean offering to join a committee at work, or looking around for non-profit groups that make a contribution in your community.

2)   **Be in the moment.** You may have casual contact with many people throughout each week. But if you're like most folks, in some interactions you're not actually paying attention. Instead of listening, maybe you're thinking about what you want to say next. Or perhaps you're worrying about another project altogether. Get more from your routine conversations by working harder to focus. In each brief encounter with a casual acquaintance, shift all your attention on the other person. Instead of spending more *time* on networking, spend more *energy*.

3)   **Network everywhere.** When you're in networking mode, it makes sense to vary your normal patterns and attend a wider variety of gatherings. But don't think of networking occasions as special events that you attend once in a while for that single purpose. Successful networkers get around a lot, and they engage with others wherever they go. Every time you are out and about, whether it's at a PTA conference or the gym, there's a chance to meet somebody who could become a friend.

4)   **Know that every person counts.** The networker who comes across as slimy is the one who always tries to wriggle close to the most important person in the room. Classy networkers understand that every individual counts. And they all figure out that some of the junior staffers they treat with kindness this year may

be buying their product or running their company some time down the road.

5) **Turn enemies into friends.** It's okay to approach folks who once were your career rivals. As time goes by, petty differences are often forgotten and shared experience becomes more important. A person you once regarded as an adversary may warmly greet you.

6) **Work the crowd in smart ways.** Use these techniques for making a success of conferences and other events:

♦ **Put in face time.** It may not feel worthwhile to attend meetings or parties where you don't know anybody, but go anyway. In networking, over the long term, you get points for just being there. People get used to seeing you, and before you know it you're part of the regular crowd.

♦ **Plan before you go.** When you meet somebody at a professional event, they are likely to ask, "What do you do?" Before you take off to that conference, practice your "elevator speech" so that you can quickly present the best version of your story. And have some questions in mind, so you can deftly refocus the attention on them. Your questions needn't be job related. I used to play the game of seeing how many people I could get talking about their pets.

♦ **Take a few risks.** Know that most people feel shy at least some of the time. So if nobody is speaking to you at an event, it might be because they don't know what to say. Even if it makes you nervous, look for people who are standing or sitting alone and introduce yourself. Keep your list of questions in mind and accept the challenge of learning about them. Here's a moment to summon up a bit of your entrepreneurial spirit. If some stranger does reject you, just let it go; remind yourself that they don't know you, and it's probably about their problem, not yours.

♦ **Be willing to serve.** If you want to attract friendly notice, watch out for opportunities to do some of the work associated with the event. Conferences often give rise to follow-up tasks and membership options. So join committees, sign up for mailing lists, and volunteer for assignments, even if it just means carrying out the coffee cups.

◆ **Follow up.** When you do meet somebody interesting, find a way to stay in touch. Let them know you enjoyed the conversation, send along information they might use, and sign up for their mailing lists. And whenever it seems appropriate, write "thank you" and congratulation notes.

Are you ready to get out there and build your network? One way to begin is connecting with a broader range of your professional peers. Contemplate your Circles, and define goals for developing existing relationships or recruiting new ones.

11

What to Say When
Your Work Is Praised

grew up believing the proper way to respond to a compliment was with modesty. If somebody said, "Great outfit," my response was something like, "Oh, it was a bargain and I've had it for years."

As a young lawyer, if I worked long hours on a tough memo and a partner said, "You did a nice job," I was inclined to answer in the same self-deprecating way. I'd belittle my efforts by saying something like, "No big deal" or "It was a team effort."

My typical response was wrong in so many ways. For one thing, it lowered the partner's assessment of the quality of my work. Instead of reading my mind and understanding that I'd struggled hard to produce a first-class draft, he might take me at my word and regard the project as not a big deal.

Beyond that, when I deflected a compliment, I drained the energy from what should have been an enjoyable moment. The partner probably felt good as he approached me to offer praise. But then my response made him feel a bit let down, instead of more upbeat. I took the fun out of the exchange with my negative comment.

Not only was my response deflating to the partner, but it was also a missed opportunity for me. With my "no big deal" attitude, I denied myself some of the benefits a compliment can bring.

It wasn't until I became a manager that I understood how the compliment exchange should go. Both the recipient of the praise and the person saying the nice things should end up feeling better after the conversation.

To your brain, receiving a compliment is like getting a prize. Think of it as comparable to somebody giving you a little reward. And research suggests that you'll perform even better after *accepting* a reward. So your first step after hearing a compliment is to pause for an instant, focus on the good wishes that accompany the complimentary words, and allow yourself to accept the full value of the message.

Then, when you open your mouth to respond, you have two goals. First, reinforce the positive evaluation that led to the compliment. Second, make the giver-of-praise feel good, and thus more likely to offer you kudos the next time.

Tips on accepting compliments on your work

Once you understand what's at play, it can be quite easy to learn how to gracefully deal with praise from your bosses and colleagues. ***With a little practice, you can master these five steps:***

1) **Say "thanks."** Begin your response to a compliment by saying "thank you." And sound like you mean it. Even if a little voice in your head says, "I don't deserve it," or "He doesn't mean it," ignore your doubt. Smile and express appreciation for the nice words.

2) **Show your pleasure at a job well done.** It's not vain to acknowledge satisfaction with your own good work. After saying "thanks," you might extend the happy moment by adding a brief phrase like, "I'm proud of this one," or "I'm so pleased that I could help."

3) **Share the credit.** You don't want to deny your contribution. At the same time, you don't want to hog the limelight if that wouldn't be fair. If it truly was a team effort, spread the praise. Add a simple comment like, "I couldn't have done it without Tom—he was terrific."

4) **Return the compliment.** You can prolong the happy moment by offering a glowing remark in return. Say something like, "Your good advice made such a difference." But this works only if your words are sincere. Fake praise can be just another way of deflecting a compliment.

5) **Keep it short.** When the compliment exchange goes on too long it can become uncomfortable. If the flow of praise feels unending, it's okay to turn it off with a light remark like, "That's enough now. You're making me blush."

Manage your "impostor syndrome"

Sometimes high achievers find it extremely difficult to hear praise, believing they don't really deserve it. If you feel like an imposter, and not really good enough to deserve such a lavish assessment, know that you're not alone. A lot of amazingly successful professionals sometimes feel, deep inside, like imposters. Try to ignore your discomfort and accept the tribute gracefully. *You might also explore these techniques for becoming more comfortable when your work gets rave reviews:*

→ **Set specific goals.** If you define precise objectives, and your bosses agree to them, ultimately everybody will know whether you are successful. If you write down measurable goals, create an action plan for achieving them, and then follow the plan, your success will be hard to miss. You will find words of approval easier to accept when they clearly reflect the facts of what happened.

→ **Ask for details.** Sometimes positive sounding feedback doesn't actually feel good because it seems vague or overblown. If you feel like you could have done much better, but they say "terrific job," it is hard to know what's really going on. If you have a good relationship with your boss, ask for a more specific critique of various aspects of your accomplishments.

→ **Calm your self-talk.** Maybe the problem isn't so much their lavish applause as it is the retort from that pesky voice inside your head. If your habitual response to praise is to tell yourself "You could have done better," it's no wonder that you don't enjoy it. Notice your internal response to positive feedback, and practice letting go of negative refrains and replacing them with phrases like, "It feels good when they recognize my hard work."

When you approach your work life like an independent entrepreneur, and accept responsibility like a CEO must, there's a danger you may feel isolated. Part of the way you get past that is to learn how to easily accept and give feedback, not just within the chain of command but across a broader web of professional relationships.

12

Give Positive Feedback in Smart Ways

The term "positivity" includes a range of thought patterns and emotions including joy, serenity, amusement, hope, and inspiration. In the last decade or so, scientists have begun to better understand how vital positivity is to the quality of your life. First, of course, it feels good, and it can have a big impact on the state of your physical and mental health. Beyond that, it actually changes how your mind works.

From a leadership perspective, it's important to understand the link between positivity and productivity. There's no longer any doubt: Most people do their best work in an environment that's predominately positive.

It's crucial to be able to discuss your team's projects in an honest way, of course, and sometimes the news is bad. But the constructive approach is to focus criticism on the work product itself, rather than on the person. And when possible, the negative assessments should be framed within a generally positive dialogue.

The human brain tends to over focus on negative cues. This may be a result of evolution. Our ancestors, who were alert to threats like lurking animals, may have survived at a higher rate than their less aware peers, who died out. In today's workplace, this tendency means that your colleagues probably over focus on negative feedback. On a day where half the boss's comments are critical, they may go home feeling like they heard not a single kind word.

Some research suggests that workers are most effective in an environment where about 80 percent of the feedback is positive. This is something not understood by Josh*, a client who was general counsel of a federal agency. He came to coaching after a staff survey suggested that many lawyers working for him felt under appreciated. They were disengaged, their morale was low, and they had real concerns about his leadership style.

Josh's initial reaction was defensive and disdainful. He said, "Grown-up lawyers shouldn't expect to be thanked just for doing excellent work. They get paid, don't they? And when I don't comment, they should know everything is okay, because I always tell them when they screw up."

We spoke about the human need to be acknowledged and appreciated. And I pointed to numerous studies demonstrating that people will be more productive in a positive work environment.

Eventually, Josh agreed to try an experiment. Every workday he put three coins in his pocket. Each time he thanked or complimented a team member he could remove one coin. And he couldn't go home until all three were gone. After the first week, Josh said he was enjoying the experiment more than he had expected. But he still felt awkward saying "good job" and "thanks," so he looked for more occasions to practice. He found times to offer compliments and say "thank you" at home, in the local cafe, and wherever he went on the weekend.

The more Josh practiced, the more comfortable he felt giving positive feedback. And he was having fun with it. "The amazing thing is not that it makes them happy, but that it makes me happy, too," he said. Soon, he quit carrying the coins because he no longer needed them. Josh said he was addicted to his "thank you" habit, and it had changed the way he looked at several parts of his life.

Well-crafted words of thanks and praise can serve as powerful positive reinforcement, guiding members of your team to achieve, change, and grow. By regularly thanking or acknowledging people for their work, you can help to shape a more positive and collaborative office culture, even if you're not the boss.

Build your "thank you" habit into a powerful leadership tool

There's some art to giving feedback that motivates and empowers the recipient. It has to be real and focused. *Practice these eight tips for giving feedback in a way that encourages people to do even better:*

1) **Be sincere.** Disingenuous flattery doesn't work. It sounds creepy and seldom fools people—at least not for long. Get in touch with your sense of gratitude when you express thanks, and speak honestly about how you feel.

2) **Be specific.** A vague, casual "thanks" isn't nearly as effective as a more detailed comment. After saying "good work," add more particulars such as, "I particularly appreciated the way you involved other team members." Precise comments not only carry more impact, but also provide powerful reinforcement for the performance you want to encourage.

3) **Fully engage.** Part of the power of saying "thank you" comes from the fact that you care enough to focus on another person. Get full value from the thanks exchange by making eye contact and listening carefully to any response.

4) **Notice what's taken for granted.** If we always perform at a stellar level, our colleagues may assume that our high standard is just normal and cease to notice it. Then it feels especially good if someone recognizes how hard we've worked to keep up the pace. When you express appreciation to a valuable team member, make it clear that you understand what goes into their good results.

5) **Calibrate your "thank you."** Elaborate kudos in response to some little thing may seem fake and can be embarrassing. And too little gratitude for a huge effort can feel insulting. The tone and style of your tribute should be commensurate with the good work you're calling out. A casual e-mail can be enough to make somebody feel appreciated for a routine task. But a face-to-face encounter is more appropriate if they pulled out all the stops.

6) **Write.** Don't forget the power of a handwritten note. It still feels good when another person takes the time to sit down and write about what we've done.

7) **Be surprising.** Formalized praise, such as during an annual review, is important, but it's not enough. With time, routine assessments feel ho-hum, no matter how positive they may be. To show you mean it, express your gratitude or admiration when it's not expected.

8) **Be quick.** Offer your commendation as soon as possible after the activity that inspired it. Words of thanks and approval (like other feedback) have more impact right after we've done the work.

The "thank you" habit can be good for you

When you regularly look for opportunities to express appreciation, you are more likely to focus on and support the values and activities that matter most.

And research suggests that taking the time to feel grateful can actually reduce your anxiety. Saying kind words to others can feel very good, and sometimes hearing their response can feel even better.

13

Get Over Your Fear of Looking Like a Suck-Up

One of the greatest TV characters ever was Eddie Haskell, Wally Cleaver's oily, conniving friend, still to be seen on reruns of *Leave It to Beaver*. Eddie was an archetype who no decent person wants to resemble—a two-faced sycophant, always scheming and currying favor to promote his plans.

The fear of looking like a brown-noser is so powerful among professionals that sometimes they shy away from obvious opportunities to make a friend or pursue a goal. Among my clients, the people who seem most likely to worry about resembling Eddie Haskell are the straight shooters who look the least like him.

A good example is Trish*, a quiet but talented financial wizard who wanted to eventually move to her dream job in another division of the company. Trish said she'd probably need support from Al, a senior colleague who knew the leaders there. She described Al as smart and accomplished, but self-absorbed and eager to be the center of attention.

I suggested Trish find ways to build her relationship with Al, and speculated that he might respond well to a bit of flattery. She said, "Yep—he probably would. But I couldn't do it. I just don't like to suck up."

Even though it could mean a lot for her future, Trish didn't want to cultivate a friendship with Al because he seemed arrogant and might expect her to kowtow. I said she needn't grovel and asked her to simply make a list of Al's strengths and areas of expertise. Next, I suggested she spot opportunities where Al's advice might actually be helpful.

Trish identified Al's types of special knowledge and found projects where she could use his insights. Then she began to ask him for occasional guidance. To her surprise, Al responded warmly and eventually became her mentor. Ultimately, he guided her into the transfer she'd been seeking. Trish's reluctance to appear unctuous had almost prevented her from getting to know the man who became her champion.

Trish is not alone. Modest but otherwise self-aware people often have a disproportionate fear of looking like a bootlicker.

Are you reluctant to offer a heartfelt tribute for fear it will be taken as apple-polishing?

Do you avoid voicing sincere admiration because people might think you have a hidden agenda? If so, you're probably overreacting. There are many times when offering a compliment is an authentic move, and it's wise to get beyond your fear of kissing ass. *Here are seven situations when you should stop worrying about seeming to suck up:*

1) **When you're supporting a positive environment.** As I mentioned in Chapter 12, research suggests people are more productive in a workplace where most of the comments are affirmative. If you consistently contribute to the environment by keeping most of your words authentically upbeat, people won't regard your praise as manipulative.

2) **When it's a boss.** Are you reluctant to say "good job" to the big boss because you don't want to seem sycophantic? Well, consider what it's like from that boss's perspective. Maybe she worked her way into this job because she's the kind of person who is motivated by getting As. Now, however, if everybody is afraid to applaud her achievements, she may start to feel unappreciated. It's not healthy

or smart when the whole team is reluctant to give a leader honest positive feedback. Stop being so self-conscious and allow yourself to be as nice to your boss as you are to your other colleagues.

3) **When you want to make new friends.** As long as you're not being untruthful or over-the-top, it's okay to express respect or gratitude to a person you'd like to know better. Finding something nice to say is a polite and acceptable way of building a relationship.

4) **When it's wise to avoid conflict.** Some people are never going to be your friends, but you have to find a way to get along with them anyway. If they are annoying, you may make things even worse if you indulge in complaints. If they are bullies, you may attract more torture if you let them see your pain. When you're dealing with difficult people, a good starting point can be to talk yourself into a mood of relaxed confidence. Then look for the good things about them, so you can diffuse the tension with a compliment that is genuine and on target.

5) **When you owe them an apology.** There are moments when groveling is justified, such as when you forgot an important deadline, or said something dreadful at the office holiday party. It's okay to cringe and humble yourself when you want forgiveness for doing something truly wrong.

6) **When it would be kind.** It is always appropriate to put people at ease or calm their anxiety, regardless of their rank or yours. If empathy makes you want to offer a flattering remark, don't be put off by concern about how observers may judge your motives. And if you can't say anything nice, maybe you really shouldn't say anything at all.

7) **When you feel shy.** When some people say, "I don't want to suck up," the real truth is that they are afraid to step forward. When you hesitate to speak up, look more closely at your motives. Do you actually think it would look bad or is it just that the thought of drawing attention to yourself gives you butterflies? It's okay to be fearful, but make a smart, conscious choice about how you will respond to that fear.

If you honestly mean it, don't hold back from offering praise or thanks just because cynics might criticize you.

14

Use Games to Create Power and Direction

George*, a fairly new manager, hesitated when I asked him about his work. Then he said, "Objectively, it's going really well. But I don't know how long I can stand it."

The good news was that, after two years of building collaboration and creating expertise, George's team was exceeding all its objectives and had been recognized as a shining "center of excellence" within the large organization.

However, now leaders in other divisions were trying to steal some of the glory and resources. They were attempting to poach George's expert staff members by having them reassigned away to other challenges. When I asked George how many team members he'd actually lost, he said, "None. But I'm so exhausted from the constant fight to protect them that I'm not sure if I can keep this up. The stress is just too much."

I thought about how much George loves board games and recalled a party where he and friends had played fiercely for hours. The intense players shouted and mocked each other. But at the end of the game they laughed about the competition and talked about what fun it had been.

I asked George whether he could take a step back from the challenges to his team and view his colleagues more like other players in a strategic game, such as the kind he enjoyed playing with his buddies. George realized that he was finding the battles at work to be tiring because they had begun to seem too personal. It felt like a slap to the face when other managers responded to his success by threatening the important program he had built so carefully.

George resolved to start taking office politics more lightly, like playing a game. He would remind himself that decisions impacting his program reflected complex patterns and were seldom about him. He became more adept at quickly disengaging from daily skirmishes and regularly stepping back and refocusing on his bigger goals. As he concentrated on keeping perspective, George found work to be fun again, and less stressful.

How to invent career games to generate energy

A game involves goals, challenges, rules, and often interaction with other players. If you're struggling to understand a problem at the office, or if you're just bored by the daily drill, try approaching parts of your work as a game. *These tips will help you to launch your game:*

→ **First, define the rules.** If a workplace issue feels like a confusing mess, look at it in a different way by framing it as a game you must learn to play. Ask yourself: What are my goals? What moves will take me in that direction? Who are the other players? What are the consequences of each type of move? Are some moves out of bounds?

→ **Play more than one game at a time.** There was a time when George was torn. His ultimate career goal was to get a prestigious government job. But it felt like he was cheating his employer when he shifted his focus from current responsibilities to building his profile in broader circles. He said, "My career took off when I finally realized that it's okay to play two games at the same time. Every morning I not only thought about how to excel at my day job, but also visualized how to prepare for my dream job. That additional target and drive made me a better employee at the same time it opened doors for the future."

→ **Understand others' games.** In your workplace you are seldom in direct competition with your colleagues. It's like you are playing your games, and they are playing theirs, and you occasionally bump into each other on the field. The best players try to understand their colleagues' goals and look for ways to offer help. Collaboration happens when you see how your goals overlap and find ways to play together.

→ **Make work more fun.** If work feels boring, think up a game that will make it more interesting. Challenge yourself to do something faster, better, or in a different way. Set a goal that involves learning a new skill, varying your habits, or broadening your network. As you find ways to make your tasks more interesting and enjoyable, you'll become more productive.

→ **Track results.** "Gamify" is a term used to describe the application of game design to a non-game process. Often, the idea is to give you a real-time view of your own or someone else's performance. People have embraced the concept of gamification in the context of exercise, where wearable devices track every step and can share summaries among selected friends. Some employers are gamifying repetitive and boring tasks by sharing performance metrics among workers, hoping a little healthy competition will make work more engaging. You can gamify your own tedious tasks by keeping track of your performance and rewarding your achievements.

If you think about your career as a very long-term game, you'll be less likely to become bogged down in this week's problems. Regularly ask yourself where you'd like to be a few years down the road, and create a game to help you develop the skills and resources that will get you there.

15

Be Prepared with Clever Ways to Brag

What if a headhunter calls today with an interesting job possibility? Can you speedily show that you're an ideal candidate? And will you be ready if a boss or client has questions about how you've been using your time?

New opportunities or unexpected challenges can pop up fast. But when you're asked to quickly explain what you've been doing on the job, you might not be prepared to gracefully describe your achievements. Some people even go blank when asked to talk about what they've done lately.

To keep moving ahead in your career, you must know how to describe where you've been. Even if you're happily entrenched in a job that feels secure, on occasion you'll need to demonstrate your worth. Perhaps you'll want to go after a raise or promotion, or show that you're ready to take on a juicy assignment.

Even if other people aren't inquiring about how you're doing, to keep growing on the job it's wise to maintain a realistic sense of your current productivity. And if you routinely keep track of which activities bring the most results, you'll know how to prioritize your time in the future.

So that you're always prepared to demonstrate your accomplishments, consider these strategies:

→ **Keep a "love me" file.** This is a handy place—also known as a "brag file"—where you immediately store a copy of any document that says something nice about you. I've seen a few "love me" files that are full of handwritten "thank you" notes and letters of praise from grateful clients. It's more likely that your file—whether it's in your desk drawer or the Cloud—will be a mixed bag. Include anything that commemorates good work or a positive evaluation, from casual "thanks" messages to press clips or training course certificates. If your file is empty, you might think about rounding up letters of reference or testimonials, just in case.

→ **Get real about "performance management."** Your organization may have an annual performance appraisal process. Typically, it begins with the establishment of goals and ends when your progress toward those goals is evaluated in the context of a discussion about compensation. Often, the process is pro forma and nobody pays much attention to it. But that's a missed opportunity. Take charge of the process and use it to get buy-in for things you want to do. Propose meaningful goals and routinely document your progress. Your records will help you create a specific picture of your most important contributions.

→ **Count activities and results.** Your resume, activity reports, and project summaries will be more useful and impressive if you include relevant numbers. Let's say you're a PR manager and a prolific writer. You can tell a prospective employer that you blog frequently and write lots of press releases. But wouldn't it be more effective to say that in the last six months you've posted 60 blog items, averaging 20,000 views each, and you've sent out 83 releases resulting in at least 327 media clips? If you keep a running log of frequent and important activities, you'll always be able to show off what you've done in a powerful, streamlined way.

→ **Note problems and solutions.** Not everything you deal with generates good fodder for your "love me" file. At times you may have to address controversies, complaints, or even clean up a mess after you make the wrong call. Smart professionals face up to tough issues and find a way to remedy errors. As time goes by, however, other people may remember the problem, but not what was done to manage it. So you may need a record of matters you've successfully handled.

If you record your activity as you go along and keep track of the positive feedback, you'll always be able to produce a quick summary of your career highlights. Beyond that, your files will bring insights into how you do your best work and reassure you when you feel discouraged.

16

Get the "It" Factor: Create Presence

Clients whom I'm coaching often ask, "How do I get executive presence?" The question is tricky because "executive presence" isn't easily defined. Most folks agree that leaders need it and great leaders have it. But it's not so simple to deconstruct its elements.

Your definition may be based on a leader you know who has a commanding aura. You know what I mean—someone who exudes confidence and attracts people like a magnet. Sometimes the value of executive presence seems most obvious when it's missing. I'm thinking of Ed*, a brilliant corporate attorney who was repeatedly overlooked when spots opened within his company's management ranks. When I asked the COO whether Ed was likely to be promoted, she said, "No. He'll always be valued as a talented technical lawyer, but we're not going to move him up. Ed just doesn't have executive presence."

The COO didn't try to define "executive presence," but I knew what she meant. The attorney could write memos like a dream. When asked a question, however, he seemed hesitant. He'd mumble, then he'd shuffle down the hall.

He just didn't have "It." He didn't radiate that assurance, that dignity, that sense of control that others see as "executive presence."

Use this checklist to build presence

Do you sometimes worry that you don't have enough of that "It" factor? Do you fear you'll miss out on career opportunities, despite your great work, because you lack a powerful demeanor? Presence is an elusive quality, like love or happiness; you can't just pick some up. But you *can* do a great deal to appear more like a leader. You can build your presence by changing the ways you look and behave, and even how you think and feel about yourself.

Here's a checklist of key factors that contribute to executive presence. If you want to enhance your gravitas, read through the questions and find points to work on:

1) **Do you have a leadership vision?** As we discussed in Chapter 5, it's easier to act like a leader when you have a clear sense of the attributes of leadership. If you can't easily describe your vision of a leader, list characteristics you admire, such as reliability, honesty, or a positive attitude. Look at your list frequently so that you're reminded to incorporate these traits into your daily behavior.

2) **Do you seem organized?** If you're typically late, if your papers are a mess, and if you have trouble meeting deadlines, then your presence is compromised. Colleagues may see you as disorganized and unable to get the job done. Suzy* is a communications consultant who thought of herself as a ditzy, creative type. She'd explain away her lateness by saying, "Oh, you know us artists." But finally she realized that her firm's partners regarded her as a bit out of control. She saw they weren't going to promote her to the role of client manager until something changed. Suzy got her calendar and other systems in order. And, significantly, she told all her colleagues that she was working with a coach to become more productive and organized. She reshaped her brand, and soon she was managing client accounts.

3) **Do you need a makeover?** It may not be fair, but physical appearance is an integral part of presence. To look like an executive, it helps to be well groomed and well dressed. If your clothes

are dated and untidy, or your hair is always messy, you may come across as unpolished and not management material.

4) **Can you make a presentation?** The ability to give a speech or contribute useful remarks at a meeting will enhance your presence. Of course, you have to be clear and concise. But it's also important to know how to engage with other people. Present your points in a way that makes them relevant to the audience. Listen carefully to questions and comments, and respond without becoming defensive.

5) **Do you say what you mean?** Whether you're speaking to a crowd or chatting one-on-one, you'll have more gravitas if you speak directly, without hesitation or self-deprecation. Ask colleagues to observe the way you talk, so they can help you spot self-critical phrasing or annoying habits like starting sentences with phrases like, "I'm not an expert, but . . ." If you sound like you're uncertain of what you're saying, you can't expect others to be convinced.

6) **How's your vitality?** Managing your presence requires taking charge of your energy level. If you're sleep deprived, bored, or out of shape, you're less likely to come across as a leader. Being frantic isn't good either, because your hyperactivity can translate into stress for those around you. To appear more powerful, be serious about maintaining good health and fitness, and stay calm with practices like meditation.

7) **Do you know how to appear more confident?** People with executive presence seem cool and ready to handle any situation. But a superb record may not be enough to give professionals a belief in their own ability to master the next crisis. And even if they do know they can perform, that knowledge may not be apparent to others. A good starting point for boosting your confidence level, and making sure it shows, is to manage the voice in your head, as we discussed in Chapter 7.

8) **What's your body saying?** Your nonverbal behavior can be even more important than your words. At least on an unconscious level, people make judgments based on your posture, facial expressions, and even your fleeting microexpressions. They may even "mirror" your smile or the way you are holding your

body, with their emotions shifting to more closely match yours. And, according to fascinating research from psychologists like Harvard's Amy Cuddy, your *own* brain also picks up those messages from your body and face. If you assume the stance of a confident person, your mind and emotions may follow, helping you to soon feel more confidence.

Although the concept of presence is complicated, I've seen professionals make speedy improvements in the way they come across. For example, there's Lydia*, an accomplished economist whose concern about details translates into successful projects. But Lydia is such a perfectionist that, when handed a new assignment, she tends to immediately start fretting about the best way to start. Her boss told me that Lydia didn't appear sure about her plans because of her worried demeanor. People hesitated to follow her directions because she often looked so anxious and uncertain.

Lydia understood that she'd be a better leader if she could appear more decisive. To work on this, she explored various forms of "self-talk" before settling on two techniques. First, before entering a meeting, she would define her intent for the occasion. It might be something such as, "I'm going to raise point X and come across as interested and positive." Then she'd encourage herself with repeated affirmations such as, "My plan is on target and I know it will work."

Lydia also became conscious of her body language, and realized that when anxious she'd bow her head, cross her arms, and hunch her shoulders. Inspired by Dr. Cuddy's moving TED Talk, "Your Body Language Shapes Who You Are," she began practicing "power posing." Before making a presentation or attending an important event, she would go through a quick series of exercises, like holding her arms up high in a V shape. She said that the poses did seem to make her feel surer of herself. She also started regular yoga classes again and found that they helped her body stop feeling—and looking—so tense.

I spoke with Lydia's boss a few months after she began working on her presence and he was surprised by her transformation in such a short time.

Building presence can mean work on many levels

There is much you can do to rapidly enhance your executive presence. And, on a deeper level, you can continue to strengthen your presence through exercises intended to develop the level of your self-awareness. ***Use these questions to check in with four aspects of yourself:***

1) **Your physical self:**

   - How is my posture? Am I tense? Shall I relax my shoulders and other parts of my body?
   - What is the expression on my face? Am I frowning? Is my jaw clenched? Can I generate a smile?
   - How is my breathing? Is it shallow or hurried? Is it time for a deep, slow breath?

2) **Your intellectual self:**

   - Has that internal voice been nagging me with worries and regrets? Shall I put them aside for now?
   - What are my top goals for the day? For the next hour?
   - What is my plan for reaching my most immediate goal?
   - Is it time to shift my focus away from my own problems and onto another person?

3) **Your emotional self:**

   - Has there been a moment today when I experienced an intense emotion? What was it?
   - Did that surge of emotion impact the way I responded to another person?
   - What am I feeling now?
   - Are there feelings I want to let go, before going back to work?

4) **Your spiritual self:**

   - What key values will help me with the decisions I must make today?
   - Have my activities so far today been in keeping with the values that matter the most to me?
   - What are three things I feel grateful for?
   - Is it time for a moment of meditation, affirmation, or a quick prayer?
   - Can I help someone?

17

To Make a Career Shift, Start with One Grain of Sugar

We all go through puzzling or difficult times. And sometimes we need a major change, perhaps even a new professional direction. You're the boss of your career. So when it's time to go another direction, you're the one who must come up with a plan.

But what do you do when you don't know where you want to go? There's no simple solution. Typically, what you must do is launch a process that sets the groundwork for your transition. From years of coaching experience, I know that the difference between just dreaming about a new phase, and actually getting there, often comes from setting up a methodical process that helps you to create change a little bit at a time.

Create your change process

Whether you want to shift professional tracks or simply pump up your performance in your current gig, setting up a change process that works for you will provide a clear starting point. When working with clients, I often suggest a technique for managing change that I've been using since I was a teenager.

When I was growing up, I followed my New Zealander parents' example and drank lots of tea. I liked it loaded with milk and sugar, but as a young teen I started worrying about the calories. I didn't want to give up my habit of drinking cups of tea every day after school, but kicking my sugar habit seemed too tough.

Then one day I was inspired to reduce the sugar so gradually that I'd never miss it. As I sat at the kitchen table, staring at the heaping pile of sugar on my spoon, I decided to make progress by removing just a few granules. In the following days, I estimated earlier volumes and tried to remove a few more grains. I kept at it, progressively lessening the amount of sugar from two or three spoonfuls to none. It took nearly a year, but I learned to enjoy sugarless tea without ever feeling deprived.

I was so intrigued by the power of creating change through small, painless steps that I applied what I called "the Sugar Grain Principle" to other aspects of my young life. For example, I became better at keeping my room neat with very small steps, like routinely shutting the closet door or spending just five minutes cleaning each morning.

I remembered the Sugar Grain Principle years later, as a senior at Ohio University. An injustice in the way female students were treated motivated me to support gender equality. I didn't expect to actually change practices that were widespread, but I thought the Principle might help to frame a satisfying gesture, just for me.

I promised myself to do at least one small "thing" in support of greater equality for university women every day. It didn't have to be much. A "thing" could be as small as a sugar grain. But I needed to come up with something—anything—every single day.

It was easy at first. A day's contribution might be as basic as speaking in class about equality. But with time it became more difficult to find my daily "thing," and I was forced to move out of my comfort zone. To meet my quota of sugar grains, I spoke at meetings, started a radio program focused on gender equality, and became the first woman to enter the university's MBA program.

As I scrambled harder to define new "things," I worried less about failure and became more creative. Eventually, the president noticed, made me his assistant, and asked me to write a detailed report on the status of women. Most of the report's recommendations were accepted, and ultimately I led

Ohio University's implementation of Title IX, the landmark federal legislation outlawing gender discrimination in education. I knew nothing about institutional change, but I found my way one sugar grain at a time.

In my job, I met individually with scores of women, often encouraging them to embark on career paths traditionally dominated by men. Still in my 20s, I was called upon to advise faculty members, and others far more experienced than I, who wanted to step into leadership or into fields traditionally closed to women.

I had no training in career development. Once again, I relied on my experience with gradual change. I developed a model that, at least inside my head, I called the "Sugar Grain Process." I used the model to help professionals rethink their goals and start taking steps in new directions.

Through the years I've repeatedly worked through the Sugar Grain Process while navigating my own varied career. And I've shared the process countless times, as a mentor, a manager, and coach.

I understand that the Sugar Grain Process is not unique and that many similar models can create success. But I have 40 years of experience in fostering career change using this approach, and I am absolutely confident that it works.

How to change careers with the Sugar Grain Process

Let's say you're bored with the kind of work you've been doing, but you don't know what you'd like to do next. *If I were your coach, I'd suggest you go through this five-part process:*

1) **Develop a vision of the career you want.** Your "vision" is a wish list of elements you'd like to see in your next career phase. Don't worry if you can't be precise. Chances are you will be surprised at how much you already know.

   ◆ **Start your list with pros and cons of your current position.** First on your list are the things you appreciate about your job—elements that you hope will continue. Then consider the negatives: Does each "con" suggest an opposite "pro" that belongs on your wish list? For example, if you don't like the isolation brought by your current project, you might add a "pro," like "more frequent social interaction," to your list.

◆ **Jump ahead and look back.** Imagine it's three years from now, and the past three years were professionally satisfying. Envision yourself feeling very successful. Now describe what made the past three-year period so productive and satisfying. What did you do, or what occurred to bring you to this good place? Maybe, in this imagined future, you met a new group of people or built your profile on social media? Does this exercise suggest elements you want to add to your vision list?

◆ **Consider elements you want in your life.** Ask yourself whether the worst part of your job is what it's doing to the rest of your life. Should your wish list include time or opportunities to pursue interests or relationships that would make your life more meaningful? For example, if what you really want is to spend more time with your kids, maybe "less weekend work" should go on your career wish list. Or perhaps you want to live in a different kind of place?

2) **State your most pressing goals.** After studying your wish list, define several achievable goals that could pave the way for your shift. For many people, three is a good number of goals for getting started. And these initial goals don't have to be precise. You might start with something like: (1) broaden my professional network; (2) learn to better manage stress; and (3) develop expertise in an important technical area.

3) **Identify some "Sugar Grains" for each goal.** Once you have identified goals, even if they're not yet specific, it's time to start finding little things—the Sugar Grains—that will move you roughly in the direction that you want to go. Start a list of Grains—small action items—for each goal. For example, your Grains on stress might include taking a meditation class and ordering a useful book. As you build out your list of future Grains, keep these points in mind:

◆ **It doesn't matter where you start.** I don't call these little items "steps" because they aren't linear. Sugar Grains don't need to take you in a logical order along a direct path. The Grains on your list needn't be related to one another. And sometimes they'll feel pretty random. What matters is that you start to build momentum by doing *something*. As you find more Grains, patterns will emerge and your goals will become clearer.

- ◆ **Grains vary widely.** Let's say one of your goals is to become more prominent in your professional circles. Your first Grains might include sending an e-mail to an old contact, attending an event you'd typically skip, spending one hour setting up your LinkedIn account, and buying a notebook to use for new writing projects. The more varied and imaginative your Grains are, the better.

- ◆ **Grains will lead to other Grains.** I love the way doing one little thing so often inspires something else. For example, if you attend a dinner where you meet somebody interesting, your next Grain could be to send a follow-up note.

4) **Commit to a specific pace of Sugar Grains.** Once you have a picture of where you want to go, decide how quickly you need to move. That will determine how many Grains you'll want to accomplish each day, or week, for each goal. For example, if you're starting the hunt for a different sort of job, but you're not in a hurry, maybe you'll promise yourself to do just one thing each week. But it's vital to set a pace and maintain it, no matter what. *This is important: The power of the Sugar Grain Process comes from your commitment to keep up your pace even when you feel like you are out of ideas or don't have the time.*

5) **Maintain records.** Keeping track of your Grains helps ensure the success of your process. Your recordkeeping will help you see your progress, bring you new insights, and inspire additional Grains. How you do it, whether it's on paper or in the Cloud, is your choice. In addition to holding onto your lists of completed things, consider using logs for tracking your activity. For example, whether you're making notes on your calendar or maintaining an Excel spreadsheet, you're more likely to stick to an exercise or other program if you record each minute you spend. Another valuable tool can be your journal. Writing about your efforts promotes self-reflection, helps you explore and keep track of new ideas, and gives you a way to manage frustration and setbacks in the course of your transition.

As with any change effort, the most difficult part of the Sugar Grain Process can be getting started. But once you build up a cadence of Grains, the Process generates its own energy. You'll start to trust it and feel sure that it's taking you somewhere interesting and important. You'll probably go through several iterations, tweaking your goals as you move closer to your destination. Then, like many of my clients, you may hear yourself saying, "I'll kind of miss the Sugar Grain Process. It was getting to be fun."

18

How to Take a Career Side Step, One Sugar Grain at a Time

In the last chapter I wrote about the "Sugar Grain Process," the approach I use to create change in my career, as well as to guide mentees and clients. The essential idea is develop a vision of what you want next, and then commit to regularly doing little things that will move you in that direction. The things you do needn't be big—they can be as small as grains of sugar—but if you keep doing them at a regular pace, the process inevitably brings positive change.

A while back I received an e-mail from Susan*, a reader whom I've not met. She described herself as a woman in her 50s who wants to find a different kind of job, while remaining in the same broad career field.

"I am physically fit and healthy, and plan on working eight to 10 more years. I want to get out of [this] environment, have a different set of responsibilities, and make more money. Can you advise me?" Susan asked.

Well, that was a big question. And if Susan were a coaching client I'd start by asking her lots of questions in return. However, because an investment in coaching doesn't seem to be an option for Susan, I told her I'd take up the challenge of laying out a plan that could lead to her new job.

If you want to stay in your field, but find a different kind of job, get started one Sugar Grain at a Time

Susan had no idea how to start her search for a different kind of job within her industry. *I applied the Sugar Grain Process and came up with this plan for launching her transition:*

1) **Write a big wish list.** Start by listing everything you want in your next phase. Dream about what would be great not only in your job, but also in the rest of your life. Sometimes we start wishing for a career shift, but part of what we want may be available without a job change. For example, if you're bored or lonely, you might create a richer life by pursuing new interests in your free time. Or, if you love your job but want more income, you might consider creating a side business.

2) **Organize your wish list.** Break your list into categories within your new life. Think broadly, and include headings like "health and fitness" or "social life," as well as "ideal job attributes." You are creating this larger vision partly because it will help you to see that not everything must be found through your work. But there may be exciting career benefits, as well, because creating positive change in *any* part of your life can bring new energy to your job. I often see that when clients make progress in one area, like their fitness program or their volunteer activity, it resonates in their work lives.

3) **Commit to regular cadence of Sugar Grains.** Once you have your categories, start moving by doing little things—the tiny Grains—to support each one. Decide how many Grains you'll undertake each week for each category. It's important to find a realistic pace, and then stick with it faithfully. For example, you might decide that each week for the first two months you will:

- ◆ **Support your job search** with three Grains. The first week might include (1) e-mailing to arrange a lunch date with a professional contact, (2) spending 20 minutes doing research on the Internet, and (3) working on your resume for 30 minutes.

- ◆ **Start exercising** by walking for 20 minutes three times during the week.

- ◆ **Take one social step,** like making a phone call to arrange a future dinner with friends.

4) **Do research and notice trends.** While you've been busy in your day job, you may not have been tracking developments in your professional area. Your job-related Grains should include looking around, identifying people who are making contributions, money, or headlines. Read everything you can, but don't stop there. Look for conferences and associations where you can learn from people working in fields not far removed from yours.

5) **Network methodically.** On your list of potential Grains will be the names of people who might be willing to brainstorm with you. Include not only those you've known well through the years, but also professional acquaintances who seem career savvy. Then work your list. Set up coffee dates, or find other ways to visit with just about anybody who might be able to spot trends or suggest opportunities. Ask your contacts if they can suggest others who might be willing to talk with you. If people are too busy to help, they'll let you know. And, if they are willing to chat, know that someday you'll be able to return the favor or pay it forward with another job seeker.

6) **Engage online.** Social media is now playing a major role in the job search arena. Today's job seekers are at a disadvantage if they don't at least have profiles on LinkedIn.com. Twitter is also a tool that allows you to connect with recruiters and others you might not be able to reach by phone or e-mail.

7) **Learn something new.** Taking classes is an excellent way to pick up new skills and broaden your perspective. When you are engaged in learning, it helps you see your routine work in new ways and become more creative. And certifications earned

through course work can demonstrate your commitment to excellence. Enrolling in classes at a local college could have the additional benefit of broadening your network. But if there's no nearby option, explore distance learning.

8) **Volunteer.** If you want to build additional skills, look for ways to get new kinds of experience. A good starting point can be to join clubs or service organizations.

9) **Find a buddy.** Making a career shift can be a lonely process. Find a friend who is also engaged in reinvention and meet regularly to share ideas, networks, and encouragement. You don't have to have similar careers. Somebody in a different line of work might offer a new way of looking at things.

I never heard back from Susan, but I've shared this plan with other readers, and more than one has reported good results.

19

Those Annoying Speech Habits May Cost You

Innovation often flows from collaboration among people who have different views, backgrounds, and skill sets. Varied teams are more likely to come up with something new than a group of professionals with similar backgrounds. When people are able to get along, diversity can give rise to startling creativity. And it can be deeply satisfying when you're part of a diverse team that clicks along.

But it's not always easy to fit within a mixed team. One thing that can hold you back is a conversational style that other members find annoying.

Here's a game to build awareness among members of the older set

In today's workplace, one way that managers are learning to foster fresh thinking is by partnering 45-and-older expert professionals with younger and more tech, and social media-savvy colleagues. Work teams cutting across generations have so much potential that it's a shame the trend isn't building even faster. However, one barrier to cooperation across the decades is that people of different ages sometimes communicate in dissimilar ways.

Let's face it: At times Baby Boomers and Millennials find each other's conversation to be boring. Ageism seems to be on the rise, and at work the communication gap may have the most serious consequences for the Boomers. People who are older than the group average can lose professional credibility if they indulge in tedious conversational patterns, whether they're speaking in meetings or during a casual lunch. And if their coworkers see them as out of date, they could be excluded from the most interesting projects.

Recently, a group of Boomer friends were talking about the tedious chatter of our age cohort. In particular, we all confessed to occasionally indulging in prolonged accounts of our various aches and pains. We bore even each other with this kind of talk and could drive a younger colleague out of the room.

So we invented "Code Blue," a game that allows us to remind each other to avoid annoying old person talk. The goal of the game is to gently cue friends to change gears when their speech is falling into a geezer pattern. The primary rule is that reminders must be offered in a spirit of kindness, and only to willing players.

To play the game, when the occasion arises, you quietly mention one of three applicable warning codes:

→ **Code Blue** (for blue hair) is our signal to end a stream of complaints about the speaker's less than perfect physical condition. I'm not talking about interrupting a serious talk about health challenges with a dear friend. Rather, the idea is to help each other resist the temptation to complain about our sore backs in any setting where the conversation would be better focused on something else. If you want to play, empower your colleague or partner to give you a gentle "Code Blue" reminder should you start to rant about the state of your body.

→ **Code Green** is a signal I invented while eavesdropping on the next table at a local bistro. There, a prosperous looking young couple was buying dinner for the man's mother, a woman in her 60s or older. Instead of expressing appreciation for the great choices, Mom embarrassed her son by going through the menu loudly complaining about the current cost of restaurant food.

When the waiter took her order, she said, "Well, what I really want is the swordfish, but I'd never let him pay that much, so bring me the pasta." The son seemed mortified and adjoining diners were rolling their eyes. This can happen in many different discussions about how much things cost today, including in a business context. So when your office pal once again wastes time with the discovery that prices have gone up since 1995, offer the gentle reminder: "Code Green."

→ **Code Golden Harvest** is used when people interrupt a discussion about a current topic with yet another story of what it was like back in the day. "Golden Harvest" was a wildly popular color for appliances and décor from the 60s into the 80s. But there's a reason people stopped using that shade and we're all still tired of it. If you're frequently tempted to reminisce when future thinking is what's needed, let your closest colleague know that it's okay to sometimes whisper "Code Golden Harvest."

Be aware of your speech habits, whatever your age

Older people aren't the only ones in danger of undercutting their professional brands with annoying talk. Individuals of all ages may make themselves unpopular by speaking way too much about topics not of interest to their audience. And even individuals with interesting content can muddle their messages with tedious or confusing speech patterns.

Recent college graduates can sometimes drive coworkers to distraction with "up-talking." You're an up-talker if you tend to end your statements with upward inflections, making them sound like questions. It's a babyish habit that can change the meaning of a sentence and make you sound timid.

We must add to the list of poor communicators anyone who indulges in too much profanity within a culture that values polite speech. And then there are the whiners—they'll never make it into the inner circle of a team that values a positive attitude. Finally, if you, uh, break up your, ah, sentences with, y'know, too many little, um, tics, your points may not be heard.

We tend not to notice our own speech patterns and may not be aware when they're interfering with our ability to be clear or connect with others. If you have doubts about how your talking comes across, ask friends to listen to you carefully and report on what they hear. Or record your next speech. Find a way to explore questions like these:

→ Do I use the same words or phrases—like, "Awesome" or "Am I right?"—over and over?

→ Is there anything about my tone that seems grating or difficult to make out?

→ Do I take too long to make my point, sometimes arguing my case even after I've won?

→ Do I speak so fast that some people may have trouble understanding?

→ Do I weaken the impact of my points with tentative preliminary phrasing like, "I'm not sure, but I think that . . ."

→ Do I constantly say "I" no matter what topic is under discussion?

If other people are bored, annoyed, or confused by the way you talk, they may tune you out. Make an effort to be aware of your speech habits, and be clear about the conversational style you'd like to have as part of your personal brand.

20

Does Your Calendar Support Your Success?

Do you feel overwhelmed by having too much to do in too little time? If you want to accomplish more without spending longer at your desk or laptop, you may need a better way to manage your schedule. But it's difficult to rethink how you keep your calendar if everything just feels like a blur.

To revise the way you manage your calendar, begin with an assessment of exactly what you're doing with all those hours at work. To get a more accurate look at how you're employing your time, keep a detailed log for a week or two. Throughout each day, record what you do and how many minutes you spend on each activity. When you study your log, you may be surprised by how much of each week is devoted to things that don't really matter.

Once you have a better handle on where your time is going, you can make adjustments to help you become more productive. Your calendar can become a more powerful tool for keeping you focused on your highest priorities and making good use of your energy, as well as your time.

These strategies can help you rethink your calendar

My client Gina* is a successful executive who earns more money, and makes bigger decisions, than she ever dreamed possible. From "360 review" interviews with several of her colleagues and clients, I know that she is widely seen as energetic, compassionate, and very smart.

But Gina came to coaching because she felt like her work life was out of control. She was spending long hours at the office, but she didn't feel efficient and her backlog of work was growing. She often arrived late to meetings and worried constantly about forgetting something important. And she was troubled by a sense that she didn't have time to focus on the big challenges she saw down the road for her team.

I asked Gina to take careful notes, for just two weeks, of how she actually employed her time in the office. As she reviewed her carefully kept log, she was startled by the true picture of her work patterns. She saw that she spent way too much time on low-value e-mail, and she let herself be frequently hijacked from her planned activities. She'd long been proud of her open door policy and reputation as a responsive colleague. But when she looked at how frequently she was interrupted, she understood the high cost. Gina was devoting relatively little attention to her most critical goals.

She decided that a key to becoming more efficient and less stressed would be to change the way she approached her calendar. To begin, we talked about how Gina's work life is shaped by a complex pattern of commitments. As each day goes along, she continues to make promises and enter into agreements. On a typical day she might say "yes" to several meetings, swear to make progress on a major project, and agree to review multiple drafts from anxious colleagues. She'd put the meetings on her calendar and maybe even block out time for her most pressing work. But then, all too often, her attention would be swept up by calls, visits from coworkers, and minor crises. She might go for hours without even glancing at her full calendar.

The log helped Gina see how frequently she missed deadlines because she was ignoring her calendar. And she had an "Aha!" moment. She realized that every time she was late or a no-show, another person might be inconvenienced or disappointed. She said, "I finally understood that one reason I felt so anxious is that I was going through life letting people down."

Gina decided to get serious about treating her calendar as a primary tool for managing both her time and her commitments. During a period of several months, she gradually rebuilt some work habits, learned new scheduling techniques, and found ways to focus more attention on her highest priorities. Once she rebuilt her relationship with her calendar, Gina felt more in control and much less stressed. ***These scheduling tips were helpful to Gina and they may help you:***

→ **Take time to plan.** Look at your calendar first thing every morning and frequently throughout the day so that you can envision what lies ahead, complete necessary preparation for the next event, and spot any problems. Notice the gaps between appointments and decide in advance how to use that available time to accomplish your most pressing tasks.

→ **Coordinate with your "to-do" list.** As you look at your task list, batch similar kinds of action items, like phone calls or brief e-mails. Then schedule blocks of time to work through each batch. For example, if you have to make a lot of phone calls, schedule one-hour blocks for quickly getting through your call list.

→ **Match your calendar to your body clock.** Many people find that they are more efficient at some times of the day than at others. Gina knew that her mind is sharpest in the morning and that she often feels too tired to think clearly by late afternoon. But she saw from her log that she often spent her morning hours answering routine e-mail, visiting with colleagues, and handling relatively simple administrative tasks. She'd put off her most challenging and important work until the end of the day, often staying late into the night when she was too exhausted to think straight. So she reorganized her routine to dedicate more of her high-quality morning hours to her top projects. Several days a week she would close her door and ignore e-mail for a couple of hours. She said the new practice changed her life.

→ **Push for shorter meetings.** Would you have more time for your top projects if you didn't have to go to so many meetings? Chances are that some of your regular meetings take longer than they should. And if you're frustrated by the wasted time, other participants probably are as well. So even if you aren't chairperson, you may be able to convince your colleagues to experiment with quicker meetings. For example, if a meeting normally takes an hour, propose restructuring so that it lasts only 45 minutes.

→ **Resist distraction.** Once your plan for the day is in place, your next big challenge may be to avoid being hijacked by phone calls, e-mails, visitors, and your own compulsion to multitask. To be more efficient, you may need to overcome old habits, like checking e-mail every 10 minutes or answering the phone every time it rings. Your log will help you notice where your plans tend to go awry. Sometimes honoring your commitments means learning how to fight off other requests and temptations.

→ **Renegotiate your schedule as you go along.** The demands you face change constantly, and life does get in the way of your carefully planned agenda. Your goal is not to be a slave to your calendar, but rather to be impeccable in the way you use it to *manage* your commitments. When you're faced with the unexpected, you can often renegotiate dates and deadlines. Gina found life to be less stressful once she learned to anticipate scheduling problems and work out alternative plans.

→ **Align your time and priorities.** Your well-kept calendar can provide a clear picture of where your time goes. As you look at it, regularly ask whether the distribution of your time is consistent with your priorities. Is most of your time going to your most important activities? Are you saying "yes" to requests when your list of current objectives suggests that you should decline? And are you building in time for things that really matter to you personally, such as working out at the gym and other ways to take care of yourself? As you schedule, remember to honor not only the promises you make to other people, but also the commitments you make to yourself.

→ **Say "no."** A chunk of your day may be devoted to activities that feel urgent but aren't really very important. Maybe you agree to attend meetings or undertake projects not because they matter to you, but because you want to be nice, because you like to avoid conflict, or because "yes" is just your knee-jerk response. If so, you should probably get better at saying "no." And saying "no" gets easier with practice as you find ways to tactfully decline proposals and opportunities that aren't consistent with your priorities. One useful technique is to pause before you say "yes," in order to ask yourself what you'll give up if you don't say "no." For example, if a coworker invites you to a meeting that sounds kind of interesting, hesitate before saying "okay," and think about what else you could do with that hour.

21

Prioritize Your Priorities

In Chapter 20 we talked about how my client Gina developed better control of her work life by rethinking the way she approached her calendar. When Gina committed to more actively managing her schedule, one of her goals was to devote more of her work time to her most important activities. But when I asked Gina to name her highest priorities, she had a hard time deciding what should go on that list.

It is tempting to just react to whatever seems most pressing as a day goes along, and Gina often fell into that trap. She sometimes lost track of her more significant objectives because at any given moment they felt less urgent than other people's demands for action or attention.

Realizing she didn't have enough time or energy to go around, Gina resolved to think more carefully about how to flag high-value work. She decided that once a week she'd arrive early near her downtown office and spend an hour or so at her favorite coffee shop, sorting out her immediate priorities as she reviewed her calendar and project list. ***Here is the seven-point system that Gina uses stay in touch with her priorities, and a similar approach might work for you:***

1) **Remember the big picture.** A good foundation for setting your priorities is to draft a list or statement about what matters most. Gina wrote a "career vision," which was basically a list of her key values and work-life goals. It included items like, "nurture my team members," "stay current in my field," and "have time for a rich social life." Gina keeps a copy of her vision with her calendar and looks at it during her weekly priority review session.

2) **Prioritize work categories.** Gina knew that the items on her lengthy task list weren't equally productive. But she tended to vacillate in gauging their importance. Her particular problem was that she was easily sidetracked by other people's sense of urgency. She decided to keep her assignments on a steady course by sorting activities into these four categories:

   Tier One: Important to her bosses, to their goals, and to their success.

   Tier Two: Important to the goals and the success of her direct reports.

   Tier Three: Related to her routine management responsibilities, like human resource and budget matters.

   Tier X: Stuff that could be done by other people.

3) **Create a daily "List of 3."** A technique that made a big difference in Gina's efficiency was her new practice of starting every morning with a list of three tasks that must be done by day's end. These are the items that are so useful or important that their completion may make the day a success, no matter what else happens. She writes the list on an index card and posts it where she'll see it frequently.

4) **Schedule time for high priorities.** Gina makes standing appointments with herself and blocks out time on her calendar for both her List of 3 and tasks related to her Tier One projects. Because she feels most productive in the morning, she often sets aside and closely guards a block of time between 10 o'clock and noon. On some days she'll use this precious time block to concentrate on a single project, and on others she'll spend the hours moving quickly through a number of small steps for a variety of important assignments.

5) **Schedule low value time for lower-value work.** Administrative and other routine tasks may be of lower priority than your major projects, but they still have to be completed in a timely way. Because Gina feels less efficient late in the day, she sets aside some afternoon hours for handling this kind of work. She often makes a game of it by seeing how fast she can speed through her list. And she rewards herself, sometimes by leaving a little early, when she completes certain tedious reports.

6) **Find the biggest bang for your buck.** Some things aren't top priority in the grand scheme of things, but they're worth doing immediately because of how much trouble they'll save you in the long run. For example, if you suspect that a quick explanatory meeting would allow you to calm down a disgruntled colleague, you might want to add it to your List of 3. If you wait, the problem may fester and ultimately the misunderstanding will require much more of your energy to resolve.

7) **Get rid of clutter.** Some activities on your "to-do" list or calendar just aren't of high enough priority to be worth doing. Yet they tend to linger on your list, sometimes distracting you or making you feel guilty. It can feel liberating to get real about your odds of finishing these low value action items. Gina now scrutinizes her calendar and task list for this kind of clutter and says it feels great to delete it.

Play with prioritization systems until you find one that works

Time management experts have written about many different ways for setting priorities. I tend to be cautious about recommending any single approach because I've found that the clients most likely to stick with a system are the ones, like Gina, who develop their own hybrid approaches.

What may be most important is that you regularly pause and evaluate the relative importance and urgency of all the things you feel you must do. *As you go through your evaluation process, ask yourself questions such as these:*

→ How would I rank the relative importance of these items?

→ How do they relate to this year's top performance objectives? To my most important long-term career goals?

→ Is this both urgent and important? Or just urgent?

→ What will happen if I don't get this done?

→ What does my boss or client want most from me?

→ What actions will assure that this is a productive day?

→ What will I learn from this? Will it help me to grow?

→ Will this help me build or improve relationships with other people?

→ Could this expand my business or job description?

→ What will it take to make this a success?

22

Getting Your Boss to Listen

How can I get the boss to listen?" That's a question I often hear from clients. Perhaps you have the same problem. Is it sometimes hard to complete a project because you can't get the boss's attention? Do you head home feeling frustrated because your boss won't give you the feedback you need? Or, even worse, does your career feel off-kilter because you and your leader are out of sync?

No boss is perfect, most managers are too busy, and some are flat out weak. But complaining won't get you anywhere, and you have too much at stake to just throw up your hands when the communication process breaks down.

Part of your strategy as an entrepreneurial professional is to communicate smoothly with your bosses and clients, no matter how difficult it may be to reach them. Your goal is to assure delivery of your key messages even when it doesn't seem fair that you have to do so much of the hard work.

These tips can help you get through to your boss

Even if you and your boss communicate pretty well, *these strategies can make your messages even more effective:*

1) **Be succinct.** Assume your boss is busy and won't want to waste time. If you ask for three minutes to discuss something important but then talk for 10 before reaching your point, the boss could be feeling impatient or annoyed by the time you make your case.

2) **Plan ahead.** Before your conversation, be clear in your mind about your points, and be prepared to state them simply and directly. To prevent confusion or distraction, limit the number of items you intend to raise. If you've requested a meeting where you'll discuss several issues, propose a brief written agenda. A simple e-mail with a sentence about each topic can set up your conversation in a good way.

3) **Be clear about your goal.** Sometimes you have to choose between having your say and having your way. It can be tempting to use your face time for venting about your problems, but that might not lead to solutions. Be strategic in the way you frame your issues, and focus on positive proposals that will support your specific objectives.

4) **Understand their communication preferences.** If you don't get through, it may not be the content of your message so much as how or when you deliver it. Different people take in and share information in different ways. For example, bosses who are extroverts may be "external processors" who want to use you as a sounding board while they explore their own thoughts. While in processing mode they might not pay much attention to your agenda, so you should wait. And introverts may find listening to be tiring, so don't make your pitch after they've been through exhausting meetings. Notice how your boss communicates with her boss or clients, and try the same techniques. If she tends to put her most important requests in writing, do the same with yours.

5) **Be a mindful listener.** Strong communicators are active listeners. Your bosses expect you to listen carefully, and good listening helps you understand what they want. But at times when we think we're listening, we're sometimes focused on something else, such as what we want to say next. When you truly concentrate on deep listening, you'll come across to your boss as alert, centered, and respectful.

6) **Let go of frustration.** If the boss doesn't seem to listen, you actually have two challenges. The first, of course, is to break through the logjam by becoming an even better communicator. But there is only so much you can do, and much of this is about the boss, not about you. So the next challenge is to learn how to not let it bother you so much. It's vital that you don't obsess, or your annoyance could make the situation worse. Writing in a journal is one way to examine your negative reactions and let go of some of the emotion.

23

Leading Upward: Manage the Boss, in a Good Way

Although successful leadership styles vary considerably, the best leaders have attributes in common. For example, most tend to have integrity, strong value systems, and a genuine desire to do the right thing. The leaders I most admire are consistently willing to step forward and serve, even if a task is menial or unlikely to lead to recognition. And their influence over other people extends in all directions. In other words, not only are they adept at managing their direct reports, but they are also able to guide other colleagues and collaborators.

Some of the stronger leaders exercise a special skill. They are able to lead upward, influencing their bosses to make better decisions and become more effective. For example, there's Sam*, who didn't expect to rise beyond his role as the VP of communications. He had five years until retirement, and he wanted during that time to contribute even more to the company he loved.

Without telling his colleagues, Sam adopted the goal of thoroughly supporting and even mentoring Joe, his young and recently arrived CEO. Because of his job, Sam had a good, comprehensive view of the company's activities and customer relationships. And he made an effort to listen to colleagues and stakeholders at every level. Sam gathered and sorted feedback and data, and relayed it in a positive, effective way to Joe. Being well informed, and having Sam as a sounding board, helped Joe to grow quickly into his job. And his private mission of fully supporting Joe made Sam's last years of work more interesting and rewarding.

In my own corporate career, the boss who taught me most about leadership was a humble guy named Dave Weatherwax. During his decade as senior VP and general counsel of Consolidated Natural Gas Company, Dave remained modest and never seemed to seek the limelight. And yet he exercised great influence, often quietly guiding the rest of the C-Suite.

During my first year with the CNG, I watched Dave carefully, trying to learn from his low-key but effective approach to management. Finally the day came when a colleague and I met with Dave to pitch a major initiative, asking his support for a public outreach project we thought might be outside his comfort zone. In making our case, I raised every argument I could think of, carefully framing my points to reflect Dave's goals, interests, and possible concerns.

Dave listened intently, and then to our surprise he approved the proposal on the spot. His only change was to set a budget much bigger than the one we'd requested. We were almost giddy with success as we left his office. Then he stuck his head out his door and called us back. He said, "I just want you to know that I saw what you were doing. But I don't mind being led, if it's done really well."

Dave let us know that upward management can benefit everyone, but it must be done adroitly and in the right spirit. ***Here are strategies to consider if you want to become better at leading up:***

→ **First, set unselfish goals.** Leading upward is not the same thing as trying to manipulate the situation so you look good or somehow score a win. "Leading" is about offering proposals, guidance, and support that serve the interests of the organization. When you step in to lead your boss, your intent should be to remain relatively invisible as you give the enterprise a helpful nudge. You quietly act like a CEO, serving the team with vision and integrity, and nobody else needs to know about it. Part of

Dave's leadership strength was his authentic humility. He had no interest in self-aggrandizement, but sincerely cared about serving the greater good.

→ **Understand what your bosses need.** If you want to influence and assist the people above you, it's critical to have a good sense of their goals and responsibilities. Develop a theory of how success will look from their perspective. Consider the organization's mission, current strategy, and primary challenges, and look carefully at what your bosses are trying to accomplish.

→ **Maintain your areas of expertise.** One reason for Dave's considerable influence was that everybody respected his judgment as a lawyer. Even after his portfolio was broadened to include a variety of functions, he was recognized as the ultimate legal expert. A good way to maximize your influence is to develop an area where you are recognized as *the* authority. Find a niche where you can excel and bring value to the enterprise by remaining current and by continuing to build your special skills and knowledge.

→ **Be gracious in managing credit and blame.** Dave understood that credit is a vast resource to be spread around, not hoarded. He worked hard to make his boss, the CEO, look good. And when things were going well in his area, he invited his team to step forward and be thanked for the good work. Though Dave was lavish in sharing credit, he didn't indulge in spreading blame. When problems arose, he took responsibility. When someone made a mistake, he typically examined the situation in a lawyer-like way, and then turned immediately to finding solutions.

→ **Report without drama.** Your boss is more likely to rely on you if she can count on you to report the facts in a simple, straightforward way. Create a strong network for gathering information and build your credibility by telling the truth without indulging in gossip, exaggeration, or negative commentary. It makes sense to be tactful, but you won't be acting like a leader if you only tell your boss what she wants to hear.

→ **Be organized.** Your bosses' time is limited, and one way you can assist them is by making sure that none of it is wasted.

When you meet with them, be prompt, stick with an agenda, and don't talk any longer than necessary. Look for opportunities to help your bosses keep things moving smoothly and find ways to save them from unnecessary stress.

A good approach for improving your upward management skills is to search for role models. Look around for people who are successful in leading upward, and learn from how they do it. And, if you already head a team, watch for times when one of the members is particularly skillful at managing *you*. Notice whether they are good at leading up because they save you time, provide you with something you need, or make you feel more positive.

24

The Jimmy Fallon Touch: Good Manners Help You Shine

I was delighted when a radio commentator reported that the National League of Junior Cotillions chose Jimmy Fallon to top its "Best-Mannered List for 2014."

According to the League's Website, Fallon was selected as Number One "for maintaining the dignity and respect of others through his comedic disposition as host of *The Tonight Show.*"

I can't think of a better choice. Part of what makes Fallon so charming is that he invariably seems delighted to be with his guests and determined to help them look good. Much of our enjoyment comes from his intense interest in their success and his whole body laughter at their jokes. Even if you don't think he's funny, you can't help but like Jimmy Fallon. Perhaps social graces like his are so appealing because they are a low-key application of the Golden Rule. The way he interacts with others seems to say: I'll be nice to you and I have confidence that you'll be nice to me.

The ideals of polite behavior may not be a topic of discussion in your workplace. But you'll know what your colleague means if he describes someone as "a real gentleman," or "a true lady." People with excellent social manners tend to stand out. And we enjoy being with polite people because they tend to notice us and are so aware of *our* needs.

For a personal brand that sets you apart from the crowd, learn from Fallon. Develop a reputation for treating everyone with respect. Of course, what counts most are the big things, like pitching in to support your coworkers in a crisis. But you can enhance your brand by consistently exhibiting good manners in even small ways. ***These seven strategies can help you develop the Jimmy Fallon touch:***

1) **Say "hello."** When we're around other people, it's always decent to acknowledge their presence. Your rude coworkers may act like others are invisible, but with a simple "good morning" you can forge a sense of connection and goodwill.

2) **Shake hands.** The perfect handshake is valued in U.S. culture, and it allows you to exude confidence and warmth. This simple gesture can help you to make a good first impression, reconnect with someone you haven't seen in a while, or say a polished "goodbye." Try these tips to perfect your handshake:

   ◆ Be quick to extend your right hand, particularly if you are the older person or have the higher authority.

   ◆ Look the other person in the eye before and during your handshake. And offer a greeting or pleasantry such as, "It's great to meet you."

   ◆ Allow your grip to be firm but not crushing.

   ◆ Shake your hand up and down, just a few inches, and not more than once or twice.

3) **Speak with basic courtesy.** Your habits of speech say a lot about you. These guidelines set a minimum standard:

   ◆ Be quick to say "please" and "thank you" to everyone.

   ◆ Say "excuse me" if you bump into or must interrupt someone.

   ◆ Avoid profanity and crude language.

   ◆ Praise or congratulate folks on their achievements, even if it requires you to bite back a twinge of envy.

4) **Be considerate of others' time.** When people are busy, it's unkind to waste their minutes and hours:

   ◆ Be punctual for meetings and appointments.

   ◆ Respond quickly to invitations (to save time spent on follow-up).

   ◆ Don't waste time with rants or lengthy accounts of small matters.

   ◆ Don't play with your phone during a meeting or conversation.

5) **Treat colleagues with class.** The way you talk about others can shape your reputation:

   ◆ Don't gossip with coworkers about coworkers.

   ◆ Don't bad-mouth your boss, your team, or your organization.

   ◆ Share credit, paying special attention to junior team members whose work might otherwise go unnoticed.

6) **Debate with civility.** Disagreement is part of the creative process and responsible professionals aren't afraid to speak up, but that's no excuse for being mean:

   ◆ Express criticism in terms of the work or the concept, and avoid making it about the person.

   ◆ When possible, frame your comments in a positive way.

   ◆ Avoid sarcasm because it's seldom amusing and can lead to misunderstandings.

   ◆ Let the other side speak, genuinely listen to their views, and imagine what it's like from their perspective.

7) **Dine with style.** Table manners are about assuring that everyone has a good time and nobody's enjoyment is ruined by someone else's gross behavior. Don't get hung up on questions about which fork to use. The point of standardized silverware rules is to make guests comfortable as they select the implement for each course. And nobody will care if you pick up the "wrong" fork. On the other hand, avoid disrupting the table by knowing which wine glass and bread plate belong to you. The standard is that

all glasses are placed on the right side of the main dinner plate ("dr*i*nk to the r*i*ght"), and other dishes are on the left ("*e*at to the l*e*ft"). Beyond that, in U.S. business circles, these rules are widely accepted:

◆   Don't object when your host indicates where you should sit.

◆   Always chew with your mouth closed.

◆   Don't speak when you have food in your mouth.

◆   Eat quietly, taking small manageable bites.

◆   Don't slurp or blow on your food to cool it—just wait until it's not so hot.

◆   Never blow your nose on your napkin.

◆   Never pick your teeth at the table.

The main point is that people with the Jimmy Fallon touch project the message that everyone matters. They're considerate. And they help build cultures where everyone can collaborate, perform well, and enjoy the work. It's no wonder that other people like being around them.

25

Do's and Don'ts of Saying "Sorry"

As we discussed in Chapter 19, people often judge you by the way you speak. If you develop annoying speech mannerisms, distracted listeners may not value your comments or perceive the full scope of your expertise. On the other hand, your personal brand is enhanced when you're seen as someone who always seems to say the right thing.

Do you aspire to be one of those tactful, well-spoken people who are welcomed into most conversations? One way to begin to speak more gracefully is to listen carefully, so you can pick up cues from the crowd and adopt the best tone. Listening to the way other people interact enhances your sense of balance; it helps you to avoid the extremes of expressing too much or too little, or coming off as too warm or too cold.

Tact also requires an awareness of the tremendous power of certain words. Some words have more consequences than others and should be used with care. One of those big impact words is "sorry." It's typically defined to include emotions like regret, sadness, and penitence. But in practice it can have many shades of meaning. And when we say the phrase "I'm sorry" in a work environment, we might be expressing anything from remorse to subservience, uncertainty, or defiance.

The nuances of the word do vary with organizational cultures. ***But here's my take on how, when, and whether to say, "Sorry":***

→ **Do say you're sorry when you've done something wrong.** When you screw up on the job, the best plan is to confess immediately, apologize sincerely, and turn quickly to rectifying the situation or making sure it won't happen again. For the victim, when you say "mea culpa" you make a bit of moral restitution. Your discomfort gives him some power over you, and he is able to decide whether to accept your apology or to withhold forgiveness. But apologizing can benefit you, as well. When you 'fess up, it's like a reset button, giving you a chance to move on and restore the normal order.

→ **Be sincere.** Not all apologies improve matters. Your "sorry" is more likely to be favorably received when you mean it. You can transmit the intensity of your regret by describing how you actually feel ("I was so upset that I couldn't sleep last night") and proposing a way to make up for your wrongdoing.

→ **Do say "sorry" even if you weren't to blame.** Sometimes we say "I'm sorry" not to express remorse, but to show our compassion. This might happen when things go wrong in some way far beyond your control, such as when horrible weather inconveniences your guests. Or you might say "I'm so sorry" to acknowledge a personal loss, such as a death in the family. Some psychological research suggests that this kind of "superfluous" apology can promote a sense of trust and connection between you and the listener, and make everybody feel better.

→ **Don't say it when you don't mean it.** Saying "I'm sorry" when you actually feel the opposite can come across to the recipient like an insult. "Sorry" is a complex word and it can be inflammatory when your nonverbal message is the opposite of regret. Don't make the situation worse by accompanying the phrase "I'm sorry" with a grimace or an eye roll. And avoid beginning your sentence with "I'm sorry, *but* . . ." When you don't feel at fault, avoid making a fake apology. Instead, focus on improving the situation and say something positive such as, "Let's see what we can do to fix this."

→ **Don't say "sorry" to soften an insult.** If you say, "Sorry, but this draft is no good," don't think your wording will make the message any easier to accept. If your remorse is genuine, make clear what it is you regret and then be direct in the way you deliver the rest of the message. You might say, "I'm truly sorry if this will ruin your weekend, but the client needs a number of changes in your draft."

→ **Don't say "sorry" when there's nothing to apologize for.** Some people repeatedly say "sorry" as a conscious way to express deference or humility. For others, the pattern may be an unconscious expression of uncertainty. Either way, constant apologies can make you look frightened or powerless. My competent and generally confident client Tina* developed the verbal tic of saying "I'm sorry" every time she was about to ask a question or make a suggestion. Her use of the phrase became so engrained she didn't know she was saying it. As soon as this habit was brought to her attention, Tina realized it made her sound like she was experiencing a crisis of confidence. Her closest colleagues admitted they found it annoying and, with her permission, they helped Tina break the habit by reminding her when there was no need to apologize.

Do you think that you say "I'm sorry" too often? Or perhaps you find it difficult to apologize and don't do it often enough? Becoming more aware of your speech patterns can help you decide whether they need some tweaking. To capture a clear picture of this kind of speech habit, keep a log for a few weeks. Write down every instance in which you apologized, noting what you were regretting and any impact from your remark. Sometimes it's hard to hear your own words, so this could be an occasion to call upon friends to gently point out your habit.

26

Find the Magic 20 Percent

My most vivid memories of business school include a few instances when professor Bill Day put aside the class syllabus and spoke vividly about phenomena that could make a difference in our lives.

In one such discussion, the professor urged us to stay focused on the important things in life by relying on the 80/20 Rule. That rule of thumb tells us that most of the results in any situation are determined by a small number of the causes. Expressed another way, the Rule predicts that about 80 percent of your achievements will flow from about 20 percent of the things you do. The numbers of "80" and "20" aren't absolute. The key point is that your bottom line isn't impacted in the same amount by each unit of your work or of your time. So a small proportion of your activity may be responsible for most of what you get done.

The Rule seems to have endless applications and has been given a variety of names, like the "Law of the Vital Few." Many accounts suggest that it was first applied as a business principle about a century ago as "Pareto's Law." Economist Vilfredo Pareto wrote that, in any situation, just a small portion of the resources will yield most of the outputs. For example, he said that if a government were to give a number of poor people money to invest in small businesses, the investors wouldn't all be equally successful. A small group (the 20 percent) would make most of the money resulting from the investments (the 80 percent).

What captured my imagination was when Professor Day told us that computer modeling can illustrate principles, like the 80/20 Rule, that demonstrate how the universe isn't just hopeless disorder. It was comforting to hear his evidence that the world operates according to some kind of logic. And I welcomed his suggestion that we can spot familiar patterns and use them to make better choices in our careers and in life.

It isn't necessary to understand *why* it works. ***If you look around, you'll see numerous applications of the 80/20 Rule:***

→ In a big organization, a few of the managers may deliver the lion's share of results.

→ Of your many clients, only a few may account for most of your income.

→ If you offer multiple products, it's likely that several will deliver most of your profits.

→ If you have lots of customers, about 20 percent of them may voice about 80 percent of the complaints.

And the Rule probably holds true in your personal life:

→ Of all the things you do, a few bring you most of the fun.

→ Of all your skills, a few deliver most of the rewards.

→ Of the many people you know, a few are responsible for much of the joy.

With these strategies, the 80/20 Rule can help sharpen your career

The Rule can remind you to stop obsessing about the lower priorities on your "to-do" list and shift your attention to your major objectives. It can help you find a place to get started when you're feeling overwhelmed. It suggests that you consider which 20 percent of your workload may make the most difference, and stop worrying about all the rest that won't count so much.

When you're in doubt about what to do next, turn to the 80/20 Rule for guidance like this:

→ **Focus on the big goal.** Don't try to pursue every opportunity that comes along. When there's too much to do, concentrate on activities most directly related to your key objectives. Shift more of your attention to the 20-or-so percent of tasks or events most likely to support your top priorities.

→ **Don't try to be great at everything.** Find ways to spend more of your time on the activities that you do well and that yield results. Let's say you're a fundraiser who is great with people but not so proficient at generating those vital follow-up reports. Instead of spending long hours struggling over your desktop, find ways to free up your time for face-to-face contact. To meet your deadlines, get smart about delegating, outsourcing, using new technology, or renegotiating the deskwork that will never be your strong suit.

→ **Choose your companions.** Make choices about how much time to spend with the various people in your life. At work, don't obsess about annoying or unproductive colleagues. As much as possible, disengage yourself from the time-wasters and naysayers. Instead, direct more of your attention to people who may become productive allies.

→ **Look at the data.** Sometimes it is worth examining the actual numbers to determine precisely how much of your time and resources result in most of your achievements. As we discussed in Chapter 21 on managing priorities, a good way to get a more realistic picture of your work patterns is to keep a log for a while. You may be surprised by how few of your activities deliver most of your success.

→ **Simplify.** Applying the Rule is sometimes simply a matter of getting rid of clutter and distractions. If everything seems too complicated, look for ways to get rid of some of the massive 80 percent, so that the vital 20 percent will become more evident. This might require delegating tasks, declining invitations, getting rid of low-value products, simplifying your routines, and reducing the archive of documents and stacks of stuff that you've been saving, just in case.

→ **Pursue your passions.** Identify which 20 percent of your life yields your greatest satisfaction, enjoyment, and sense of well-being, and reflect that knowledge in the way you schedule your time. If being in nature helps to keep you feeling balanced and there's no time on your calendar for a walk in the park, it's time to make a shift.

27

How to Create Mentoring that Works Both Ways

Back in the 1970s, feminists seized on mentoring as a way to help women ease their way through the men's club atmosphere then dominating so many American offices. Through the years, the idea has become mainstream and now there's a widespread understanding that having supportive mentors helps both women and men to advance professionally. But the definition of "mentor" varies widely, and not all career-focused mentoring programs succeed.

What makes structured programs and individual efforts so difficult to get right is that mentoring involves building a relationship between two people. And strong human relationships require a delicate mix of hard work, honest communication, and good luck.

As with any healthy relationship, a mentoring partnership prospers only when both parties receive value. Initially, the mentor may be motivated simply by a desire to give back and to be a good citizen. And early in a relationship the mentee usually does get the most benefit, including sympathetic advice and, sometimes, an active champion at critical moments. But when the relationship really clicks, the mentor eventually receives at least as much as she gives.

If you're the mentor, one of the first rewards is the pleasure of having someone listen to you and the good feeling that flows from him or her following your advice. Then, as a relationship grows, the mentee's questions and feedback can give you a chance to pause and gain a new perspective. Through the long term, your conversations tend to become truly two-way, with both of you seeking advice, sharing insights, and exploring delicate career questions in an environment of trust.

Several of my dearest friendships began decades ago when I agreed to serve as a mentor, motivated simply by a desire to support deserving young professionals. I can't think about mentoring without feeling a wave of gratitude for two particular mentees, Andrea Wilkinson and Sherry Little. When I met these two best friends they were young congressional staffers, thrilled to be working on Capitol Hill, but not always sure about how to build careers in the government.

First Andrea, and later Sherry, asked me to serve as a mentor. Both were obviously talented and I enjoyed their company, so I said "yes" without giving it much thought. At the beginning, we spent much of our time together talking about their work challenges. But soon I was hearing as much good advice as I could offer. Through the years, Andrea and Sherry have pushed me beyond my career comfort zone, sent along clients and opportunities, challenged me to be less self-deprecating, and have been there for all my biggest events.

These strategies can help you create powerful mentoring relationships

Being involved in mentoring can be enormously rewarding, whether you're the guide or the protégée. *If you want to attract additional mentors, or strengthen the relationships you already have, try these tactics:*

→ **To identify mentors, begin with casual connections.** If you hope to recruit a mentor, don't start with complete strangers. Most of these people are too busy and unlikely to make time for you. Instead, look to your network. As we discussed in Chapter 10, your network extends from your inner circle all the way out to communities of folks you haven't even met yet, like members of your professional groups or your college alumni association. Think about the people with whom you have even a slight connection and gradually strengthen some of those relationships, slowly and steadily, one Sugar Grain at a time.

→ **To recruit mentors, request a bit of advice.** All too often, young professionals ask higher-ranking colleagues to serve as mentors, are told "yes," but then nothing happens. Usually it's more effective to gradually engage advisors, starting with a small request and encouraging further involvement as they get to know you better. For example, you might approach a senior colleague and say something like, "I want to get better at X, and I notice that you are great at X, so I wonder if you could give me advice about this X-type challenge?"

→ **For more help, make a specific request.** Some mentors would like to do more, but they don't know where to start. They can't read your mind, and it's often up to you to explain when you need more than advice. So make an explicit request when you want something from a mentor. If programs, procedures, or deadlines are involved, do all the homework, so you make it as easy as possible for them to put in a good word or fight your battles. And understand that it isn't fair to ask for action if your mentor doesn't have suitable rank, access, or knowledge.

→ **Welcome honesty.** At times a mentor's most important contribution is to give constructive feedback, even when it's unpleasant for you to hear it. If you're working on a project in which your mentor has expertise, ask for suggestions about how to improve your chances for success. Don't allow yourself to be offended by honest feedback, even if it is hard to swallow, and resist the urge to respond defensively.

→ **Aim for two-way relationships.** Mentoring works best when both parties make an effort and enjoy some benefit. If you are trying to forge a stronger bond with your mentor, ask yourself what's in it for them. Can you, the mentee, make the relationship more valuable by serving as a source of information and support? Do you know what they care about most? Have you figured out the kinds of activities and venues they prefer?

→ **Practice sponsoring and mentoring.** To learn how to create better relationships, look for opportunities to practice *being* the mentor. Even if you are at the bottom of your hierarchy at work, you can find mentees through alumni and nonprofit networks. As you find ways to make contributions to your mentees, you will get a better sense of how to manage upward and energize your own mentors.

Although there are many reasons to be a mentor, much of the joy comes from helping someone else. If others guided you along your professional path, now is a good time to pay it forward. If you didn't have the help you needed, break the negative cycle by giving someone else the kind of support that would have made your life easier. *If you want to be a great mentor, consider these suggestions:*

→ **Listen.** You can't solve everything. But you can always help by asking questions in a positive way and genuinely listening to the answers.

→ **Request plans.** When mentees identify realistic goals, suggest that it's time to create a plan. Help them identify action steps and milestones, and hold them accountable for moving forward.

→ **Make connections.** Be alert to opportunities to tap into your own network on behalf of mentees who need information or introductions. Once you build up a bank of mentoring relationships, it can be particularly gratifying when your long-term protégées agree to help out your newest crop of mentees.

→ **Meet regularly.** Don't let strong mentoring relationships fade away after the initial challenges have been addressed. If the match between the two of you still feels right, suggest ways to continue the conversation, even if there is no pressing need. You've both made an investment, and the best part of your partnership may be just beginning.

Reciprocal mentoring can be powerful

The classical image of mentoring involves a relationship where an older, capable person helps to guide someone with less experience and knowledge. That idea of a wise, generous senior advisor leading us along a career path can be wonderful and soothing, but it's not always available or even desirable.

Here's what can make mentoring really hum: creating relationships intended to work both ways.

I thought about this new style of mentoring during a long weekend at our Virginia farmhouse, as I dropped in and out of a three-day conversation between my husband, Andy Alexander, and one of his much younger professional pals. Andy was the longtime Washington bureau chief for the Cox Newspapers chain, where he also ran the international news operation. He won journalism awards and served a term as ombudsman of *The Washington Post*. Once a classic newspaper guy, these days his work includes teaching and fostering media innovation, mainly at Ohio University's Scripps College of Communication.

Andy's 20-something friend Ryan Lytle has racked up an impressive resume as a multimedia expert. An outstanding 2010 Scripps College graduate, today Ryan is a rising star at Mashable.com, a global source of news "for the digital generation."

As the two men brainstormed about trends in delivering the news, what fascinated me about their interaction was the way each one listened so intently and seemed to be learning from the other. When I asked about it, Ryan said one thing he learns from veterans who grew up in a very different news business is how to build organizations and grow leadership. Andy said, "Everything I do professionally is about the future of journalism. And part of being engaged is staying in touch with the people, like Ryan, who are creating that future."

Andy and Ryan didn't create a formal mentoring relationship. But their style of dialogue illustrates the benefits of an emerging concept: *reciprocal* mentoring, where each partner is both teacher and student. Both men enjoy and benefit from their talks. The differences in their age, skill set, and experience are what make their sharing so interesting and valuable. ***If you're ready to give reciprocal mentoring a try, consider this approach:***

→ **Think about the potential exchange.** As a starting point, define what you want to learn and some of the strengths you have to offer. If you have potential partners in mind, approach them with the idea of mutual mentoring. If the problem is that you don't know where to start, spread the word about what you're seeking. Professional, community, and alumni circles can provide venues for meeting people of different generations and backgrounds.

→ **Identify needs and goals.** It's not enough for partners to begin with a vague sense that they'd like some career help. Each partner should enter the process with clear ideas about issues to explore and forms of assistance that would be welcome. Later, when the relationship is successfully launched, it might grow in surprising directions.

→ **Consider logistics.** It's great if you find a mentor in your neighborhood and can meet over coffee or lunch. But what if you go through your national group and find an ideal partner who lives across the country? Explore options like phone calls or video chats, and set a schedule that's comfortable and convenient for both of you.

28

Don't Be Sabotaged by Your Own Frustration

Years ago I learned something about career resilience by watching how two women in the same large organization handled their work-related frustration. Mary* had an abusive boss who bullied her and made her days miserable. She was from a humble background and not as highly educated as some of her colleagues, and she felt shy about confiding in coworkers when the boss insulted and demeaned her. Senior management finally became aware of the boss's ugly habits when he was investigated and fired for unrelated wrongdoing.

Mary knew that she had strong grounds for complaint, but she decided to let go of her hurt and anger and become strategic. In spite of her bad experience, she wanted to stay with the organization, and she convinced management to provide her with training and opportunities in a different professional field. Mary became an excellent student and her confidence grew. As the years went by, she was promoted and ultimately she built a new career that brought her great pride.

Elsewhere in the organization, Cheri* was passed over for several management slots. She was smart, polished, and technically proficient, but was told that she wasn't a good fit for the leadership track she hoped to pursue. Cheri felt entitled to a promotion and was angry about not moving up in the way she'd expected. Instead of listening to the feedback and trying another approach, she fumed and grumbled to anyone who would listen. As Cheri allowed her resentment to grow, her coworkers tired of the chip on her shoulder.

Nobody was sad to see Cheri go when she was hired away by a start-up company. And she didn't resist the urge to fully express her bitterness. In her last week on the job, Cheri told her bosses just what she thought of them. When the start-up quickly failed, nobody on her old team wanted to write her a favorable recommendation. Cheri ultimately had to take a lower-level job in a different field.

Move out of your own way and let go of workplace frustration

Do you arrive home from work too anxious to relax and enjoy your evening? Do you find yourself waking up in the middle of the night, fuming about what they're doing at the office? Do you hear yourself complaining to colleagues about how things are done around here?

Professional life has always been full of annoying jolts and tedious challenges. Some career paths have become increasingly bumpy in recent years, with belt-tightening and increasing demands for production. It's understandable if you're feeling discouraged and indignant about how you've been treated.

But just because there are strong reasons for your negative emotions doesn't mean you can afford to indulge in them. You are in charge of your career. If you hope to stay where you are, and you want things to improve, you need to come up with a plan.

And before you can implement your plan, you may need an attitude adjustment. ***Here are reasons to stop fuming and let go of your preoccupation with the bad stuff at work:***

→ **You must be present.** If you want to move to a better
   career phase, you have to operate in high gear. But if you're

preoccupied with how you were treated last week or last year, you can't be fully engaged in what's happening today. If you give in to annoyance, you could be less alert to new opportunities, less creative, and more likely to make mistakes.

→ **You must be energetic.** When you're trying to launch a new plan, it helps to be in great shape. But if you can't let go of your angst, you won't sleep as well, your stress level will slow you down, your health might suffer, and you won't be able to do your best work.

→ **It's best to come across as an upbeat team player.** Your best friends may be willing to listen to the story of your bad breaks, but even they will grow tired of you if you don't move on. Most folks prefer working with positive people, and they tend to avoid the high maintenance whiners. When you find a way to release your negativity, you'll be more productive, work better with others, and attract more opportunities.

Do you feel more like Cheri than Mary? Is it possible that your continuing frustration is undercutting your good work and limiting your career mobility? *If it's time to lose your negative attitude, these strategies can help:*

→ **Notice.** Becoming aware of your frustration can be the first step in letting it go. Take a careful look at how you've been feeling and be honest with yourself about the consequences. Consider keeping a journal of your feelings. Once you have specifically described your misfortune and the pain it caused you, it's much easier to move past it all.

→ **Be grateful.** Neuroscience research suggests that we don't experience gratitude and anxiety at the same time. As a result, your ire will naturally dissipate when you focus on things that cause you to feel thankful. So make a list of things for which you're most grateful and read that list a few times a day, including first thing in the morning and last thing at night.

→ **Take breaks.** By pausing and shifting your focus, you can dispel pent-up antagonism and feel refreshed. Whether it means chatting with a friend, taking a short walk, or spending a few minutes meditating, take frequent breaks throughout the workday. And remember that regular exercise provides a change of pace and can help you feel more cheerful.

→ **Forgive.** When you can't stop being upset about how management has treated you, you're likely to remain bogged down in the past. But when you elect to stop blaming people, you can move beyond yesterday, enjoy today, and look forward to tomorrow. Many spiritual traditions offer guidance about the benefits of and the path to forgiveness.

29

Yes, You Can Do Something about Difficult Colleagues

Does it feel like your job would be more fun if you could work with a different crowd? Are you surrounded by whiners, chronic pessimists, backstabbers, or other difficult people? Or is going to the office less pleasant because of that one person whom you just can't stand?

In any workplace there may be folks who are hard to get along with. Sometimes you can reduce the pain by staying out of their way. But avoiding their company may not be an option. *Here are five suggestions for dealing with your difficult colleague:*

1) **Don't escalate the problem.** The first rule is to not make things worse by indulging in petty revenge, sulking, or gossip about what a jerk that guy is. Even if he started it, the wise move is to take the high road. If you spend too much time complaining behind his back, your colleagues may think that you're just as

bad as he is. When you disagree with him about a project, limit your comments to the work itself. And never get personal.

2) **Confide in a trusted friend or colleague.** Though you don't want to indulge in public rants, it can be helpful to describe the situation to another person. If you're feeling angry, hurt, or frustrated, it's hard to objectively assess your options. Brainstorming with someone may help you identify ways to address the problem and move on.

3) **Understand other personality types.** Just as some are born left-handed and others are right-handed, people tend to fall into various broad personality categories. For example, some of us are extroverts, and we like to brainstorm out loud, sharing our thoughts long before we've reached our conclusions. This can be annoying to introverts who may prefer a quieter environment where people don't start to talk until they know what they want to say. As you learn more about basic personality types, it's easier to recognize when other people's behavior is not about you—it is just how they are made. Tools such as the readily available Myers-Briggs Type Indicator can help you to understand what makes you tick, and suggest strategies for communicating with people whose approach to work is different than yours.

4) **Listen to them in a new way.** Once we start thinking of people as "difficult," we tend to stop hearing what they say. As they speak, we feel defensive, and we start working on our rebuttals instead of paying attention to their points. Most humans aren't skillful at hiding what we feel, so at some level they know we're ignoring them, causing their obnoxious behavior to intensify. You can often defuse a tense situation by putting aside your distrustful response and concentrating on what is being said. By listening closely, you may forge a connection and launch a new era of healthy communications.

5) **Manage your attitude.** Although you can't control other people, you can shift the dynamic by changing how you respond to them. Because you can't really hide your feelings, if you approach someone in a mood of anger, annoyance, or contempt, he'll have some sense of it. And his answer to your negative attitude might

be an even stronger display of fury or rudeness. You can break the negative cycle by adjusting your own emotional state. If you learn to shift the way you feel, you can dramatically change relationships that traditionally have been rocky. ***Try this approach to adjusting your reaction to a colleague:***

- Start by quietly recalling the emotions you experienced the last time you clashed with your difficult colleague. Did you feel hurt, tense, or frustrated? Where in your body did you experience the feelings and tension? Was it in your shoulders or your stomach?

- Now take a few deep breaths. As you breathe, relax your shoulders, clenched fists, or other body parts that feel tight. Visualize each breath as a flow of calm energy, helping to release that tension.

- Now that you're more relaxed, try to imagine an alternative emotional state that might feel better and make it easier for you to deal with the colleague. For example, might it help if you could look at that guy with some sense of compassion?

- Come up with a simple phrase to describe that alternative emotional state such as, "I am calm and have compassion in my heart." Through the next few days, practice repeating the phrase. As you do so, experiment with using it to help yourself feel more relaxed and upbeat.

- Once you've practiced in safe places to summon up your more positive emotional state, try out the technique in more challenging situations. You might use the technique when you're annoyed with a waiter, or placed on hold by a call center. When you feel like you have the knack, call up your positive attitude when you're actually with your difficult colleague. Now that you're able to put aside your bad feelings, they won't have so much power over you. And you might find that their attitude changes, as well.

As we discussed in the last chapter, you won't be able to change many of the frustrating situations in your career. But it's easier to move forward once you've learned how to put your frustration aside.

30

Find or Build Communities

When pundits describe the characteristics of successful entrepreneurs, they may emphasize independent thinking, a tolerance for risk, or the willingness to break rules. But when I try to predict the success of either business owners creating their own thing, or intrapreneurs making their way within large organizations, I tend to look at something else. I find that, though their personalities vary widely, most effective entrepreneurial thinkers seem to share one trait: They understand the power of their networks.

In Chapter 10 we talked about how you might visualize your network as a series of four concentric circles, starting with your core group in Circle #1 and moving out to your far-flung communities in Circle #4. Not everyone actively manages that fourth Circle, but in building your career like an entrepreneur, it's smart to explore the power of your communities.

A "community" is a group that has members, rather than a collection of unconnected people. Membership may be informal or unacknowledged, but the community members are linked by common values or interests. And often they have some feeling of belonging, as well as a sense of mattering—of being able to make a difference to the group.

Among your communities are your neighbors, people with a history or interest similar to yours, professionals who share your training and challenges, and members of the clubs and associations you have formally joined.

Your communities are packed with people you may never have met. But when you approach someone as a member of your group, it's unlikely he'll treat you like a stranger. Your communities are a source of business intelligence, customers, mentors, referrals, and friends.

There's a growing body of research that links good health with one's degree of social connection. That reflects not just relationships within your inner circle, but also your interaction with broader communities. Reasons for the health impact might be that supportive communities can help you to manage stress, gain perspective, and maintain healthy habits.

Beyond that, your emotions and behaviors can be influenced by the emotions and behaviors of those in your extended communities. Research on human networks suggests that your attitude and habits may be shaped or reinforced not only by your close contacts, but also by your contacts' contacts, and their contacts as well. If the people in your communities are energetic, helpful, and creative, their positive vibes can be contagious, helping you to stay positive as you push your boundaries.

No matter how busy they might otherwise be, successful entrepreneurs are often highly attuned to their business, customer, and social communities, looking to them for inspiration, technical knowledge, clients, and empathy. Molly Peterson, the photographer who shot the photo on the back of this book, is a fine example of a modern entrepreneur who is investing in her communities as she continues to invent her multifaceted career.

Molly's documentary-style photos are beautiful and authentic and have been widely published. She is known particularly for her food and farm shots, and she took the pictures for *Growing Tomorrow*, a 2015 book with portraits of 18 sustainable farmers. Photography is only one of Molly's professions. She and her husband run Heritage Hollow Farms, where they raise grass-fed livestock and also operate a farm store in Sperryville, Virginia.

Although it seems that two active careers would take up all Molly's time, she's one of those natural givers and connectors, active in both community and online groups. I bump into her at meetings of a nonprofit board and also via social media, where she has built a broad following. It was through customer and online communities that Molly came up with one of the farms' distribution channels. She noticed that many Washington, D.C., residents care about the benefits of sustainable meat but can't always make the two-hour drive to

Sperryville or be available for a scheduled delivery. So she arranged for meat orders to be delivered to freezers installed in Washington area Crossfit Gyms.

When I asked Molly why she's so active in the community, despite her heavy schedule, she said, "I was taught from a young age by both of my parents to be curious, connected, and 'well rounded.' They were both entrepreneurs, as were many of my extended family members. I've always been curious and interested in a world outside of my own: Why do people do what they do, is there a deeper reason for it, what makes them 'tick'? I also feel it never hurts to ask; nothing frustrates me more than when I'm told that something can't be done simply because that isn't the way it's usually done."

Molly also said, "Outside of my careers I have a genuine care and concern for my community and the Earth and how to make it better, more joy-filled, healthier—whether that's through my photography as art, through the way we raise our livestock that ultimately feeds families, or through my time. It's a fine balancing act to strive to keep all the pieces in line, but my brain rarely slows down. I carry a notebook with me everywhere to make sure I keep on track with all of the daily tasks and requests."

Become active in your existing communities, or discover new ones

Staying in touch with a range of supportive communities can be key to building your resilient career. *These strategies can help you to develop deeper community involvement:*

→ **Identify your communities.** Start by listing groups of people with whom you are already associated. This might include groups related to places where you worked or went to school, professional associations, neighborhood committees, and online groups. Then think about topics or activities that interest you, and search for additional organizations of like-minded people. If you're an Italian American who likes to raise herbs and cook, look around for a garden club, gourmet group, or Italian-American association.

→ **Become active.** Study the list of the organizations you belong to now, as well as those you might like to join. Target a few communities where you'd like to raise your profile and build relationships. Then look for opportunities to make a

contribution. This might mean volunteering for a service project, joining a committee, or simply attending functions.

→ **Care about an issue.** Many communities are built around
causes or local needs. If your family has been touched by cancer, you may want to join a committee that raises money for
research. If you're concerned about children in your town who
live in poverty, join the local pantry organization or a big sisters
group. The best way to get to know people can be working with
them to address a problem you all care about.

→ **Be a mentor.** To connect with a younger crowd or make your
network more diverse, offer to serve as a mentor. Contact a professional association, or get in touch directly with someone who
is starting something new, and volunteer to share your skill set
or be an advisor.

→ **Give money.** If you're overwhelmingly busy right now, you can
quietly begin to build name recognition by making contributions to nonprofit groups. If your name shows up repeatedly on
donor lists, group leaders may eventually beg you to become
more actively involved.

→ **Launch a new group.** If you're passionate about an activity or
cause, don't be discouraged if you can't find an organization
for people who feel the same way. It can be surprisingly easy to
start your own group. Use social media, community bulletin
boards, newspaper ads, or other mechanisms to publicize your
interest. Your first event might be anything from a Twitter chat
to a coffee date with one other person. Other people love communities, and they might be willing to join yours, particularly
if you're willing to do a lot of the work.

31

Make Your Meeting Time More Productive

How much time do you devote to meetings? You might want to say, "Too much!" But seriously, do you have any idea what percentage of your work life is spent meeting with people? Try calculating it. If meetings take just 20 percent of your time, and you work 40 hours a week, 50 weeks a year, that's a whopping 400 hours annually.

Just think about what you'd be able to accomplish if you could retrieve only 10 percent of that meeting time. You would have a whole week to devote to your top priorities.

In fact, if you start to rethink your approach to meetings, you can find ways both to spend less time at conference tables, and also to get more value from the meetings that you do attend. ***Start by trying out these strategies to reduce the hours you spend in meetings:***

→ **Cut them short.** Explore with your colleagues whether some regular meetings could be shortened. For example, if your team always gathers on Monday mornings for 90 minutes, aim for a new time limit of one hour. And if other meetings typically last one or one-half hour, could you all agree to cut them down to 45 or 20 minutes? An extra bonus of shortened meetings will be the gap between your standard ending and starting times. Participants in your 10 o'clock will be late less often because they'll now have a chance to take a break or check their e-mail after their nine o'clock ends at 9:45 a.m.

→ **Stand up or walk around.** Another way to encourage shorter meetings is to occasionally schedule quick standing meetings, where nobody takes the time to sit down. And an approach that works well for some kinds of topics is the walking meeting, where two or three of you will stroll for half an hour, as you talk through your issues. This can happen inside, in large or connected buildings, or outside, perhaps in nearby parks. I know a leader who twice a week has a 30-minute walk-and-talk time block on her calendar. Any staff member can sign up to be her walking companion, and if the slot is left open, she may invite a staffer she rarely has a chance to see.

→ **Say no.** You might also reduce your time in meetings by getting better at declining invitations. Of course, many meetings are useful or required. But sometimes your participation isn't all that important, and you can be excused simply by explaining that you have another commitment (which might mean your scheduled time at your desk).

→ **Create a no-meeting day.** Finally, consider working out an agreement with your team members for a meeting-free time zone. If you all decide to keep Wednesday free of meetings, you can plan on one day a week for telecommuting or concentrating on your top priority projects.

When you run the meetings, keep them productive with these strategies

Some of your most valuable meetings are the ones where you're in charge. And if you're the leader, you have an opportunity to make better use of your time and theirs by tweaking the routine. *Here are nine basic rules for running effective meetings:*

1) **Know the purpose.** Before you send out invitations, be clear about your goals in calling a meeting. When no business is pressing, or work can be accomplished more easily in another way, be flexible about cancelling regular meetings. Leaders known for holding pointless meetings may have a tough time attracting participation when they really need it.

2) **Have an effective invitation process.** For successful meetings, you might have to be assertive about sending invitations and reminding participants of the details.

    ◆ Even if it's a regular meeting and everybody knows the drill, specify the date, day, time, and place.

    ◆ Routinely send at least one reminder, at the last minute.

    ◆ If you're using e-mail for invitations or reminders, put the details in the subject line.

    ◆ If it might be useful, share the proposed attendance list.

3) **Create an agenda.** A written list of discussion items helps to shape participants' expectations and keep the meeting on target. This is true even when the gathering consists of just two or three team members talking through their issues over coffee. It often makes sense to ask attendees for discussion items and to distribute the agenda in advance.

4) **Build in structure.** Even informal meetings should feel intentional. As the leader or convener, plan to include in each meeting:

    ◆ **An opening** in which you state the purpose and the desired outcome.

    ◆ **A middle** in which agenda items are discussed, with each one being moved forward by at least a baby step.

    ◆ **A closing** when you may sum up the conclusions, action items, and assignments, and perhaps mention next steps or future events. It is also appropriate to thank people for their attendance and contributions.

5) **Warm it up.** There's a legitimate social component to many meetings, and you may make more progress if all the participants feel engaged and comfortable about offering comments. You can

address some social needs and establish a cordial mood for the event by devoting the first five or 10 minutes to a warm-up phase in which everyone is invited to offer information, suggestions, or concerns. This can be as simple as brief introductions, or you might request brief answers to a question such as: "Do you have any good news to report?"

6) **Set the tone.** Treat all participants with courtesy, give speakers your full attention, and don't work on other projects during the meeting. If you have trouble staying focused, try taking notes of the discussion. Show your respect for attendees by making sure your meetings always start and end on schedule.

7) **Establish ground rules.** Regular meetings will flow more smoothly if everybody understands the etiquette. Set the rules or build a consensus on matters such as:

   ◆   Attendance.

   ◆   Arrival times.

   ◆   Participation in discussions.

   ◆   Use of cell phones and other devices.

   ◆   Confidentiality.

8) **Keep track.** Every meeting should have someone designated to keep a record, at least of key conclusions and assignments. This can be as simple as your rough notes—the ones that you, the leader, use when you summarize the meeting in your closing remarks.

9) **Follow up.** After the meeting, be sure that both the participants and the invitees who couldn't attend are sent a copy of the notes. Consider touching base with participants who left with assignments, checking that they have everything they need, and are moving forward on their tasks. If nothing seems to come of your meetings, people will lose interest and stop taking them seriously.

Get more from the meetings you don't run

No matter how well you manage the meetings you run, and how successful you are at avoiding some others, you probably still spend a big chunk of your work time convening with colleagues. So your next challenge is to make that remaining meeting time as productive as possible.

That was a valuable lesson for my client Sharon*, who didn't understand why she hadn't been given the chance to lead a team. Sharon groused to her mentor, "If I didn't have to waste so much time sitting in their useless meetings, I could really show them what I can do."

The mentor countered, "You can't get out of those meetings, so why not make better use of them? That's where people see you in action, so think of those sessions as a chance to show off your strengths. Instead of coming in late and acting distracted, aim to look like one of the most productive people there."

Convinced it was worth a try, *Sharon developed a five-point plan for being a stellar attendee at each required meeting:*

1) **Prep.** She'd rearrange her priorities to allow a little time for preparation, like reading the agenda and the background materials sent out in advance.

2) **Plan remarks.** While prepping, she'd identify at least two comments or questions to contribute to the discussion.

3) **Focus on the purpose.** She'd ask herself, "What's the goal of this meeting? And what can I do to help get us there?"

4) **Create goals.** Before arriving, she'd set a personal objective like, "Today I'll come across as calm and organized."

5) **Focus through writing.** Once the discussion began, she'd listen carefully to each speaker, taking notes to help her stay focused.

Sharon's plan worked. Meeting leaders began noticing that she seemed more engaged and was adding to the discussion. They started to count on her active participation, and that led to her getting better project assignments. After six months, she was appointed team leader for an exciting project.

To her surprise, once Sharon launched her five-point plan, she found it brought other benefits beyond just looking like a more effective meeting participant. Once she developed the habit of always being prepared, her job started to feel more interesting and satisfying. Also, she became aware that the growing respect for her as a participant continued after each meeting. Soon she felt more connected to her colleagues. And she had fewer moments of boredom and frustration. "By trying to *act* engaged," she said, "I found out that it's more fun to *be* engaged."

The fact is that meetings represent a big part of your life as a professional. And as long as you have to spend the time, why not get more back from it? *Here are six strategies for maximizing the return on the hours you spend in other people's meetings:*

1) **Do the homework.** You won't fool anybody when you're searching through your papers or tablet, trying to catch up with the crowd. When you put the meeting time on the calendar, schedule some time for any necessary preparation.

2) **Be prompt.** Even if the culture tolerates casual start times, late arrivers show a lack of respect for their more punctual colleagues. By typically being there at the appointed hour, you can help to set a more productive tone. And once you're there, you can make use of any delay by reviewing the materials or networking with the crew.

3) **Understand the intention.** It's easy to dismiss many meetings as pointless, but that doesn't get you anywhere. Somebody had something in mind or you wouldn't be sitting in that room. You'll be able to make a bigger contribution if you have some sense of the objective. Dig a little, and you may find several reasons why you've all been called in, such as:

   ◆ Sharing information.

   ◆ Brainstorming and solving specific problems.

   ◆ Establishing goals, making plans, and keeping track of milestones.

   ◆ Creating a collective sense of purpose.

   ◆ Encouraging collaboration by helping people get to know each other.

4) **Set your own goals.** Of course, you always want to do your part to make the meeting productive. But beyond that, you'll get more out of your participation if you have your own games to play. For example, if you're trying to broaden your brand, your objective might be to speak knowledgeably about areas outside your normal portfolio.

5) **Listen.** One reason so many sessions feel useless is that attendees just aren't paying attention. If just one or two of you start really

listening, you can change the tone. And if you make a habit of being truly engaged, chances are that when it's your turn somebody will hear what you have to say.

6) **Follow up.** Often, the success of a meeting depends on what happens next. Do your bit. Keep track of any commitments you make and do that work. If you're particularly interested in aspects of the conversation, find ways to continue the dialogue later. And let people know if you found their remarks to be helpful.

If meetings are part of the job, complaining about them is simply a waste of time. Instead, strategize to get as much as you can from the hours spent around a conference table.

32

How to Love
Your Work Again

Author Kerry Hannon, who wrote the foreword to this book, is a noted authority on work and career. For the last two decades, she has been covering all aspects of business and personal finance as an author, columnist, editor, and writer for leading media organizations including the *New York Times*, *Forbes*, *Money*, *PBS*, *U.S. News & World Report*, and the *Wall Street Journal*. Although I've learned much from Kerry's careful research, what has inspired me the most is her own career path.

Kerry started as a traditional print journalist, earning a salary from major publications. Then about 14 years ago she struck out on her own, freelancing for some of the nation's top magazines and newspapers. But she does so much more. Kerry has become a prolific author, a peripatetic speaker, a frequent radio and TV guest, and an expert panelist at conferences. This entrepreneurial dynamo has become a one-woman media company. And all along the way she has helped other writers, given generously of her time to nonprofits, pursued her love of horses, traveled with her husband, and stayed in touch with her friends.

In recent years, Kerry has published countless articles and several books about how to follow your heart in order to find the work you love. Pursuing the topic of "second acts," she has traveled back and forth across the country, interviewing folks who have reinvented their work lives, and speaking frequently about how to navigate midcareer transitions.

Kerry says that many people dream of starting over with an entirely different kind of career. But what she's been hearing is that, all too often, that kind of big shift may not be practical. So, in a 2015 book, Kerry changed gears to focus on how to make your *current* job more satisfying. I had the pleasure of serving as an expert for the book and loved the chance to brainstorm with Kerry, learning from her many stories, and talking about the rapidly changing American workplace.

Kerry Hannon says you can find more fun and meaning at your current job

Love Your Job: The New Rules for Career Happiness is Kerry's guide for people who are looking to find or reignite purpose and joy in their work. She says, "If you want to be happier, you have to do something, to take action." That doesn't always mean a big swerve from the past. "It does, however, often call on the courage to make necessary but sometimes uncomfortable and even painful changes." ***If you are ready to take action, here are seven tips from Kerry's book:***

1) **Begin with a journal.** Kerry suggests you dedicate a notebook or computer file to your "Job Remodeling Journal." Launch your effort by writing for 20 minutes every day for a week. Let yourself go as you talk about what you'd love to see in your dream job. Perhaps you can list people who seem happy at work so you can ask them about what they enjoy in their career. Next, try writing about the times your professional life was most rewarding. Kerry recommends that you create a "budget" in which you list the pros and cons at work. From there, start planning action steps for building on the best parts of your job and addressing the liabilities.

2) **Know when it's burnout.** Sometimes you're feeling miserable, but the problem is not really that you hate your job. As you journal, you may realize that the biggest issue is you're just too tired.

Job burnout can be experienced as physical, emotional, or mental exhaustion combined with self-doubt and uncertainty about the value of your work. If you're feeling burnt out, the solution must start with you and goes beyond what happens at the office. Consider taking a vacation, or perhaps a series of shorter breaks. And look closely at your health and fitness programs.

3) **Stop complaining.** According to Kerry, "It's remarkably easy to fall into the trap of whining and grumbling about a boss, coworker, or employer, but it rarely makes things better." Her advice is blunt: "Do something. Get over it." Sometimes you can't make progress until you "stop the looping chatter." Kerry suggests that you read over your journal, looking for the specific things you can change. Start working on those aspects of your job by identifying small steps.

4) **Get in shape financially.** Human resources professionals say that personal financial challenges are a frequent cause of employee stress, poor health, and low productivity. If money problems keep you up at night, your work suffers. On the other hand, Kerry says, being financially fit gives you the freedom to make choices because "you are not trapped and held ransom by your paycheck." Kerry urges you to do everything possible to eliminate debt. The relief can transform your work life.

5) **Enrich your job.** Kerry says that making a number of small tweaks to your current job can help it become more interesting and full of opportunity. As a start, stay informed about the trends in your field. "Just being in the know can inspire you to think of projects and tasks." Also, find ways to do even more of the kind of work you like best. And, at the same time, search for additional kinds of duties. When your bosses ask you to take on another task, "accept the invitation gratefully . . . and then figure out how to do it," she says. Another strategy for job enhancement is to network more actively with colleagues. Reach out to people you don't know well, look your coworkers in the eye, find opportunities to smile and chat—and keep building new connections.

6) **Create more flexibility.** "When I ask people to name one thing that would make them happier about their jobs, they say independence in some way, shape, or form," Kerry says. The option to

work flexibly gives us a sense of autonomy, and that is a good way to make your work life immensely more enjoyable. Two increasingly popular ways to give you back some control are telecommuting and flexible work schedules. "When you feel trapped and micromanaged in your office environment, the sense of control of your own time and virtual freedom can do wonders to help you get reconnected with your work again," she says.

7) **Learn new tricks.** "If you're feeling stuck in your job and don't know what to do next, charge up your brain cells," Kerry says. Even if you have only a hazy notion of what interests you, start exploring libraries, classes, or the Web, and learn something new.

The core message from Kerry's book, in her words, is that "*you* can turn it around and rebound from your malaise or grim work environment. *You* have to own it. *You* consciously choose whether to continue being unhappy or pick an alternate path and change it up, even if it's in baby steps."

33

Make Social Media Work for You

My normally cheerful client Brian* was aggravated. He'd been assigned to find productive work for Jason*, a new hire. The problem, he said, is that "we can't give Jason a project because he doesn't know how to do anything at all."

Jason had polished manners, an Ivy League education, and a distant family connection to the CEO. Brian's boss had recruited Jason from his last job, where he'd maintained a fairly high profile as a "senior policy advisor."

"Does he really not understand those policy issues?" I asked.

"Oh, he knows the issues alright," Brian said. "But that's irrelevant because he can't *do* anything. We're going to have to find a way to let him go."

It turned out that Jason had enjoyed one of the last remaining old-school jobs, where he wrote all his papers on a legal pad. "He doesn't even know how to use e-mail," Brian said. "In this company, not even the CEO writes longhand drafts for some secretary to type up. I don't care how smart or connected he is. There's no room here for a guy without basic skills."

The fact is that there's no room in most corporations for a professional without basic communication skills. But the definition of those skills can vary widely. During the interview process, nobody at Brian's company asked Jason whether he could use a laptop because it seemed inconceivable that an expert could operate in the policy arena without the "basic skill" of turning out quick drafts and distributing them electronically to the world.

In regard to communications, "basic skills" may seem to include whatever technologies you happen to be using now, but not much more. Too many professionals seem to share the view of my client who said, "I have all the communication skills I need and I'm not going to go messing around with a time sink like social media."

Consider this statement as a SHOUT: Understanding social media is now a *basic skill* in the world of business, academia, or government. That doesn't mean that you have to know how to *do* everything. But you absolutely must understand the fundamental concept and potential power of these rapidly evolving media. Even if you're in your 20s, you'll sound like a dinosaur if you make derisive comments like, "Oh, I just think Twitter is silly. Why would I want to see what some stranger has for lunch?"

Every professional needs a social media strategy

In Chapter 4 we talked about how—whether you know it or not—you have a personal brand that is impacting the opportunities that come along in your career. One factor shaping your brand is the way you show up online. And—whether you know it or not—you do have an online image. If there isn't much information online about you, you may come across as someone not well connected in the world of work.

You are in charge of your career, and it's your responsibility to think about how the Internet and social networking may impact your professional brand. *If you are just starting to think about your social media strategy, consider these four tips:*

1) **Know who's using it.** Most businesses and large organizations now have some kind of social media presence. It's smart to know how your employer, your customers, and your competitors are showing up. If you do nothing else, remain aware of messages flowing from the organizations that matter to your work life.

2) **Set up a profile.** LinkedIn.com, by definition, is a professional networking tool, and many people now use it as a digital address book. It's a great way to gather data and keep track of most of your business associates in one place. But it's become much more than that. Hiring organizations and executive search firms use it on a regular basis to locate talent. And there's a good chance that anyone you meet will use LinkedIn to quickly check you out. So here's a chance to tweak your brand: Create a LinkedIn profile that at least describes your current professional persona.

3) **Get news.** Until you get the hang of it, Twitter feels like a large, random crowd of people shouting about trivia. But once you understand how to organize the flow, it's a tool for connecting with people all over the world in real time. If you want instant feedback from an audience or customer group, Twitter works as well as anything out there. And if you want to know what people are talking about right now, Twitter is your tool.

   Many users never Tweet a word, but they manage Twitter as their primary source of incoming news. Twitter allows you to organize reports from all the major media companies, as well as the specialized journals and commentators you most respect. And it brings fast access to crowdsourced reporting when there's breaking news like an earthquake or security breach. If you'd rather use Facebook or other social options for getting the news, that's fine. But when there's a crisis it helps to be plugged in to some kind of social media stream.

   And if you want to give Twitter a try, please follow me at: @beverlyejones.

4) **Don't mock what you don't understand.** There are so many new channels that it's easy to become bored or confused. Don't think you have to understand it all or feel pressure to sign up for everything from Facebook and Pinterest to Scoop.it and Academia.edu. If you're just starting out, a smart goal is to try one or two tools immediately, and gradually learn more about some of the other options. What you don't want to do is self-righteously refuse to try the tools that your colleagues are using, or make fun of media that you're unwilling to use.

Social media can help you put your best foot forward and stay abreast of developments that are critical to your professional life. If you refuse to even try them, you may find yourself on the wrong side of a great divide. Like today's elderly who don't hear from grandkids because they can't text or e-mail, you might eventually be cut off from your younger or sharper friends and colleagues. The challenge is to understand what is technically possible, and what avenues are your best choice for staying in touch with the people and activities you care about.

34

Stress Is Contagious and Debilitating— but Manageable

You're still tired from working late last night. Your commute this morning was a nightmare and you reached the office 30 minutes behind schedule. Your boss was waiting for you when you arrived, in a hurry to hand over a tedious project with an unreasonable deadline. And you need immediate relief from a coworker who's been grouchy and uncooperative for days.

Feeling stressed out?

You're not alone. Surveys suggest that work is the leading cause of adult stress, and a growing number of workers are experiencing physical or emotional symptoms of job-related stress. Many of my clients not only suffer from stress themselves, but also worry about how a stressful environment might be hurting their teams.

For you, the modern professional, there's bad news and good news. The bad news is that the consequences of chronic stress can be serious, even deadly. The good news is that there are many options for dealing with stress, and you *do* have the power to stop feeling so stressed out.

Understand that stress poses a serious health risk

In some work circles, it seems like the symptoms of stress carry a certain prestige. And occasionally when you complain about feeling stressed, you're actually a bit pleased with yourself and are letting folks know that you've been working hard for the good of the team.

If that rings a bell, please take a careful look at what stress can do to you and get serious about taking control of your health and well-being.

To understand how stress operates, think of it as associated with the "fight-or-flight response," which is our normal reaction to some form of threat or challenge. That response is a kind of survival mechanism that allows humans to automatically react to possible danger. In effect, stress reactions start out as your body's helpful way to generate a bit more oomph when you need it.

Imagine that you're strolling along a country path and you spot a snake up ahead. You freeze for a moment, staring at the snake. While you pause, still uncertain, your brain starts sending messenger chemicals like adrenaline and cortisol that change operations throughout your body. For example, your pulse and blood pressure go up, and more blood flows to your heart and brain. Your body is getting ready to tackle the snake or turn around and run. At the same time, to free up resources, cortisol and other chemicals slow body functions that aren't critical in an emergency, like digestion, your immune system, and your reproductive drive.

This is an example of "acute stress"—a one-time reaction that gives you a burst of energy and helps you fight with or escape from something threatening. Occasional acute stress reactions might even be good for you, strengthening your immune system and helping you to become stronger.

Now let's imagine that, as you stand staring at the snake, you realize that it's actually just a stick lying across the path. Wow, what a relief. You now experience a "relaxation response," which is the opposite of your "fight or flight" reaction. Your chemical balances return to normal, your breathing and heart rates go down again, and you're ready to resume your walk.

On a workday, the stimulant that triggers your stress reaction might be anything from a physical threat to worrisome thoughts. It could come in the form of aggressive drivers cutting you off on the road, your boss giving you that annoying project, or a nasty comment from your obnoxious colleague. But unlike the snake scenario, the moment of stress isn't quickly resolved. Before you can relax, the first stressor is followed by a difficult client call, then a problematic e-mail message, and a plea for help from a panic-stricken colleague.

What you're experiencing now is chronic stress set off by a continuing stream of stimuli. Instead of dropping to normal, your level of hormones like cortisol stays elevated. It's possible to fall into a downward spiral, where stressful events trigger your physical and psychological symptoms, which in turn make your stress level feel even worse. The long-term activation of your stress-response system can disrupt many of your body's processes, threatening your health in many ways.

Chronic stress is associated with numerous health and emotional problems, including:

→ **Physical aches and pains,** such as headaches, back pain, sore necks, and shoulders, and other symptoms such as indigestion.

→ **Sleep difficulties** and feelings of fatigue even when you do sleep.

→ **Cognitive difficulties,** including forgetfulness, constant worry, and an inability to concentrate, be creative, or make decisions.

→ **Emotional symptoms,** including crying, anxiety, anger, loneliness, and a sense of being powerless.

→ **Depression,** which is magnified by stress and can also lead to more stress.

→ **Excess weight,** in part because cortisol can stimulate your appetite and stimulate enzymes to cause fat to be stored in your fat cells.

There are many ways to address stress

There is no single solution to the problem of workplace stress. At times you can address some of the underlying issues. For example, if your long commute is getting you down, perhaps you could arrange to telecommute a day or two a week. But many factors contributing to a stressful environment are beyond your control.

However, even where you can't do much to change your situation, you *can* change your reaction to some of those stressors. You can start feeling better quickly by using one or more of the many techniques shown to be effective in addressing the *symptoms* of stress. Research suggests that just knowing you have a plan in place can be enough to help you calm down and start to mend.

Your doctor and many kinds of therapists and programs might help you come up with a comprehensive plan. Meanwhile, ***here are some of the many practices that can help bring your stress to a more tolerable level:***

→ **Exercise.** Regular walking or other aerobic exercise can significantly reduce the physical symptoms of stress and improve your mood. Repetitive or rhythmic exercises, such as jogging, dancing, or biking, seem to be particularly effective.

→ **Talk to somebody.** The sense of isolation that hits some overworked professionals can magnify the impact of other stressors. Find ways to have meaningful conversations more frequently. Beyond that, make eye contact, actually listen to other people, and try to connect with them in casual ways throughout your day.

→ **Connect with nature.** Research suggests that being in nature—or being aware of nature through something as simple as looking at houseplants—can reduce your stress symptoms. For some people, regular lunchtime walks in a park can make a big difference.

→ **Be creative.** It can be healthy to focus on something different, and stimulate the creative part of your brain. Try painting or playing a musical instrument, working in your garden, taking a cooking class, or taking up a repetitive craft like knitting.

→ **Write about it.** Keeping a journal is a great way to develop insights, change your perspective, and grapple with tension. Try writing about your stressors, describing precisely how they make you feel. Then write about the good parts of your situation, and the things that make you feel grateful. Describe your goals, and the kind of work life you intend to create in the future.

→ **Look at the big picture.** An immediate problem can lose its impact when you place it in perspective. One way to do this is to make a list in your journal about the things that matter most in your life. Then ask yourself: how does the current problem affect your list of big-picture goals or values?

→ **Simplify.** A common source of stress is having too much going on. You may be able to reduce your stress by finding ways to streamline. Look for activities and responsibilities that could be reduced or restructured. And find ways to get rid of physical clutter; getting rid of piles of stuff can feel quite liberating.

→ **Help other people.** In her TED talk, "How to Make Stress Your Friend," health psychologist Kelly McGonigal describes research suggesting that people who reach out to other people reduce their own stress level and build resilience. Your caring for others is associated with a release of the hormone oxytocin, which helps to heal stress induced damage.

→ **Meditate.** In recent years, a wave of studies has explained some of the physiological benefits of meditation. There's evidence that it not only can make you feel more peaceful and physically relaxed, but it also promotes cognitive and psychological changes that enhance your performance and bring a feeling of contentment. In working with clients, I find that it's worth trying a few approaches in order to select a style of meditation that feels comfortable. ***Here's a very simple meditation exercise to get you started:***

1) Pick a focus word, short phrase, or prayer that has meaning for you, such as "peace," "Hail Mary, full of grace," or "I am calm and connected."

2) Sit quietly in a comfortable position.

3) Close your eyes.

4) Relax your muscles, progressing from your feet to your calves, thighs, and abdomen, and up to your shoulders, neck, and head.

5) Breathe slowly and naturally, and as you do, say your phrase silently to yourself, each time you inhale and exhale.

6) When thoughts come to mind, just notice them and gently return to your repetition. You might say to yourself, "Oh well," or "That's just a thought."

7) Some instructors suggest that you continue for 10 to 30 minutes, but I find that even a few minutes can be helpful.

Help your team by managing your stress

If you're thinking like a CEO, you want the other members of your team to feel motivated, energetic, and positive. And that requires addressing the level of stress in the environment. If you're the leader and some of the stress is associated with a tough situation, keep your team informed about what's going on and show that you're there to support them. And don't micromanage. It's easier for workers to cope with difficult challenges when they have some control over how to get things done.

What could be most important in difficult circumstances is how you handle yourself. Regardless of whether you're the leader, you can often improve a situation by working hard to stay positive and being willing to listen. Beyond that, the way you manage *your* level of stress can impact the stress level of your colleagues. That's because a stress reaction can be contagious. You can make a difference to colleagues by staying calm and modeling healthy habits, such as taking walking breaks. If your stress level is under control, not only will you be healthier and happier, but also other people will enjoy being around you.

35

Snap Out of It: Coping with Career Rejection

A highly qualified professional went after his dream job. Paul* has an extraordinary record of accomplishment, and he was confident that he'd be the winning candidate. Then he felt devastated when he didn't get the job. Paul wrote me about the intensity of his reaction.

"I hate how this news makes me feel," Paul said. "Not only did I miss out on a job that I really wanted, but the company hired someone against whom I stacked up very well."

"Aside from frustration and sadness, I also have second-order emotions about this decision," Paul said. "Namely, I'm angry at myself for feeling sad and frustrated. These aren't becoming emotions of a gentleman, and certainly I know rationally that they aren't the 'right way' to deal with rejection."

That was almost two years ago, and Paul has long since bounced back. He suggested that his struggles and our e-mail dialogue about career rejection might be useful to others trying to get over a career disappointment. ***These tips helped Paul, and they might help you if you don't get that job:***

→ **Know that pain is normal.** As someone who has read a lot of history, Paul realized that all great leaders face setbacks on their paths to glory. But that knowledge didn't help him feel better. He was embarrassed about experiencing such pain from something that happens to everyone.

"I understand your frustration and the other emotions swirling around," I wrote to Paul. "This is a normal passage for all high achievers. Everybody gets rejected eventually, and the pain is tougher when you are not used to it." Knowing it's normal to feel bad was helpful to Paul, and he chose to let go of those secondary emotions, such as guilt for feeling grief.

→ **Write about your pain.** A useful way of dealing with emotional or physical pain is to examine it. When you carefully notice details about your pain, you can develop some distance from it. I suggested that Paul take notes about exactly what he was experiencing. I asked him, "What does it feel like to be 'sad and frustrated'? Can you describe your feelings precisely? Where do you feel tightness or discomfort in your body? What thoughts keep popping into your head? Are you making yourself feel worse by speculating what this disappointment could mean for the future?"

→ **Share with your inner circle.** A key to Paul's rapid recovery is the support he received from his partner and a few close friends. "I found it really helpful just to share my anxieties with them because good friends who know you well can help you maintain perspective," he said.

→ **Understand what you lost.** When you face professional rejection, some of your sadness is a sense of loss because you won't have the opportunity you sought. But sometimes people feel awful about not getting a job they didn't even care about. They like winning and feel bad about losing whether or not they care about the prize. It may help you refocus on the future if you can clearly identify what hurts. Are you mostly concerned about the opportunity, the prestige, or the money? The more you understand the true cause of your disappointment, the better you will be at articulating your next goals and shifting your focus to the future.

→ **Keep a gratitude journal.** As we've discussed, one of the best antidotes for negative emotion is gratitude. When you feel grateful, the part of your brain associated with anxiety quiets down. So you can pull yourself out of a bad place by summoning up a sense of appreciation for the things in your life and career that are going well. A useful exercise is to take a few minutes at the end of every day to list five things for which you're grateful.

→ **Be gracious in defeat.** Though Paul was honest about how he felt with a trusted few, for most of the world he put on his game face, thanked everyone involved in the hiring process, and avoided any show of disappointment. That worked out well for him because one of the executives involved in the hiring decision kept him in mind. Later, she reached out to him and helped him win a job that was an even better fit.

In the depth of his despair, Paul asked, "What's the silver lining here?" One answer is that you can learn how to navigate career transitions, and overcoming setbacks is part of the learning process. And, I said, "Now that you finally have this big disappointment out of the way, you'll start to build up antibodies for the next time, like with chicken pox."

36

How to Foster Great Teams, Even if You're Not the Leader

When I want a quick sense of whether a new client is working well with a team, I take a look at how the members communicate.

Jenna* was an agency branch chief who wanted to help her 14 direct reports become more innovative and productive. Years ago, her branch had been organized into cascading layers, with three deputy chiefs each managing two to four people. That kind of top-down organization made sense when it was the only way to assure the distribution of accurate information. But the old command-and-control model became out of date with the advent of e-mail and other technology. Now that the agency was much flatter, its leaders were exploring new ways to arrange the workload.

To foster collaboration and mentoring, Jenna had organized her group into project-focused teams. Because each person might be on more than one team, and some teams included professionals from other branches, Jenna was keeping her eye on six teams, each with three to five members. Several teams were active, energetic, and highly productive. But a couple of them had gone dormant even before they really got started.

As part of an effort to evaluate and restructure the teams, Jenna asked me to interview each branch employee. Don*, an experienced and technically gifted lawyer, led one of the teams that hadn't gelled. When I asked Don about how his team operated, he said he called meetings "only when they were absolutely necessary." He said he was available to answer individual questions, but he didn't want to encourage people "to waste time talking about each other's problems."

I said to myself, "Wow! Don's poor team never had a chance." Don had no idea that frequent and effective communications are key to building an effective team.

It's long been intuitively obvious that talking is a basic step in teambuilding. But recent research, including studies from the new science of mapping communication patterns, suggests that *how* team members talk with one another may be more important than what they say. Frequent contact is so vital that regular social conversation during breaks could be as crucial as business talk during formal project meetings.

In a flourishing team, communication is constant. Members connect directly with one another, and not just with the leader. Also, the leader circulates actively, visiting with everyone, listening at least as much as talking, and making sure all members get a chance to express their views.

Though communication is key, teams also need structure

Even if you're not the designated leader, you can help shape the culture, support other members, and clarify processes that will help your team to be productive. *These six strategies can help you to strengthen your team:*

1) **Define it.** Be clear about the basics. Members should know who is on the team and who is not, as well as what they're supposed to be doing together.

2) **Model respect and positivity.** Be relentlessly upbeat and treat everyone with respect. In healthy teams, every member's contribution is recognized. Observe each person's strengths and look for ways to help each one to shine.

3) **Share leadership.** Even where there is a designated leader, every member should take responsibility and share accountability for success. It can be helpful if all members have an opportunity to take the lead when their particular kind of expertise is needed.

4) **Address the desire to belong.** Humans have a fundamental need to be part of communities, particularly those that allow us to make contributions that are appreciated by others. So focus on the power of belonging and find ways to reinforce it. Even silly ways to embrace membership, such as T-shirts or mottoes, can enhance team spirit.

5) **Celebrate little victories.** Team members are most likely to feel satisfied and motivated when they believe they're making progress on meaningful work. To keep up the team energy level, find appropriate ways to celebrate even small wins, such as meeting deadlines or being congratulated by the boss.

6) **Create norms.** Even if leadership is loose, high-performing teams need some structure. For example, when the team conducts group meetings, members should agree on elements such as:

   ◆ Scheduling.

   ◆ Attendance requirements.

   ◆ Promptness.

   ◆ Participation in discussions.

   ◆ Cell phone usage and other interruptions.

   ◆ Ways to track and follow up on action items.

There's no single formula for creating a great team. But a good starting point is to think about a configuration that suits your tasks, allows regular discussion among members, provides a way to acknowledge contributions, and lets everyone enjoy the camaraderie that team membership can bring.

37

Celebrate Your Wins and Theirs

D o you worry so much about what could go wrong that you can't seem to focus on what's going right? If so, you're missing important opportunities.

That was the case with my client Joe*, who led a government branch composed of seven communications specialists. His team had been in place for several years and generally was meeting its goals and coping with constant deadline pressure. The problem, Joe said, was that it felt like his people had "run out of juice." Too often they seemed bored or exhausted, and he was tempted to micromanage in order to prevent mistakes.

We talked about how Joe might restructure the unit's activities not only to deliver more value to the agency, but also to reengage staffers and encourage them to grow. He worked hard to create a new vision for the team, and after a few months built upper management support for a plan to reorganize the branch's responsibilities. The plan dropped several of the team's old projects and added a new one that would require the development of additional skills. After much discussion, Joe's team members welcomed the change and began to seem more enthusiastic about work. But Joe worried that once the group was past the excitement of building something new, the old malaise would quickly return.

At that point, Joe began to tweak his leadership style. In the past, he'd kept careful track of deadlines, and after the team met one target he'd immediately redirect its attention to the next one. This approach kept everything moving, but it seldom allowed people to pause, consider what had gone well, and explore ways to make their work products even better.

Also, by shifting so quickly to the next assignment, Joe had repeatedly missed the ideal time to positively reinforce good work. The most effective time to give feedback is immediately after a task is completed. But Joe tended to save up his praise for each staffer's required annual review. That often left some team members feeling unappreciated or uncertain about whether they were giving Joe what he wanted.

After reading about the importance of a positive work culture, Joe launched a six-month experiment. He promised himself that at least twice each month he would find a way to celebrate his team's good work, or perhaps to draw attention to any good luck. Then, in honor of various accomplishments, he started his new regimen by staging a surprise pizza party, arranging for a big boss to express thanks at an all-hands meeting, and taking individual staffers out for lunch or coffee.

Once he began looking for opportunities to celebrate, Joe found that he was focusing more intently on his team's best efforts. He realized that he'd been taking some high performers' output for granted, because they invariably did so well. He spotted additional ways for staffers to learn from each other's smartest strategies. And, as he involved his customers in some of the team's celebrations, he became more adept at promoting its achievements.

By the end of the six months, Joe was feeling remarkably positive and was committed to celebrating work as part of his leadership brand.

Workplace celebrations can lead to even more success

Celebrations can enhance a positive workplace culture and encourage teams to perform well. Creating a celebration can be a wonderful way to acknowledge achievements and motivate people to continue to excel. Affirmative feedback is a powerful motivator, and a celebratory event is a meaningful way to reinforce an accomplishment. Sharing appreciation for success and good fortune can support the well-being of individuals, foster a sense of community, and promote the health of your whole organization.

If you take note of even modest achievements, it can help you and your colleagues to remain focused on the kinds of details that will lead to further success. Celebrations provide times when coworkers come together, get to know each other better, and develop a shared perspective. Enjoying festive occasions helps workers become friends, and having friends at the office helps you do your best. Arranging celebrations can provide a moment for reflection, allowing people to develop a collective focus on the right stuff. It's a way to direct attention to the organization's goals and values, and to remind participants that they work at a great place.

Of course, the style and magnitude of a celebration should vary with the situation. A few triumphant events may call for a big blowout, but even routine achievements may deserve a brief toast. ***Here are 13 ways to celebrate at work:***

1) **Set the meeting tone.** Kick off regular meetings with a brief time to acknowledge recent achievements and thank individuals for their contributions. "Thanks" and "attaboys" can be expressed by the leader or anyone else in the room. A gratitude ritual can set a positive tone and support an atmosphere where it's normal to thank colleagues for what they do.

2) **Arrange a chance to show off.** When your team does well, find an opportunity for members to talk about their activity to senior management or an external audience. If they're shy, you do the talking and let them bask in the glow.

3) **Create an award for overlooked contributions.** Sometimes we stop noticing the people who keep things moving by reliably doing terrific work. Create a Keystone Award and occasionally honor colleagues whose routine excellence is vital to the team effort.

4) **Have a retreat.** Acknowledge the group's importance by taking people out of the office for an event that is about bonding rather than problem solving. Dress casually, share a good meal, and structure activities that allow members to chat casually and have some fun.

5) **Go home early.** If you're the boss, after a big effort, express appreciation by inviting everybody to head out before normal closing time.

6) **Throw a surprise party.** Call an important meeting to ensure everyone will attend; then surprise the employees with a festive event to thank them for a recent success.

7) **Create a media event.** Whether it's a classy video presentation, a picture in the company newsletter, or a photomontage on the bulletin board, honor people for their production by showing it off.

8) **Notice milestones.** People feel more satisfied if they believe they're making progress toward something that counts. So don't wait until the end of a major initiative to celebrate. Express appreciation for key steps along the way. Consider a special lunch party or small gifts to acknowledge the halfway point of a big project. It will help to build enthusiasm for reaching the finish line.

9) **Buy T-shirts.** Even though the items may seem tacky, people often enjoy receiving shirts, paperweights, stuffed animals, and other little gifts decorated with the team logo or slogan. Order T-shirts or mugs for team members who contribute to a stellar effort.

10) **Buy lunch.** It could be a pizza party in the conference room or an elegant meal at a nearby restaurant, but people always like it when you buy lunch. And, during the meal, offer a few heartfelt comments about what you appreciate.

11) **Call on local talent.** Does somebody in your group sing, play an instrument, or do a bit of stand-up? Can you recruit a small group to perform a funny skit? Turn a meeting or pedestrian lunchtime into a party by coming up with some entertainment.

12) **Write notes.** Share a quiet moment of gratitude by taking a few minutes to sit down and write a note to someone who has done well or given you a hand.

13) **Take a break.** To be at your creative best, you should take regular rests. That might include frequent mini-breaks, such as a few minutes of meditation, or it might be longer interludes, such as a couple of hours away from your desk for a massage. When you've completed a tedious or thorny task, celebrate by yourself with a little time off. Even taking a few minutes to chat with a friend can help you to get back to work with new purpose and energy.

Whether it means planning a party for the whole team, or quietly reward-ing yourself for taking on a tough task, take time to shine a light on work well done. Even if you're not yet a leader, celebrating gracefully can become a vital part of your flourishing work life and can help you to build a supportive pro-fessional community.

38

It's (Usually) Not Okay to Be Late

I dislike being late. It makes me feel anxious and disorganized, and I'm uncomfortable at the prospect of disrupting somebody else's schedule.

On the other hand, I generally don't mind being kept waiting if I'm meeting a friend or client. I always have a book and phone with me, I treat the waiting period as found time, and I catch up on messages or read something I enjoy.

However, there are two conditions to my tolerance. First, I want a heads-up. When I'm not alerted the other person is running late, I worry that I'm in the wrong place, or at the wrong time, or that something awful has happened. Second, I don't want to be made late if it means that I, in turn, will be late for somebody else.

But that's just me. Punctuality can be a surprisingly emotional issue, and attitudes about timeliness vary widely. Some people are angered or insulted if they are kept waiting, believing it shows a lack of respect. Others are annoyed or exhausted by unending demands to stay on schedule.

Flexible attitudes about punctuality can work well where people in a community know what to expect. For example, a 30-minute delay is no problem if everyone in the social group understands that the "seven o'clock dinner" really starts at 7:30.

In the context of your career, however, your standard approach should be to stay on schedule. American business etiquette requires that you show up for meetings and events at the appointed hour. In some organizations the rule is tougher, and to be considered "on time" you must actually arrive a little early. This strict approach to punctuality isn't just an arbitrary tradition. If your lateness causes others to lose minutes of productivity, you've just stolen some of their most valuable resource.

But cultures and expectations vary. In some circles, a fanatical preoccupation with the clock could come across as silly or obnoxious. If you wonder whether you have the right approach to punctuality, look around to see how closely your habits are aligned with those in your environment. *As you ask yourself whether your approach to timeliness is good for your brand, consider these six strategies:*

1) **Know the rules.** The organizations you deal with may have explicit policies about punctuality, but sometimes the general practice is nothing like the policy manual. When you start interacting with a new group, inquire about preferences for meeting start times. Does that 10 o'clock meeting really begin on the hour, or is it considered polite to chat for a few minutes with other attendees?

2) **Bank goodwill.** If you're a person who finds it tough to get to places on time, work hard to be prompt as often as possible. If you can establish a reputation for being punctual, people are more likely to be tolerant when you really can't help being late.

3) **Know the message your behavior sends.** When you're typically late, a colleague may take offense, interpreting your tardiness as an overblown sense of your own importance. On the other hand, if you always make a big deal about starting on the dot, you might come across as intolerant. To be effective, you must understand what your approach to punctuality is saying to those around you. If your lateness says that you just don't care, it's probably time to change your message.

4) **Lighten up.** Getting upset when you're kept waiting is a waste of your energy. The first step in letting go of your negative emotion is to acknowledge that when others are late, it's probably not about *you*; it's a reflection of what's going on in *their* lives. For example, the late arrivers could be struggling with traffic. Instead of fuming, use the waiting time productively or enjoy a quiet moment for reflection.

5) **Respect your team.** If you're a leader, you have a special obligation to stay on time. If you're seldom prompt, the efficiency of the whole group is impacted. And if you are on time for your superiors but not for your direct reports, you're modeling a culture where junior staffers are not respected.

6) **Negotiate the rules.** If you and your colleagues have different views about the value of being punctual, it might be useful to talk. Whether you tend to be tardy, or you're the one who's always kept waiting, you can smooth relationships by forging shared standards of punctuality. It can be helpful for teams to openly discuss questions such as these:

   ◆ Are meeting times a bit flexible, reflecting travel and other uncertainties? For example, is it acceptable to arrive 15 minutes late for a lunch across town? Does the person who travels the furthest get more flexibility?

   ◆ Is it sometimes fine to be really late, such as when the team has to start the weekly meeting without you because the big boss had a question?

   ◆ When is lateness just plain unacceptable, such as when you are having dinner with a client?

   ◆ What's the best way to take the sting out of being late, like giving early notice, apologizing profusely, or doing better next time?

39

Measuring Progress Makes Your Goals Powerful

Throughout this book we discuss how building a resilient career and leading like a CEO require you to stay focused on your goals. Whether you're framing major long-term objectives or simply making your plan for a productive week, how you actually articulate your goals can have an impact on your ability to reach them.

You might start with a general picture of what you want to accomplish. But from there, the way to make your goals truly useful is to decide precisely how you will record and evaluate your headway.

You may have heard about the importance of "measurable goals" more times than you can count. The basic idea is that, in order to keep moving toward your goals, you must come up with specific ways to gauge your progress. For example, if you've always wanted to write a book, a measurable goal could be to write a specific number of words per week. If your book will have about 60,000 words, and you write at least 1,000 words each week, you will come up with a draft manuscript in a little more than a year.

You'll still make progress if you accomplish only a little at a time. As we discussed in Chapter 17, the action steps that move you forward might not be large—they could be as small as sugar grains—but eventually you *will* approach your target if you maintain a steady pace.

I'm sometimes surprised by talented professionals who resist the notion of quantifying their progress. Maybe the concept of metrics strikes them as time consuming, complicated, or boring? Or perhaps they think that some values just can't be counted? *If you're reluctant to define your goals in measurable terms, consider these four points:*

1) **Measuring creates awareness.** If you regularly count something, you tend to keep it in mind. So if you're working on a new habit, coming up with a metric will help you to keep on the path. For example, many dieticians predict that if you're trying to lose pounds, you're more likely to stick to your diet if you consistently log your food, weigh yourself, and chart your weight. And it's the same for organizations. In businesses, government units, and nonprofits, attention tends to focus on the things that get evaluated and recorded.

2) **Quantity can lead to quality.** When you regularly count your steps, you're likely to take more of them. That's the theory behind fitness tracking devices, like the one I use, the popular Fitbit. And the more you practice an activity, the better you may get at it. My favorite book about the power of practice is Geoff Colvin's *Talent is Overrated.* Colvin examined research about "what really separates world-class performers from everybody else." He concluded that great performers—whether in music, sports, or business—are the ones who practice intensely. Quantity doesn't always produce quality, but often the more times you do something, the more you learn. And when learning is involved, quantity does lead to quality.

3) **Measurement helps build self-control.** "If you can measure it, you can manage it." That quote is often attributed to management guru Peter Drucker, but his take on measurement in the workplace was actually more nuanced. In his great book *Management*, he wrote of the danger that measurement "could be used to control people from the outside and above— that is, to dominate them." He suggested that the better use

of measurement is to "make self-control possible." Drucker thought metrics should be used by every manager "to appraise his own skill and performance and to work systematically on improving himself."

4) **Measurement can replace micromanagement.** As a coach, I've encountered many situations where managers want to delegate but can't seem to do it. Sometimes they hover annoyingly over a project because they want a better sense of how it's going. But when the manager and the project leader are able to come up with the right metrics, suddenly the problem disappears. A good measurement and reporting system can create transparency. That makes it easier both to solve problems and to recognize progress. When you're able to quantify and describe your accomplishments, it's easier for your manager to let go of control.

Explore different types of data and metrics

At times people are slow to create a measurement system because it's not obvious what should be counted. But whereas it's not always easy to quantify the impact or value of your work, grappling with the selection of metrics can contribute to your ultimate success. Choosing your approach to keeping track requires you to ask important questions. The first step may be to break a large goal into smaller pieces. Then you'll want to consider which factors actually matter.

Suppose your New Year's resolution is to get to the office earlier. You start to build a picture by recording your daily arrival times. For two weeks you count how many minutes you arrive before or after the official nine o'clock start time. And then you begin to wonder: Why is it harder to be prompt on some days than on others? So you expand your log to note your bedtime, your hours of sleep, and whether you lay out your next day's clothes before going to bed. You realize that the way to get to work before nine is to go to bed earlier, so you change your evening routine. You start getting out of the house sooner, and your commitment to reach work earlier is reinforced by that little ping of pride each morning when you record your arrival.

It can be useful to experiment a bit as you choose data to show how you're doing. As you explore options, ***consider these three approaches to measuring progress toward your goals:***

1) **Measure progress toward actually completing the mission.** Some goals can be framed in numerical terms, which make it easy to chart your achievements. Suppose, for example, that you want to raise your profile by energizing your blog. It's a simple matter to set numerical targets, such as the number of posts you intend to publish during the next year.

2) **Count important activities.** Often, things that impact the completion of your mission are beyond your control. In that case, observe the things you *can* control. Determine which activities are most likely to contribute to your success and start measuring them. Let's say your committee wants to raise money for a foundation, but a tough economy means that donors may give less. As you think about goals for committee members, identify their most important fundraising activities, like calling supporters and meeting with potential donors. A direct measurement approach would count output from the members' efforts, like how much money they raise each month. But the measure that motivates your team could be one that gives credit for their actions—their inputs to the process—such as the number of people they call or visit.

3) **Create capacity.** Complex goals may require a phased approach to measurement. Often, you can't start racking up actual results until you put the tools, systems, and resources in place. If your fundraising goal requires something substantial like creating a new task-force to raise the money, map the whole process and break it into stages. Perhaps your first stage will involve recruiting the task force members, and a key milestone will be the initial meeting. In the beginning of your work, the way you evaluate progress will be to monitor the capacity build-out. Once your structure is in place, you can shift to more direct measures of success, like the number of dollars being raised.

Your wishful thinking can turn into a tangible goal when you describe your target and start doing things to move you in that direction. Your goal becomes powerful when you begin to track the things that will help you make progress.

40

Use Those Amazing Checklists

It's wonderful when one simple tool can help you streamline your work and organize your group. That was the case with my client Sarah*, who's an excellent technical writer. Sarah enjoys reporting on complex situations, and she's proud of her ability to present complicated data in a clear way.

Sarah loved her job preparing reports for a large institution, but she felt panic-stricken when she suddenly was made manager of her department. Although Sarah maintained high standards in her own work, she didn't know how to articulate those standards for use by her team members. She said that she wanted them to do excellent work, but she struggled to describe what "excellence" would look like.

During coaching, Sarah decided to put her writing skills to work to assist her team. She drafted detailed checklists as a way to lay out the key elements of three of the group's routine reports. Sarah used the checklists not only to serve as report templates, but also to encourage a dialogue with her writers. First, she invited them to improve her drafts. Then, after the first round of reports was completed, she convened the team to revisit the checklists, evaluate their usefulness, and suggest ways to make them even more helpful and complete. At the start of her new job, Sarah felt shy about criticizing the work completed by her former peers. But by focusing discussion on the checklists, she was able to establish standards of excellence without making comments that felt personal.

The extraordinary power of checklists attracted public attention in 2007, when the World Health Organization (WHO) urged operating room personnel to save lives by using one during surgical procedures. The WHO "Surgical Safety Checklist" specifies 19 steps, some as basic as confirming the patient's name and the scheduled procedure. Although all the steps are routine, research showed that without reliance on a checklist, even experienced surgeons might miss at least one step. According to the WHO's Website, a 2009 study found that its surgical checklist "reduced the rate of deaths and serious complications during surgery by more than one-third across all eight pilot hospitals."

The operating room checklist process is much like the procedure that airplane pilots have followed successfully for decades. Proponents say that the aviation checklists not only prevent busy or distracted crews from forgetting steps, but also promote communication and teamwork.

Checklists promote safety, accuracy, and speed

In professions where lives are at stake, protocols increasingly call for checklists because they break complex projects into manageable parts and combat the human tendency to take shortcuts. Checklists are low-tech tools that can also help the rest of us to become more effective. *Here are examples of ways that you might use checklists to make your work go more smoothly:*

→ **Shape reports.** Use checklists to specify the content, style, and organization of routinely prepared documents.

→ **Assure accuracy.** Whether you are writing or editing, checklists can promote thorough fact-checking with questions like, "Have you checked the spelling of all names?" and "Are the quotes accurate and properly attributed?"

→ **Organize events.** If you plan meetings, conferences, or parties, smooth the process with a comprehensive planning list. Note every possible element, from invitations and RSVPs to the nametags and the menu. After each event, review your standard checklist to make sure that it addressed every development.

→ **Get packing.** Though some checklists include tasks and procedures, others simply describe items that you might need. Ease your travel anxieties with a standard list of everything that you might want to take along on a trip.

→ **Consider candidates.** Whether you are hiring an assistant or choosing a service provider, make a list of the skills and expertise that matter most to you. It may be easier to make a decision if you use the same checklist to evaluate each option.

→ **Assure best practices.** Checklists can help you avoid mistakes in challenging situations like conducting a difficult staffer's performance review or running the annual meeting. And emergency checklists can help you rise to the occasion if the worst occurs, whether the building is on fire or the CEO makes a public relations gaff.

41

Overcome Big Project Letdown

I wasn't surprised when my client Lisa* cancelled our phone meeting because I knew she was completing a big project. Her assignment was to organize a large conference, accompanied by a media blitz, designed to launch a new product for her company.

From what I read online, the conference and all the surrounding hoopla were a success. The activity reached a crescendo on a Friday, and I expected to speak with Lisa during the following week, when I hoped she'd be enjoying a victory lap around the corporate headquarters.

But when we finally spoke, Lisa was on the verge of tears. She couldn't forget the tiny things that had gone wrong, and she worried about people who might be disappointed. On top of that, routine marketing work had piled up during preparation for the product launch and the tall stack of requests now felt daunting. Lisa needed a plan to quickly get through the backlog, but she was reluctant to ask for extra work from her exhausted staff. ***Lisa had a bad case of Big Project Letdown and this is what she felt:***

→ **Exhaustion.** Because the project was so important, Lisa had been working long hours without taking time out for her normal life. At night she was tossing and turning. She'd quit going to the gym, she hadn't spoken with her girlfriends in weeks, and she couldn't remember her last quiet dinner with her husband.

→ **A sense of loss.** Although the project had been rewarding, it had also been invigorating. For its duration she was included with the senior team, and for the first time she spoke frequently with her CEO. And though the pressure was on, her staff rose to the occasion, following her lead and making her proud. Now that the big push was over, everything felt dull and flat. The prospect of tackling overdue routine work felt like drudgery compared to the creative activity involved in the special event.

→ **Depression.** Lisa realized that she was tired and also frustrated at the thought of turning to all the overdue tasks. But she felt so very blue that she was disconcerted. She said, "I know it was a success, so why do I feel so awful? What's wrong with me?"

You can manage Big Project Letdown

Lisa felt better as soon as she realized that it's normal to experience a sense of anticlimax after you've made a big effort. One reason is that during a big push your brain chemistry changes to help keep you going. Perhaps your dopamine spikes in a major meeting, or working with the big boss triggers your serotonin. But when your mood-enhancing chemicals return to their normal levels, it feels like something is wrong with your world.

After taking a day off, Lisa gradually bounced back from her postproject crash. Since then, she has learned to plan ahead to assure a speedy recovery after each major event. *Strategies like these helped Lisa and can help you to avoid or recover from Big Project Letdown:*

→ **Manage expectations.** Part of Lisa's problem was that for weeks she told people, "I'll get back to you right after the conference." So when she came into the office that Monday, a barrage of "can we talk now?" messages made her feel like she was under attack. These days she uses project management software to help make realistic commitments about when her team will fulfill routine requests after a special event is over.

→ **Take breaks.** Lisa's unrelenting pace disrupted the pattern of her life, causing stress at home and in the office, and keeping her awake at night. Now she has learned to keep up her fitness routine and build some quiet time into her schedule. She has found that taking regular brief rests, including quick outdoor walks, can help her stay calm and feeling creative.

→ **Plan ahead.** Lisa is happier if she is looking forward to something. When there was nothing new on the horizon after the conference, the future felt bleak. So now she lines up interesting projects and fun events down the road. By planning activities and vacations far in advance, she always has something to anticipate.

→ **Debrief.** One thing that helped Lisa is that, immediately after the conference, she and her team carefully reviewed what went right and what could be improved in the future. By examining the project details, she had a good understanding of the many things that went well, as well as of ways to be even more successful next time. In the following days, when she had moments of feeling like a failure, she was able to snap herself out of it by remembering the evidence of her success.

→ **Celebrate.** Lisa realized that she probably wasn't the only one who was feeling down in the days after the conference. She wrote notes to the many people who had helped, and she scheduled a festive lunch to thank team members for their hard work. She continued to celebrate by taking her patient husband out to dinner. As she drew other people into her celebration, her satisfaction with the success continued to grow.

It's normal to feel emotional after a significant project or a long-anticipated event. Sometimes the best way to move forward is to notice what you are feeling, and maybe even write about it. And look for ways in which the end of one big project can be transformed into the start of your next one.

42

Know When to Forget about Status

Initially, my friend Robert* was excited when his company offered him an opportunity to move to a different kind of job. He told me that he'd been bored at work for years and the new position could put him on a career track with more interesting opportunities than in his current role. But then he saw the problem. Although the transfer would bring Robert a small bump in pay, it would mean losing his "vice president" title.

I felt sorry for Robert. He had a chance to try something that looked exciting, but he was tortured by the thought that his colleagues would think he was being demoted. And so he was about to decline the offer, even though he was sick of his dull, topped-out VP position.

Soon after Robert and I chatted, I read a compassionate passage in Michael Korda's entertaining book *Horse People*. Writing about the herd behavior of horses, Korda said, "However peaceful horses may look grazing in their fields or dozing solemnly on their feet in their stall, they are always busy, in the sense that their mind is constantly aware of their status, and brooding over anything that might seem likely to change or challenge it. In short, it ain't easy being a horse..."

That's just like Robert and many other people. As social animals, humans may become preoccupied by their status, fretting over anything that challenges it. They might even pass up a wise move because others could regard it as a step down. In short, it ain't easy being human.

Unlike herd animals, however, we don't have to always give in to the pressure from the crowd.

Of course, it's normal to want respect from our colleagues. In his classic theory of human motivation, psychologist Abraham Maslow identified the need for esteem as a basic driver of human behavior. And leaders understand how important it can be for team members to feel accepted and valued by the group.

At work, the desire to look like a winner can keep us hustling when we secretly want to just throw in the towel. And praise and appreciation from our peers can make it all feel worth it once a big effort is over.

But although the desire to move up and look good can bring energy to your career, it also can lead you astray. There are times when the wish for status or accolades can waste your time or lead you to the wrong choices. *Here are five situations when the wiser move may be to let go of your all-too-human yearning for standing or prestige:*

1) **When you're the leader.** Have you worked for a manager who was preoccupied with the trappings of her position? Perhaps she'd insist on an early meeting, but then show up late and play with her phone once the discussion began. Weak leaders may play power games to underscore their high title. Stronger leaders tend to treat everyone with respect, focus on the work, and forget about symbols of rank.

2) **When you get a promotion.** In the first months of a new role, it may be tempting to talk a lot in order to demonstrate your qualifications and knowledge. And it can feel reassuring to show off the power that comes with senior standing. But now that you have the position, be modest about it. Instead, concentrate on listening, learning, and building relationships.

3) **When a job change could bring opportunities.** The idea that your career should keep you moving up some kind of hierarchical ladder is old-fashioned and can be self-destructive. These days, our long professional lives are more complicated and may include lateral shifts and even fresh starts. If you're starting to

feel stuck or insecure on your current track, be open to a change in direction. A short-term loss of grade or title is a small price to pay for a shift that could recharge your professional life. Tell yourself to put aside concerns about what other people think. Eventually, smart observers will recognize a good strategic move.

4) **When you're ready to reinvent yourself.** If you want to smoothly navigate a major work-life transition, the starting point may be your willingness to look like a beginner. I struggled with this when I chose to retire from law and business and start a new career as an executive coach. As an attorney, I drew confidence from my areas of expertise. I had to reframe my thinking before I was comfortable going back to school to learn something new.

5) **When you feel anxious or obsessed.** It's healthy to want respect from others, but self-respect is even more important. If you need public recognition in order to feel good about yourself, it may be time for reflection or counseling. A neurotic need for prestige, or an outsized fear of embarrassment, can make you miserable and jeopardize the success you want so much.

Even if we're not teenagers anymore, we want to look cool. But healthy grown-ups understand that working our way into the "in" crowd is mostly a game. One way to keep your need for prestige under control is by staying in touch with the things that matter to you most in life. Keep focusing on the big picture so it won't be so hard to stop worrying about status symbols when they're holding you back or tripping you up.

And if you're tired of your team members' preoccupation with the petty symbols of their standing, have a little compassion. Fretting too much about rank can be an indicator of pain. Remember: It just ain't easy being human.

43

To Lead without Authority, Know How to Herd. Cats

Do you know how to run a committee in a way that gets things done? Or to direct a work group when you don't really have a manager's authority?

Much of the work getting done today comes from fostering collaboration among people who don't share identical goals. But whether you're brainstorming a start-up with entrepreneurial pals, chairing a committee, or serving as counsel to a blue ribbon panel, leading folks who don't report to you can be frustrating. It can be like herding cats.

A person who is adept at leading across functional, political, and organizational lines is my friend and longtime mentee Sherry Little. In 2009, Sherry became a founding partner of Spartan Solutions, L.L.C., a company that develops and administers large infrastructure projects. As a result, Sherry often plays a lead role in the creation of public-private partnerships to build things like subway systems, trolley lines, or ferries. Sherry learned political skills as a senior staffer in the U.S. Senate, where crafting transportation legislation required negotiating across party lines. And then, while she was still in her 30s, and before the formation of Spartan, Sherry managed a $6 billion budget as acting administrator of the U.S. Department of Transportation's Federal Transit Administration.

Today, Sherry's work requires her to forge coalitions among people who may have different objectives, interests, and areas of expertise. When I asked her to share her favorite strategies for building an effective committee or task force, *Sherry offered four tips for "herding cats"*:

1) **Start strong.** The first meeting of a new group sets the tone for the future. It's vital that the initial meeting, and the invitation process, be smoothly organized. Be sure to structure the discussion and prepare the written materials so that every member leaves with a clear idea of the group's mission.

2) **Allocate tasks.** Make sure every member of the work group is given something specific to do, even if it's minimal. Sherry says that when people don't have even a small assignment, they are more likely to sit back and criticize.

3) **Track action items.** Whether an elected secretary prepares formal minutes or participants take turns e-mailing timely informal notes, it's important to keep track of action items and group decisions. Sherry makes sure that all assignments are put in writing to keep members accountable and on the same page.

4) **Explain decisions.** Regardless of whether you have direct authority, Sherry advises that in a collaborative group, you, as leader, should listen to everybody's views. Then, once you decide upon a course of action, explain the reasoning behind your decision. She says it's particularly important to describe how you took contrary opinions into account. When team members understand and respect the process, they will feel valued. Furthermore, Sherry says, they'll be more likely to go along with your decision this time, and to participate positively in the next debate.

Use the "Herding Cats Triangle" to plan your strategy

As Sherry knows, leading a collaborative effort requires a mix of strong organizational skills and softer skills, such as recognizing what each person needs and wants. In talking with clients, I often use a little model I call the "Herding Cats Triangle" to help work out a leadership strategy for a team or committee. The model, which consists of three questions, is loosely inspired by the "Strategic Triangle" described by Mark Moore in his book *Creating Public Value*. *If leading your group does feel like herding cats, keep things moving ahead by regularly running through these three questions:*

1) **What's the mission?** It's important for all participants to understand why the group exists. That doesn't mean that goals can't evolve with time, but the members must always have a shared, clear view of their collective purpose and responsibilities. If the committee or team is part of a larger organization, be sure your activities are consistent with the bigger vision. And, as you look at a specific project or challenge, define the likely deliverables and structure them so they support the organizational mission.

2) **Who are the stakeholders and what do they need?** As a starting point, learn as much as possible about all group members, including what they want from their membership and what interest sectors they represent. The more you know about the needs and interests of participants, the easier it will be for you to foster cooperation and compromise. Beyond the immediate participants, think about the interests of other possible stakeholders, because they have the potential to offer support or limit your progress. Regularly consider whether additional groups and individuals might be interested in or impacted by the group's activities.

3) **Are the right meeting logistics in place?** Running productive meetings is a key part of your job as leader. To start, make sure that you have the necessary capacity for tasks such as distributing the agenda and minutes, and keeping track of assignments. Chapter 31 describes more techniques for structuring meetings to keep your group moving forward.

To lead a relatively unstructured group, you must be highly organized. At the same time, you should recognize that, to some degree, participation in the effort is voluntary. That requires you to pay attention to every participant and be sensitive to the way each person is likely to be motivated.

44

How Bigger Goals Can Take You Further

When I first met Gayle Williams-Byers in the early 90s, I was impressed by her determination. At the time, she had begun a coveted internship in the White House. She was supposed to be writing a paper about her learning experience as an intern, for 12 hours of academic credit from Case Western Reserve University, where she was a junior.

Gayle's problem was that the only assignment her White House bosses had given her was to make photocopies. She needed those credit hours, but she didn't feel she'd be able to claim them because she wasn't learning anything.

Gayle found her way to my Washington office through an acquaintance. She requested a few minutes of my time, then pretty much announced that she'd be transferring her internship to my team at Consolidated Natural Gas Company. She said that she'd do anything, that she'd make it worth my while to take her on, but that she needed a challenge and she absolutely had to learn something.

Today, both of Gayle's parents have PhDs, but when she was growing up, no one in her family had attended college. And as one of her family's first college students, Gayle was anxious to learn as much as possible. She regarded the semester in Washington as the opportunity of a lifetime, important not just to her, but also to her extended family. She wanted a full experience, even if it meant walking away from the White House and inventing something new.

Gayle returned to my office after graduation and kept working for the company while completing a joint JD/MPA program. Then, during her last years in D.C., she was counsel to a Senate committee. In her early 20s, Gayle encountered many challenges, from racism to breast cancer, but I never doubted her ultimate success. I knew she wouldn't quit hustling to develop her potential because her future meant so much to her supporters.

During a 2011 Kwanzaa celebration, a community group in the Cleveland suburb of South Euclid gave Gayle a Kujichagulia Award to honor her self-determination. That was just one of the celebrations that followed her election, at age 37, as South Euclid's first African American municipal court judge.

I agree with Gayle's neighbors that she is a model of self-determination, and I'm so proud of her. She has always kept pushing toward her goals, even when life seems to have stacked the odds against her. A low point came during her election campaign, when she was going door-to-door, talking about her plan to bring change to the South Euclid Municipal Court system.

At the first house on a long street, an angry man refused to listen to her pitch. He jabbed her with his finger saying, "We don't want to hear it. We've already made up our minds. You got no chance, kid." Gayle was tired. She looked down the row of about 30 houses and thought, "I don't think I can do this again."

Her candidacy was a long shot and Gayle almost gave up. I asked her why she didn't. She said, "That's what self-determination is. You dig really deep when you don't want to, and you decide to take one more step toward your goal."

Gayle shares her parents' belief that, no matter how humble your beginning, you can become just about anything you want. She says, "If you can imagine it, you can do it." The most important thing to know is that "it's easier to keep going when you have a goal that's bigger than yourself."

For her judicial race, Gayle developed a comprehensive plan for a more transparent, service-focused court. And when she felt discouraged, she tried to stay focused on what the change could mean for her community. I've often seen the same thing with my clients. Having a vision about something important to a community makes you feel powerful and energetic, whereas personal ambition alone might just make you anxious. ***Here are six suggestions from Judge Gayle on building an outsized career:***

1) **Define big goals.** Look for ways that you can contribute to or create change for a broader group, not just for you. Identify a mission—for your team, family, or community—that will get your juices flowing. If you feel like you're too busy to worry about a larger mission, ask yourself why your job matters so much. Are you working this hard for your family? Or perhaps because you believe in what you're doing? You are more likely to persevere once you realize that more than your own ego is already at stake.

2) **Control what you can control and work to accept the rest.** When Gayle had cancer during law school, she faced difficulties that she couldn't change. But she focused her energy on studying hard and on taking care of herself. She says she couldn't control the fact of having cancer, but her "gift from cancer" was that she learned to control how she spent her time.

3) **Find mentors and role models.** Gayle deeply respects her parents and continues to learn from them. And, as I know well, she has never been shy about recruiting other mentors. She says that it is easier to keep going in the tough times if you've built yourself a cheering squad. And with practice, you get better at asking for help.

4) **Act like you have self-discipline.** Do you sometimes think about how much you could accomplish if only you were more disciplined? Gayle suggests that you identify the steps you would take toward your goal if you did in fact have that necessary self-discipline. For example, to start turning in your weekly report by the noon Friday deadline, would you draft it before leaving work on Thursday? Once you have a vivid picture of what you'd do if only you were more disciplined, start acting like that. Work on your report on Thursday afternoons. And each time you decide to "act like that" you'll exercise your self-discipline "muscle" and build your self-control.

5) **Laugh at yourself.** There's a danger that self-determination can morph into arrogance or self-righteousness. A good way to avoid that trap is to keep your sense of humor, particularly when it comes to your own failures and mistakes. Gayle says she looks pretty silly when she walks around her community in her sweats at 5:30 in

the morning, hand delivering "door-knockers" to inform citizens about how to access the resources of their court system.

6) **Build your confidence.** A powerful career aimed at big goals requires a good deal of self-confidence. One way to become surer of yourself is to define and achieve a series of small goals. Each time you reach one little target, you'll feel a bit stronger and you'll gradually become ready to aim for larger targets. Meanwhile, try to keep acting *as if* you were confident.

When you contemplate your long-term goals, it can seem presumptuous to feel passionate about making the world a better place. You might think, "How can I make that kind of difference, with my puny skills and resources?" To get past that kind of thinking, imagine what your goals could be if you *were* a smarter, braver, more confident person. What would you aim for, if you were an extraordinary person like Judge Gayle? Well—here's the secret: You *are* an extraordinary person, just like Judge Gayle. What you need to do is to imagine those big goals, then get started, even if you move forward just one sugar grain at a time.

45

You Might Hesitate, but Keep Going

This chapter explores an issue that seems to impact a disproportionate number of women: Why do so many talented professionals hesitate to reach for major career opportunities when the time seems right? I've heard executives worry about how often their female star performers seem reluctant to go after a higher job. And I've heard clients struggle with that tendency in their own behavior. Some never feel quite ready to step up, even when they see less-qualified men successfully moving into leadership.

In recent years public conversations have asked why, in at least some fields, so many talented women appear reluctant to go after the plumb jobs. Particularly in areas like law and technology, why aren't women moving to the top of the hierarchy at the same pace as their male colleagues?

The discussion about this phenomenon doesn't seem to be an us-against-them, women-versus-men thing. I've heard insightful men express concern that too few women are reaching their full professional potential. For example, two male professors recently asked me why their outstanding female business students seem to have lower job aspirations than their less-qualified male classmates. And I've heard some of the most accomplished American journalists—men and women—talk about how leading print and digital newsrooms are still dominated by a male culture, despite the fact that university journalism programs often have more women than men students.

Part of the problem may be lodged in the workplace culture resulting from the experiences of early women to enter many professions. When I joined the first big wave of women moving from law schools to Washington law firms, it was wonderful and exciting. But at times being a "first woman" was frightening. Even where there was no hazing or explicit double standard, it could be exhausting and bewildering to join all-male teams.

Many "old girls" who fought for professional acceptance decades ago, and who went on to success after success, say they still feel scarred. And these highly accomplished women still experience surprising flashes of uncertainty when they know it's time to seize an opportunity. In some cases it feels like exhaustion; it gets tiring to keep pushing when it feels like the odds are against you.

Notice your hesitation and adjust your timid behavior

Do you experience an unreasonable reluctance to step up when, intellectually, you know it's time to reach for the opportunity you've worked so hard to get? Your hesitant behavior may not be an isolated response that holds you back only when it's time for your big career move. If you look closely, you may see that it's part of a broader behavior pattern—a pattern that you can elect to change.

If you practice managing your hesitancy in small moments, you'll learn to deal with it more effectively in the face of bigger challenges and opportunities. *Here are little ways your uncertainty may show up, and strategies you can use to get past it:*

→ **Self-deprecating speech.** Some people undercut their otherwise professional presence, and their own feeling of confidence, by repeatedly using overly modest phrases such as "I'm probably wrong, but . . ." when a simple statement would be stronger. If that sounds like you, pause before saying, "I think perhaps it might be a good idea to try X." Instead, practice saying, "Let's do X."

→ **Excessive risk aversion.** When they first had access to law, engineering, and finance degrees, female students were sometimes mocked or intimidated. This exacerbated academic and job pressures, causing some women to grow less sure of themselves and, eventually, become overly fearful of career risks. Regardless of the underlying cause, and whether you're male or female, do you think that your outsized concern about the potential for failure might somehow be holding you back at work? If you know that you're more risk averse than your average colleague, you can choose to manage the way you approach opportunities. Imagine how you would act if you *didn't* feel so tentative. Now, look for occasions to practice acting more like *that*.

→ **Apologizing.** Feeling unwelcome at work may have been why some women started saying "sorry" even when they weren't at fault. It was tempting to blame themselves when things weren't going well. For some, it's still a challenge to face problems quickly and move the conversation on to solutions. Chapter 25 has suggestions about when to get over your urge to say "sorry."

→ **Dithering.** That hesitant feeling can leave you frozen, caught between staying or going, like the proverbial donkey between two handfuls of straw. Often, the worst decision is the one you don't really make. If you feel like you can't make up your mind, you might be better off tossing a coin than agonizing endlessly. Give yourself a time limit on decision-making. Choose one of the options even if your choice feels arbitrary. And move forward decisively, whatever you decide.

Notice your hesitation and move on anyway

Successful dieters know you don't have to eat just because you're hungry.

When you feel a little pang of hunger, instead of reaching for the cookie jar, you can elect to take a deep breath and just ignore that urge to munch. It can be the same when you have a sudden pang of inadequacy. You *don't* have to react just because of a little momentary discomfort. If you simply notice your feeling of hesitation and act anyway, your uncertainty may soon pass.

It helps to recognize that each of us—male or female—experiences fear at times. And it's normal to pause when we're facing an unfamiliar situation. But just because you experience a twinge of uncertainty doesn't mean you have to remain immobile. Once you've assessed the obstacles, you have the option to *act* like a confident person and forge ahead.

46

Ageism Is Real: Deal With It Sooner than Later

While finishing her MBA at a top tier university, Sarah* was aggressively recruited by a large company. She accepted their offer to join the marketing department. Once there, she connected with a powerful mentor who helped her snag plum assignments. For several years Sarah was the most junior professional in her group, and she enjoyed being treated like a young star.

But then the growing company made a wave of new hires and Sarah began to feel neglected. She felt stuck with the routine work, while the more interesting new projects went to her younger colleagues.

Sarah was asked to supervise the internship program, but she told me she didn't enjoy the work. She said the interns didn't have the right work ethic and were obsessed by technology. And one day, as she entered the office kitchen, she heard them making fun of her for being clueless about the power of social media.

When Sarah came to coaching, she complained that she was past her career peak. She felt like she was cut off from the company's high potential challenges and might be too old to compete for another good job elsewhere. Sarah was 34 at the time.

Sarah believed she was struggling with age discrimination and to some degree her concerns were well founded. Ageism is rampant in the workplace and can be hard to fight. And even 30-somethings like Sarah can find themselves sidelined by employers seeking fresh talent.

To improve her situation, Sarah found ways to demonstrate energy and enthusiasm. And soon she worked her way out of her slump. One thing that helped her was finding examples of older professionals whose age did not seem to limit their success. She noticed that whereas some coworkers were dissed for being out of date, these others seemed timeless despite their years.

Try these strategies for overcoming ageism

If you're facing subtle age bias at work and you want to stay where you are, you need to come up with a plan. A starting point for getting past ageism is to understand the negative stereotypes on which it's based. Then make it clear that the stereotypes don't fit you. *Consider these seven strategies for avoiding the burden of age discrimination:*

1) **Be tech savvy.** You don't have to *enjoy* sharing on Instagram, Skyping, or building a Twitter community. But if those are the ways that your colleagues or customers communicate, you need to participate. If you want to stay in the game, keep up with the technology. Take classes or find help to buy the devices you need and do whatever it takes to keep your skills current. And when you don't understand the latest developments, avoid the temptation to indulge in a Luddite rant. Express an interest, ask for assistance, and get on board.

2) **Look and act fit.** Some employers and younger workers believe that their older colleagues may have physical limitations that will prevent them from performing their fair share of the work. And your boss or clients won't offer you new challenges if they think you are about to have a heart attack. If you want to maximize your career options, it is vital not only that you stay healthy but that you also *look* healthy and exude energy.

3) **Talk healthy.** Most of us have health issues from time to time, but we can manage the way they impact us in the workplace. As

we mentioned in Chapter 19, it's possible to sabotage yourself by talking too much about your symptoms or crises. If you endlessly discuss your health challenges, not only will you sound boring, but people may start to think of you as frail and over the hill. Talk about the great hike you took last weekend instead of how sore you felt on Monday morning.

4) **Be stylish.** Looking shabby may seem cool when you're 22. But the older you get, the more important it is to look polished and up to date. If your clothes, hairdo, or glasses seem out of style, you may seem like you are past your prime. That doesn't mean you should dress like a kid, but you should aim for a look that feels current.

5) **Don't bring up your age.** If you are older—or younger—than the people you work with, it is very tempting to keep mentioning that fact. But if you can refrain from alluding to the age difference, chances are your coworkers will forget about it. And avoid reminding people of your age by endlessly telling stories about the good old days.

6) **Build a varied network.** If you are accustomed to hanging out with friends of all ages, you are more likely to blend easily into a group of younger or older workmates. If you don't allow age to be a barrier in your social life, you will be more comfortable talking and keeping up with different age groups at the office.

7) **Listen to your colleagues.** A great starting point for building strong relationships at work is to genuinely listen to what other people have to say. If you're part of the older set, show an interest in what younger colleagues say and learn from their perspective.

If you put aside your own prejudices about age and look for opportunities to work on projects with people of all generations, you'll become more skillful at avoiding age bias.

47

How to Stay Steady When Change Is Constant

A longtime mentee, Andrea Wilkinson, asked me to give a talk about how to survive in an organization that's going through a multiyear transition. Andrea is an executive who leads global government affairs initiatives to launch strategies for biopharmaceutical products and she wanted me to speak to group of women in her industry.

But when I heard the topic, I was surprised. That's because I can't think of anybody more skillful than Andrea at navigating a satisfying career through an industry experiencing prolonged change. She has survived multiple mergers, division liquidations, and company restructurings. And, from the time she was a young congressional staffer, Andrea has been adept at jumping ship at the right time, making perfect landings and always creating goodwill along the way.

Then I realized that Andrea didn't have questions herself, but was concerned about her industry colleagues. She saw some of them worrying and frozen with anxiety, instead of hustling to come up with her kind of survival strategies. So in preparing my remarks, I used Andrea as a model for thriving in the midst of uncertainty and transition. *Here are Andrea's tips for steering a steady career course even when the environment gets stormy:*

→ **Know that it's not about you.** Organizational change is like a torrential rain storm. It's pouring everywhere, not just on you. Complaining won't help and bitterness can make your situation worse. It's vital to job survival that you look at the big picture and focus on the future. Let go of any anger at finding yourself in a game you didn't sign up for, and concentrate on playing the cards you've been dealt.

→ **Understand your industry and its environment.** One reason Andrea keeps landing on her feet is that she always puts in the time to understand her company's business, as well as the surrounding market, regulatory framework, and political situation. She knows a lot about the competition, she's alert to the needs and interests of customers, and she's well informed about the winds of innovation. By thinking like a CEO, Andrea can spot the trends and be ready when the next wave hits.

→ **Know your bosses' goals.** Your longtime supervisor may fondly recall your contributions from a few years back, but that's probably not enough to save you when the going gets tough. Your most valued colleagues are the ones solving today's problems and contributing to the achievement of tomorrow's goals. If you want to do well in the coming months, be sure you understand your bosses' immediate objectives. Ask yourself: what do they need in order to be successful? And are there more ways I can help them succeed?

→ **Network! Network! Network!** One reason Andrea does so well is because she is so widely connected. She makes friends wherever she goes, she keeps in touch even when she's busy, and she's always willing to offer help or ask for it when she needs it. As we've discussed throughout this book, whether you are looking for a new job or a new idea, your position will be stronger if you have a broad network. Andrea urges that you take the time to listen when you meet someone, join groups, volunteer for projects, and find other ways to get to know people throughout your organization and beyond it.

→ **Find stability in other places.** Some folks are less at ease with uncertainty than others. If the constant state of change at work is getting you down, find people and communities to rely upon in other aspects of your life. Although she can be a bit of a workaholic, Andrea is smart about building a balanced life. She is active in her church, she works hard to stay connected with many friends, and she finds the time to visit widely scattered family members, as well as mentors like me. Andrea has created structures in her life that give her a place to rest when everything at work seems crazy.

→ **Be in great shape.** Let's face it: Change can be exhausting. When the world seems to be shifting, it takes extra energy just to get through the basics. So, although working around the clock might be the answer in an emergency, it's a shortsighted strategy when transition is the new normal. You need sustained energy for the long haul. Andrea is not an athlete, but she has learned that a regular fitness routine and enough sleep are critical to strong performance during difficult times.

→ **Reduce financial pressures.** One thing that has helped Andrea keep her jobs is that she has never become desperate at the thought of losing one. For a while she dreamed of buying a larger home, but instead she's held onto her little stone house and diversified her investments. When times are uncertain, it's wise to build up your rainy day fund or lay the groundwork for alternative sources of income. And there could be another benefit to pursuing some sort of entrepreneurial sideline. I've noticed that when clients start a side gig, whether it's consulting or a part-time job, it sometimes brings new energy to their day job. Creating your small business can inspire your entrepreneurial thinking and refresh your career enthusiasm.

48

Art Can Boost Your Creativity at Work

As a resilient, entrepreneurial professional, you must be able to change with changing circumstances and constantly find ways to make your work product a bit more valuable. And that requires you to be innovative—to be always open to learning and willing to create something new. But it's difficult to innovate when you're exhausted.

So how can you be at your creative best when your workload is already overwhelming? The answer is this: To do your best work you *must* stay in shape, physically, emotionally, and spiritually. You already know that a key to flourishing is to commit to your health and fitness program, which will support all aspects of your life. But that's just the starting point. One way to stimulate your innate creativity, and promote your well-being at the same time, is to engage with art.

Merry Foresta, an expert on American art, is the author of numerous books, including two in 2015: *Artists Unframed*, which features spellbinding snapshots of legendary artists; and *Irving Penn, Beyond Beauty*, featuring 161 of the great photographer's iconic images.

As an art historian and curator, Merry has long been fascinated by the relationship between art and innovation. For example, in studying the 19th century she was intrigued by the rich contributions of artist/scientists like Samuel Morse. He was one of America's great painters and then went on to invent the telegraph; and for good measure he also introduced photography to this country. Morse was prolific, but his combination of interests wasn't unusual in his circles. According to Merry, up until the 20th century, studying art was one of the ways that leaders were educated and encouraged to develop critical thinking.

For more than three decades, I've enjoyed learning from my friend Merry and brainstorming with her about ways to encourage innovation. Our first big project together was in the early 90s when Merry was curator of photography for the Smithsonian Institution's American Art Museum and I was leading external affairs for the Consolidated Natural Gas Company. At that time, the Smithsonian had rarely partnered with a company, but we worked through the institutional concerns and came up with a new collaborative model. The result was a CNG Collection of Photography at the Smithsonian, including a lovely book and a series of exhibitions.

Merry's final role as a full-time Smithsonian executive was to create its groundbreaking Photography Initiative, an online entrance to the Institution's vast collection of photographs. These days, while occasionally serving as a guest curator, Merry works with museums, universities, and other organizations in new ways. They call her when they want to reexamine their assumptions and foster innovation in their programs. Along the way, Merry helps clients rediscover that art can inspire original thinking, allow people to make new connections among complex issues, and inspire them to achieve in satisfying new ways.

Merry uses the now-popular term "Creative Culture" to describe a workplace or other environment where, she says, "creative ideas are encouraged, supported, protected, and nurtured for further development, until their true value can be understood and appreciated. Creativity brings imagination, curiosity, experimentation, and idea sharing into all manner of daily activities. And Creative Culture can bring imagination, diversity, curiosity, experimenting, and idea sharing into our work."

One path to fostering an organization's Creative Culture is to provide access to art, whether it means sponsoring a field trip or installing artworks throughout the office space. "Even the language of art resembles the language of innovative leadership," Merry says. "Art is often about surprise, finding a new perspective, seeing things we had never before noticed, developing a vision, and communicating that vision with others. So is leadership."

"By engaging in art, or simply looking at art," Merry says, "we see new things, make new connections, and learn that it is fine to ask questions and push boundaries. Some businesses are leading the way, using art to encourage employees to break out of their limited thinking and invent new ideas."

In the last year or so, Merry has been particularly intrigued by the concept of spending more time with fewer things as a way to experience art in a profound way. The idea was introduced by Peter Clothier in his 2012 book, *Slow Looking*, and is now gaining attention at a number of museums that see this approach as a way to more deeply engage their audiences.

Merry describes the concept as "an antidote to contemporary life." Often, when busy people visit a museum they dash through, glancing at as many works of art as they possibly can. The "slow art" alternative approach might start with 30 minutes of strolling from room to room, but then the viewer would return to a favorite painting and study it for the next half hour.

"Sometimes you're rewarded more than you might have thought possible if you're able to deeply look and consider a single painting over a longer period of time. As you contemplate it minute after minute, you begin to draw conclusions and gather ideas about art and perhaps even about creativity itself," Merry says.

It's not clear why long, deep looking can be so transformative, but one theory is that it becomes a form of meditation. "This kind of viewing can change your patterns of thought. It fosters your ability to get out of your rut, and think in entirely different ways," Merry says.

Refresh creativity by engaging with art

If you want to bring new creativity to your team, or simply to your own work, one way to begin is by looking at art. ***Consider these strategies for stimulating innovation through art:***

→ **Do some team building.** Instead of your normal quick lunch, arrange with colleagues to visit a local art museum. Encourage people to get to know each other better by talking about what they like and don't like. Merry says, "There is no such thing as 'good' or 'bad,' just 'intriguing' and 'interesting'!" Discussing exhibits can be a great way to bridge cultural, age, and other gaps.

→ **Try "slow looking."** Find a piece of art you like and study it for 20 or 30 minutes. At first, it may seem that you can't stay still for so long, but as you continue to focus, you'll begin to see more and more.

→ **Try another type of museum.** Merry says that whether you're in the butterfly gallery at the Natural History Museum in Washington, or viewing the collection of First Ladies' gowns in the nearby American History Museum, you can find art and beauty in almost any kind of exhibition. So if your group is turned off by the idea of an "art" museum, try another kind of exhibit.

→ **Redefine your book club.** Do you belong to a book club or some other kind of social group? Vary your regular program by suggesting that one meeting be scheduled at a local museum.

→ **Take a course.** Museums are finding new ways to engage and educate their patrons, and many schools and universities offer continuing education programs touching upon the arts. Stimulate your creative self by taking a course or signing up for a workshop.

→ **Take art home.** Museum stores offer postcards and posters that make it possible to take home exciting art at a reasonable price. And, of course, the Web makes it possible for us all to look at art, no matter where we live or work.

49

The Right Way to Move On

Most smart professionals understand the importance of getting off to a great start in a new job. But some don't take full advantage of that other opportunity in a transition: the chance to tie up loose ends in the old job and turn the experience into a building block for the future.

Bill* is a young lawyer who was let go from his law firm after the leaders of his energy group left the partnership, taking their clients with them. Bill started his week as an associate with a bright future, but by Friday he was ushered out of the office with a small severance payment and a cardboard carton of personal items.

Bill was stunned and then angry. However, on the advice of a mentor, he controlled his emotions and quickly launched a plan that paid off later. Bill saw that the firm's senior lawyers were furious with the departing energy group and associated him with the traitors, even though he hadn't been invited to join their new enterprise. And he recognized that he'd been unwise during his time at the firm in not making an effort to get to know colleagues outside the busy energy practice. Most worrisome, he feared that former colleagues who weren't his friends would describe him as not competent enough to either stay in the firm or be invited to join the departing unit.

Determined to make the best of his situation, Bill launched a process that changed the way his former firm remembered him and ultimately led to a new job. In the days after his departure, he methodically contacted the law firm leaders and staff and found ways to thank each of them for something. Even though it often felt like a reach, he wrote notes expressing appreciation for the collegial atmosphere, the training in managing client accounts—for any kindness or strength he could describe without being insincere. And as a few years went by, he found ways to stay in touch, even referring a little business to a friend in the old firm.

What Bill did so well was reframe his law firm experience in the minds of his former colleagues. Most of them probably didn't remember him vividly, but now they did think of him positively. This was reflected in the fact that they occasionally sent him energy work they could no longer handle. And when they eventually decided to rebuild the firm's energy capability, they remembered Bill and recruited him to rejoin, this time as a partner.

Use these strategies for a departure that will pave your way in the future

Whether you're sad to go or can't wait to get out the door, it's normal in a career transition to focus more on the future than on the past. But if you're smart, you'll do what it takes to create a classy departure. In today's fluid job market, it's inevitable that you'll bump into some of these people again. And, when that happens, what they may remember is your last few days on the job. *Here are five tips for leaving your job the right way:*

1) **Give proper notice.** Once you've decided to accept another opportunity, tell your boss immediately, before word gets around. The boss may not like being surprised by your departure, but it'll be much worse if the news drifts in through the grapevine. Give as much notice as possible—two weeks or a month is common, but more could be better. And follow up your conversation with a very brief resignation letter that clearly states your last day on the job.

2) **Resist the urge to speak up.** You may have fantasized about how great it would feel to tell the team what you really think. Don't

do it! Your goal now is to end things on a good note, not point out the error of their ways. Even formal exit interviews should be approached with caution because you can't really count on confidentiality.

3) **Finish your work and leave a trail.** Your last days on the job are a great time to show that you have what it takes. If you can't complete your projects, leave them in good shape so the next person will know where to get started. Write notes about your tasks, contacts, and responsibilities to help your coworkers or your replacement keep things moving. If you leave things in a mess, that's how they'll always think of you.

4) **Say "thanks."** Think about every person, at every level, who has been helpful to you in some way. Don't dramatize. But write notes, stop by your colleagues' desks, or find other appropriate ways to thank them for what they have done or what they have meant to you. The more specific you make your "thank you's," the more effective and appreciated they will be.

5) **Make plans to stay in touch.** Make sure everybody has your new contact information and confirm that you have theirs. If you haven't connected with them on LinkedIn, do it now. You're likely to see many of these people again, but don't leave it all to chance. Think about the people you most want in your future and promise yourself that you will find ways to make it happen.

In a career market where people change jobs frequently, knowing how to say "goodbye" with grace has become an important skill. An essential part of your smooth transition is treating each one of your old colleagues as though they still matter.

50

Choose to Be an Optimist

During my second year of law school, I hit a low point. I was exhausted from long hours of work and feeling sorry for myself because I was paying my way through school. And somehow I got it in my head that I wouldn't be able to find a good job after graduation. I dragged through, day after day, with a little voice in my head saying, "I'll never get a job. I'll never get a job."

Then my sister Helen reported that a routine exam had shown our brother Dick to have a tumor on his spine. Helen, a nurse, said the spine was a dangerous place for a tumor and if it were malignant, Dick might not have long to live. Dick was rushed immediately into surgery. Happily, we soon heard the good news that the lump was just a harmless cyst, and Dick was in no danger.

The next morning I woke up in a wonderful mood. My career worries had drifted away, I was confident that things would work out, and life felt good.

Then I noticed: My life was no different than it had been the day before Helen's call. But my depression had lifted and I once again felt confident and ready to face the world. The scare about Dick's health had pulled me out of my self-pity and given me a chance to focus on the big picture.

So I wondered: If a momentary scare could shake me out of my pessimism, shouldn't I be able to do that for myself? I knew I was born a worrier, but I decided that from then on I'd make better choices about whether to let my worries take over my life.

I experimented with various ways of holding my pessimism in check, like refocusing on the bigger picture and talking back to the voice in my head. And I found that when I kept an optimistic outlook, my career did indeed tend to flow smoothly. Years later, I came across a book that helped me understand that I was on the right track. I was captivated by *Learned Optimism: How to Change Your Mind and Your Life* by leading psychologist Martin E.P. Seligman.

Often called "the father of Positive Psychology," Dr. Seligman has spent years studying "well-being" and ways that normal people can choose to become happier and more fulfilled in life. Reading his work reinforced my own belief, developed through trial and error, that optimism is a choice and we don't have to be controlled by our innate tendency toward pessimism.

Practice techniques for choosing optimism

Optimism is a positive attitude that carries with it an expectation that things will probably work out for the best. A growing body of research from multiple disciplines suggests that optimism can set you up for career success, improve your social life, help you overcome stress and many kinds of difficulties, and support your efforts to stay healthy.

Pessimism, on the other hand, can undercut your level of achievement, weaken your immune system, and make it more likely that you'll become depressed. In the workplace, pessimism is valuable in performing tasks that require an awareness of risks, such as drafting legal documents. Even for lawyers, however, a pessimistic style can be a burden when it's time to woo clients or manage projects. Generally, it's the optimists who enjoy more fruits of success.

Some lucky optimists are just born that way, but the rest of us need not despair. Dr. Seligman documented that you can build optimism by modifying your internal dialogue. The trick is to recognize and dispute your pessimistic thoughts. For example, if you catch yourself thinking "I'll never get this right," you can argue back to yourself that you're just starting out and will get much better with practice.

In my own life, and working with clients, I've seen good results using these techniques pioneered by Dr. Seligman:

→ **Catch that thought.** Learn to identify self-defeating thoughts that automatically run through your mind, particularly when you're feeling down or discouraged. Simply noticing your frequent negative attitudes—such as, "I'm so bored" or "This will never work out"—will help to tame them.

→ **Argue back.** As we discussed in Chapter 7, you can talk back to the voice in your head. Once you observe a negative refrain, dispute it, just as you would in conversation with a dear friend who was putting herself down. If you notice a voice saying, "I'm a loser," respond with something like, "You have what it takes to start winning."

→ **Test the accuracy.** One simple way to dispose of a pessimistic thought is to demonstrate that it's just not true. Look to external evidence, and then dismiss exaggerated statements such as, "I always fail at things like this."

→ **Find other explanations.** Most situations have many causes, but pessimists tend to cling to the worst possible options. They may leap to the most permanent and pervasive explanation imaginable, such as, "I'm just too old to do this." Dispute negativity by proposing alternative explanations, like: "Maybe I didn't prepare enough this time, but I can do better next time."

Here are more suggestions for developing a more optimistic approach to life:

→ **Make lists.** Carry around a small notebook in which to list each negative phrase that plays repeatedly inside your head. Periodically review the list and create a new list by reframing each pessimistic thought into a positive statement. For example, "I'm too fat," may become "Today I will eat consciously" on the new list. Read the positive list at least daily.

→ **Appreciate the good stuff.** You can generate a surge of optimism by refocusing your attention on the more positive aspects of any situation. For example, if you're frustrated with the stresses of your job, look at the total picture and list five things you appreciate about your professional life. Review the list frequently.

→ **Make goodwill deposits.** Each time you say something kind or positive to another person, or go out of your way to do a good deed, there will be at least two impacts. First, it will be as though you've made a deposit in an account where that person can store up positive feelings about you. And you'll know that the goodwill might come in handy in the future. Second, your positive gesture toward another person will probably provide a lift in your own attitude.

→ **Resist naysayers.** Sometimes that negative dialogue isn't all in your head. Pessimistic people can drain your energy and pull whole groups off track. Avoid negative people when you can and try not to let them bring you down when their company is unavoidable. When you must deal with angry or disrespectful clients or coworkers, try to summon up a feeling of compassion for their angst. Then observe your negative emotions stimulated by their attitude or behavior, and imagine that you are opening your heart and letting those feelings float away.

→ **Talk to people.** Pessimists may isolate themselves when facing difficulties, which can make things worse. When things aren't going well, resist your urge to curl up in a hole. Instead, seek ways to enjoy even small positive connections with other people. If things are troublesome in one sector, like work, find new energy and renewed optimism by structuring happier interactions in other parts of your life.

→ **Plan for the worst.** If you have a strong pessimistic streak, you naturally start thinking about all the things that could go wrong. If you're worrying about developments that are out of your control, remind yourself that there's no point in torturing yourself when there's nothing you can do. But when you're thinking about things that are within your span of control, your best bet may be to create a contingency plan. When you have a worst case plan in place, it's easier to shift your focus away from your worries.

→ **Smile.** If you put on a happy face and act like an optimist, you're likely to actually experience an emotional lift. And the upswing in your mood may continue to build when other people return your smile.

→ **Spend time in nature.** There's growing evidence that spending time outdoors can help you to overcome moderate depression, particularly if you walk or engage in other active pastimes. I've had many clients who've found a daily walk to be helpful in keeping up their positive outlook.

→ **Get help.** If your anxiety feels out of control or you always wake up grouchy, it may be time to seek professional help. Many kinds of therapy can help you to tackle your depression and rediscover your optimism. For example, cognitive behavioral therapy—including emerging online versions—may help you to manage your moods by replacing pessimistic thoughts.

→ **Pray.** There's much evidence that prayer can make you feel better, even if you're not sure what to believe in.

Just choose

Sometimes no tricks are needed. You can simply *choose* optimism. Every morning as you head to work, you can *decide* to face the day with an optimistic attitude. Your elevated mood may not last, but each time a client is rude or your boss is unreasonable you'll have an opportunity to choose again. Throughout the day you'll have opportunities to let go of negativity and notice the positive. Some choices will be more challenging than others, but with repeated attempts at optimism your brain will change, and it will be increasingly easy to opt for the positive choice.

Learning how and why to be optimistic is something I've had to absorb more than once. Like everyone, I've had ups and downs. And I've discovered and rediscovered that managing my attitude must be part of my formula for working past the down times.

Choosing optimism is what I'm doing now, in this later phase of my professional life. I'm excited about the rapidly evolving new career options, and I'm electing to stay part of it all, rather than retire.

You also have the power to choose optimism in ways that can transform your career and enrich your life.

I wish you well.

BIBLIOGRAPHY

Allen, David. *Getting Things Done: The Art of Stress-Free Productivity*. New York: Penguin Books, 2001.

Baker, Dan, and Cameron Stauth. *What Happy People Know: How the New Science of Happiness Can Change Your Life for the Better*. Emmaus, PA: Rodale, 2003.

Begley, Sharon. *Train Your Mind, Change Your Brain: How a New Science Reveals Our Extraordinary Potential to Transform Ourselves*. New York: Ballantine Books, 2008.

Benson, Herbert, and William Proctor. *Beyond the Relaxation Response: How to Harness the Healing Power of Your Personal Beliefs*. New York: Times Books, 1984.

———. *The Breakout Principle: How to Activate the Natural Trigger that Maximizes Creativity, Productivity, and Personal Well-Being*. New York: Scribner, 2003.

Breuning, Loretta G. "What a Let-Down! When Your Happy Chemicals Dip, Your Brain Concocts Failure." *Psychology Today* (blog). Accessed October 10, 2014. https://www.psychologytoday.com/blog/your-neurochemical-self /201107/what-let-down.

Buckingham, Marcus, and Donald O. Clifton. *Now, Discover Your Strengths*. New York: Free Press, 2001.

Buettner, Dan. *The Blue Zones: Lessons for Living Longer from the People Who've Lived the Longest*. Washington, D.C.: National Geographic, 2008.

Buzan, Tony, and Barry Buzan. *The Mind Map Book: How to Use Radiant Thinking to Maximize Your Brain's Untapped Potential*. New York: Plume, 1993.

Carnegie, Dale. *How to Win Friends & Influence People*. New York: Pocket Books, 1998.

Carson, Richard David. *Taming Your Gremlin: A Surprisingly Simple Method for Getting out of Your Own Way*. New York: Quill, 2003.

Chaleff, Ira. *The Courageous Follower: Standing up to and for Our Leaders*. San Francisco: Berrett-Koehler Publishers, 1995.

Chopra, Deepak. *The Seven Spiritual Laws of Success: A Practical Guide to the Fulfillment of Your Dreams*. San Rafael, CA: Amber-Allen Publishing, 1994.

———. *The Spontaneous Fulfillment of Desire: Harnessing the Infinite Power of Coincidence*. New York: Harmony Books, 2003.

Chopra, Deepak, and Rudolph E. Tanzi. *Super Brain: Unleashing the Explosive Power of Your Mind to Maximize Health, Happiness, and Spiritual Well-Being*. New York: Harmony Books, 2012.

Collins, James C. *Good to Great: Why Some Companies Make the Leap—and Others Don't*. New York, NY: HarperBusiness, 2001.

Colvin, Geoffrey. *Talent Is Overrated: What Really Separates World-Class Performers from Everybody Else*. New York: Portfolio, 2008.

Covey, Stephen R. *The 8th Habit: From Effectiveness to Greatness*. Philadelphia: Running Press, 2006.

Coyle, Daniel. *The Little Book of Talent: 52 Tips for Improving Skills*. New York, NY: Bantam Books, 2012.

Cuddy, Amy. "Your body language shapes who you are." Accessed June 21, 2015. http://www.ted.com/talks/amy_cuddy_your_body_language_shapes_who _you_are.

Dalai Lama, and Howard C. Cutler. *The Art of Happiness: A Handbook for Living*. New York: Riverhead Books, 1998.

Davidson, Richard J., and Sharon Begley. *The Emotional Life of Your Brain: How Its Unique Patterns Affect the Way You Think, Feel, and Live—and How You Can Change Them*. New York: Hudson Street Press, 2012.

Dean, Jeremy. *Making Habits, Breaking Habits: How to Make Changes That Stick*. Richmond: Oneworld, 2013.

Drucker, Peter F. *The Age of Discontinuity: Guidelines to Our Changing Society*. New York: Harper & Row, 1969.

———. *Management: Tasks, Responsibilities, Practices*. New York: Harper & Row, 1974.

Duhigg, Charles. *The Power of Habit: Why We Do What We Do in Life and Business*. New York: Random House, 2012.

Dyer, Wayne W. *Excuses Begone!: How to Change Lifelong, Self-Defeating Thinking Habits*. Carlsbad, Calif.: Hay House, 2009.

Gallwey, W. Timothy, Edward S. Hanzelik, and John Horton. *The Inner Game of Stress: Outsmart Life's Challenges and Fulfill Your Potential*. New York: Random House, 2009.

Gerber, Michael E. *E-Myth Mastery: The Seven Essential Disciplines for Building a World Class Company*. New York: HarperCollins Publishers, 2005.

————. *The E-Myth Revisited: Why Most Small Businesses Don't Work and What to Do about It*. New York: CollinsBusiness, 1995.

Goleman, Daniel. *Emotional Intelligence*. New York: Bantam Books, 1995.

————. *Social Intelligence: The New Science of Human Relationships*. New York, NY: Bantam Books, 2007.

————. *The Brain and Emotional Intelligence: New Insights*. Northampton, MA: More Than Sound, 2011.

————. *Focus: The Hidden Driver of Excellence*. London: Bloomsbury, 2013.

Goulston, Mark. *Just Listen: Discover the Secret to Getting through to Absolutely Anyone*. New York: American Management Association, 2010.

Hannon, Kerry. *Great Jobs for Everyone 50+: Finding Work That Keeps You Happy and Healthy and Pays the Bills*. Hoboken, NJ: Wiley & Sons, 2012.

————. *What's Next?: Follow Your Passion and Find Your Dream Job*. San Francisco, Calif.: Chronicle Books, 2010.

————. *Love Your Job: The New Rules for Career Happiness*. Hoboken, NJ: Wiley & Sons, 2015.

Heath, Chip, and Dan Heath. *Made to Stick: Why Some Ideas Survive and Others Die*. New York: Random House, 2007.

————. *Switch: How to Change Things When Change Is Hard*. New York: Broadway Books, 2010.

Horstman, Judith. *The Scientific American Healthy Aging Brain: The Neuroscience of Making the Most of Your Mature Mind*. San Francisco: Jossey-Bass, 2012.

Iacoboni, Marco. *Mirroring People: The New Science of How We Connect with Others*. New York: Farrar, Straus and Giroux, 2008.

Jaworski, Joseph, and Betty S. Flowers. *Synchronicity: The Inner Path of Leadership*. San Francisco: Berrett-Koehler Publishers, 1996.

Jones, Beverly E. "No Girls Aloud: A Report on the 'report on the Status of Women at Ohio University' during the 1970s." 2005 Archives Lecture. Athens, Ohio. Lecture.

Koch, Richard. *The 80/20 Principle: The Secret to Success by Achieving More with Less*. New York: Currency, 1999.

Korda, Michael. *Horse People: Scenes from the Riding Life*. (Illustrations by the Author.) New York, NY: HarperCollins, 2003.

Kouzes, James M., and Barry Z. Posner. *The Leadership Challenge*. San Francisco, CA: Jossey-Bass, 2008.

LaFrance, Marianne. *Why Smile?: The Science Behind Facial Expressions*. New York: W.W. Norton, 2013.

Langer, Ellen J. *Counter Clockwise: Mindful Health and the Power of Possibility*. New York: Ballantine Books, 2009.

———. *Mindfulness*. Cambridge, MA: Lifelong Books/Da Capo Press, 2010.

Leonard, George. *Mastery: The Keys to Long-Term Success and Fulfillment*. New York, NY: Dutton, 1991.

Loehr, James E., and Tony Schwartz. *The Power of Full Engagement: Managing Energy, Not Time, Is the Key to High Performance and Personal Renewal*. New York: Free Press, 2005.

Maslow, Abraham H. *Motivation and Personality*. New York: Harper & Row, 1970.

McGonigal, Kelly. "How to make stress your friend." www.ted.com. June 2013.

Moore, Mark H. *Creating Public Value: Strategic Management in Government*. Cambridge, MA: Harvard University Press, 1995.

Norcross, John C., Kristin Loberg, and Jonathon Norcross. *Changeology: 5 Steps to Realizing Your Goals and Resolutions*. New York: Simon & Schuster, 2012.

Pantene. "Sorry, Not Sorry." Advertisement. Accessed June 18, 2014. https://www.youtube.com/watch?v=rzL-vdQ3ObA.

Pentland, Alex "Sandy". "The New Science of Building Great Teams." *Harvard Business Review*, April 2012. https://hbr.org/2012/04/the-new-science-of-building-great-teams/arl1.

Pink, Daniel H. *A Whole New Mind: Why Right-Brainers Will Rule the Future*. New York: Riverhead Books, 2006.

Pollan, Stephen M., and Mark Levine. *Second Acts: Creating the Life You Really Want, Building the Career You Truly Desire*. New York: HarperResource, 2003.

Price, Beverly Jones. *Report on the Status of Women at Ohio University*. Rep. no. 213296587. Athens, Ohio: Ohio U Libraries, 1972. Print.

Pritchard, Forrest, and Molly Peterson. *Growing Tomorrow: A Farm-To-Table Journey in Photos and Recipes: Behind the Scenes with 18 Extraordinary Sustainable Farmers Who Are Changing the Way We Eat*. New York: The Experiment, 2015.

Rahe, Richard, and Tores Theorell. "Workplace Stress." www.stress.org. The American Institute of Stress, June 2013. Web.

Rath, Tom, and Donald O. Clifton. *How Full Is Your Bucket?: Positive Strategies for Work and Life*. New York: Gallup Press, 2004.

Ryckman, Pamela. *Stiletto Network: Inside the Women's Power Circles That Are Changing the Face of Business*. New York: AMACOM, 2013.

Sandberg, Sheryl, and Nell Scovell. *Lean In: Women, Work, and the Will to Lead*. New York: Knopf, 2013.

Seligman, Martin E.P. *What You Can Change and What You Can't*. New York: Vintage Books, 1993.

———. *Authentic Happiness: Using the New Positive Psychology to Realize Your Potential for Lasting Fulfillment.* New York: Free Press, 2002.

———. *Learned Optimism: How to Change Your Mind and Your Life.* New York: Vintage Books, 2006.

Silverman, Craig. *Regret the Error: How Media Mistakes Pollute the Press and Imperil Free Speech.* New York: Union Square Press, 2007.

Strozzi-Heckler, Richard. *Holding the Center: Sanctuary in a Time of Confusion.* Berkeley, Calif.: Frog, 1997.

Sweeney, Camille, and Josh Gosfield. *The Art of Doing: How Superachievers Do What They Do and How They Do It so Well.* New York: Penguin Group, 2013.

Tracy, Brian. *Eat That Frog.* Offenbach: GABAL, 2002.

"Twenty-five Best-Mannered People of 2014." The National League of Junior Cotillions. Accessed January 2, 2015. http://www.nljc.com/tenbest mannered.html.

Watkins, Michael. *The First 90 Days: Critical Success Strategies for New Leaders at All Levels.* Boston, MA: Harvard Business School Press, 2003.

Wheeler, Claire Michaels. *10 Simple Solutions to Stress: How to Tame Tension & Start Enjoying Your Life.* Oakland, Calif.: New Harbinger Publications, 2007.

Whyte, William Hollingsworth. *The Organization Man.* New York: Simon and Schuster, 1956.

Winston, Stephanie. *Organized for Success: Top Executives and CEOs Reveal the Organizing Principles That Helped Them Reach the Top.* New York, NY: Crown Business, 2004.

Zander, Rosamund Stone, and Benjamin Zander. *The Art of Possibility.* New York: Penguin Books, 2002.

INDEX

ABOUT THE AUTHOR

Beverly Jones is a master of reinvention. She led university programs for women before trailblazing her career as a Washington lawyer and Fortune 500 energy executive. Throughout her varied work life she has mentored other professionals and leaders to grow and thrive.

Since 2002, Jones has been a respected executive coach and leadership consultant, helping professionals of all ages to advance their careers, shift directions, and become more productive. Based in the nation's capital, she works with clients spread across the country, including accomplished leaders in Congress, at major federal agencies, NGOs, universities, large corporations, and small businesses.

Jones is a popular speaker and facilitator, and creates workshops and retreats around the needs of her clients. She is a visiting executive with Ohio University's Voinovich School of Leadership and Public Affairs. Her podcasts are distributed through WOUB Digital, and her blog posts and e-zine archive are found on her Website: *www.clearwaysconsulting.com*. Jones is active on Twitter: @beverlyejones.

PROBLEMS OF THE MODONOMY

The Battle Against Unemployment and Inflation

PROBLEMS OF THE MODERN ECONOMY

General Editor: EDMUND S. PHELPS, *Columbia University*

Each volume in this series presents
prominent positions in the debate of an
important issue of economic policy

THE BATTLE AGAINST UNEMPLOYMENT AND INFLATION

CHANGING PATTERNS IN FOREIGN TRADE
AND PAYMENTS

THE GOAL OF ECONOMIC GROWTH

MONOPOLY POWER AND ECONOMIC PERFORMANCE

PRIVATE WANTS AND PUBLIC NEEDS

THE UNITED STATES AND THE DEVELOPING ECONOMIES

LABOR AND THE NATIONAL ECONOMY

INEQUALITY AND POVERTY

DEFENSE, SCIENCE, AND PUBLIC POLICY

AGRICULTURAL POLICY IN AN AFFLUENT SOCIETY

THE CRISIS OF THE REGULATORY COMMISSIONS

The Battle Against Unemployment and Inflation

Edited by

MARTIN NEIL BAILY
THE BROOKINGS INSTITUTION

ARTHUR M. OKUN
THE BROOKINGS INSTITUTION

THIRD EDITION

 W · W · NORTON & COMPANY

NEW YORK   LONDON

Published simultaneously in Canada by
Penguin Books Canada Ltd,
2801 John Street, Markham, Ontario L3R 1B4.

PRINTED IN THE UNITED STATES OF AMERICA

The text of this book is composed in Caledonia, with display type set in Bulmer. Composition by The Vail-Ballou Press. Manufacturing by The Maple-Vail Book Group.

Library of Congress Cataloging in Publication Data
Main entry under title:
The Battle against unemployment and inflation.
3rd edition.
    (Problems of the modern economy)
    1. United States—Economic policy—1971–1981—
Addresses, essays, lectures.   2. Unemployment—
United States—Addresses, essays, lectures.
3. Inflation (Finance)—United States—Addresses,
essays, lectures.   4. Macroeconomics—Addresses,
essays, lectures.   I. Baily, Martin N. (Martin Neil)
II. Okun, Arthur M.   III. Series.
HC106.7.B375   1982   339.5'0973   82-8230
ISBN 0-393-01381-2
ISBN 0-393-95055-7 (pbk.)

W. W. Norton & Company, Inc., 500 Fifth Avenue, New York, N.Y. 10110
W. W. Norton & Company Ltd., 37 Great Russell Street, London WC1B 3NU

4 5 6 7 8 9 0

Contents

Introduction

PROSPERITY IS RIVALED only by peace as the key political issue in the United States. Unemployment and inflation are always near the top of any opinion poll's list of major matters of concern to the populace. In presidential and congressional election campaigns, the record of economic performance by the "ins" and the promises of the "outs" represent one of the central issues. The Employment Act of 1946 declared that "It is the continuing policy and responsibility of the Federal Government . . . to promote maximum employment, production, and purchasing power."

The Employment Act's conclusion that social action to curb unemployment is necessarily desirable was neither trite nor self-evident. Until the 1930s, most economists believed that the private enterprise system, functioning competitively, had an automatic tendency to balance supply and demand in the aggregate at the right level. Wide fluctuations in economic activity and excessive unemployment were generally interpreted as either inevitable features of a growing economy or the results of misguided government interferences in economic life. Such views pointed toward a hands-off policy of neutrality for the government.

The Great Depression had a permanent impact on attitudes toward public policy against unemployment. At the depths of the depression, one-fourth of the nation's labor force was unemployed; and the unemployment rate did not fall below 14 percent throughout the 1930s. No individual escaped the impact of this great collapse and no individual could combat it on his own. With the sole exception of the Civil War, no episode in our nation's history has so strained the fabric of American society. The public refused to accept this deep and persistent depression as inevitable, nor could it be convinced that the depression was attributable to the errors of the government. The call of social action was insistent and persuasive. At a theoretical level, the great British economist John Maynard Keynes developed a model in which Say's Law, the doctrine that supply creates its own demand, did not hold. Thereby he attacked the logical foundation for faith in the basic stability of the private economy. Thus, the battle of public policy against unemployment took shape in the 1930s.

The golden era of Keynesian economics in the United States was the 1960s, when fiscal and monetary policy combined to pull the economy out of recession and into a period of stable rapid growth with low inflation. By the mid-1960s there was almost a consensus in the country that macroeconomic policy could and should be used to promote economic stability.

In the wake of the adverse economic experience of the 1970s that consensus has completely collapsed. High unemployment, accelerating inflation and declining productivity growth have brought into question the effectiveness and desirability of the policies of aggregate demand control. Few if any economists today are pure Keynesians. The Keynesian income determination model supplemented by the Phillips curve can no longer provide an adequate basis either for theory or for policymaking. But there is sharp disagreement about what should come next.

One group of economists argues that while Keynesian analysis may have been inadequate, it was not wrong. They suggest that the stubborn momentum of inflation in the 1970s confirms the relevance of the Keynesian assumption of sticky wages and prices. This means that contractionary policy that slows nominal GNP growth will indeed induce a decline in real GNP and employment, and they point to the effect of tight money in 1974–1975 and in 1980 as examples.

They argue that inflation began in the late 1960s because of the political decision to fight the war in Vietnam and the War on Poverty at the same time, not because of mistaken stabilization policies. Inflation has been exacerbated in the 1970s because of several factors, particularly sharp changes in the relative prices of food, oil, and housing. And because of the momentum of wages and prices, these price shocks have created an upward rachet, so that the economy is now stuck at a very high rate of inflation. This could be ended by contractionary policy, but only at a cost of lost output and employment that is extremely high.

On the theoretical side these economists have tried to provide a more rigorous basis for macroeconomic theory, where the arbitrary assumption made by Keynes about the behavior of wages and prices and other variables are replaced by rational or at least sensible models of decision-making.

Another group of economists argues that the problems of high inflation and high unemployment that have emerged have signaled the failure of the intellectual core of Keynesian analysis. Attempts to promote rapid growth of output and employment have lead to rapid expansion of the money supply. The result has been high inflation and, at best, no reduction of unemployment. Only by abandoning Keynesianism and the Phillips curve, with what they see as their arbitrary assumptions about wages and prices, can a new macroeconomic theory be developed. And a key feature of the new theory is that it implies no role for government policy in stabilizing the economy. On the contrary, they argue, erratic government policies have been a major cause of the cycle.

Both Arthur Okun and I fall into the first of these two groups of economists. And this is reflected in the choice of readings in this volume. But we have given, if not equal time, at least a clear voice to the alternative viewpoint. The readings are divided into six parts. The first tries to examine the nature of unemployment and inflation and some of their costs. Part Two looks at the relationship between unemployment and inflation and whether or not there is a trade-off between them. Parts Three and Four consider the respective roles of monetary and fiscal policy and their influence on aggregate demand and inflation. Part Five reviews the record of stabilization policy and the pro and con arguments for its effectiveness. Part Six considers alternative strategies to fight inflation and then takes a look at the slowdown in the growth rate of real output and productivity. There is now a third group of economists who have come on the scene—supply-siders. Their approach and a critique of it form the last two selections.

In 1978, Arthur Okun and Donald Lamm at Norton asked me to work on a new edition of Okun's book of readings *The Battle Against Unemployment*. I agreed, and we had pretty much completed the selection of readings when Okun died suddenly on March 23, 1980. Saddened by his death, progress pretty much stopped, and when it resumed, both Don Lamm and I felt we should take advantage of some new papers and ideas that had appeared in the interim. So this volume contains mostly readings selected by both Okun and myself, but not completely.

Arthur Okun was, to my mind, the best policy-oriented macro-economist of his time. His voice was influential in Washington, but not influential enough or the economy would be in better shape today. These are difficult times for the economy and interesting times for economists. Okun's contributions to macroeconomic theory and policy will be greatly missed.

Martin Neil Baily
Washington, D.C.
1981

Part One   The Nature of Unemployment and Inflation

Oral History:
Three Unemployed Workers Talk about Their Experiences

> *Each month the Current Population Survey samples households to determine the number of people (a) with jobs, (b) looking for jobs, or (c) out of the labor force. The number looking for jobs as a percent of the total labor force is the unemployment rate.[1]*
>
> *Unemployment insurance and other income-support programs have softened the hardships inflicted by joblessness. And the severity of economic fluctuations has been much less since World War II than before. But the economic and psychological costs of prolonged unemployment can be very severe as our first extract from* Hard Times *by Studs Terkel illustrates. A worker describes his experiences during the period of massive unemployment of the 1930s.*
>
> *The second and third pieces are from a recent oral history—Not Working by Harry Maurer. The contrast between the attitudes and opportunities of the two young people interviewed in the 1970s is very striking. They represent the opposite ends of the spectrum of people who are unemployed.*

STUDS TERKEL *Hard Times*

Ed Paulson, a laborer born in 1912, describes his experiences in San Francisco in 1931. · I'D GET UP at five in the morning and head for the waterfront. Outside the Spreckles Sugar Refinery, outside the gates, there would be a thousand men. You know dang well there's

---

1. Workers on layoff waiting for recall are also counted as unemployed even if they are not looking for other jobs. The total labor force includes the employed plus unemployed.

1

only three or four jobs. The guy would come out with two little Pinkerton cops: "I need two guys for the bull gang. Two guys to go into the hole." A thousand men would fight like a pack of Alaskan dogs to get through there. Only four of us would get through. I was too young a punk.

So you'd drift up to Skid Row. There'd be thousands of men there. Guys on baskets, making weird speeches, phony theories on economics. About eleven-thirty, the real leaders would take over. They'd say: O.K., we're going to City Hall. The Mayor was Angelo Rossi, a dapper little guy. He wore expensive boots and a tight vest. We'd shout around the steps. Finally, he'd come out and tell us nothing.

I remember the demands: We demand work, we demand shelter for our families, we demand groceries, this kind of thing. . . . Half the guys up there making the demands were Negroes. Now there wasn't a big black colony in San Francisco in those days. But they were pretty cagey, the leaders—they always kept a mixture of black and white.

I remember as a kid how courageous this seemed to me, the demands, because you knew that society wasn't going to give it to you. They'd demand that they open up unrented houses and give decent shelters for their families.[2] But you just knew society wasn't yielding. There was nothing coming.

This parade would be four blocks long, curb to curb. Nobody had a dime. There were guys on the corner trying to sell apples to this moneyless wonder. [*Laughs.*]

The guys'd start to yell and there come some horses. They used to have cops on horseback in those days. Then there'd be some fighting. Finally it got to killing. I think they killed three people there that day, besides the wounded. It really got rough because the guys had brought a bunch of marbles and threw them on the street, and the horses were slipping and sliding around. This made the cops mad and they got rough.

There'd be this kind of futile struggle, because somehow you never expected to win. We had a built-in losing complex. That's the way

2. "Thirteen public aid families squatted in a vacant building . . . they defied the police to evict them. Most were victims of a recent fire. The others decided to abandon their substandard housing in favor of a three-story building. . . . 'Man, we're going to stake out those apartments just like the early settlers when they took it away from the Indians,' announced Mrs. Pearl Moore, a Tenants' Union representative." (*Chicago Daily News*, February 21, 1969.)

those crowds felt. A lot of them would drift back into the Sally.[3] By now it's one o'clock, and everybody's hungry. We were a gentle crowd. These were fathers, eighty percent of them. They had held jobs and didn't want to kick society to pieces. They just wanted to go to work and they just couldn't understand. There was a mysterious thing. You watched the papers, you listened to rumors, you'd get word somebody's gonna build a building.

So the next morning, you get up at five o'clock and you dash over there. You got a big tip. There's three thousand men there, carpenters, cement men, guys who knew machinery and everything else. These fellas always had faith that the job was gonna mature, somehow. More and more men were after fewer and fewer jobs. So, San Francisco just ground to a halt. Nothing was moving.

We were always trying to get to sea, but I didn't have any ticket. Oh, I made that waterfront a thousand times. There used to be those great old liners that sailed out to Hawaii. You could hear the band play "Aloha Away," and all the guys were standing there with tears in their eyes. As though you had somebody going some place. And you didn't know a damn soul. [*Laughs.*]

HARRY MAURER *Not Working*

Robin Landau was 24 years old at the time of this mid-1970s interview • I THOUGHT publishing would be exciting because you're around all these books. What a *drag* publishing is. . . . And it was really hot. It was last summer. And all I did—you had to memorize like two hundred names of people. It's so big. And these salesmen would call up from around the country and go [*mocks deep voice*], "Well, Brentano's in Ohio just ordered fifty thousand copies of such-and-such!" . . . It was just a lot of phone work and a lot of names and a lot of bullshit. All mass production. I quit after two weeks.

I didn't collect unemployment until three months after I quit. 'Cause I'm scared to ask people for favors. I was scared to go back to the place I worked before the publishing company and say, "Could you please say that you laid me off instead of I quit?" And I left there on very good terms. I still see the people. So finally one of my friends said, "You're a stupid idiot; why don't you just go and ask?" After three months I got up enough courage to go. Otherwise I

3. The Salvation Army.

wasn't going to get unemployment. Now that I look back on it, it was so stupid of me. Why not ask? So you get a rejection? It's just that I can't take rejection either [*laughs*].

Interviewer: How did you feel about taking the unemployment money?

Great! Oh, it was the best thing that ever happened to me. It was like a free $85 a week. Just to enjoy myself and fool around with, for doing nothing. For doing *nothing*. I mean when I was working, I was taking home maybe $40 more. Busting my ass. Well, not busting my ass, but just being very depressed and wasting a lot of time for $40 more a week. And here I was collecting $85, doing nothing. It was the best thing that ever happened to me. It was like a gift from heaven. Pennies from heaven. Dollars. It's terrific.

And I certainly feel no guilt whatsoever about taking the $85. I think this government and the whole world is crazy and war-happy and that I wasted a large part of my life by working for these people, doing nutty jobs. That's not what life is about, sitting in an office nine hours on your ass. So I feel they owed it to me.

Steve Lacainere was twenty five and living in New Mexico at the time of this interview • AS SOON AS I GRADUATED from high school, I went to work. This was in Boise. I started doing roofing. Ever since I was twelve, I've known how to do roofing work because my father's a carpenter and all my uncles are carpenters and all my brothers are carpenters. I learned roofing from them. So I went on my own when I was about nineteen and worked for four years. Making good money.

But then everybody stopped buying roofing. Really, it was strange. There was a fuel shortage, and then all of a sudden everything went haywire. Nobody was buying roofs. I couldn't find work nowhere. I'd been working for this one company almost three years, and I couldn't believe it when they went into that slump. 'Cause they had kept me busy through the snow and everything. There was always work, even in the hard winter up there. And all of a sudden they hit that slump, and there was *nobody* hiring.

I called all the roofing outfits and they didn't need me because they already had men that had been working for them five or six years. So I went to the unemployment office and used their job service to look for a while. But the situation was just too bad. There wasn't that many openings. You had to have college education for most of them. And I was looking for *anything*, from car wash to anything else. I'd get out to the car wash and find thirty-year-old men washing cars. It was like everything just went crazy all of a sudden. And I started to go stir crazy. You get frustrated, going to job interview after interview with these little referral cards. You go out there and all they do is tell you, "Well, we can accept it but we can't give you a job because we already got somebody. We'll keep you on referral." In four months I must've put out over a hundred referral cards. That's just too many to get nothing, not even a response.

So what do you do all day? You go home and you sit. You become a real TV bug. And you begin to get frustrated sitting at home. Everybody in the household starts getting on edge. They start arguing with each other over stupid things 'cause they're all cramped in that space all the time. I was living with my brother and my sister and my mother. And we all got hit. My brother got laid off, and then my sister was out of work. My mother was retired. The whole family kind of got crushed by it. That's a lot of frustrated people, sitting there together so long.

To burn up your energy, you start getting crazy. I didn't like that. I felt like decking the people at the unemployment office, right? 'Cause when you had to go there and sign up for your checks, that's about the worst humiliation you ever have to go through. A lot of these people seem to feel like you're taking it out of their pocket. Actually it's the money you put away for this. But the way they treat you, you really get pretty mad. I've seen a lot of people get mad down at the unemployment office. I've seen it to the point where one guy actually knocked another guy down. But I try to forget about it [*laughs*]. That was a really bad time. It was just so hopeless.

I was out of work four months that time. Frustrated.

The Nature of Unemployment Spells
KIM B. CLARK AND LAWRENCE H. SUMMERS

When the Current Population Survey (CPS) is taken and a respondent answers that he or she is unemployed, the person is then asked how long they have been unemployed up to that time. It is possible to impute from this information the answers to two important questions: How long on average does a person who becomes unemployed remain unemployed? Of all the weeks of unemployment experienced during a year by all persons, what fraction of these weeks are due to long-term unemployment? The answers are surprising. Most spells of unemployment are short, but most of the weeks of unemployment are attributable to long spells.

In the selection below, Kim Clark and Lawrence Summers build on earlier work and present information answering the two key questions given above. They also emphasize the high fraction of workers—particularly young workers—who cease to be unemployed not because they find jobs, but because they stop looking for jobs.

Other aspects of the unemployment picture are revealed by comparing high unemployment years (like 1975) with average years (like 1974) and by comparing high unemployment groups (like teenagers) with low unemployment groups (like adult males).

The Clark-Summers table shows also that when the unemployment rate increased from 5.6 percent in 1974 to 8.5 percent in 1975, the average length of a spell rose only 14.4 percent (from 1.94 months to 2.22 months). Thus two-thirds of the increased unemployment came from an increase in the frequency of spells. The same story is even more true across different groups during a given year. Teenagers had an unemployment rate of 16.0 percent in 1974, but shorter average spells than adults.

RECENT RESEARCH on unemployment has emphasized the distinction between the frequency and the duration of spells of unemployment. We begin our reexamination of unemployment dynamics by analyzing the distribution function of the duration of completed unemployment spells.[1] The estimated spell distributions provide the

---

1. The distribution function tells you what fraction of workers who become unemployed will spend one month unemployed, what fraction two months, three months, and so on. (*Editor*)

basis for estimating characteristics such as the average duration of a completed spell, which have been the focus of earlier work. The distributions can also be used to calculate a different concept, the fraction of total unemployment attributable to spells of different durations. To see the importance of the difference between these measures, consider the following example. Suppose that, each week, twenty spells of unemployment began lasting one week, and one spell began lasting twenty weeks. The mean duration of a completed spell of unemployment would be 1.9 weeks; but half of all unemployment would be accounted for by spells lasting twenty weeks. In a steady state, the expected length of time until a job was found, among all those unemployed at any instant, would be 9.5 weeks. Focusing on the mean duration of a completed spell would not convey this picture of the underlying unemployment experience.[2]

We calculate the distribution of completed spells using the gross-flow data of the U.S. Bureau of Labor Statistics, which is derived from monthly CPS data. Individuals are included in the CPS sample for four months, then are dropped for eight months, and return for four additional months. By matching individual survey responses in successive months, flows between labor-force states can be estimated.

Various features of the completed spell distribution are indicated in Table 1. The data are presented for male and female teenagers and adults and are based on average transition probabilities in 1974. We chose 1974 because it represents the most recent year for which data are available when the economy operated at high employment levels. The distribution of spells for the total population in 1969 and 1975 are also shown.[3]

The first two rows of figures confirm the traditional conclusion that the typical spell of unemployment is quite short. Sixty percent of all spells in 1974 were completed within a month, and the mean duration of a completed spell was slightly less than two months. In

2. None of the concepts considered in this paragraph corresponds to the published statistics on the duration of unemployment. These statistics provide the mean amount of unemployment already experienced by persons currently unemployed. They thus apply to interrupted rather than to completed spells. In our numerical example the mean duration for those currently unemployed would be approximately five weeks.

3. Our calculations do not appear to be sensitive to the choice of years. For example, the results for 1973, which some might regard as more typical than 1974, differ negligibly from the 1974 results.

TABLE 1. *Characteristics of Completed Spells of Unemployment, by Demographic Group, 1974, and for All Groups, 1969 and 1975*

| | 1974 | | | | | 1969 | 1975 |
| | Males | | Females | | | | |
Characteristic	16–19	20 and over	16–19	20 and over	All groups	All groups	All groups
Completed spells of unemployment							
Proportion of spells ending within one month	0.71	0.47	0.70	0.60	0.60	0.79	0.55
Mean duration of a completed spell (months)	1.57	2.42	1.57	1.91	1.94	1.42	2.22
Proportion of spells ending in withdrawal from the labor force	0.46	0.26	0.58	0.55	0.45	0.44	0.46
Proportion of unemployment[a]							
By length of spell (months)							
2 or more	0.55	0.80	0.55	0.69	0.69	0.49	0.75
3 or more	0.34	0.63	0.33	0.48	0.49	0.24	0.58
4 or more	0.23	0.48	0.21	0.34	0.36	0.12	0.45
5 or more	0.15	0.37	0.14	0.25	0.26	0.06	0.35
6 or more	0.11	0.28	0.09	0.18	0.19	0.03	0.27
Spells ending in withdrawal	0.47	0.26	0.59	0.58	0.47	0.46	0.48
Spells ending in employment, by length of spell (months)							
2 or less	0.36	0.29	0.28	0.24	0.28	0.42	0.23
3 or less	0.42	0.39	0.33	0.30	0.36	0.49	0.30

SOURCE: Derived from authors' calculations of the distribution of unemployment spells, using gross-flow data from the Current Population Survey of the U.S. Bureau of Labor Statistics. The procedure is detailed in an appendix available from the authors upon request.

a. Expressed as a fraction of the total weeks of unemployment within the specific age-sex category.

1975, when the unemployment rate rose precipitously, the mean duration of a spell increased by about a week. The response to cyclical movements appears to be quite asymmetric. Almost 80 percent of all unemployment spells lasted less than one month in 1969 when the unemployment rate was 3.5 percent. The finding in previous work that young people have shorter mean durations of unemployment than older persons is also confirmed.

Short spells of unemployment can be the result of either easy entrance into new jobs or high rates of withdrawal from the labor force. These two causes obviously have different implications. The relative importance of spells of unemployment that end in exit from the labor force is examined in the third and fourth rows of Table 1. In the aggregate, 45 percent of spells ended in withdrawal in 1974. This proportion varies substantially across demographic groups, from 26 percent for men over twenty years of age to almost 60 percent for young women. The high rates of exit from the labor force indicate the inadequacy of the duration of completed spells as an indicator of the ease or difficulty of finding work. The point is well illustrated by comparing young and older men. Adult men have unemployment spells that are about 50 percent longer than those of teenagers. This differential is largely attributable to the much higher withdrawal rate of teenagers.

The fact that most spells are short does not imply that most unemployment is due to short spells or that most unemployed persons at any point in time will leave unemployment soon. If, for example, all the unemployed had a probability of one-half of escaping unemployment in a given month, the mean duration of completed spells would be two months, but three-quarters of unemployment would be due to spells lasting more than two months. Of those unemployed at a point in time, ultimately half would have experienced more than three months of unemployment. If the probability of escape from unemployment declines with duration, the concentration of unemployment in the longer spells would be even more pronounced.

The lower half of Table 1 weights spells by their length to portray the distribution of months of unemployment. The results present a different picture of unemployment from that suggested by the spell distribution. While 60 percent of spells in 1974 ended within a month, almost half of all unemployment was attributable to spells lasting at least three months—that is, of all those unemployed at any moment in 1974, half experienced three months of unemployment or more before terminating their spell.[4] The concentration of unemployment in long spells is even more pronounced, among adult men, almost 50 percent of whose unemployment is contained in spells lasting four or more months. The 1969 and 1975 figures reveal sharp cyclical changes in the concentration of unemployment. While only 3 percent of total weeks of unemployment in 1969 was found among those who experienced long-term unemployment—spells lasting six months or longer—the share of long-term unemployment rose to 27 percent in 1975.[5]

The proportion of unemployment attributable to spells ending in withdrawal from the labor force is shown in the third row of Table 1. It is marginally greater than the proportion of spells that end in employment because withdrawal spells last slightly longer than those terminating with a job.

The final rows of the table demonstrate the unrealistic features of the view of unemployment that stresses relatively easy access to jobs after a brief spell of unemployment. For the entire population, only about one-third of unemployment is due to spells ending in a job within three months. The view that most of the unemployed are in the midst of short transitions between jobs is simply wrong. *Even during the strong 1969 peak, less than half of the unemployed found jobs within three months.*

4. This calculation requires the assumption of a constant flow into unemployment during the year.

5. These statistics contrast sharply with published data on the distribution of interrupted spell lengths. In 1974, for example, on average 7.3 percent of the unemployed had already experienced six months of unemployment, yet almost 20 percent would do so before their unemployment spell ended.

Potential GNP: Its Nature and Significance

ARTHUR M. OKUN

"How much output can the economy produce under conditions of full employment?" That is the question addressed in Arthur Okun's 1962 paper. He defines full employment as 4 percent unemployment, on the grounds that pushing aggregate demand harder than this will generate inflationary pressures. The level of GNP consistent with 4 percent unemployment Okun calls potential output. It grows over time as the productive capacity of the economy grows.

As well as the importance of the concept of potential output for policy analysis, there is another important lesson from Okun's paper. Unemployment can be costly in itself, but just as importantly, unemployment changes are a barometer of the state of the economy. In a recession, GNP falls below its trend path. Investment, profits, the stock market, average weekly hours worked and other important measures of the economy are depressed. The relationship linking the gap between actual and potential GNP and the unemployment rate has become known as Okun's Law. This "Law" remains a tool of policy analysis, but it has required amendments for the 1970s and may need more in the 1980s. The change in the demographic composition of the labor force (there are now more young people and women) has raised the estimate of the full-employment rate to between 5 and 6 percent (because young people, and also women, are more unemployment prone). Low productivity growth in the 1970s has lowered the estimates of the growth of potential output.

POTENTIAL GNP AND POLICY

"HOW MUCH OUTPUT can the economy produce under conditions of full employment?" The concept and measurement of potential GNP are addressed to this question. It is a question with policy significance because the pursuit of full employment (or "maximum employment" in the language of the Employment Act) is a goal of policy. And a target of full employment of labor needs to be linked to a corresponding target of full employment output, since policy measures designed to influence employment operate by affecting aggregate demand and production. How far we stand from the target of full-employment output is important information in formulating fiscal and monetary policy.

The evaluation of potential output can also help to point up the enormous social cost of idle resources. If programs to lower unemployment from 5½ to 4 percent of the labor force are viewed as attempts to raise the economy's "grade" from 94½ to 96, the case for them may not seem compelling. Focus on the "gap" helps to remind policymakers of the large reward associated with such an improvement.

THE 4 PERCENT UNEMPLOYMENT RATE

Potential GNP is a supply concept, a measure of productive capacity. But it is not a measure of how much output could be generated by unlimited amounts of aggregate demand. The nation would probably be most productive in the short run with inflationary pressure pushing the economy. But the social target of maximum production and employment is constrained by a social desire for price stability and free markets. The full-employment goal must be understood as striving for maximum production without inflationary pressure; or, more precisely, as aiming for a point of balance between more output and greater stability, with appropriate regard for the social valuation of these two objectives.

It is interesting and perhaps surprising that there seems to be more agreement that a 4 percent unemployment rate is a reasonable target under existing labor market conditions than on any of the analytical steps needed to justify such a conclusion. Economists have never developed a clear criterion of tolerable price behavior or any quantitative balancing of conflicting objectives which could be invoked either to support or attack the target of a 4 percent rate. Indeed, I should expect that many economists who agree on the 4 percent target would disagree in estimating how prices and wages would behave if we were on target.

Having said what the 4 percent unemployment rate is not, I shall now state that it is the target rate of labor utilization underlying the calculation of potential GNP in this paper. The statistical and methodological problems would not be altered if a different rate were selected; only the numbers would be changed.

POTENTIAL GNP AS A SHORT-RUN CONCEPT

In estimating potential GNP, most of the facts about the economy are taken as they exist; technological knowledge, the capital stock, natural resources, the skill and education of the labor force are all data, rather than variables. Potential differs from actual only because the potential concept depends on the assumption—normally contrary to fact—that aggregate demand is exactly at the level that yields a rate of unemployment equal to 4 percent of the civilian labor force. If, in fact, aggregate demand is lower, part of potential GNP is not produced; there is unrealized potential or a "gap" between actual and potential output.

The failure to use one year's potential fully can influence future potential GNP; to the extent that low utilization rates and accompanying low profits and personal incomes hold down investment in plant, equipment, research, housing, and education, the growth of potential GNP will be retarded. Because today's actual output influences tomorrow's productive capacity, success in the stabilization objective promotes more rapid economic growth.

THE MEASUREMENT PROBLEM

As it has been defined above, potential output is observed only when the unemployment rate is 4 percent and even then must be viewed as subject to stochastic variation. At any other time, it must be regarded as a hypothetical magnitude. The observed actual measures of labor utilization tell us by a simple arithmetic calculation how much employment would have to increase, given the labor force, to make the unemployment rate 4 percent. But they do not offer similar direct information on other matters that might make labor input at full employment different from its observed level:

a) how average hours worked per man would be altered if the level of aggregate demand were consistent with full employment;

b) how participation rates in the labor force—and hence the size of the labor force—would be affected under conditions of full employment.

Nor do the actual data reveal directly what aggregate labor productivity would be under full-employment conditions. There are many reasons why productivity might be altered in the aggregate: the added workers, changed average hours, possible alterations in the sectoral distribution of employment, higher utilization rate of capital, and altered efficiency in the use of employees all could make a difference in productivity at full employment.

THE LEAP FROM UNEMPLOYMENT TO OUTPUT

Ideally, the measurement of potential output would appraise the various possible influences of high employment on labor input and productivity and evaluate the influences step-by-step, developing quantitative estimates for each adjustment to produce the desired measure of potential. While I shall discuss the steps individually below, the basic technique I am reporting consists of a leap from the unemployment rate to potential output rather than a series of steps involving the several underlying factors. Strictly speaking, the leap requires the assumption that, whatever the influence of slack economic activity on average hours, labor-force participation, and manhour productivity, the magnitudes of all these effects are related to the unemployment rate. With this assumption, the unemployment rate can be viewed as a proxy variable for all the ways in which output is affected by idle resources. The measurement of potential output then is simplified into an estimate of how much output is depressed by unemployment in excess of 4 percent.

The answer I have to offer is simple and direct. In the postwar period, on the average, each extra percentage point in the unemployment rate above 4 percent has been associated with about a 3 percent decrement in real GNP.[3]

When the unemployment rate is 4 percent, potential GNP is estimated as equal to actual; at a 5 percent rate of unemployment, the estimated "gap" is 3.2 percent of GNP. In the periods from which this relationship was obtained the unemployment rate varied from

3. In the article from which this is drawn, Okun presents regression estimates of the relation between unemployment and GNP. (*Editor*)

about 3 to 7½ percent; the relation is not meant to be extrapolated outside this range. I have no reason to expect the 3.2 coefficient to apply if unemployment were either 1 or 15 percent of the labor force.

THE STEPS

The findings above assert that a reduction in unemployment, measured as a percentage of the labor force, has a much larger than proportionate effect on output. To appraise and evaluate this finding, it is necessary to inspect the steps which were leaped over in the statistical relationships between output and unemployment. Clearly, the simple addition of 1 percent of a given labor force to the ranks of the employed would increase employment by only slightly more than one percent: $100/(100\text{-}U)$ percent to be exact. If the workweek and productivity were unchanged, the increment to output would be only a little more than 1 percent. The 3 percent result implies that considerable output gains in a period of rising utilization rates must stem from some or all of the following: induced increases in the size of the labor force; longer average weekly hours; and greater productivity.

LABOR FORCE

Participation in the labor force as we measure it consists of either having a job or seeking actively to work. The resulting measures of labor force are not pure reflections of supply; they are affected by job availability. In a slack labor market, people without a job may give up when they are convinced that job-hunting is a hopeless pursuit. They then may be viewed as having left the labor force though they stand ready and eager to work. Furthermore, there are secondary or passive members of the labor force who will not actively seek employment but would accept gainful employment if a job came looking for them. This latter group suffers little or no personal hardship in not having work, but the output they would contribute in a fully employed economy is a relevant part of the nation's potential GNP.

There may be induced changes in the labor force in the opposite direction: e.g., the loss of a job by the breadwinner of a family might increase the measured labor force by leading his wife and teenage children to seek work. The prewar literature debated the probable net effects of these opposing influences on participation rates. However, the postwar record has convincingly delivered the verdict that a weak labor market depresses the size of the labor force. But the magnitude and timing of the effect is not clear.

Even the conceptual problem of defining a potential labor force is difficult—we should not wish to count only the secondary labor-force members who would appear for work tomorrow morning; on the other hand, we would not want to include all those who might be attracted by many years of continued job availability. The response of participation rates is likely to be a complicated lagged phenomenon which will not be closely tied to the current unemployment rate. While this aspect of the difference between potential and actual output is hard to quantify, zero is certainly not a satisfactory estimate. At the end of 1960, the Bureau of Labor Statistics estimated the difference between actual and "normal" labor force at 561,000. If this figure is taken as the induced effect of poor opportunities for jobs, it implies that, in those recession conditions, for every ten people listed as unemployed over and above the 4 percent rate, there were three additional potential workers who were not actively seeking work.

HOURS

Taking into account the normal secular decline in hours worked per man, there is a clear relationship between movements in average hours and in output. When output has been rising rapidly, average hours have expanded—or, at least, have not contracted. On the other hand, periods of low growth or decline in GNP mean more rapid declines in average hours per man. The data point toward the concept of a full-employment path of average annual hours. But the concept of full-employment hours is hard to quantify: e.g., in a rapid rise of output toward full employment, the amount of overtime might well push the workweek above the level consistent with steady full employment. Furthermore, economy-wide data on average hours are notoriously poor. However, using what evidence is available, we find that each 1 percent difference in output is associated with a difference of 0.14 percent in hours per man, including both over-time and part-time work.

Returning to the finding that a 1 percentage point reduction in the unemployment rate means 3.2 percent more GNP, the hours-output estimate above indicates that it will also be accompanied by an increase of nearly one half of one percent in hours per man, or an addition of about 0.2 of an hour to the workweek. With an allow-ance for induced gains in labor force, based illustratively on the 1960 estimate cited above, the reduction of one point in the unem-ployment rate means perhaps a 1.8 percent increase in total labor input measured in manhours. Then, to get the 3.2 percent incre-ment in output, manhour productivity must rise by about 1.4 per-cent.

PRODUCTIVITY

The direct checks that could be made on productivity data were consistent with this implication of the output-unemployment rela-tionship. The record clearly shows that manhour productivity is depressed by low levels of utilization, and that periods of movement toward full employment yield considerably above-average produc-tivity gains.

The implications and explanations of this phenomenon are in-triguing. Indeed, many *a priori* arguments have been made for the reverse view—that depressed levels of activity will stimulate pro-ductivity through pressure on management to cut costs, through a weeding out of inefficient firms and low quality workers, and through availability of more and higher quality capital per worker for those employees who retain their jobs. If such effects exist, the empirical record demonstrates that they are swamped by other forces working in the opposite direction.

I have little direct evidence to offer on the mechanism by which low levels of utilization depress productivity. I can offer some spec-ulation and try to encourage other researchers to pursue this prob-lem with concrete evidence at a microeconomic level. The positive relationship between output and labor productivity suggests that much of labor input is essentially a fixed cost for fairly substantial periods. Thus, high output levels permit the spreading of labor overheads, and low production levels raise unit fixed costs of labor.

At times, we may take too seriously our textbook examples which view labor as a variable factor, with only capital costs as fixed. Even the most casual empiricism points to an overhead component in labor costs. There are many reasons why employment may not be easily variable:

1. *Contractual commitments* may tie the hand of management in a downward direction—employees may have guaranteed annual wages, supplementary unemployment compensation, rights to severance pay, etc., as well as actual contracts for a term of employment.

2. *Technological factors,* in a broad sense, may also be important. A firm plans on a division of labor and degree of specialization attuned to "normal" operations. If operations fall below normal, there may be marked indivisibilities which prevent the firm from curtailing its employment of specialists, clerical and sales personnel, and supervisors in parallel with its cutback in output.

3. *Transactions costs* associated with laying off labor and then, in the future, doing new hiring may be another influence retarding the adjustment of labor input to fluctuations in sales and output.

4. *Acquired skills* that existing employees have learned on the job may make them particularly valuable to the firm so that it pays to stockpile underemployed labor rather than run the risk of having to hire untrained men when business conditions improve.

5. *Morale factors* may also make layoffs undesirable.

All of these factors could help explain why slack economic activity is accompanied by "on-the-job underemployment," reflected in depressed levels of manhour productivity. Firms obviously do lay off labor in recessions but they do so reluctantly. Their problems may be mitigated, in part, by the presence of voluntary quits which permit a downward adjustment of employment without layoffs. In part, the impact of slack on manhour productivity may be reduced by shortening average hours to spread the work and the wage-bill without a cut in employment. But these appear to be only partial offsets.

To the extent that the productivity losses of recessions are associated with fixity of labor costs, they would not be maintained indefinitely. If the recession was of long duration—or merely was expected to last a long time—firms would adjust their employment more drastically. On this reasoning, in an era when business-cycle dips are continually short and mild, one might expect productivity to bear more of the brunt of recession and labor input to be less affected, even relative to the decline in output.

Thus far, I have ignored the dependence of labor productivity on plant and equipment capacity. The entire discussion of potential output in this paper has, in effect, assumed that idle labor is a satisfactory measure of all idle resources. In fact, measures of excess capacity in industrial plant and equipment do show a close relationship to unemployment—idle men are accompanied by idle machines. But the correlation is not perfect and operating rates in industry should be considered along with employment data as an indicator of the gap between potential and actual output. Obviously, if capital were fully employed while there was much unemployed labor, this would hold down the productivity gains that could be obtained through full employment of labor. Robert Solow did use capital stock data together with unemployment data in fitting a production function for 1929 to date.[4] His estimates of potential output for the post-Korean period agreed remarkably well with those I am reporting.

Still, I shall feel much more satisfied with the estimation of potential output when our data and our analysis have advanced to the point where the estimation can proceed step-by-step and where the capital factor can be explicitly taken into account. Meanwhile, the measure of potential must be used with care. The trend line yields a point-estimate of the "gap," e.g., $31.3 billion for the second quarter of 1962. But that specific figure must be understood as the center of a range of plausible estimates. By my personal evaluation of its degree of accuracy, I find potential output useful—and superior to substitute concepts—for many analytical purposes.

4. See the *American Economic Review* of May 1962

The Intelligent Citizen's Guide to Inflation

ROBERT M. SOLOW

It has been argued that while unemployment hurts only the minority that are unemployed, inflation hurts everyone. Most economists would agree with neither part of the argument. Okun showed in the preceding selection that a rise in unemployment is associated with a fall in real output that affects most people. In the following piece, written in 1975, Robert Solow explains what inflation is and that not all inflations are alike. There are some serious costs to inflation, he says, but there are misapprehensions about the costs. And some people do gain from inflation.

TWO BROADLY OPPOSITE frames of mind seem to dominate the current discussion of inflation. One says that we are beset by some utterly mysterious plague of unknown origin. If it is not stopped soon, it will cause unimaginable, or at least unspecified, disasters. The only hope is that some Pasteur or Jenner or Ehrlich will discover The Cure. The other view is that it is all quite simple. There is some one thing we have failed to do: control the money supply or balance the budget or legislate price controls or abolish the unions. As soon as we do it, the problem will then go away.

This essay is written in the belief that both these currents of opinion are wrong. I do not, however, have an alternative solution to offer. Indeed, I rather doubt that there is a Solution, in the sense of some policy that your average mixed capitalist economy can reasonably be expected to pursue which will drastically reduce the tendency to inflation, without substituting some equally damaging and intractable problem instead.

What I can hope to do is to explain the vocabulary and intellectual framework evolved by economists for discussing and analyzing inflation. By itself, this will contribute to clarity of thought—much, perhaps most, of current popular discussion is hopelessly confused. I hope to be able to go further than that, however. There are some positive statements one can reasonably make about the behavior of modern mixed economies. Where I verge on speculation, or where there are real differences of opinion within the economics profession, I will try to be honest about it.

WHAT IS INFLATION?

Inflation is *a substantial, sustained increase in the general level of prices*. The intrinsic vagueness of "substantial" is harmless. One would not want to use a heavyweight word to describe a trivial rise in the price level; granted, it will never be perfectly clear where to draw the line, but neither can it be important since only a word is at stake. "Sustained" is a little trickier. One would not want to label as inflationary a momentary (six-month? one-year?) upward twitch of the price level, especially if it is soon reversed. There is no point in being forced to describe mere short-term fluctuations in prices as alternating bouts of inflation and deflation. "Sustained" also carries some connotation of "self-perpetuating" and that raises broader questions. It is obviously important to know whether each step in an inflationary process tends to generate further inflation unless some "outside" force intervenes, or whether the inflationary process is eventually self-limiting. The answer need not be the same for all inflations, and it certainly depends on what you mean by "outside." So it is probably best not to incorporate this aspect as a part of the definition.

It is the notion of the "general price level" that will lead us somewhere. Economists make a sharp and important distinction between the system of relative prices and the general price level. Relative prices describe the terms on which different goods and services exchange for *one another;* the general price level describes the terms on which some representative bundle of goods and services exchanges for *money*. Imagine an economy in which the only goods produced are meat and vegetables, and first suppose that all exchange is barter; some people trade meat for vegetables with other people who want to trade vegetables for meat. If one pound of meat exchanges for three pounds of vegetables, then the relative price is established. But since there is no money, there is no such thing as the general price level. Notice that inflation is inconceivable in a barter economy. It would be logically contradictory for "all prices" to rise at the same time. Suppose that, because of a change in tastes or a natural catastrophe, one pound of meat should come to exchange for six pounds of vegetables. One could say that the price of meat (in terms of vegetables!) had doubled. But that is exactly the same thing as saying that the price of vegetables (in terms of meat!) had halved. A carnivorous farmer would find himself worse off; but a vegetarian rancher would be sitting pretty.

So inflation has intrinsically to do with money. Now let us introduce some greenbacks to serve as money in our meat-and-vegetables economy. Suppose meat goes for $1.50 a pound and vegetables for $0.50 a pound—i.e., one pound of meat for three of vegetables, as before. Now suppose that at a later time meat goes to $3.00 a pound and vegetables to $1.00. The relative price is unchanged. From most points of view the meat-and-vegetables economy goes along as if nothing has happened, and from most points of view nothing has. (Not quite nothing: A tradesman or a miser who happened to be sitting on a load of greenbacks at the time will have taken quite a beating.)

We can go a step further. Suppose the average daily diet consists of one pound of meat and one pound of vegetables (though very few individuals may actually consume exactly the average diet). We could agree to measure the general price level by the money cost of the average consumption bundle. In that case, we would say that the price level was 200 in the initial situation, and 400 after the price increases. (It is the custom to choose some year as "base year" and set its price level arbitrarily at 100. If the initial year is the base year, then the later price level would be 200.) In any case, we would certainly want to say that the general price level had doubled, and if it had doubled in exactly 12 months, we would say that the rate of inflation had been 100 percent a year.

Since the prices of all goods and services had exactly doubled, it is no trick to say that the general price level had doubled. But we now have a routine that will take care of less obvious situations. Suppose meat goes from $1.50 to $2.40 a pound and vegetables from $0.50 to $0.60. The price of meat has risen by 60 percent, that of vegetables by 20 percent. But the cost of the average consumption bundle rises from $2.00 to $3.00 (or the price index from 100 to 150). So we could say that the price level had gone up by 50 percent. Notice also that this time relative prices have also changed: A pound of meat exchanges for four pounds of vegetables at the new prices. The vegetarian rancher gains at the expense of the carnivorous farmer, but *that is because of the change in relative prices*. In the case of "pure inflation," when *all* prices change *in the same pro-*

portion, nobody loses (except owners of money) and nobody gains (except owers of money).[1]

Perhaps the simplest way to define inflation is as a loss in the purchasing power of money. That has the merit of emphasizing the fact that inflation is essentially a monetary phenomenon. But there is a possible semantic trap here. Some economists believe that the whole inflationary mechanism is primarily or exclusively monetary, in particular that the main or only cause of inflation is too rapid a growth in the supply of money. They may be right or they may be wrong. (I happen to think that doctrine is too simple by half.) But the mere fact that you can have inflation only in a monetary economy is neither here nor there, just as the fact that you can't have a drowning without water doesn't prove that the way to understand drowning is to study water. I will come back to this analytical question later.

MEASURING INFLATION

In the real world there are thousands of goods and services, whose relative prices are changing all the time in complicated ways. The measurement of the general price level thus becomes a major statistical enterprise. But it is done, and generally according to the principles just described. In fact, the American reader is confronted with at least three separate indexes of the general price level: the consumer price index (CPI), the wholesale price index (WPI),[2] and the GNP deflator. Since there are some conceptual differences among them, and since they may occasionally say different things, it is worthwhile to understand exactly what each of them means.

The CPI (what is sometimes called the cost-of-living index) is produced and published monthly; it is closest in principle to the kind of price index described earlier. At intervals of a decade or more, the Bureau of Labor Statistics (BLS) conducts an expensive survey

1. The smart kids in the class will now ask: If meat gets more expensive relative to vegetables, won't consumers buy less meat and more vegetables, and won't that change the make-up of the average consumption bundle, and what will that do to the price index? They can go on to the course in Index-Number Theory, but they will find it dull.

2. Since this was written the name has been changed to the producer price index, or PPI. (*Editor*)

of the spending habits of families of different size, income, and other characteristics. From this survey it calculates the typical budget of a middle-income, urban wage-earner or clerical worker with a family of four. Then each month it actually prices out that budget in a number of cities around the country. If the cost of that bundle goes up or down by one percent, the CPI goes up or down by one percent.

That is certainly a reasonable and meaningful price index, but it does have some drawbacks. (Of course, any method of reducing all those thousands of price changes to a single number will have drawbacks.) It relates only to consumers; the prices of industrial machinery and raw materials could go sky-high, and the CPI would register that fact only later, when cost increases filtered down to retail prices. Moreover, the CPI relates only to some consumers—those middle-income, urban, wage-earning families of four. Old people, or poor people, or oil millionaires, who buy different bundles, may have different experiences. Finally, economists have a technical reservation. The CPI covers, as its concept dictates it should, everything consumers spend money on, including sales taxes, monthly mortgage payments, used cars, and so on. It reflects changes in state and local taxes, interest rates, used-car prices, etc. For some purposes, economists would prefer a price index confined to currently produced goods and services. Certainly it matters whether a rise in the CPI reflects mainly higher sales taxes and interest rates or higher prices for food and clothing.

The WPI, also available monthly, is based on prices collected at the wholesale level. Its coverage is wide but rather peculiar, for several reasons. For one thing, it omits all services, medical care, house rents, etc. For another, it counts some prices over and over again, and thus gives them more weight than they deserve. For example, a change in the price of raw cotton will appear first as a crude material, then again as it is reflected in the price of cloth, then again as it is reflected in the price of clothing. This pyramiding overemphasizes crude material prices and can cause the WPI to behave quite erratically, especially when the prices of materials are changing.[3] Its main utility is that, just because of its coverage of the

3. Because of the problems Solow describes, the BLS has now deemphasised the overall index and instead emphasizes producer price indexes for finished, intermediate, and crude goods separately.

early stages of fabrication, it often catches price developments early. The WPI, like the other indexes, is broken down into sub-indexes (in the case of the WPI, farm products, processed foods, industrial materials, various categories of finished manufactures, etc.), and these may be very informative.[4]

THE GNP DEFLATOR

The GNP deflator is by and large the economists' favorite. Unlike the CPI, it covers only currently produced goods and services, and unlike the WPI, it avoids all double-counting. But it is constructed in a more complicated way. The Department of Commerce calculates every quarter the country's gross national product. This is essentially the value at current market prices of the current flow of newly produced final goods and services. (The force of "final" is that one omits goods and services which are immediately used up in the production of something else, because their value will be included in the value of the final product.) At the same time, Commerce also calculates the GNP "in constant prices." That is, it takes the current flow of final goods and services, but instead of valuing them at this quarter's prices, it values them at the prices of some fixed year, currently 1958.* For instance, in 1973 the GNP in current prices was $1,295 billion, but the GNP in 1958 prices was $839 billion, because 1958 prices were lower than 1973 prices.

How much had prices risen between 1958 and 1973? The natural computation is $1,295 / $839 = 1.54, for an increase of 54 percent. If the 1973 flow of output valued in 1973 prices is 54 percent higher than the *same* flow of output valued in 1958 prices, then the obvious inference is that the general level of prices must have risen by 54 percent since 1958. So the general formula for the GNP deflator in year X is: GNP in year X in current prices / GNP in year X in base-year prices.

Economists like this price index for the analysis of inflation not because it is obscure, but for the reasons I mentioned before: It eliminates double-counting, and it focuses on the pricing of cur-

---

4. For more on the WPI, and for a very informative and interesting article complementary to this one, I recommend "Inflation 1973: The Year of Infamy" by William Nordhaus and John Shoven in the May / June 1974 issue of *Challenge* magazine.

* Since this article was written, the base year has been changed to 1972. (*Editor*)

rently produced goods, not existing assets. For that very reason, of course, it may not reflect exactly the experience of consumers. Another disadvantage is that the GNP deflator is available only at quarterly intervals.[5]

All price indexes suffer from a common difficulty. Commodities change in character and quality. How can the BLS price the same consumer bundle in 1955 and 1975 when many of the things consumers buy in 1975 did not exist, and so had no prices, in 1955? How can the Commerce statisticians value 1975 GNP in 1958 prices, when there were no 1958 prices for some of the items entering the 1975 GNP? If the price of an ordinary shirt rises 10 percent in the course of a year, but simultaneously the wrinkle-resisting properties of the shirt are improved, how is one to decide how much of the 10 percent represents the greater value of an improved product and how much represents pure price increase? The agencies do the best they can, but it is hardly a job that can ever be done perfectly. It used to be thought that there was systematic underallowance for quality improvements to such an extent that an annual rise of 1 or 2 percent in the measured price level could be ignored as not being a true price increase; but no one knows for sure. Perhaps the best conclusion is that one ought not to attach great significance to small changes in price indexes.

This discussion of price indexes has given us another concept of absolutely fundamental importance for rational discussion. GNP in constant prices is in an important sense a "physical" concept. It is an attempt to measure the size of the flow of actual production in a way that is independent of inflationary and deflationary aberrations. When GNP in constant prices changes, it is because the production of goods and services has changed, not because prices have changed. In terms of my earlier example, the difference between the 1968 GNP of $707 billion in 1958 prices and the 1973 GNP of $839 billion in 1958 prices permit us to say that "aggregate output" rose by 18.7 percent between those years. In the jargon, GNP in constant prices is called "real GNP" or "real aggregate output." We will be coming back to it.

---

5. There is another minor problem. The basis for putting a price on the output of governments—education, police services, "plumbers' " services, etc.—is pretty tenuous, though these are all part of the GNP. It is possible to produce a price index for privately produced GNP, nearly all of which is actually sold on a market.

WHY IS PURE INFLATION A BAD THING?

There seems to be universal agreement that rising prices are a cause for alarm and perhaps fear. Candidates for office accuse incumbents of having fostered inflation or failed to prevent it, and promise to eliminate it themselves. Incumbents announce that they are working on the problem. And surveys of public opinion show that very many ordinary people regard inflation of the price level as one of the most serious problems they face, or at least as an important background worry. Yet it is fair to say that public discussion offers no insight at all into the precise way in which a rising price level damages the current or prospective welfare of the representative citizen. Occasionally, the implied mechanism in the background makes no sense at all. Such a peculiar situation clearly deserves the most thorough investigation.

For the sake of clarity, let us first make an abstraction and think about a "pure" inflation, during which all prices rise at the same proportional rate—so many percent per year—so that relative prices are unchanged throughout. Real inflations don't happen that way; but if we are to understand how and why inflation is a burden on society, we had better be able to understand the hypothetical special case of a pure inflation. After all, relative prices can change without any change in the general price level; we ought not to confuse the effects of the one with those of the other.

Well, then, who gets hurt in a pure inflation? If you think back to our meat-and-vegetables economy, it is hard to see how producers, including workers, suffer at all. So long as the prices of meat and vegetables, and wage rates in both industries, go up at the same percentage rate, every participant in the economy continues to have the same purchasing power over all goods and services as before. The inflation appears to have no "real" effects. The general point is that a person's economic welfare depends on the prices of the things he or she buys and sells, including labor and the services of property; if the prices of all those things go up or down in the same proportion, then economic welfare stays the same.

Now there is an optical illusion that clearly plays some role in popular discussions of inflation. Many people see no connection between the prices of the things they buy and the prices of the things they sell. The ordinary person works hard and feels that each year's wage increase is deserved. When it turns out that prices have also increased, so that all or part of the wage increase is illusory, the ordinary person regards that price rise—inflation—as a form of theft, a hand in his or her pocket. But of course, wages could not have increased had prices not increased. I cannot estimate how widespread this illusion may be, but there can hardly be any doubt that such an illusion does exist.[6]

If you want to know how the country as a whole is doing, then the course of the price level will not tell you. In narrowly economic terms, the proper measure of success is the flow of goods and services produced and made available to the society for consumption and other uses. The closest thing we have to look at is the real GNP, which we have already met. GNP in constant prices is the most comprehensive available measure of the performance of the economy in doing what it is supposed to do—the generation of want-satisfying commodities. It is far from perfect for reasons that involve the treatment of depreciation, environmental effects of economic activity, the organization of work, the "quality of life," governmental activity, and other things, but none of them has to do with inflation. So if inflation is a net burden to society, that ought to show up in a reduction of real GNP, or at least a slowing-down of its normal upward trend. But that is not what happens; in fact the opposite is more nearly true. Periods of prosperity are somewhat more likely to coincide with periods of inflation and periods of recession are somewhat more likely to coincide with intervals of stable or more slowly rising prices.[7]

Is the social cost of inflation a mirage? There is one earlier hint that needs to be followed up. In a monetary economy—the only

6. No one could make that mistake in the simple meat-and-vegetables economy. But the real world is more complicated. For instance, the timing of price and wage increases is irregular, with some temporary advantage from getting in early, and some loss from getting in late. Moreover, the normal experience is that standards of living rise as productivity improves. Then only part of a wage increase is eroded away by price increases, but even the loss of that part is felt as robbery.

7. There is an exception to all this, but it need not concern us. Imagine a country which must import a large fraction of its basic necessities, like food and oil, and pay for them with exports of other commodities. Such a country may experience steady or rising real production, but if world food and oil prices are rising faster than the prices of its exports, its own standard of living could deteriorate. The United States is not in that position because it is so nearly self-sufficient; but of course it is hardly a hypothetical possibility for Japan and some European countries.

kind that can have inflation—holders of cash see their real wealth eroded by a rising price level, even in a pure inflation. So do creditors who hold claims for payment fixed in money terms. Offsetting at least some of these losses are the gains of debtors, who can pay back in dollars of smaller purchasing power what they had borrowed and spent in dollars of higher real value. Perhaps the true social costs of inflation are to be found among the holders of money, or among cash creditors more generally.

ANTICIPATED INFLATION

Another distinction—this time between anticipated and unanticipated inflation—is required for this analysis. So let us take the strongest case first: a pure inflation which is confidently and accurately expected by everyone in the economy. Suppose you lend me a dollar today and I agree to pay back $1.05 a year from today. Then we have agreed on an interest rate of five percent annually. (You laugh, somewhat bitterly. But it's just an example.) If we both correctly expect the general price level to be quite steady during the next year, then that is all there is to it. You as lender and I as borrower are both willing to make the transaction at an interest rate of 5 percent a year. Now imagine instead that we both confidently expect the general level of prices (which means each individual price and wage, since we are talking about a pure inflation) to be 4 percent higher a year from now. I would be delighted to take your dollar today and pay you $1.05 in a year. Why not? If meat is a dollar a pound today and will be $1.04 a pound in a year, then in effect you would be lending me a pound of meat today, and I would be obliged to pay you only 1.05 / 1.04 or about 1.01 pounds of meat next year. In *real* terms, you would be getting interest at 1 percent a year, not 5 percent. Of course for the same reasons that I would be pleased at the transaction, you would not be. In fact, if we were both prepared to make the deal at 5 percent with stable prices, we ought both to be prepared to make the deal at 9 percent when we both confidently expect the price level to rise at 4 percent a year; in the real purchasing power terms that matter, you will then be collecting interest at 5 percent per year. In the professional jargon, the *real* rate of interest (5 percent) is the *nominal* or *money* rate of interest (9 percent) less the expected rate of inflation (4 percent). Thus the very high interest rates of early 1974 have to be read against the substantial inflation of the same period. Real rates are not as high as nominal rates; in fact, they are lower by about the expected future rate of inflation—about which we can only guess. Of course, anyone who borrows long and is locked in at high interest rates is left holding the bag if the inflation should unexpectedly slow down or stop.

What follows? *If* the inflation is fully anticipated by everyone, *if* everyone has complete access to the capital markets, and *if* all interest rates are free to adjust to expectations about the price level, and do so quickly and smoothly, then borrowers and lenders will be able to protect themselves against inflation. Once again, the inflation would seem to have no real effects.

Well, not quite. Those qualifications are pretty strong. Obviously, we will have to consider the case of unanticipated inflation; but even before we get to that there are some important things to say. First of all, some assets bear no interest at all: the important ones are currency and balances in ordinary checking accounts. They constitute the money supply. It would be mechanically difficult for the Treasury to pay interest on currency. Commercial banks are restrained by law from paying interest on checking accounts.[8] (They do the next best, thing by providing financial services free of charge, or at a fee that diminishes with the size of balance; but that is hardly the same thing and cannot in any case serve the same purpose as a nominal interest rate in adjusting to expectations about rising prices.) So, even if the inflation is correctly anticipated, holders of currency and checking accounts will suffer (as they would symmetrically gain if deflation should ever come back into style). These losses to holders of money are not, so to speak, net losses to society, because there are corresponding gains to others. In the case of checking accounts, the gainer is the bank and its stockholders, who earn the higher nominal interest rates on their own assets and pay no interest—except for those free financial services—on deposit liabilities. In the case of currency, the United States government, in the person of the Federal Reserve, is the issuer of the paper, but it is rather special paper, and a special kind of liability, and in any case not very important.

8. The law has changed since this was written. NOW accounts paying interest are legal in all states. (*Editor*)

THE "DEADWEIGHT LOSS"

Since anticipated inflation redistributes to others part of the wealth of holders of money, it is natural that businesses and people should try to reduce their holdings of money when they expect prices to be rising. One can hardly do without any cash in the modern world, but nevertheless it is usually possible to substitute effort for liquidity. Corporations can buy relatively liquid short-term securities and try correspondingly harder to synchronize inflows and outflows of cash. Individuals can rely more on savings banks as a repository of funds, making correspondingly more frequent trips downtown to deposit and withdraw cash, and to transfer funds to a checking account just before large payments have to be made. Indeed they can, and the figures suggest that they do. It is true that this minimization of cash holdings costs time, trouble, and shoe leather. Clever comptrollers are thinking about cash management when they could be worrying about higher things. Moreover, and this is the point, these expenditures of time and effort are a real net burden to society, not merely a transfer to others. They are sometimes described as a "deadweight loss" to emphasize this. They are a true cost of inflation in the same sense that the maintenance of expensive police forces is a cost of crime. Some economists seem to regard these losses as the main social cost of pure inflation. But in that case, something very peculiar is afoot, because one finds it hard to believe that they amount to much. For *this,* governments tremble and people cry on the pollster's shoulder? Even if you add in the computational difficulties of planning with changing prices, the discomfort that comes from not knowing whether your anticipations about future price levels are approximately right or dangerously wrong, it is hard to get excited.[9]

There is one other important "real" effect of anticipated pure inflation; it works through the tax system. Think of any progressive

9. In very rapid inflations—what are usually called "hyperinflations"—the losses from holding money are so great that one observes a genuine flight from the currency, whence come the stories from Germany in the 1920s of children meeting their fathers at the factory gate to bicycle madly into town and spend the day's pay before it has had a chance to depreciate further. In such cases there may be a return to barter. This kind of disorganization of the economy and society can be very costly, but it is not what we have to talk about. Even at relatively small rates of inflation, a little ingenuity can sometimes invent substitutes for the non-interest-bearing checking account—e.g., the NOW account.

tax, a tax that takes a higher fraction of a higher income than of a lower income. Now let all prices, and thus all before-tax incomes, rise in the same proportion. Nobody's purchasing power has changed. But the general rise in nominal incomes will drive everyone into a higher tax bracket. If the general rise in prices amounted to X percent, incomes after tax will rise by less than X percent, because of the higher effective tax rate, and the government's revenues will rise by more than X percent, for the same reason. So taxpayers suffer a loss in purchasing power after taxes, and their loss is the Treasury's gain. Our tax system is not as progressive in action as it is on paper, but nevertheless this effect is quite real. The sharpest case is that of someone whose income is low enough not to be taxable at all; pure inflation can push such a person into the taxable range and thus impose a loss of real income.

In summary, a perfectly anticipated pure inflation imposes a small deadweight loss on society, mostly through a waste of effort directed toward economizing on the holding of money; in addition, it redistributes wealth, from holders of cash and checking accounts to banks, and from everyone to the Treasury. Not good, one is tempted to say, but no worse than a bad cold. Real GNP, for all its faults, is the best measure we have of the current production of valued goods and services; that's the number to watch.

UNANTICIPATED INFLATION

Now real-life inflations are not perfectly anticipated. Neither do they come as a complete surprise. But different people have different opinions about the future of the price level; not all of them can be right, and most of them can be wrong. The consequences of this fact are important, but still special. Interest rates cannot adjust to cushion both debtors and creditors from the effects of pure inflation. Some people will be caught with their pants down: those creditors who have locked themselves into long-term loans at interest rates that do not fully reflect the particular rate of inflation that happens, and borrowers who have agreed to pay high nominal interest rates in the expectation of faster inflation than actually materializes. Of course, for each of these unlucky lenders and borrowers, there is a lucky borrower or lender. Needless to say, when the losers include the broad class of pensioners whose expectations of a viable old age are dashed, it is not a trivial matter.

These gains and losses are not restricted to loans. *Anyone* who has concluded a long-term contract of any kind, stipulated in money terms, stands to gain or lose, depending on which side of the contract we are talking about and whether the rate of inflation turns out in fact to be higher or lower than had been expected when the terms of the contract were agreed. (If rapid inflation continues, we can expect to see more long-term contracts with renegotiation clauses, or with rates of payment explicitly tied to some index of prices. These are a form of insurance against windfall gains and losses from unexpectedly fast or slow inflation.)

Finally, it should be realized that many people, especially non-rich people, are more or less excluded from the benefits of higher nominal interest rates in an inflationary period. Small savers lack either the knowledge or the minimal stake needed to gain access to the sorts of assets whose yields will provide protection against inflation. The small saver is limited in practice to savings accounts and Series E government bonds. The rate on Series E bonds is not set by a market but is managed by the Treasury, and usually kept low enough to constitute a swindle on the nonrich. (One wonders what would happen if Secretaries of the Treasury were required by law to keep all their private wealth in Series E bonds.) The maximum deposit rate payable by savings banks is also limited by law, and by the peculiar role of those institutions as essentially nothing but mortgage lenders. Heaven does not protect the working girl.

The net result of all this is that imperfectly anticipated inflation—the only kind we have—generates massive redistribution of wealth between some borrowers and some lenders, some buyers and some sellers. From a very lofty point of view, these are still transfers, not a net burden on society as a whole. But that doesn't make them good. Moreover, in the public mind these transfers come to look like a net loss: The gainers attribute their gains to their own perspicacity, energy, and virtue; the losers attribute their losses to inflation.

"IMPURE" INFLATION

Pure inflation is an abstraction, though a necessary and useful one. If you can't understand the workings of pure inflation, you will never be able to understand what is actually happening. What is actually happening, of course, is a mixture: The general price level is rising, and at the same time relative prices are changing, sometimes drastically. The price indexes I described earlier are supposed to measure the pure inflationary component of the complicated set of price changes we experience. When I tell you that in the 12 months between June 1973 and June 1974 the CPI rose by 11.1 percent, the WPI by 14.5 percent, and the GNP deflator by 9.7 percent, I am saying something like: It is approximately as if there were a pure inflation of about 10 percent, accompanied by a "pure" change in relative prices around a stationary level. In fact, I can add such information as this: The price of food went up by 14.7 percent during the year, while rents went up by 4.7 percent, so there was clearly a rise in the price of food relative to rental housing.

That is conceptually clear (though not quite as clear as I am pretending). The trouble is that what you observe and feel in the course of the year is the Total Experience, and it is by no means easy to sort out in one's mind the causes and consequences of a rising general level of prices and the causes and consequences of simultaneous changes in relative prices. This difficulty is complicated further by the fact that price movements are not synchronized. Even if, when all is said and done, the price of A and the price of B are both going to rise by X percent, A may take off first and B only later. You would think that these timing differences would all come out in the wash, but they may actually have important independent consequences of their own.

The important thing to say about an inflation in which some prices and some incomes rise faster than others is that the *redistribution* of income can become both quite drastic and quite haphazard. It may be that real GNP is high and rising, so that the country as a whole is not being deprived of goods and services and the satisfactions they bring. But definable groups in the population may find their own standards of living deteriorating, either because the prices of the things they buy are rising faster than the average, or because the prices of the things they sell—including their labor—are rising slower than the average of all prices. And often enough it will appear to them that the inflation is the cause of their troubles, when in fact the real thief is the accompanying change in relative prices. Some economically and socially pointless or harmful redistributions can happen just because certain prices and incomes are less flexible than others and adapt sluggishly to a generally inflationary climate.

Customer Markets and the Costs of Inflation

ARTHUR M. OKUN

Several writers have suggested recently that long-term trading arrangements between buyers and sellers (including those between firms and workers and between borrowers and lenders) play a crucial role in understanding both the behavior of inflation and the costs of inflation. These trading arrangements determine how wages and prices are set over time. They may be explicit legal contracts or else just be informal implicit understandings. They will generally be found where there are long-term buyer-seller relationships.

The existence of formal or informal contracts helps to explain the observed momentum of inflation. Once inflation is well underway a short bout of recessionary excess supply may create lots of unemployment but does not cause much revision of wage or price agreements that have a long-term time horizon. But if contracts have an effect on the path of inflation, they are also, in turn, affected by inflation in ways that may impose serious costs on the contracting parties. When the value of the dollar is changing it becomes much harder to enter into new mutually agreeable buyer-seller agreements. Past agreements do not produce the outcome that was expected and have to be revised more frequently.

In the next selection, Okun points to the disruptive effects of inflation on wage or price contracts and to other costs of inflation. His view differs from Solow's in stressing the inevitable differences between any actual inflation and what Solow calls "pure" inflation.

Realities of the Wage-Price System • IN A SMALL AND SHRINKING sector of the United States economy, products are traded in organized auction markets in which prices vary from day to day to keep supply and demand in balance. Those prices respond promptly and sharply to recession. For example, prices of sensitive industrial raw materials fell by 15 percent between May 1974 and March 1975. That area, which matches the textbook model, offers a striking contrast to the rest of the economy.

Most of our economy is dominated by cost-oriented prices and equity-oriented wages. Most prices are set by sellers whose principal concern is to maintain customers and market share over the long run. The pricing policies designed to treat customers reasonably and maintain their loyalty in good times and bad times rely on some standard measure of costs. Prices are set to exceed costs by a percentage markup that displays only minor variations over the business cycle.

Similarly, the key to wage decisions in both union and nonunion areas is the common long-run interest of skilled workers and employers in maintaining their job relationships. Employers make investments in a trained, reliable, and loyal work force as well as in plant and equipment. They know that if they curbed wages stringently in a slump, they would pay heavily for that strategy with swollen quit rates during the next period of prosperity. Thus, during recession and slack periods, nonunion firms with workers on layoff and queues of eager job applicants find it worthwhile to raise the wages of their workers, in order to protect their longer term personnel relationships.

In those nonunion areas where workers have rapid turnover and thus employers and employees have little stake in lasting relationships, wages respond more noticeably to the level of unemployment. In most areas, however, personnel policies are sensibly geared to the long run with an emphasis on equitable treatment. The basic test of equity is that the pay of workers is raised in line with the wage increases of other workers in similar situations. Such a strategy introduces momentum in the rate of wage increase; it creates a pattern of wages following wages.

The customer and career relationships that desensitize wages and prices from excess supplies and demands in the short run have a genuine social function. They are not creations of evil business monopolies or unduly powerful labor unions, but rather efficient arrangements for a complex interdependent economy in which customers and suppliers, workers and employers benefit greatly from lasting relationships. The resulting influence on prices and wages cuts two ways. When total spending in dollars starts to expand rapidly, most of the increase takes the form of a bonus in output and employment, with little added inflation. In that sense, these institutions make inflation slow starting. But when the dollar value of GNP slows down, most of the decline consists in a loss of production with little relief from inflation. So inflation becomes slow stopping.

Adapting to Inflation · As people recognize the persistence of inflation, they change their behavior in ways that make inflation more rapid and more tenacious. Before the 1970s, the United States economy had a basically noninflationary environment in which average inflation rates in peacetime rarely exceeded 2 percent for any sustained period. Wage and price decisions relied heavily on the dollar as a yardstick, as a scorekeeping device, and as a basis for planning and budgeting. People had a reasonable notion of the wage increase that was par for the course. And so labor and management were willing to sign contracts that fixed wage rates over a three-year interval. Firms set their prices on the basis of known actual costs that they had paid for their labor and supplies, rather than on hypothetical calculations of replacement costs. Salesmen accepted orders for the future delivery of products at guaranteed prices. Catalogs carried price lists that were subject to change only infrequently, often at stated intervals. Public utility and other regulatory commissions needed to review rates only occasionally.

During the 1970s, these institutions changed as Americans adjusted to the persistence of inflation. The notion of par for the course for wage increases was revised upward. Escalator clauses spread through the major collective bargaining contracts and thus made wages respond promptly to inflation in the cost of living. Businessmen began to adjust their pricing to reflect the growing gap between replacement costs and actual historical costs. They shortened the intervals at which they raised prices, and many stopped taking fixed-price orders. These adaptations to chronic inflation speed up the spiral, transmitting higher wages and other costs into higher prices, and higher prices into higher wages even more rapidly.

THE PRINCIPLE OF MALIGN NEGLECT

Because reliance on the dollar is so heavily embedded in our economic practices and thinking, these adaptations to inflation have really just begun. If the inflation rate is not reduced, they are bound to spread much further as people keep adjusting to inflation in self-defense. In a sense some of these adjustments represent ways of learning to live with inflation, and hence they are welcomed by some economists. But while they can reduce the amount of pain per point of inflation, they are bound to increase the number of points of inflation. In my judgment, they are more a disease than a cure. If these institutional adaptations keep spreading, the inflation rate will keep ratcheting upward. Inflation tends to feed on itself rather than to correct itself. Thus, the neglect of inflation is, in principle, malign rather than benign.

Adaptations to chronic inflation contributed to the bad news of 1978. Nonunion wages, which had been rising much less rapidly than union wages during the preceding few years, began to catch up. Because of the wide gap between historical and replacement costs, businessmen felt a need to raise their mark-ups when the markets for their products strengthened—long before excess demand, in any objective sense, appeared. These developments should not have surprised anyone; they were entirely predictable.

To be sure, food and energy have contributed to the acceleration of inflation during the past year. But the prices of those products tend to spurt and slow down; indeed, the major inflationary danger they pose over the longer run stems from the way they can get into the wage-price spiral. Over the entire four years of economic recovery since March 1975, food and fuel have not raised the inflation rate significantly. Since March 1975, the consumer price index has risen at an average annual rate of 7.2 percent; the average for all items except food and energy has been nearly as large—7 percent. Thus we have been experiencing primarily a wage-price-spiral inflation—not an inflation caused by food, fuel, or other special factors.

The American people identify inflation as domestic public enemy no. 1 in opinion surveys. They did so by an overwhelming margin even during 1976 and 1977, when inflation proceeded at a fairly steady 6 percent rate and was well predicted. And they are concerned for good reasons. Only a small minority of Americans have obtained cost-of-living escalators that effectively protect their real incomes from inflation. They do not find opportunities in financial markets to protect their wealth against inflation and still preserve their liquidity. The stable interest rates on passbook deposits that once provided them with a predictable, reasonable return on liquid assets now do not even allow their principal to keep up with the price level—not even on a before-tax basis. Common stocks have been miserable failures as inflation hedges, because the era of stagflation brought higher volatility and lower growth of real corporate earnings. The single-family home has been the one good investment for most Americans, but many who have taken advantage of that opportunity have had to sacrifice liquidity and some have plunged over their heads with commitments for cash payments on mortgages. For the long run, no American can plan effectively in a world in which the dollar remains the yardstick, but shrinks in real value at an uncertain rate.

Moreover, the ratcheting up of inflation has produced a serious credibility gap between citizens and their elected officials. Americans have been told again and again that inflation would be curbed. The acceptable rate of inflation in policymaking rose from 1.5 percent in the early 1960s to 3 percent in the early 1970s. Anyone familiar with that history must wonder whether the present inflation rate of about 8 percent will be reduced, or whether it will be just one more turn of the ratchet.

Finally, inflation has increased social divisiveness. It is not easy for families to know where they stand in the wage-price race. They feel threatened by it and regard it as unfair. Many undoubtedly feel that they are behind in the race, even when that may not be objectively the case. And so they believe they have been given the short end of the stick and are convinced that someone else must have the long end. The principal new product of the American economy in the decade of the 1970s has been sticks with two short ends.

Part Two   Unemployment and Inflation

The Citizen's Guide: The Trade-Off View
ROBERT M. SOLOW

*In Part One the nature and costs of both unemployment and inflation
were examined. The question for Part Two is: What is the relationship
between the two? In the 1960s economists were optimistic that acceptable levels of unemployment and inflation could be sustained. A year
like 1965 when the unemployment rate was 4.5 percent and falling and
inflation was less than 2 percent gave good reason for such optimism.
It was also widely believed at that time that there was a clear trade-off
between inflation and unemployment—the famous Phillips curve. A little less unemployment could be purchased by a little more inflation. In
the following selection, Robert Solow turns from his discussion of the
nature of inflation to its causes. This theme will be picked up later by
James Tobin, but first Solow explains the trade-off view and links it to
an important issue dividing macroeconomists: What is the relation
between the "real" economy (things like real GNP and unemployment)
and the monetary economy (things like inflation and the money supply)?*

THERE IS A VAST AND SUBTLE literature on the causes of inflation
and the mechanism of the inflationary process. One of the central
issues in the theory of the subject—with roots going back hundreds
of years in economics—concerns the nature of the connection
between monetary goings-on and the real economy of production,
consumption, and relative prices. The very concept of inflation presupposes a monetary economy. Moreover, a simplified meat-and-
vegetables economy, you could imagine two identical islands, one
of them (A) with unchanging prices and the other (B) experiencing
perfectly anticipated pure inflation at X percent per year, but with
exactly the same *real* events taking place on both of them. The main
preconditions for this conclusion are (1) that the money supply should
be increasing X percent a year faster on Island B than on A, so that

the amount of purchasing power represented by the money supply could be the same in both places, and (2) that it be possible to pay interest on whatever is used for money, say bank deposits, so that the nominal interest rate could be X percent per annum higher on Island B, to keep the real rates of interest equal.

Now that is pretty abstract; but the further development of such reasoning leads one school of economists to conclude that the real and monetary spheres are in principle separate, and that the true and only cause of inflation is excessively fast expansion of the money supply. It follows that the only way to reduce or stop inflation is to slow down the growth of the money supply. Moreover, if the real and monetary spheres really are separate, then doing so will not have real effects and thus will be quite harmless. (Of course, one can argue that if inflation has no real effects, or negligible ones, there is hardly any point in stopping it.)

I hasten to say that this is a caricature. This school of thought recognizes perfectly well—and the recognition goes back to David Hume—that real-life inflations are not pure and perfectly anticipated. Any attempt to slow or stop an inflation by tightening money will certainly have redistributional effects and may well cause recession, diminished production, unemployment, and excess capacity. All the "new Quantity theorists" claim is that these real consequences will not last forever. Eventually, as the new state of affairs comes to be embedded in expectations and business decisions, the real effects will disappear. Island B will get to be like Island A. The intervening period of bad times has to be regarded as an investment whose payoff is the reduction of inflation, whatever that is worth.

A practical man would want to know how long that period of bad times is likely to last. The new Quantity theorists are not really able to say, and it is hard to blame them. It is a difficult question, and the experiment has never been tried. The sterner protagonists of this view have occasionally hazarded the guess that the period of purification might conceivably last a long time, to be measured more nearly in decades than in quarters. A political figure like Herbert Stein will not say that, but he did say that inflation is "a serious and dominant problem which will require the maintenance of a policy of restraint for the remainder of this year and beyond that."

This question of timing is an analytical question as well as a practical one. The opposing school of thought holds—to caricature once again—that there is a permanent connection between the monetary sphere and the real economy. But what does "permanent" mean? Presumably it does not mean literally forever; nothing is forever. If it means "a long time"—as, for instance, decades—then the distinction between the two schools seems to be more a matter of emphasis or taste than of principle, more a matter of applied economics than of pure theory. But those questions of application are terribly important, as we will see.

THE "TRADE-OFF" VIEW

I shall give a grossly oversimplified sketch of one version of the alternative doctrine. It is based on the famous "Phillips curve," named after A. W. Phillips, who started the whole thing with a purely statistical study of British figures. Let us take it for granted that for extended periods of time in many countries there is a reliable inverse relationship between the unemployment rate (to be thought of as a measure of the degree of prosperity) and the contemporaneous percentage rate at which the level of wages rises. That is to say, in a year in which the economy is strong and the labor market is tight, workers—individually or through their organizations—will be inclined to hold out for relatively large wage increases, and employers will be inclined to offer them; in a depressed year, when the unemployment rate is high, workers will push less and employers will feel more hard-pressed and hard-boiled. Naturally, there are other forces affecting the behavior of wage rates, but this is the one we are concentrating on. Observe carefully: The Phillips curve is a relation between the rate of increase of wage rates (a *monetary* magnitude) and the unemployment rate or level of production (a *real* phenomenon). I have given a plausible but casual rationalization of such a relation; I must warn you that this apparently simple proposition has been the object of whole volumes of the most subtle theoretical and empirical research, which is only beginning to converge. There are still wide differences of opinion within the profession.

So much for wages. If there were no improvements in productivity, labor costs per unit of *output* would move along in step with wage rates (i.e., labor costs per *hour*). Since productivity is generally rising, though not uniformly, labor costs per unit of output rise more slowly than wage rates. In fact—subtleties aside—unit labor costs rise when wages rise more rapidly than productivity in percentage terms, decline when the opposite holds true, and remain constant when wage rates and productivity both rise at the same percentage rate.

But we are interested in prices, not only wages. The simplest acceptable preliminary explanation of the behavior of the price level in the private nonfarm economy is that it is cost-determined. Market conditions are clearly part of the story too—think of oil!—but for simplicity let us just keep that in the background. Suppose that the general price index simply comes out as a mark-up on unit cost of production. That is practically the same thing as a mark-up on unit labor cost, since labor costs amount to more than three quarters of all costs in the economy as a whole. If the price level is roughly proportional to unit labor costs, then the price level will rise when unit labor costs rise, fall when they fall, and stay the same when unit labor costs are stable. So the price level will rise, fall, or remain unchanged according to whether wage rates are rising faster than, slower than, or at the same pace as productivity.

But the wage level—apart from the other market forces we are now ignoring—rises faster when the unemployment rate is low, and slower when it is high. And so the price level—again ignoring other market forces—rises when unemployment is low and the economy prospers, and falls when unemployment is high and the economy is depressed. This is the famous "trade-off between inflation and unemployment" that has found its way into everyday talk. A stable price level can be achieved only at that unemployment rate that allows wages to rise about as fast as productivity is increasing.

According to this line of argument, the real and the monetary are intimately connected. The rate of inflation is governed by the real condition of the economy, in particular by its "tightness" or prosperousness. Moreover, the options for policy are clear but limited. Society can have a slower rate of inflation or no inflation at all, if and only if it is prepared to generate and maintain enough unemployment and excess capacity to hold prices and wages in check. Years ago, Paul Samuelson and I conjectured that the corresponding unemployment rate might be in the neighborhood of 5.5 percent of the labor force; and events suggest that it would now be higher. If the policy choice is really limited by the "trade-off" then there is no avoiding the question: How much is it worth to reduce the rate of inflation, and how much does it cost to live with higher unemployment and lower production? If you think back to our discussion of the social costs of inflation, at least of moderate inflation, it is hard to avoid coming away with the impression that they are minor compared with the costs of unemployment and depressed production—especially since the redistributive costs could in principle be cancelled out by actions designed to protect or compensate the potential losers.

The reply of the trade-off school to the monetary school is: Yes, tight money and balanced budgets can stop inflation, but only by depressing the economy for a long time, perhaps a very long time. The "old-time religion" is (as Karl Kraus said of psychoanalysis) the disease of which it purports to be the cure.[1]

The doctrinal dispute I have been describing obviously goes deeper at the level of analytical principle than at the level of practical economic policy. At the analytical level, there are wheels within wheels that I haven't even mentioned. So far as policy is concerned, it seems to be mainly a matter of timing. Whatever their sterner members mutter, the monetary school acts as if you could squeeze the inflation out of the system in real time; the period of restraint and unemployment would not be so long as to be impractical or worse. Their opponents estimate the period to be longer, and they are less willing to swallow the intervening unemployment anyway. So there is a difference, but a vital difference, mainly in tone.

1. I should mention two quite different policy options, though I don't want to discuss them in detail. One is the imposition of wage and price controls of varying degrees of stringency. There are arguments and counter-arguments as to whether such controls can be effective, and, if they are stringent enough to be effective, whether they are likely to have destructive side-effects on the working of the system. The second option is an organized attempt to "improve the trade-off"—i.e., to make a lower rate of wage and price increase correspond to any given unemployment rate, either by union-busting or trust-busting, or by a program of manpower policies designed to improve skills and open up labor markets. Some people say that recent experience shows that manpower policy doesn't work; others point to the small size and piecemeal character of the programs and argue (as Bernard Shaw said of Christianity) that manpower policy has not failed, it hasn't been tried.

Inflation and Unemployment

MILTON   FRIEDMAN

*The leading monetarist economist is Milton Friedman. The next piece
is drawn from his Nobel prize address delivered in 1976. He argues
forcefully that the Phillips curve is a bad guide to policy. Any trade-off
between inflation and unemployment is transitory and results only from
unexpected changes in aggregate demand. He sees a total breakdown
of the Phillips relation in the 1970s and suggests that attempts to exploit
the short-run trade-off have actually caused the problem of simultaneous high unemployment and high inflation known as stagflation.*

STAGE 1: NEGATIVELY SLOPING PHILLIPS CURVE

PROFESSIONAL ANALYSIS of the relation between inflation and unemployment has gone through two stages since the end of World
War II and is now entering a third. The first stage was the acceptance of a hypothesis associated with the name of A. W. Phillips that
there is a stable negative relation between the level of unemployment and the rate of change of wages—high levels of unemployment
being accompanied by falling wages, low levels of unemployment
by rising wages. The wage change in turn was linked to price change
by allowing for the secular increase in productivity and treating the
excess of price over wage cost as given by a roughly constant mark-
up factor.

Unfortunately for this hypothesis, additional evidence failed to
conform with it. Empirical estimates of the Phillips curve relation
were unsatisfactory. More important, the inflation rate that appeared
to be consistent with a specified level of unemployment did not
remain fixed: in the circumstances of the post–World War II period,
when governments everywhere were seeking to promote "full
employment," it tended in any one country to rise over time and to
vary sharply among countries. Looked at the other way, rates of
inflation that had earlier been associated with low levels of unemployment were experienced along with high levels of unemployment. The phenomenon of simultaneous high inflation and high

45

unemployment increasingly forced itself on public and professional notice, receiving the unlovely label of "stagflation."

Some of us were skeptical from the outset about the validity of a stable Phillips curve, primarily on theoretical rather than empirical grounds. What mattered for employment, we argued, was not wages in dollars or pounds or kronor but real wages—what the wages would buy in goods and services. Low unemployment would, indeed, mean pressure for a higher real wage—but real wages could be higher even if nominal wages were lower, provided that prices were still lower. Similarly, high unemployment would, indeed, mean pressure for a lower real wage—but real wages could be lower, even if nominal wages were higher, provided prices were still higher.

There is no need to assume a stable Phillips curve in order to explain the apparent tendency for an acceleration of inflation to reduce unemployment. That can be explained by the impact of *unanticipated* changes in nominal demand on markets characterized by (implicit or explicit) long-term commitments with respect to both capital and labor. Long-term labor commitments can be explained by the cost of acquiring information by employers about employees and by employees about alternative employment opportunities plus the specific human capital that makes an employee's value to a particular employer grow over time and exceed his value to other potential employers.

Only surprises matter. If everyone anticipated that prices would rise at, say, 20 percent a year, then this anticipation would be embodied in future wage (and other) contracts, real wages would then behave precisely as they would if everyone anticipated no price rise, and there would be no reason for the 20 percent rate of inflation to be associated with a different level of unemployment than a zero rate. An unanticipated change is very different, especially in the presence of long-term commitments—themselves partly a result of the imperfect knowledge whose effect they enhance and spread over time. Long-term commitments mean, first, that there is not instantaneous market clearing (as in markets for perishable foods) but only a lagged adjustment of both prices and quantity to changes in demand or supply (as in the house-rental market); second, that commitments entered into depend not only on current observable prices but also on the prices expected to prevail throughout the term of the commitment.

STAGE 2: NATURAL RATE HYPOTHESIS

Proceeding along these lines, we (in particular, E. S. Phelps and myself) developed an alternative hypothesis that distinguished between the short-run and long-run effects of unanticipated changes in aggregate nominal demand. Start from some initial stable position and let there be, for example, an unanticipated acceleration of aggregate nominal demand. This will come to each producer as an unexpectedly favorable demand for his product. In an environment in which changes are always occurring in the relative demand for different goods, he will not know whether this change is special to him or pervasive. It will be rational for him to interpret it as at least partly special and to react to it by seeking to produce more to sell at what he now perceives to be a higher than expected market price for future output. He will be willing to pay higher nominal wages than he had been willing to pay before in order to attract additional workers. The real wage that matters to him is the wage in terms of the price of his product, and he perceives that price as higher than before. A higher nominal wage can therefore mean a lower *real* wage as perceived by him.

To workers, the situation is different: What matters to them is the purchasing power of wages not over the particular good they produce but over all goods in general. Both they and their employers are likely to adjust more slowly their perception of prices in general—because it is more costly to acquire information about that— than their perception of the price of the particular good they produce. As a result, a rise in nominal wages may be perceived by workers as a rise in real wages and hence call forth an increased supply at the same time that it is perceived by employers as a fall in real wages and hence calls forth an increased offer of jobs. Expressed in terms of the average of perceived future prices, real wages are lower; in terms of the perceived future average price, real wages are higher.

But this situation is temporary: let the higher rate of growth of aggregate nominal demand and of prices continue, and perceptions will adjust to reality. When they do, the initial effect will disappear and then even be reversed for a time as workers and employers find themselves locked into inappropriate contracts. Ultimately, employment will be back at the level that prevailed before the assumed unanticipated acceleration in aggregate nominal demand.

This analysis is, of course, oversimplified. It supposes a single unanticipated change whereas, of course, there is a continuing stream of unanticipated changes; it does not deal explicitly with lags, or with overshooting, or with the process of formation of anticipations. But it does highlight the key points: what matters is not inflation per se but unanticipated inflation; there is no stable trade-off between inflation and unemployment; there is a "natural rate of unemployment" which is consistent with the real forces and with accurate perceptions; unemployment can be kept below the level only by an accelerating inflation; or above it only by accelerating deflation.

The "natural rate of unemployment," a term I introduced to parallel Knut Wicksell's "natural rate of interest," is not a numerical constant but depends on "real" as opposed to monetary factors—the effectiveness of the labor market, the extent of competition or monopoly, the barriers or encouragements to working in various occupations, and so on.

For example, the natural rate has clearly been rising in the United States for two major reasons. First, women, teenagers, and part-time workers have been constituting a growing fraction of the labor force. These groups are more mobile in employment than other workers, entering and leaving the labor market, shifting more frequently between jobs. As a result, they tend to experience higher average rates of unemployment. Second, unemployment insurance and other forms of assistance to unemployed persons have been made available to more categories of workers and have become more generous in duration and amount. Workers who lose their jobs are under less pressure to look for other work, will tend to wait longer in the hope, generally fulfilled, of being recalled to their former employment, and can be more selective in the alternatives they consider. Further, the availability of unemployment insurance makes it more attractive to enter the labor force in the first place, and so may itself have stimulated both the growth that has occurred in the labor force as a percentage of the population and its changing composition.

The determinants of the natural rate of unemployment deserve much fuller analysis for both the United States and other countries. So also do the meaning of the recorded unemployment figures and the relation between the recorded figures and the natural rate. These issues are all of the utmost importance for public policy. However, they are side issues for my present limited purpose.

The connection between the state of employment and the level of efficiency or productivity of an economy is another topic that is of fundamental importance for public policy but is a side issue for my present purpose. There is a tendency to take it for granted that a high level of recorded unemployment is evidence of inefficient use of resources, and conversely. This view is seriously in error. A low level of unemployment may be a sign of a forced-draft economy that is using its resources inefficiently and is inducing workers to sacrifice leisure for goods that they value less highly than the leisure under the mistaken belief that their real wages will be higher than they prove to be. Or, a low natural rate of unemployment may reflect institutional arrangements that inhibit change. A highly static rigid economy may have a fixed place for everyone whereas a dynamic, highly progressive economy, which offers ever-changing opportunities and fosters flexibility, may have a high natural rate of unemployment. To illustrate how the same rate may correspond to very different conditions, both Japan and the United Kingdom had low average rates of unemployment from, say, 1950 to 1970, but Japan experienced rapid growth, the United Kingdom, stagnation.

The "natural rate" or "accelerationist" or "expectations-adjusted Phillips curve" hypothesis—as it has been variously designated—is by now widely accepted by economists, though by no means universally. A few still cling to the original Phillips curve; more recognize the difference between short-run and long-run curves but regard even the long-run curve as negatively sloped, though more steeply so than the short-run curves; some substitute a stable relation between the acceleration of inflation and unemployment for a stable relation between inflation and unemployment—aware of but not concerned about the possibility that the same logic that drove them to acceleration will drive them to ever higher order rates of change.

Much current economic research is devoted to exploring various aspects of this second stage—the dynamics of the process, the formation of expectations, and the kind of systematic policy, if any, that can have a predictable effect on real magnitudes. We can expect rapid progress on these issues. (Special mention should be made of the work on "rational expectations.")

STAGE 3: A POSITIVELY SLOPED PHILLIPS CURVE?

Although the second stage is far from having been fully explored, let alone fully absorbed into the economic literature, the course of events is already producing a move to a third stage. In recent years higher inflation has often been accompanied by higher, not lower, unemployment, especially for periods of several years in length. A simple statistical Phillips curve for such periods seems to be positively sloped, not vertical. The third stage is directed at accommodating this apparent empirical phenomenon. To do so, I suspect that it will have to include in the analysis the interdependence of economic experience and political developments. It will have to treat at least some political phenomena not as independent variables—as exogenous variables in econometric jargon—but as themselves determined by economic events—as endogenous variables. The second stage was greatly influenced by two major developments in economic theory of the past few decades—one, the analysis of imperfect information and of the cost of acquiring information; the other, the role of human capital in determining the form of labor contracts. The third stage will, I believe, be greatly influenced by a third major development—the application of economic analysis to political behavior.

The apparent positive relation between inflation and unemployment has been a source of great concern to government policymakers. Let me quote from a recent speech by Prime Minister Callaghan of Great Britain: "We used to think that you could just spend your way out of a recession and increase employment by cutting taxes and boosting government spending. I tell you, in all candour, that that option no longer exists, and that insofar as it ever did exist, it only worked by injecting bigger doses of inflation into the economy followed by higher levels of unemployment as the next step. That is the history of the past 20 years."

The same view is expressed in a Canadian government white paper: "Continuing inflation, particularly in North America, has been accompanied by an increase in measured unemployment rates."

These are remarkable statements, running as they do directly counter to the policies adopted by almost every Western government throughout the postwar period.

Some Evidence • More systematic evidence for the past two decades is given in Table 1 which shows the rates of inflation and unemployment in seven industrialized countries over the past two decades. According to the five-year averages in Table 1, the rate of inflation and the level of unemployment moved in opposite directions—the expected simple Phillips curve outcome—in five out of seven countries between the first two quinquennia (1956–60, 1961–65); in only four out of seven countries between the second and third quinquennia (1961–65 and 1966–70); and in only one out of seven countries between the final two quinquennia (1966–70 and 1970–75). And even the one exception—Italy—is not a real exception. True, unemployment averaged a shade lower from 1971 to 1975 than in the prior five years, despite a more than tripling of the rate of inflation. However, since 1973 both inflation and unemployment have risen sharply.

Annual data tell a similar, though more confused, story. In the early years, there is wide variation in the relation between prices and unemployment, varying from essentially no relation, as in Italy, to a fairly clear-cut year-to-year negative relation, as in the United Kingdom and the United States. In recent years, however, France, the United States, the United Kingdom, Germany, and Japan all show a clearly marked rise in both inflation and unemployment—though for Japan the rise in unemployment is much smaller relative to the rise in inflation than in the other countries, reflecting the different meaning of unemployment in the different institutional environment of Japan. Only Sweden and Italy fail to conform to the general pattern.

Of course, these data are at most suggestive. We do not really have seven independent bodies of data. Common international influences affect all countries so that multiplying the number of countries does not multiply proportionately the amount of evidence. In particular, the oil crisis hit all seven countries at the same time. Whatever effect the crisis had on the rate of inflation, it directly disrupted the productive process and tended to increase unemployment. Any such increases can hardly be attributed to the acceleration of inflation that accompanied them; at most the two could be regarded as at least partly the common result of a third influence.

Both the quinquennial and annual data show that the oil crisis cannot wholly explain the phenomenon described so graphically by

TABLE 1. *Inflation and Unemployment in Seven Countries, 1956–75: Average Values for Successive Quinquennia* (DP = Rate of Price Change, Percent per Year; U = Unemployment, Percentage of Labor Force)

Years	France		Germany		Italy		Japan		Sweden		United Kingdom		United States		Unweighted average seven countries	
	DP	U	DP	U	DP	U	DP	U	DP	U	DP	U	DP	U	DP	U
1956 through 1960	5.6	1.1	1.8	2.9	1.9	6.7	1.9	1.4	3.7	1.9	2.6	1.5	2.0	5.2	2.8	3.0
1961 through 1965	3.7	1.2	2.8	0.7	4.9	3.1	6.2	0.9	3.6	1.2	3.5	1.6	1.3	5.5	3.7	2.0
1966 through 1970	4.4	1.7	2.4	1.2	3.0	3.5	5.4	1.1	4.6	1.6	4.6	2.1	4.2	3.9	4.1	2.2
1971 through 1975	8.8	2.5	6.1	2.1	11.3	3.3	11.4	1.4	7.9	1.8	13.0	3.2	6.7	6.1	9.3	2.9

NOTE: *DP* is rate of change of consumer prices compounded annually from calendar year 1955 to 1960; 1960 to 1965; 1965 to 1970; 1970 to 1975; *U* is average unemployment during five indicated calendar years. As a result, *DP* is dated one-half year prior to associated *U*.

Callaghan. Already before the quadrupling of oil prices in 1973, most countries show a clearly marked association of rising inflation and rising unemployment. But this too may reflect independent forces rather than the influence of inflation on unemployment. For example, the same forces that have been raising the natural rate of unemployment in the United States may have been operating in other countries and may account for their rising trend of unemployment, independently of the consequences of inflation.

Despite these qualifications, the data strongly suggest that, at least in some countries, of which Britain, Canada, and Italy may be the best examples, rising inflation and rising unemployment have been mutually reinforcing, rather than the separate effects of separate causes. The data are not inconsistent with the stronger statement that, in all industrialized countries, higher rates of inflation have some effects that, at least for a time, make for higher unemployment. The rest of this paper is devoted to a preliminary exploration of what some of these effects may be.

A Tentative Hypothesis • I conjecture that a modest elaboration of the natural rate hypothesis is all that is required to account for a positive relation between inflation and unemployment, though of course such a positive relation may also occur for other reasons. Just as the natural rate hypothesis explains a negatively sloped Phillips curve over short periods as a temporary phenomenon that will disappear as economic agents adjust their expectations to reality, so a positively sloped Phillips curve over somewhat longer periods may occur as a transitional phenomenon that will disappear as economic agents adjust not only their expectations but their institutional and political arrangements to a new reality. When this is achieved, I believe that—as the natural rate hypothesis suggests—the rate of unemployment will be largely independent of the average rate of inflation, though the efficiency of utilization of resources may not be. High inflation need not mean either abnormally high or abnormally low unemployment. However, the institutional and political arrangements that accompany it, either as relics of earlier history or as products of the inflation itself, are likely to prove antithetical to the most productive use of employed resources—a special case of the distinction between the state of employment and the productivity of an economy referred to earlier.

Experience in many Latin American countries that have adjusted to chronically high inflation rates is consistent, I believe, with this view. The version of the natural rate hypothesis summarized above pertains to alternative rates of fully anticipated inflation. Whatever that rate—be it negative, zero, or positive—it can be built into every decision if it is fully anticipated. At an anticipated 20 percent per year inflation, for example, long-term wage contracts would provide for a wage in each year that would rise relative to the zero-inflation wage by just 20 percent per year; long-term loans would bear an interest rate 20 percent higher than the zero-inflation rate or a principal that would be raised by 20 percent a year; and so on—in short, the equivalent of a full indexing of all contracts. The high rate of inflation would have some real effects, by altering desired cash balances, for example, but it need not alter the efficiency of labor markets, or the length or terms of labor contracts, and hence it need not change the natural rate of unemployment.

This analysis implicitly supposes, first, that inflation is steady or at least no more variable at a high rate than at a low—otherwise, it is unlikely that inflation would be as fully anticipated at high as at low rates of inflation; second, that the inflation is, or can be, open, with all prices free to adjust to the higher rate, so that relative price adjustments are the same with a 20 percent inflation as with a zero inflation; third, really a variant of the second point, that there are no obstacles to indexing of contracts.

Ultimately, if inflation at an average rate of 20 percent per year were to prevail for many decades, these requirements could come fairly close to being met, which is why I am inclined to retain the long-long-run vertical Phillips curve. But when a country initially moves to higher rates of inflation, these requirements will be systematically departed from. And such a transitional period may well extend over decades.

Consider, in particular, the United States and the United Kingdom. For two centuries before World War II for the United Kingdom, and a century and a half for the United States, prices varied about a roughly constant level, showing substantial increases in time of war, then postwar declines to roughly prewar levels. The concept of a "normal" price level was deeply imbedded in the financial and other institutions of the two countries and in the habits and attitudes of their citizens.

In the immediate post–World War II period, prior experience

was widely expected to recur. The fact was postwar inflation super-imposed on wartime inflation; yet the expectation in both countries was deflation. It took a long time for the fear of postwar deflation to dissipate—if it still has—and still longer before expectations started to adjust to the fundamental change in the monetary system. That adjustment is still far from complete.

Indeed, we do not know what a complete adjustment will consist of. We cannot know now whether the industrialized countries will return to the pre–World War II pattern of a long-term stable price level or will move toward the Latin American pattern of chronically high inflation rates—with every now and then an acute outbreak of super- or hyper-inflation, as occurred recently in Chile and Argen-tina—or will undergo more radical economic and political change leading to a still different resolution of the present ambiguous situation.

This uncertainty—or more precisely, the circumstances produc-ing this uncertainty—leads to systematic departures from the conditions required for a vertical Phillips curve.

The most fundamental departure is that a high inflation rate is not likely to be steady during the transition decades. Rather, the higher the rate, the more variable it is likely to be. That has been empiri-cally true of differences among countries in the past several decades. It is also highly plausible on theoretical grounds—both about actual inflation and, even more clearly, the anticipations of economic agents with respect to inflation. Governments have not produced high inflation as a deliberate announced policy but as a consequence of other policies—in particular, policies of full employment and wel-fare-state policies raising government spending. They all proclaim their adherence to the goal of stable prices. They do so in response to their constituents, who may welcome many of the side effects of inflation but are still wedded to the concept of stable money. A burst of inflation produces strong pressure to counter it. Policy goes from one direction to the other, encouraging wide variation in the actual and anticipated rate of inflation. And, of course, in such an environment, no one has single-valued anticipations. Everyone rec-ognizes that there is great uncertainty about what actual inflation will turn out to be over any specific future interval.

The tendency for inflation that is high on the average to be highly variable is reinforced by the effect of inflation on the political cohe-siveness of a country in which institutional arrangements and financial contracts have been adjusted to a long-term "normal" price level. Some groups gain (e.g., homeowners); others lose (e.g., owners of savings accounts and fixed-interest securities). "Prudent" behavior becomes in fact reckless, and "reckless" behavior in fact prudent. The society is polarized; one group is set against another. Political unrest increases. The capacity of any government to govern is reduced at the same time that the pressure for strong action grows.

An increased variability of actual or anticipated inflation may raise the natural rate of unemployment in two rather different ways.

First, increased volatility shortens the optimum length of unindexed commitments and renders indexing more advantageous. But it takes time for actual practice to adjust. In the meantime, prior arrangements introduce rigidities that reduce the effectiveness of markets. An additional element of uncertainty is, as it were, added to every market arrangement. In addition, indexing is, even at best, an imperfect substitute for stability of the inflation rate. Price indexes are imperfect; they are available only with a lag and generally are applied to contract terms only with a further lag.

These developments clearly lower economic efficiency. It is less clear what their effect is on recorded unemployment. High average inventories of all kinds are one way to meet increased rigidity and uncertainty. But that may mean labor hoarding by enterprises and low unemployment or a larger force of workers between jobs and so high unemployment. Shorter commitments may mean more rapid adjustment of employment to changed conditions and so low unemployment, or the delay in adjusting the length of commitments may lead to less satisfactory adjustment and so high unemployment. Clearly, much additional research is necessary in this area to clarify the relative importance of the various effects. About all one can say now is that the slow adjustment of commitments and the imperfections of indexing may contribute to the recorded increase in unemployment.

A second related effect of increased volatility of inflation is to render market prices a less efficient system for coordinating economic activity. A fundamental function of a price system, as Hayek emphasized so brilliantly, is to transmit compactly, efficiently, and at low cost the information that economic agents need in order to decide what to produce and how to produce it, or how to employ owned resources. The relevant information is about *relative* prices—of one product relative to another, of the services of one factor of production relative to another, of products relative to factor services, of prices now relative to prices in the future. But the information in practice is transmitted in the form of *absolute* prices—prices in dollars or pounds or kronor. If the price level is on the average stable or changing at a steady rate, it is relatively easy to extract the signal about relative prices from the observed absolute prices. The more volatile the rate of general inflation, the harder it becomes to extract the signal about relative prices from the absolute prices: the broadcast about relative prices is, as it were, being jammed by the noise coming from the inflation broadcast. At the extreme, the system of absolute prices becomes nearly useless, and economic agents resort either to an alternative currency or to barter, with disastrous effects on productivity.

Again, the effect on economic efficiency is clear, on unemployment less so. But, again, it seems plausible that the average level of unemployment would be raised by the increased amount of noise in market signals, at least during the period when institutional arrangements are not yet adapted to the new situation.

These effects of increased volatility of inflation would occur even if prices were legally free to adjust—if, in that sense, the inflation were open. In practice, the distorting effects of uncertainty, rigidity of voluntary long-term contracts, and the contamination of price signals will almost certainly be reinforced by legal restrictions on price change. In the modern world, governments are themselves producers of services sold on the market: from postal services to a wide range of other items. Other prices are regulated by government and require government approval for change: from air fares to taxicab fares to charges for electricity. In these cases, governments cannot avoid being involved in the price-fixing process. In addition, the social and political forces unleashed by volatile inflation rates will lead governments to try to repress inflation in still other areas: by explicit price and wage control, or by pressuring private businesses or unions "voluntarily" to exercise "restraint," or by speculating in foreign exchange in order to alter the exchange rate.

The details will vary from time to time and from country to country, but the general result is the same: reduction in the capacity of the price system to guide economic activity; distortions in relative prices because of the introduction of greater friction, as it were, in all markets; and, very likely, a higher recorded-rate of unemployment.

Diagnosing Inflation: A Taxonomy

JAMES TOBIN

One of the leading proponents of views at variance with those of Friedman is James Tobin. He suggests that the problems of the 1970s have not resulted primarily from deliberate and misguided attempts to exploit a short-run trade-off between unemployment and inflation but rather from a series of shocks, disturbances and policy reactions that have led to high unemployment and high inflation. Then the inertia or momentum of the inflation, once it is established, makes it hard to eliminate. Tobin explains and critiques alternative views of the inflation problem in this 1979 paper.

INTRODUCTION

FOR NEARLY A DECADE the advanced democratic societies of Western Europe, North America, and Japan have been struggling with inflation and losing. Their problem, still as far from resolution as ever, has been to keep price inflation under control at low rates while sustaining economic growth and high employment. While the OECD (Organization for Economic Cooperation and Development) countries, individually and collectively, have failed to reconcile these goals, the aspirations of their peoples have not shrunk nearly enough to fit actual performance.

In diagnosing the malady and prescribing remedies, the economic physicians of the West have exhibited as much disarray as their sick patients. One important reason, I shall argue, is that there are several kinds of inflation and several diseases of which inflation is a highly visible symptom. Some of our countries suffer from one of these maladies, some from another, some from more than one simultaneously or sequentially. Some cure themselves, some are easy to remedy, some are intractable. Anyway there is no single sovereign remedy.

A MONETARY PHENOMENON?

What I have just said may sound like heresy to those who recall Milton Friedman's famous aphorism: "Inflation is at all times and

58

everywhere a monetary phenomenon." It certainly is, if only by definition. Since inflation means generally increasing *money* prices of commodities, or generally declining commodity value of the monetary unit, it necessarily is a monetary phenomenon. The author of the quotation and other monetarists mean much more than that. They mean to attribute all inflation to excessive rates of expansion of monetary aggregates, excessive relative to the sustainable growth of real output. For example, if the growth of labor supply and other productive resources, augmented by the normal technological trend of productivity, is 3 percent per year, then monetary expansion that brings about a growth of more than 3 percent per year in nominal spending for goods and services is excessive. Insert the word "continuously" before "brings" in the last sentence and it too is almost tautological. The difficult questions remain: Why does the monetary authority acquiesce in "excessive" growth of monetary aggregates and nominal spending? What would happen if it did not?

A purely *monetary inflation* is one variety of the disease. It is far more than a logical possibility, as the historical inflations resulting from surges of gold production attest. But modern central bankers do not capriciously or gratuitously expand money supplies, and they are not friends of inflation. There are several explanations why central banks have nonetheless been engines or accomplices of inflation.

One explanation, offered by Friedman himself, is simply intellectual error. Central banks didn't know what they were doing. They misunderstood the monetary and financial system and the economy, and inadvertently overexpanded money supplies. They paid too much attention to nominal interest rates or to credit-market conditions. Underestimating the lags in transmission of their monetary impulses, they destabilized the economy like an idiot trying to regulate the temperature of a shower or the thermostat of a home furnace. Whatever the merit of these allegations, they do not apply to the inflation of the 1970s, our current concern. This inflation has coincided with the conversion of central bankers to monetarist theories, statistics, and targets.

EXCESS DEMAND AND TRADE-OFF INFLATIONS

It is more credible that central banks have assisted their governments in pursuing fiscal and macroeconomic policies with inflationary consequences. Classic *excess demand* inflation occurs when new government demands for resources are piled onto labor and product markets without slack capacity. The government does not have the courage to tax its citizens enough to obtain the needed resources in an orderly way, and the central bank lacks the will or the power to raise interest rates enough to release the resources from private use. Pressure to keep the Treasury's borrowing rates low when the government is selling securities has often constrained the central bank.

In the United States, our most recent example of excess demand inflation was quantitatively modest in historical perspective but turned out to be important beyond all expectation and proportion in the genesis of the inflation that still plagues us. It was the financing of the Vietnam War in 1966–69. In the United States, it raised the inflation rate by three points, from 2 percent in 1965 to 5 percent in 1969 and 1970.

A variant of excess demand inflation, somewhat different both in theory and in motivation, could be called *trade-off inflation*. The Phillips curve blurred the line defining excess demand into a continuum of trade-offs, with increasing marginal cost in inflation for additional employment and production. In its primitive form, the theory certainly understated the long-run inflation cost of low rates of unemployment and excess capacity.

Today a widespread version of recent history is that governments deliberately sought higher inflation in order to reduce unemployment (as was clearly and explicitly done in the first Roosevelt administration, 1933–36) and underestimated the severity of the trade-off. As an explanation of recent inflation in the United States, I believe this account is enormously exaggerated. In 1961–65 the Kennedy-Johnson administration sought successfully to reduce unemployment from 7 percent to 4 percent, its estimate of full employment or of what would later be called the "natural rate of unemployment." Far from welcoming inflation, the administration adopted "wage-price guideposts" to hold it down during the hoped-for recovery. In the event, the 4 percent unemployment goal was reached in 1965 with inflation still no higher than 2 percent. The 1966–69 ride up the Phillips curve was not a conscious choice of novel macroeconomic strategy but a timeworn political decision about wartime finance. Against the advice of his Keynesian advisers, President Johnson chose for his own reasons of domestic and international politics not to ask the Congress for increased taxes to finance his ill-starred escalation of the conflict in Indochina.

In 1971, President Nixon and Treasury Secretary Connally, frustrated by the failure of the 1970–71 recession to cure inflation (it actually reached new heights while unemployment was rising by 2½ points), slapped on wage and price controls and shifted into stimulative monetary and fiscal gear. The recovery of 1971–74 ended with double-digit inflation and 5 percent unemployment. The abrupt counter-inflationary response brought the worst recession and highest unemployment of postwar history. The subsequent recovery of 1975–79 is ending with double-digit inflation and 6 percent unemployment. Whatever the reasons for these misfortunes, it is clear that none of these episodes can be fairly described as an attempt to make full employment fuller by inviting higher inflation.

THE POLITICAL BUSINESS CYCLE

Observers within and outside the economics profession claim to discern a political rhythm in the stop-go alternation of expansionary and restrictive macroeconomic policies. (It is widely believed, for example, that the Federal Reserve's monetary expansion of 1972 was a deliberate assist to Nixon's campaign for re-election. I don't know the inside facts, but I observe that the policy was understandable in the economic circumstances and was within the normal range of "leaning against the wind" characteristic of recovery periods.) The incumbent administration, it is alleged, times prosperity for pre-election months, calculating that the inflation pain will come later. Cooling off the economy comes after the election, long enough before the next one, to be forgotten and to set the stage for the next well-timed "go" policy. These commentators have an extravagant view of the precision of fine-tuning, as well as a contemptuous view of voters and politicians. The more cynical among them regard expansionary policies as purely political, never seeing intrinsic economic benefit in reducing unemployment and raising production. In any event, the theory of the political "stop-go" business cycle, resting as it does on the premise that votes depend not on levels of economic activity but on the rate of increase of real incomes in the year prior to election, implies an inflationary trend only on the assumption that the structure of the economy is so asymmetrical that symmetrical cycles in real economic activity generate irreversible accelerations of inflation. The assumption is realistic, but recognition of the bias suggests that the causes and conditions of inflation are not solely monetary and political but structural as well.

ACCOMMODATION

Whether or not they engage in "stop-go" electoral calculations and manipulations, the makers of macroeconomic policy are always seeking politically acceptable compromises. There is really no great mystery why governments and central banks have in the 1970s allowed monetary expansions "excessive" in relation to actual and sustainable real growth rates. They have usually accommodated ongoing inflation because they regarded the consequences of non-accommodation as unacceptable economically and politically. Those consequences are exemplified by the severe worldwide recession of 1974–75, which may be attributed to nonaccommodative policies, deliberate or accidental.

INERTIAL INFLATION

The inflations of the 1970s confronted monetary and other macroeconomic policymakers with cruelly difficult choices. To describe these inflations, I must add two more types to the taxonomy I have gradually been introducing. I will call them *inertial inflation* and *specific-price inflation*. By "inertial inflation" I mean the self-replicating pattern of wage and price inflation with which we have all become familiar. Whatever the historical origins of the inflation, once it is built into the system in a consistent manner it continues very much on its own. A natural habitat of such a closed system is the nonagricultural private sector of the United States economy. Unions and employers relate their wage increases to recent settlements in other markets and to recent price trends. Employers mark up the increases in labor costs, with allowance for normal productivity gains. These mark-ups determine price trends that in turn feed into the wage increases.

The behavior that sustains these patterns may be interpreted as backward-looking—emulating the behavior of other unions and other industries, catching up with reference groups, passing through historical costs, fulfilling explicit or implicit contractual agreements and mutual understandings. Or it may be interpreted as forward-look-ing—estimating from past experience and other information the likely course of other prices and of market conditions during the periods of decision. It is doubtless both, and the two are tied together. In any case, what matters is the stubborn persistence of the built-in pattern, in particular its resistance to slowdown in monetary demand. Refusal to accommodate inertial inflation will not cause the pattern to collapse. Rather it will bring severe contraction in employment and production for several years, while the built-in wage-price pat-tern subsides very slowly. This is the fear that motivates accommo-dative policies.

SPECIFIC-PRICE INFLATION

Similar dilemmas of accommodation arise when nonmonetary events raise prices in specific markets, and as a result raise econ-omy-wide price indexes. A few years ago, admitting the possibility of "specific-price inflation" would have invited excommunication from the guild of monetary economists. The important distinction between absolute and relative prices is still fundamental. It is still vulgar fallacy to refer to the declining prices of computers and digi-tal watches as "deflation" and to rising oil prices as "inflation." These are not monetary but real phenomena!

Nevertheless, the same wage- and price-setting institutions that sustain inertial inflation make it impossible to keep dramatic changes in specific prices out of the average price level. Given the stubborn-ness of built-in patterns of wage and price inflation, it was inevitable that absorption of quadrupled oil prices would create a bulge of gen-eral inflation. Indeed OPEC's blow was a prototypical stagflationary shock, transferring money and real income and wealth to non-spenders at the same time it was raising prices. Fully accommoda-tive macro policies not only would have covered the rise in prices but would have compensated for the contractionary diversion of purchasing power. A nonaccommodative policy was bound to lead to recession unless wages and prices in sectors and markets other than oil were very quickly flexible donwward. They were not.

Specific price shocks are not always inflationary, though since 1973 we in the United States can be excused for thinking they are. In addition to oil and energy, we have suffered from increases in food prices, from the dollar price consequences of exchange depreciation, and from various "self-inflicted wounds." The latter included farm price supports and crop restrictions that deprived us of the full counter-inflationary advantages of favorable agricultural developments; import restrictions; increases in payroll taxes and other indirect taxes; increases in minimum wages and unemployment insurance benefits; and environmental and safety regulations.

EQUILIBRIUM PATHS

The discussion so far has taken for granted the existence of a viable economic and political equilibrium of real outcomes, a path along which expectations of relative prices and real incomes are mutually consistent and are by and large fulfilled. Such an economy can have any rate of inflation—or even any other path of nominal prices—to which it has adapted its conventions, institutions, and expectations and to which it accommodates its monetary and fiscal policies.

That is surely the view of monetarists, old-fashioned and new. It is also the view of those who diagnose current inflation as basically inertial. They would say there is no intrinsic difference between the United State's economy of 1965 and that of 1978 to explain the difference between their wage-price patterns, 4 percent wage and 2 percent price in 1965, 9 percent and 7 percent in 1978. The inflation difference is purely historical in origin. If the slate could be wiped clean of the patterns of behavior and expectation that keep the inflation going, the economy could go on its merry way with lower inflation or even with stable prices. Unlike the monetarists, the diagnosticians of inertial inflation don't think it's easy to wipe the slate clean. That's why they favor incomes policies rather than restrictive macro policies unassisted.

These diagnoses are consistent with the possibility that the amount of structural, frictional, and voluntary unemployment has risen since the 1960s and 1950s. A number of reasons, varying in plausibility, have been advanced and need not be reviewed here. Some of them say merely that, for various demographic and statistical reasons, the official overall unemployment rate is higher for the same essential tightness of labor and product markets. It is more disturbing if at the same degree of resource utilization we now experience greater acceleration of prices. Moreover, deterioration of both kinds may be an unintended and unwelcome by-product of the counter-inflationary macroeconomic measures of the 1970s. I have in mind that slowdown in capital investment can turn Keynesian unemployment into classical structural unemployment, the lack of jobs for cohorts of teenagers and young adults can make them unemployable, that extensions and improvements of unemployment insurance and other measures to relieve economic distress can convert some involuntary unemployment into voluntary. Maybe there are several equilibrium paths, and we have shifted to a less desirable one.

CONFLICT INFLATION

Quite a different diagnosis is that inflation is the symptom of deep-rooted social and economic contradiction and conflict. There is no real equilibrium path. The major economic groups are claiming pieces of pie that together exceed the whole pie. Inflation is the way that their claims, so far as they are expressed in nominal terms, are temporarily reconciled. But it will continue, and indeed accelerate, so long as the basic conflicts of real claims and real power continue.

Will restrictive macroeconomic policies resolve *conflict inflation?* If the players cannot agree how to divide a larger pie, will they agree how to divide a smaller one? The hope is that the exclusion of more and more people from the game weakens the more assertive groups. The fear is that the shrinking of the pie just makes the insiders more intransigent and protectionist. Reasoning by competitive logic does not help us in this syndicalist world.

There are a number of possible scenarios of conflict inflation in the 1970s. A common story is that a combination of misfortunes—OPEC, long-run energy shortage, environmental dangers, and costs—has sharply lowered the paths of potential output, real wages, and real returns on capital investment. But it has not lowered the standards of real income progress to which employed workers are accustomed, or the profit rates that managers and shareowners expect.

Workers expect their employers and unions to continue to deliver the usual gains, and they are willing to exert their organized power to that end. Presumably in the long run, workers and unions adapt to whatever rate of productivity growth the economy can provide.

But in a painfully long meanwhile, those workers whose jobs are protected by seniority may push for higher wages, even at the expense of jobs for new workers. Similarly, unrealistic profit goals result in excessive mark-ups and exaggerated hurdles for new investment.

In this scenario the relative price shocks of the mid-1970s are the source of serious and lasting conflict, not simply of a temporary bulge of inflation statistics. If hamburger and gasoline become more expensive, will urban workers accelerate wage inflation for decades in hopeless quest for compensation from employers who profit from neither beef nor petroleum? Will they do the same when sales or payroll or income taxes are raised? One theory of British inflation goes along the following lines: Although they voted for MPs who gave them the welfare state, British workers didn't really regard the benefits for which they were taxed as the equivalent of take-home pay. Consequently they sought to get them back at the bargaining table.

Among OECD countries there were large differences in the paths of real wages following the adverse shift of terms of trade with OPEC and with producers of food and materials. In the United States, money wages stayed pretty close to their inertial trend, and labor, organized as well as unorganized, absorbed absolute reductions in real wages, as well as declines in the growth of real disposable incomes. In Britain, thanks partly to untimely indexation and partly to political power, major unions were able to maintain real wages and via accelerated inflation shunt the national losses to other social groups. One lesson we should all learn, incidentally, is the danger of casual indexing by cost-of-living measures inclusive of prices that represent unavoidable costs to the whole society. Somebody has to pay OPEC for oil, and not everyone can have incomes, wages, or social benefits insured against such risks.

The distinction I have tried to make between inertial inflation and conflict inflation invites a metaphor. Consider a stadium where everyone stands up to see the spectacle. They can all see equally well if everyone sits down. The problem is to get people to sit down. But that's the only problem. A more serious situation occurs when there are not enough places in the stadium, and no way to agree on taking turns.

I am not sure how to classify the inflations of our countries in this decade. I have been pretty sure that United States inflation, initiated by various factors, has been sustained by the inertial process I described above. But I would not exclude the possibility that more fundamental social conflict is arising from the frustrations of continued economic reverses. In either event, we face problems much more serious than their inflationary symptoms, problems that we cannot expect a central bank to solve.

PART THREE   Fiscal Policy

Understanding Fiscal Policy
CONGRESSIONAL BUDGET OFFICE

The area of fiscal policy is one of lively controversy at the present time. In this first selection of Part Three, the mainstream or orthodox view of fiscal policy is presented. This says that the main impact of tax and expenditure changes is on aggregate demand. An income-tax-rate-change affects disposable income and hence spending. A change in government purchase of goods and services directly adds to or subtracts from total spending. Fiscal policy changes, particularly tax-rate changes, are then made either to cut total spending, to restrain demand and reduce inflationary pressure, or to boost spending to reduce unemployment.

In the following selection, and then again in Part Four, it will be debated whether or not the attempts to use discretionary fiscal policy and / or the size of the government sector have in fact been the cause of the stagflation problem. But start with the mainstream position. This is developed here by the Congressional Budget Office. The CBO was set up by Congress in 1975 to provide bipartisan assistance to Congress on budgetary and economic matters. It thus parallels the Council of Economic Advisers that gives such assistance to the president. In this selection, alternative budget measures are considered, and the differences among the various fiscal policy instruments are described.

THIS PAPER CONSIDERS the problems of designing fiscal policy. First, it reviews some of the overall measures of fiscal policy—the federal deficit is the best known of these—and their usefulness as a guide to making fiscal policy. Second, it discusses specific fiscal instruments—tax rebates, permanent tax cuts, and others—and suggests some of the special characteristics which affect the impact that each of these instruments has on the economy.

SUMMARY MEASURES OF FISCAL POLICIES

The Unified Budget Deficit · The unified budget deficit, voted by the Congress in its budget resolutions, is the best-known, single-number summary of fiscal policy. The deficit has been very large in recent years—$45 billion, $66 billion, and $45 billion in fiscal years 1975 through 1977, respectively, compared to an average of $14 billion in the earlier 1970s.

All too often, the unified budget deficit is taken to suggest that fiscal policy has been enormously expansionary. While it is essential for accounting purposes, the unified deficit, unfortunately, is a very misleading indicator of discretionary fiscal policy because it responds very sensitively to changes in the economy that do not necessarily have anything to do with fiscal policy. Most importantly, weakness or strength in private demands and incomes cause revenues to fall or rise and hence affect the unified budget deficit. Reinforcing this tendency is the automatic response of income support programs, such as unemployment insurance, to a deterioration or improvement in economic activity. A severe recession causes the unified budget deficit to rise not only because the fall in incomes depresses revenues but also because the fall in real incomes increases payments for unemployment compensation, food stamps, and other outlays. The recession of 1973–75 and the subsequent failure to close fully the gap between actual and potential output that opened up at that time is the main cause of the large unified budget deficits of recent years.

Federal outlays respond not only to changes in real income but also to inflation. Some major federal programs—social security is the most important—are tied automatically to the rate of inflation, and certain other categories of outlays tend to rise semiautomatically when prices go up. A boom, which drives up the level of prices, thus increases outlays of certain kinds as well as increasing revenues. If the outlay effect were as large as the revenue effect, then the deficit would be unaffected; but in fact, the revenue effect tends to be stronger than the outlay effect. The main reason for this is that inflation drives households into higher income brackets and personal income taxes consequently increase more than in proportion to inflation. On balance, therefore, the deficit is reduced by a general increase in prices.

The National Income and Product Accounts Deficit · Thus, the unified deficit is sensitive to a whole host of developments in the private economy that have no necessary connection with congressional policy changes. In addition, there are other shortcomings of the unified deficit. One of them is the fact that it records taxes at the time the money is collected, rather than at the time the liability is incurred. In the case of corporations, the effect of taxes on economic behavior appears to be more closely related to taxes on a liability, or accrual, basis than to taxes on a cash payment basis. Another problem with the unified budget deficit is that certain financial transactions, such as oil leasing on the Outer Continental Shelf and the direct lending activities of government corporations, such as the Farmers Home Administration, are included in the unified deficit, although their effect on the overall economy is much smaller per dollar than the impact of general spending and tax receipts.

These conceptual shortcomings in the unified deficit from the point of view of its economic impact are corrected by moving from the unified budget deficit to the deficit as recorded in the National Income and Product Accounts (NIPA) of the United States. The NIPA deficit generally parallels movement in the unified deficit but displays occasional differences because of these timing and financial adjustments. For fiscal year 1977, the NIPA deficit was $48 billion, compared to a unified deficit of $45 billion. The NIPA deficit shares with the unified deficit the sensitivity to a host of private economic changes that makes it unsuitable as a single indicator of federal fiscal policy.

REFINEMENTS OF THE SURPLUS-DEFICIT CONCEPT

Full-Employment Budget · The full-employment budget was the earliest attempt to correct the unified or NIPA budget for the key difficulty—considered as an indicator of fiscal policy—of responding to developments in the private economy. The method of doing so is to express receipts and outlays not at their actual historical value but at what they would be were the economy at some standardized rate of unemployment. The rate of unemployment chosen was usually 4 percent in the past, but full-employment budget numbers now use somewhat higher rates for recent years.

As has often been pointed out, the full-employment budget adjusts only for departures from a standard unemployment rate, but not for changes in the rate of inflation. The full-employment budget remains quite sensitive to the rate of inflation, and the complications arising from the varied sources of inflation in recent years have made the interpretation of this fiscal policy measure extremely difficult.

In addition, the full-employment budget has other defects that require further adjustments. One difficulty is that this budget evaluates discretionary changes in fiscal policy by the effect that they would have at full employment (at least in theory—in practice, this is often modified) rather than at actual employment levels. Thus, enactment of an expansionary program which would "trigger out" before the economy reached a low rate of unemployment would in theory have no effect on the full-employment budget, although it has an effect on the actual economy.

Another problem with the full-employment budget is that, like the actual budget, it weighs each fiscal policy move according to the number of dollars involved and not according to some measure of its impact on the economy. Thus, in spite of the fact that corporate tax changes are generally viewed as having smaller short-run effects on output and prices (per dollar of tax) than personal income-tax changes, the full-employment budget gives the two types of changes equal weight.

Standardized Budget • A variation on the full-employment budget, the so-called "standardized budget surplus," attempts to correct for some of these defects. The standardized budget surplus measures changes in discretionary programs at the actual position of the economy, rather than at some hypothetical full-employment rate. In doing so, it correctly includes policy changes that have an impact at the time they are enacted but would fade out before full employment. By restricting itself to new discretionary policy actions, it also largely eliminates the automatic effects of the rate of inflation on receipts and on certain categories of expenditures. The standardized surplus does not, however, make any change in the practice of using budget cost, rather than some measure of budget impact on the economy, as the yardstick for fiscal policy measurement.

SOME MAJOR FISCAL INSTRUMENTS

Since no single number is an adequate summary of all of the important dimensions of fiscal policy, it is important to remain aware of the special characteristics of the commonly used instruments of stabilization policy. Accordingly, this section comments briefly on the time lags, economic impact per dollar, and other features of the main taxing and spending instruments available to the Congress.

An ideal instrument of stabilization policy, if there were one, would have at least four characteristics. It would first of all be easy to implement as well as to remove or reverse promptly. Secondly, it would have a favorable, or at least minimally unfavorable, unemployment-inflation trade-off—that is, it could either be used to reduce unemployment with a minimal effect on inflation or be used to reduce inflation with very little cost in extra unemployment. Thirdly, it would have a favorable jobs-deficit trade-off, requiring as small as possible a net budget cost per job created. Finally, it would interfere as little as possible with the efficiency of the private economy. Although none of the common fiscal instruments has all of these advantages, the list of advantages is a useful standard against which to compare each instrument.

The Individual Income Tax • Promptness is the great advantage of changes in the individual income tax for stabilizing the economy. At times, the Congress has been able to work out a tax-change bill within two to four months, and the Treasury is able to translate a completed action into changes in the take-home pay of millions of Americans within weeks after enactment. Not only are income-tax changes prompt in taking effect, they are also easily reversible from a technical point of view, although politically tax reductions are much more popular than tax increases, of course.

A rebate of income taxes is even more prompt than a permanent change in tax rates or deductions. A $10 billion rebate can be paid out entirely within two or three months after enactment, while the direct effects of a $10 billion annual change in tax rates or deductions are generally spread out over a year. There is widespread doubt, however, whether a rebate has nearly as much impact on the economy per dollar of cost (gross or net cost) as does the first year of a permanent cut in taxes. Many economists view consumption decisions as influenced more by long-run income prospects, which are affected by a permanent tax cut but not a rebate, than by windfalls such as a one-time rebate.

According to most analyses, even a permanent income-tax cut is a relatively expensive way of reducing unemployment in terms of budget dollars (net or gross costs) per additional job. The contention that a permanent cut in individual income tax generates enough revenue so that its net cost is zero is one which careful analysis does not support. Nor does a change in individual income taxes, according to most analyses, have any special advantage in avoiding inflation. A few dissenters from this view feel that low income taxes increase the willingness of some persons to hold jobs or work longer hours, and thereby lift the potential non-inflationary level of output of the economy; but this is not a widely held position. Another aspect of the individual income tax that needs to be considered is that proposals to change provisions inevitably raise distributional issues as well as macroeconomic ones.

Corporate Income Taxes · Like the personal income tax, the corporate income tax can be changed promptly and—subject to the same political constraints—can be reversed easily.

There is much less agreement about the economic impact of the corporate income tax than there is about the personal tax. One channel of influence is that the increased cash flow accompanying a cut in business taxes may increase investment, but this channel has not been found to be very important in recent investment analyses. Some models of the economy translate changes in the corporate income tax into movements in stock prices, with significant effects on personal wealth and hence on consumer spending. It is safe to say, however, that most changes in the corporate income tax in the past have not been based on any precise view of their economic impact, but rather on the grounds of preserving equity between personal taxes and corporate taxes.

Investment Tax Credits · A growing number of models of the economy find a powerful GNP impact per dollar for the investment tax credit. Other changes in the tax treatment of capital spending, such as accelerated depreciation or inflation-adjusted depreciation, should also have powerful effects if the investment tax credit does, since they have similar effects on the after-tax return on investment. Changes of this kind, furthermore, are easy to enact and to implement. The investment tax credit has, in fact, been varied a number of times since it was first introduced in 1962.

Time lags in economic impact are the great shortcoming of the investment tax credit as a stabilization device. Because of the long lags involved in business investment decisions, it may be a matter of a year or two before a change in the investment tax credit begins to have substantial effects on employment and output. This is a contrast with the personal income tax or with federal purchases, which may not reach their *peak* effects for a year and a half, but which begin to have substantial effects long before that.

A special effect of the investment tax credit is that it promotes an increase in the amount of capital per employee and thus in the long run leads to a more capital intensive economy. According to some economists, this shift to more capital per employee is accompanied by a shift in the demand for labor from blue-collar to white-collar workers and frequently also by a shift toward greater energy use. These possibilities need to be considered along with the short-run macroeconomic impact in assessing the value of this fiscal device.

Payroll Taxes • The employee share of the social security tax has macroeconomic impacts similar to those of the individual income tax. Both taxes reduce take-home pay and thereby influence consumer spending, and both taxes raise revenues and thereby reduce the size of the deficit. Changes in both can be implemented promptly.

The incidence of the two taxes is quite different; a much higher proportion of payroll taxes than income taxes is paid by low-income workers, while a much higher proportion of income taxes than payroll taxes is paid by middle- and high-income households and property income recipients. This difference in incidence could lead to a difference in overall impact if the saving behavior of the rich differed greatly from the poor. Contrary to most popular speculation, what facts there are on saving by income class do not suggest large differences in the proportion of lifetime income saved at the margin.

The way in which costs, prices, and incomes adjust to changes in the employer share of payroll taxes—both social security and unemployment insurance—is less understood. Most analyses indicate that the principal initial impact is on business costs and prices. The higher prices that are set in response to an increase in employer payroll taxes reduce the real value of wealth and cause higher interest rates, and thereby depress real output and employment. Possibly there is another type of depressing effect on output if the higher payroll taxes were to cause employers to offer lower wages. According to this analysis, in summary, raising the employer payroll tax worsens both inflation and unemployment.

Why then has the payroll tax been raised so frequently? Clearly, economic stabilization is not the reason; from the point of view of stabilization goals, *lowering* payroll taxes would be an advantageous move. Rather, the payroll tax has been raised to maintain the solvency of the social insurance trust funds in spite of effects on the general economy. This conflict between the trust fund effects and the aggregate economic effects of payroll taxes is one of the difficult dilemmas facing policymakers at the present time.

Transfer Payments · From the point of view of impact on the economy, transfer payments—social security payments, veterans' benefits, unemployment compensation, and other payments to individuals—are the opposite of personal income taxes. An increase in social security payments adds to the money households have to spend and adds to the deficit, while an increase in personal income taxes reduces money households have to spend and reduces the federal deficit. Like personal income taxes, transfer payments can be changed promptly; however, there are very few actual instances of reductions in transfer payments other than automatic ones caused by a decline in the number of persons eligible. Decisions about transfer payments, like decisions about taxes, have special power to affect the incomes of particular groups—the retired, the unemployed, and veterans, among others.

Probably most changes in transfer payments, like changes in personal taxes, have less economic impact per dollar than federal purchases of goods. Transfers need not be equivalent to personal taxes in this respect if the persons directly affected by a tax change have different spending-saving patterns from those directly affected by transfer programs. Unemployed household heads, for example, probably spend a higher fraction of any addition to their income than do employed household heads. It follows that payments to unemployed household heads should generate more GNP per dollar than a cut in taxes that is spread among all taxpayers. There is, however, very little data useful for measuring whether the difference is significant. Perhaps for this reason, models of the economy generally do not allow for such differentials.

Again like the income tax, most transfer programs respond automatically to changes in economic conditions. A recession and the accompanying rise in unemployment raises transfer payments; unemployment compensation and welfare payments rise; and possibly, through changes in the number of early retirements, social security benefits rise. These changes, like the drop in revenues during a recession, illustrate the tendency of the federal deficit to grow when the private economy weakens and thereby helps cushion the impact of a recession.

In the case of a step-up in the rate of inflation the response of transfer payments is also to increase—automatically in the case of social security and semiautomatically in the case of unemployment compensation which tends to be linked to recent levels of wage rates. These responses succeed in protecting the beneficiaries against inflation by preserving the real purchasing power of old age payments and the real value of unemployment insurance. At the same time, however, these responses add to total spending and hence increase the overall inflationary pressure in the economy. The automatic response of transfer payments to inflation is thus stabilizing from the point of view of the individuals directly involved, but—unlike personal tax payments—is not stabilizing for the economy as a whole.

Public Works · Public works is the new construction of public facilities such as schools, hospitals, dams, sewage treatment plants, and mass transportation structures. Like public service employment, it has been a part of recent efforts to stimulate the economy.

Evidence supports two propositions about public works as a fiscal instrument. First, it is relatively powerful per dollar of direct budget cost. Like other federal purchases of goods, it is more powerful in this respect, according to almost all models, than general tax cuts or transfer payments. Secondly, there are long lags in starting up or terminating public works projects. Because of the long lags, it is probably a more appropriate fiscal instrument when there appears to be a need for fiscal stimulus or restraint extending several years into the future than when the needs of the economy are known for only a short period ahead. The lags are a disadvantage in using public works to counter short-run swings in the private economy.

Other Federal Spending Programs • There are many types of federal expenditures that have not been covered in this discussion. Usually, these programs satisfy a very specific public need—such as defense, aid to education, medical research, and health care delivery—so that a rapid expansion and subsequent contraction of outlays, which might serve the interest of stabilization policy, could markedly reduce the effectiveness of these programs in meeting their long-term goals. Often, the timing of these programs needs to be designed carefully for technical reasons and they require sustained long-term effort to yield benefits. For this reason, outlays of this kind—say, for health care delivery—are less amenable to countercyclical action than public works. The latter consists of investment projects whose date of completion can be altered without tremendous loss, since the finished investment is likely to last for a long time and thus will render a continuous stream of services once it is completed.

In sum, most spending programs outside the areas of cash transfer payments, revenue sharing, public service employment, and public works at either the local or federal level, are difficult to organize as an instrument of stabilization policy. This is not to say, however, that with careful planning and attention, these other types of expenditures could not also be utilized to help make government outlays a stabilizing tool. Such an approach would require more than simply an appropriation of funds; it would require careful follow-up on the speed and efficiency with which funds are channeled into the private economy, and perhaps authority to change the allocation of funds if bottlenecks develop.

A Debate on Taxes and the Budget
WALTER HELLER AND ARTHUR BURNS

In June 1978, Proposition 13 was passed in California, mandating a major reduction in property taxes. This event stimulated much discussion of the impact of taxation and government spending on the economy. And looking back, we can see in that vote a sign of the shift of public opinion that lead to Ronald Reagan's election, with what he sees as a mandate to cut taxes and spending at the federal level.

In the wake of Proposition 13, several proposals surfaced, that are now very much alive as policy options. These include the Kemp-Roth proposal to cut personal income-tax rates by 30 percent in three years, a constitutional amendment to force a balanced budget, and a proposal to limit government spending to some fraction of GNP. Shortly after the passage of Proposition 13, Walter Heller, former chairman of the Council of Economic Advisers, and Arthur Burns, former chairman of the Federal Reserve Board, debated these proposals, with Ben Wattenberg and David Gergen moderating.

One point to remember while reading this debate is the following. The decisions on (1) the appropriate size of the government sector and (2) the use of fiscal policy to stabilize the economy are separate. It is quite possible to have a small government sector, but at the same time to use tax or expenditure changes to provide stability. In policy debates, the two issues are often linked much more than need be.

Ben Wattenberg (moderator): *Since the passage of Proposition 13 in California in early June, the country has been awash in learned and semi-learned explanations of that specific legislation, the econometrics and economics of it, cross tabulations of the vote, attitudes toward it, and its impact across the country.*

But our purpose in convening this conversation is to deal with— as they say in the polling business—"none of the above."

Economic policy at its root is successful or unsuccessful only insofar as it correctly understands human nature, or, if you will, the aggregate opinions of the public.

Accordingly, we seek here not fact but wisdom, not data but direction.

All the tax revolt hoopla seems to be predicated on the idea that something very new has happened—that a stark change in the pub-

*lic psyche has taken place. That seems an appropriate point to begin
our discussion. Dr. Heller, is all this really new? Or is it an old
drama played out on a new stage?*

Walter Heller: Ever since the 1930s when I was a graduate student
in public finance, and as long as I can remember, people have
rebelled against high taxes. There have been movements, if you
will, that have reflected that rebellion, most notably in the 1950s
when Colin Clark, in a sense, sparked one by saying that any nation
whose taxes went above 25 percent of its national income was bound
to go into unrelenting inflation.

Then, too, there was a constitutional amendment movement in
the 1950s to limit federal income and estate taxes to a top rate of 25
percent. They tried the route of memorializing Congress to call a
constitutional convention, and some 30 states took action, although
how many of those were legal was always a matter of great controversy. And I find that some of my colleagues cite that experience as
a kind of precedent for today's tax revolt and say that this, too, is
going to fall of its own weight. I disagree.

I believe there are sharp differences between those more or less
sporadic movements of the past and this taxpayer revolt of the present. Today we see a strong reaction to what people regard as excessive government, as inefficient spending, and as inroads of inflation
that are unfair in terms of their property and income taxes, in particular.

Mr. Wattenberg: *Do you agree with that, Dr. Burns, and, particularly, let's expand the horizon for a moment, looking not just at the
United States but around the world? Is this a familiar and cyclical
phenomenon, or is this new?*

Arthur Burns: I have been hoping for a good many years that we
might have a taxpayer revolt. I don't remember the revolt of the
1950s that Walter speaks of. It made very little impression on me.

I think we are closer to having a tax revolt in this country
at present than at any time in the past that I can recall, but I am not
yet convinced that the American public has spoken clearly on the
subject. This may be a passing mood; I hope not. But if it is a tax
revolt, I am delighted and I hope it prospers.

Mr. Wattenberg: *Does the situation we are now in have any obvious
analogues to either of you in terms of other countries in years past?*

Dr. Burns: I don't recall any. Do you, Walter?

Dr. Heller: No, I don't. One thinks of Sweden with 50 percent of its GNP going to taxes, and France, Britain, and Germany well above our United States level of nearly 30 percent, and yet I haven't heard of any great tax rebellion or revolt there.

Dr. Burns: I hear a great deal about the frustrations of people, especially from the people I meet in Britain and all over Europe, but I can't think of anything that I would describe as a taxpayer revolt.

The fact is that the middle class and business people generally are psychologically submissive. They tend to act as if the world we live in, with government doing what it does, and taxes being what they are, and regulators doing their bit in growing numbers, they almost act as if God created the world that way and that they therefore have to adjust to it. However, they too are sometimes stirred to anger and protest.

Dr. Heller: I think you have to look at Proposition 13 as part of a movement. After all, there is a constitutional amendment in Tennessee that limits new state spending to the increase in personal income and also has a truth in taxation provision. There are new statutory limitations on state spending in Colorado and Michigan. Also, there is every indication that the California vote is going to have a mimicking effect.

But at the same time, I think we should recognize that certain aspects of Proposition 13 are *sui generis:* they really are Californian. What happened was that there were zooming property tax revenues at the state and at the local level which in good part were inadvertent in the sense that they were caused by inflation and a particularly big boom in property values and immediate assessment response in southern California. And instead of, in effect, *returning* the bounty to the people in the form of lowering tax rates, they just went right ahead and *spent* it. At the same time, they were piling up a huge $5 billion surplus at the state level. So, you had overspending at the local level, overtaxing at the state level, and just a surge of reassessments, reevaluations, and so forth.

And there is another characteristic in California, and I *do* fault the legislature and the governor of California for not doing something about this. The local governments there have had to spend a lot more on public assistance and Medicaid and a higher proportion on education out of property taxes—by far—than in the country at large. The Medicaid and public assistance bills should be paid by the state. But the state just never made any major adjustments with all those extra revenues.

Mr. Wattenberg: *Dr. Burns, assuming that there is a tax revolt, why have you long awaited it, why is it good, what is it telling us about the people in this country? What are they saying beyond "lower my taxes," if anything?*

Dr. Burns: I think people have been watching our government grow at the federal, state, and local levels, year in and year out, pretty much. People have come to feel that while taxes have been going up and governmental spending has been going up, they were not getting their money's worth in the way of governmental services.

They see a huge bureaucracy all around them. They see the government becoming ever bolder as a redistributor of income. People in the middle class—which is the more creative and the more productive part of our economic society—feel that they have been neglected. And to a large degree, they are right.

To be sure, we have had cuts in income taxes at the federal level, but these reductions have applied to people in the lower income brackets. Taxes for the middle and upper income groups have been rising. And people at all income levels have been suffering from inflation.

More and more people are therefore saying to themselves: "We see our government doing more, spending more, taxing more, but our problems—economic and social—are not going away; they are not being solved." So, there is a great deal of unhappiness and frustration in our country, particularly on the part of the middle class.

Mr. Wattenberg: *And you are suggesting that if that tax revolt succeeds, it will be beneficial to the society as a whole?*

Dr. Burns: I have little doubt about that. Our federal government is fundamentally responsible for the inflation that we have been having. Our government is largely responsible for the decline in business and consumer confidence. The huge increase in spending has not solved our urban problems. If anything, it has added to them.

Our economy is not functioning as it should. Business capital investment is lagging. To restore confidence in our nation's economic future, we ought to cut back on governmental spending, cut back on taxes, cut back on regulation. And I think that this is what people feel to an increasing degree.

One thing that surprises me and why I am uncertain about the genuineness of a tax revolt is that, as yet, I don't see anything significant in the Congress in the way of reaction to the Jarvis-Gann proposition in California.

The Congress seems to be going on its old-fashioned way. Yes, we have had a few cuts here and there, but they don't amount to much.

Dr. Heller: I take quite a different view of this. First of all, yes, of course, there is a lot of unrest about taxes, and the middle class is particularly restive. But the idea that they have been taking the major beating from tax increases as against the lower income groups is open to considerable question.

The fastest growing tax in the United States has been the payroll tax. And that certainly is about as regressive a tax as one could find. While we have been cutting income taxes, with recent emphasis on the lower income groups, the payroll tax has been growing very sharply and rapidly as a percentage of the total tax take.

Now, that is just a question of fact and, while I would agree that the delivery systems of government leave a great deal to be desired, that we are not getting as much as we should for our governmental dollar and, while I would also agree that we should be cutting taxes from time to time—I have been associated with some fairly sizable tax cuts in this country and I have been advocating a tax cut now—at the same time, I think it is terribly important to ask: What does this tax revolt accomplish?

Does it accomplish efficiency of government? Does it accomplish a cutback of what we might consider government supernumeraries, and superfluous services, and so forth, or does it just blindly hobble local government?

At the moment, I am very concerned that Proposition 13, and if there should be other actions like that, represent an assault on responsive, responsible, representative local self-government. What is happening in California? The local governments are running "hat-in-hand" to Jerry Brown and the state legislature and asking for largesse of $5 billion.

One of the things I have always been interested in—and this is one of the reasons I was an early advocate of no-strings revenue sharing back in 1957—is seeing that we have strong, decentralized, pluralistic self-government at the local level. I think this is an attack on that.

Secondly, what happens to services when you have a tax revolt like this? What services are cut down eventually? In the California case, they will buffer it for a year or so, but in the last analysis, who wins? Who loses? Is it the poor? Is it the aged? Is it the ill? Is it the disadvantaged—at the expense of preserving services for the middle class? I think the jury still has to be out, and I doubt that the tax revolt is a very good way of getting an efficient solution to that problem.

Furthermore, I don't like it if it ties up government with constitutional limitations. One of the ways in which democratic representative government can be effective is by responding to changes in the economic situation, changes in preferences, changes in circumstances. I don't like to see those things embedded in the Constitution.

One has a whole array of questions that have to be answered before we can decide whether the effects of the tax revolt are going to be negative or salutary.

Furthermore, as far as the overall federal, state, and local tax levels are concerned, I don't know whether this is much comfort to the American people—obviously, it isn't at the moment—but our United States taxes are less than 30 percent of the gross national product.

Mr. Wattenberg: *As compared to rates in European countries in the high 40s or so?*

Dr. Heller: In the 35–40, 45–50 range. The only major industrial country below us is Japan.

The questions of fairness in the distribution of tax burdens, efficiency in the delivery of services, inadvertent tax increases that arise from inflation—in other words, where inflation takes the place of the legislature, in effect, and stealthily and inadvertently increases taxes—I think those questions need to be faced. We have a big agenda there. I just don't think that this slashing and crashing about in taxes, the way Jarvis-Gann has done, is the way to go about it.

Dr. Burns: I would have preferred a more rational approach to cutting back on governmental spending and on taxation than the Jarvis-Gann way. I still hope that might happen in the future.

I was an enthusiastic proponent of the Congressional Budget Reform Act, but I am disappointed with what has been accomplished under it. I don't see rational techniques accomplishing the result that Walter seeks and that I, too, seek. A meat-axe approach, arbitrary though it be, may perhaps be the only way, the nature of man in the political arena being what it is, to cut back on governmental spending.

Governmental spending is a larger factor in our economy than the figures you cite would suggest, Walter. According to my calculations, governmental expenditures at all levels now constitute 37 percent of the net national product and about 33 or 34 percent of the gross national product. And the proper comparison is with the net national product—in other words, the dollar value of the nation's true production of goods and services. That proportion has been growing steadily across the decades.

I have asked myself the question, "What would I have done if I were a Californian?" I would have been somewhat unhappy voting for the Jarvis-Gann proposition, but I still would have voted for it in order to force economies on our governments.

Walter, you speak of weakening of local government. Well, here you have a state government accumulating a surplus of $5 billion; I think this was a shocking performance. It is not Governor Brown's money. Why didn't he reduce the debt? Why didn't he cut taxes? What was he holding out for?

That is enough to cause dismay and anger on the part of citizens.

As things now stand, the citizens of California have a year in which to carry through rational adjustments in the level and direction of local expenditure. I am not willing to assume that essential services will be cut while frills are still being accommodated through the budget.

Dr. Heller: That is a terribly "iffy" thing. And when the property tax is such a high proportion of the revenue sources of local government and such a variable proportion as among counties, cities, school districts, and special districts, it is going to be extremely hard to avoid cutting into muscle and bone along with fat. It would be great if we could just cut fat, but I know no method has ever been found for that.

Dr. Burns: In any event, I think that an increasing number of Americans feel that there is a great deal of fat in governmental outlay and I agree with them. I have been around this city for many years and from my post of observation there is waste and excessive spending everywhere.

I have been asked time and again, when I have appeared before congressional committees, where would I do the cutting. My answer has consistently been, "I would cut everywhere." I see this country experiencing a fairly rapid expansion of economic activity. I also see the federal budget deficit—instead of diminishing or vanishing, as used to be American practice during business-cycle expansions—I see the budget deficit mounting. True, the rhetoric that we hear about the budget is conservative, but that is an old and familiar story.

Dr. Heller: Well, let's take a different cut at it. We are agreed that it did get up to 23 percent or so of the GNP in the early 1970s. We can also agree that if Carter is able to carry out his 1979 plan, 1½ percent real growth in federal spending as against 3 to 4 percent growth projected in GNP, the proportion will drop and continue the move toward Carter's target of 21 percent of GNP. And that, it seems to me, is a valid if not by any means complete answer to the charge that government is expanding like some kind of protoplasmic blob. This is a genuine effort and one on which there will be very considerable congressional cooperation.

Dr. Burns: I like Mr. Carter. I don't question his striving for a balanced budget eventually. All I say is that the net result so far of his efforts and congressional efforts has been to expand the federal budget deficit at a time when economic activity is increasing quite rapidly.

Walter, you know as well as I do that in the kind of world we live in, sooner or later a recession is likely to come along. Make the assumption quite arbitrarily that a recession will get under way this year sometime, or next year, or the year after. Now, if we run budget deficits of the magnitude that we have been having, the deficit in a year of recession could easily rise to $100 billion or $125 billion. I am very much afraid that if we ever got into a situation like that, it might take ten or twenty years for this country to get back to anything like economic or financial stability.

Dr. Heller: Arthur, you paint too black a picture. Our governmental budget deficits, as a whole, are a smaller proportion of GNP than in Germany and Japan, among others. And as long as state and local governments run a $30 billion surplus and foreign governments run a near-$25 billion trade surplus against us, the federal deficit mainly serves to offset those surpluses. Undesirable as the big federal deficit may be, it's not about to do us in.

Dr. Burns: At the risk of shocking you, Walter, I would like to see the federal government proceed on the principle that if there is to be a budget deficit of any magnitude, it should be voted by a three-fifths or a two-thirds majority of the Congress. Now, that is a reform that I would like to see carried through.

Dr. Heller: That is shocking. In terms of sensible, sound, responsible economic management, Arthur, I am shocked.

Dr. Burns: I think we need to introduce some firm discipline into the management of fiscal affairs. Simple majority government has led us into the position in which we now find ourselves—with deficits persisting year in and year out, with deficits feeding inflation year in and year out, with inflation itself accelerating in this country at a time when the rate of inflation is diminishing in most other parts of the world. The legislating of deficits by simple majority rule has led to a depreciation of the dollar in foreign exchange as well as in domestic markets. It has led to great uncertainties about the future of free enterprise in our country. It has led also to a lowering of our national prestige.

Dr. Heller: I surely agree that we need far better economic and financial management, but that involves, for example, a much better coordinated Federal Reserve monetary policy and government fiscal policy. If you, in effect, tie one hand—the fiscal hand—behind your back, I think it will distort the management of United States economic policy.

It seems to be that when you have the kind of slide you had in 1974–75 in the economy, you absolutely need the assurance that the federal deficit will serve as an economic balance wheel.

Dr. Burns: And if it is that clear, and I would say at that time it was that clear, then I am confident we would get more than a bare majority of the Congress voting for it.

Dr. Heller: Well, as I say, I think it would hobble budget management for stability and growth and worsen expectations.

Dr. Burns: It would make it certainly more difficult to run large deficits.

Dr. Heller: Yes, it would.

That, of course, raises the question: What is the source of our inflation in this country? You attribute it all to deficits. I didn't hear anything about monetary policy or the quantity of money, but I would just as soon pass on that.

Dr. Burns: You are granting too much, Walter.

Dr. Heller: Yes, I am, in order to underscore the point that so much of our inflation today is upstream from both monetary and fiscal policy. It is a cost push phenomenon.

THE KEMP-ROTH APPROACH

Mr. Gergen (moderator): *Dr. Heller, you were one of the chief architects of the 1964 tax cut which is now being cited by the Kemp-Roth advocates as proof that you can cut taxes by a very large amount and still increase government revenues. What are your views of the Kemp-Roth proposal in the context of today's economy?*

Dr. Heller: In 1964, when this tax cut was introduced into the economy, inflation was running at a rate of only 1.2 percent a year, and unemployment was running at 5.6 percent, at a time when the full-employment target was 4 percent. In other words, prices were stable and excess capacity was ample. Our estimates were—and subsequent developments seemed to confirm this—that there was $30–35 billion of slack in the economy, something like 5 percent of the GNP. So the supply capacity already existed, and the tax cut released the purchasing power, both to individuals and to business, to absorb that supply capacity. Not that we ignored incentives for more investment and higher productivity. But the basic objective of that tax cut was to increase aggregate demand to absorb the existing supply capacity of the economy. It worked that way and, at the same time, it did facilitate a continued growth in productivity and in the economy's productive potential.

But for Kemp-Roth advocates to cite the 1964 cut as a pure and simple illustration of how a huge tax cut causes an enormous surge in the supply capability of the economy is to misread the facts.

Mr. Gergen: *Your conclusion would be, then, that the Kemp-Roth tax cut would cause larger deficits and more inflation?*

Dr. Heller: Tomorrow morning, before the Joint Economic Committee, I'm going to say that it would cause "soaring deficits and roaring inflation."

Dr. Burns: Let me make a factual comment or two before I try to address this matter.

One of the things that I admired about the Kennedy-Heller tax reduction of 1964 was that it applied to individual incomes across the board, and to corporate incomes as well as to individual incomes. It didn't raise any significant questions of income redistribution; it didn't cause social tensions. Therefore, in concept, it was a constructive measure.

Second, as a point of history, during the 1920s we kept on cutting taxes, the economy kept expanding, government revenues kept on increasing, the new surpluses led to further tax reductions and so it went.

In the case of Japan, Walter, you may recall my coming back from Japan in 1962, when I went to see President Kennedy and informed him of the Japanese experience. The Japanese followed a policy of reducing taxes every year; one year for individuals, another year for corporations, still another year for both. And the policy worked marvelously in Japan. Therefore, there is some historical basis that one can draw upon, but one has to be very careful how one uses history.

I think, at the present time, we have virtually full employment in our country, as far as skilled labor is concerned. We have little surplus of skilled, experienced labor. We don't have a significant unemployment problem in that area. Our present unemployment is largely of a structural character.

And I therefore think that if we now had a massive tax reduction not accompanied by a large reduction in governmental spending, the chances are the effects would be serious; that is, the rate of inflation would be magnified.

PART FOUR   Monetary Policy

Some Issues of Monetary Policy
COUNCIL OF ECONOMIC ADVISERS

Both the structure of the banking system and the ways in which monetary policy is made have been changing. The Keynesian view of monetary policy is that it should be coordinated with fiscal policy to reduce the fluctuations of the business cycle and to steer a course between excessive inflation and excessive unemployment. Many Keynesians argue that monetary policy's effectiveness in slowing an overheated economy has come about in the past partly through credit rationing. Because commercial banks, savings banks, and savings and loan associations had controlled interest rates (Regulation Q), they found it difficult to compete for funds when money became tight. This meant mortgage and other credit became scarce.

Interest-rate ceilings and other restrictions on the financial system have gradually been lifted, so things are changing. But to review monetary policy in historical perspective, the next selection presents the Keynesian view as described in the 1969 Annual Report of the Council of Economics Advisers. The Council at that time consisted of Arthur Okun, Merton Peck, and Warren Smith.

THE RECORD OF the past eight years demonstrates that flexible, discretionary monetary policy can make an effective contribution to economic stabilization. The economy's gradual return to full productive potential in the early 1960s was partly attributable to a monetary policy which kept ample supplies of credit readily available at generally stable interest rates. And in early 1967, the prompt recovery of homebuilding after the 1966 slowdown was the direct result of timely and aggressive easing of credit conditions by the Federal Reserve.

The most dramatic demonstration of the effectiveness of monetary policy came in 1966, however, when a dangerously inflationary situation was curbed primarily by a drastic application of monetary restraint. Credit-financed expenditures at the end of that year appear to have been as much as $8 billion below what they might have been had monetary policy maintained the accommodative posture of the preceding five years. And there were substantial further "multiplier" effects on GNP as these initial impacts reduced income and consumption spending.

THE CONDUCT OF MONETARY POLICY

The primary guides for monetary policy are the various broad measures of economic performance, including the growth rate of total output, the relation of actual to potential output, employment and unemployment, the behavior of prices, and the nation's balance-of-payments position. Extensive research, together with the experience of the last few years, has increased our knowledge of the complex process by which monetary policy influences these measures. While there are still major gaps in our knowledge of the precise chain of causation, some conclusions seem well established.

Like fiscal policy, monetary policy affects economic activity only after some lag. Thus actions by the Federal Reserve must be forward-looking. In considering the prospects ahead, however, an assessment must be made of both the expected behavior of the private sector and of the likely future course of fiscal policy. As noted earlier, the inherent flexibility in the administration of monetary policy permits frequent policy adjustments to take account of unexpected developments in either the private or the public sector.

Sectoral Impacts • Monetary policy can affect spending through a number of channels. To some extent it works by changing the terms of lending, including interest rates, maturities of loans, downpayments, and the like, in such a way as to encourage or discourage expenditures on goods financed by credit. There may also be market imperfections or legal constraints and institutional rigidities that change the "availability" of loans as monetary conditions change— that is, make it easier or more difficult for borrowers to obtain credit at given terms of lending. Under some circumstances, purchasers of goods and services may finance their expenditures by liquidating financial assets, and changes in the yields on these assets produced by a change in monetary policy may affect their willingness to engage in such transactions. Changes in monetary policy may also, on occasion, change the expectations of borrowers, lenders, and spenders in ways that affect economic conditions, although these expectational effects are rather complex and dependent upon the conditions existing at the time policy is changed.

Monetary policy affects some types of expenditures more than others. The extent of the impact depends not only on the economic characteristics of the activity being financed but, in many instances, on the channels through which financing is obtained and the legal and institutional arrangements surrounding the financing procedures.

The sector of the economy most affected by monetary policy is residential construction. Although the demand for housing—and for mortgage credit—does not appear to be especially responsive to mortgage interest rates, the supply of mortgage funds is quite sensitive to several interest-rate relationships.

The experience of 1966 clearly demonstrated how rising interest rates can sharply affect flows of deposits to banks and other thrift institutions and thereby severely limit their ability to make new mortgage loans. In the first half of that year, the net deposit gain at savings and loan associations and mutual savings banks was only half as large as in the preceding six months. These institutions could not afford to raise the rates paid on savings capital to compete with the higher rates available to savers at banks and elsewhere because of their earnings situation—with their assets concentrated in mortgages that earned only the relatively low rates of return characteristic of several years earlier. Commercial banks experienced a similarly sharp slowing in growth of time deposits in the second half of the year, as the Federal Reserve's Regulation Q prevented them from competing effectively for liquid funds. This forced banks to make across-the-board cuts in lending operations. . . . Savings and loan associations and mutual savings banks together supplied less than 10 percent of total funds borrowed in 1966, well below their 22 percent share in the preceding five years. This was the main factor limiting the availability of household mortgage loans. The effect on homebuilding was quick and dramatic, as the seasonally adjusted volume of new housing units started fell by nearly half between December 1965 and October 1966.

In 1967, as interest rates in the open market retreated from their

1966 highs, the thrift institutions were able to regain their competitive position in the savings market. A good part of their funds was fairly quickly channeled into the mortgage market. By fall, housing starts had recovered nearly to the level of late 1965. Many factors—including several significant institutional reforms, sharply improved liquidity positions, and the widespread expectation that monetary restraint was only temporary pending passage of the tax bill—helped to moderate the adverse effects of renewed monetary restraint on mortgage lending in 1968. But the thrift institutions again experienced some slowing of deposit inflows when market interest rates rose to new heights, and mutual savings banks switched a good part of their investments away from the mortgage market to high-yielding corporate bonds.

State and local governments also felt the effects of monetary restraint in 1966. These governments cut back or postponed more than $2.9 billion, or nearly 25 percent, of their planned bond issues that year.

It is difficult to determine precisely what caused these postponements. In cases involving more than half the dollar volume, the reasons given related to the prevailing high level of interest rates. In some instances, the interest costs simply exceeded the legal ceiling governments were permitted to pay for borrowed funds. In other cases, finance officers decided to delay bond issues for a few months in the expectation that interest rates would decline.

This sizable cutback in borrowings had a relatively small effect on state and local government expenditures. Larger governments apparently were able to continue most of their projects about as scheduled by drawing down liquid assets or borrowing temporarily at short term. Smaller governmental units, however, cut their contract awards by a total estimated at more than $400 million.

Because of the problems state and local governments often face in raising funds, the Administration is proposing the establishment of an Urban Development Bank, which could borrow economically in the open market and then lend in the amounts needed to individual local governments. The Bank could lend at federally subsidized interest rates, with the federal government recovering the cost of the subsidy through taxation of the interest income earned by holders of the Bank's securities.

The 1966 credit squeeze undoubtedly also had some effects on business and consumer spending, though the amount of impact is not easily determinable. Most theoretical and empirical studies find that business firms in some way balance the cost of borrowed capital against the expected returns from their capital projects. Some small firms may also simply not be able to obtain funds during tight money periods. In 1966, bank lending to business did slow sharply during the second half of the year. Many of the larger firms shifted their demands to the open market—and paid record high interest rates for their funds—but some of the smaller ones probably were forced to postpone their projects.

Household spending on durable goods—particularly automobiles—has been shown to be affected by changes in the cost and availability of consumer credit, as reflected in the interest rate, maturity, downpayment, and other terms. While it is difficult to sort out cause and effect, households borrowed only two-thirds as much through consumer credit in the second half of 1966 as in the preceding half year. Capital gains or losses on asset holdings accompanying changes in yields may also induce consumers to spend more or less on goods and services.

Active and Passive Elements · Monetary policy, like fiscal policy, has what might be termed active and passive components. Recognition of this distinction played an important role in formulating the accommodative policy of the early 1960s. In the 1950s, economic expansion had generally been accompanied by rising interest rates, which tended to produce an automatic stabilizing effect somewhat similar to the fiscal drag of the federal tax system. The large amounts of underutilized resources available in the early 1960s made such restraint inappropriate, and credit was expanded sufficiently to prevent it from occurring.

It is especially important to distinguish between these elements in monetary policy at cyclical turning points. If, for example, private demand weakens and causes a decline in economic activity, interest rates will generally fall as credit demands slacken, even without any positive action by the Federal Reserve to push rates down. This induced fall in the interest rates can help to check the decline in economic activity but may not, by itself, induce recovery. Similarly, as the economy rises above potential, the induced rise in interest rates may only moderate the expansion but may not bring activity back into line with capacity.

An active monetary policy during such periods requires positive effort by the Federal Reserve to produce further changes in interest rates and in availability of credit beyond those that would occur automatically. Since expectational responses may either accentuate or moderate the effects of the initial action, it is sometimes difficult to know in advance precisely how much of a policy change is needed. But the main point is clear—at such turning points, interest rate movements alone are not likely to provide an accurate reflection of the contribution of monetary policy to economic stabilization. Careful attention must also be paid to credit flows, particularly those to the private sector of the economy.

MONETARY POLICY AND THE MONEY SUPPLY

Examination of the linkages between monetary policy and various categories of expenditures suggests that, in the formulation of monetary policy, careful attention should be paid to interest rates and credit availability as influenced by and associated with the flows of deposits and credit to different types of financial institutions and spending units. Among the financial flows generally considered to be relevant are: the total of funds raised by nonfinancial sectors of the economy, the credit supplied by commercial banks, the net amount of new mortgage credit, the net change in the public's holdings of liquid assets, changes in time deposits at banks and other thrift institutions, and changes in the money supply. Some consideration should be given to all of these financial flows as well as to related interest rates in formulating any comprehensive policy program or analysis of financial conditions.

Much public attention has recently been focused on an alternative view, however, emphasizing the money supply as the most important—sometimes the only—link between monetary policy and economic activity. This emphasis has often been accompanied by the suggestion that the Federal Reserve can best contribute to economic stabilization by maintaining growth in the stock of money at a particular rate—or somewhat less rigidly, by keeping variations in the rate of growth of the money stock within a fairly narrow band.

There are, of course, numerous variants of the money view of monetary policy. The discussion below focuses only on the simple version that has captured most of the public attention.

Money and Interest Rates • In a purely theoretical world, abstracting from institutional rigidities that exist in our financial system and assuming that relationships among financial variables were unvarying and predictable, it would make little difference whether monetary policy were formulated in terms of interest rates or the money supply. The two variables are inversely related, and the alternative approaches would represent nothing more than different paths to precisely the same result. The monetary authorities could seek to control the money stock, with interest rates allowed to take on whatever values happen to result. Or alternatively, they could focus on achieving the interest rates that would facilitate the credit flows needed to finance the desired level of activity, allowing the quantity of money to be whatever it had to be.

But financial rigidities do exist that often distort flows of credit in response to swings in interest rates. And financial relationships have changed steadily and significantly. Just since 1961, several important new financial instruments have been introduced and developed, including negotiable time certificates of deposit and Eurodollar deposits. Attitudes of both investors and lenders have also undergone marked shifts, with sharp variations in the public's demand for liquidity superimposed on an underlying trend toward greater sensitivity to interest rates.

There is, to be sure, enough of a link between money and interest rates at any given time to make it impossible for the Federal Reserve to regulate the two independently. But this linkage is hardly simple, and it varies considerably and unpredictably over time. The choice between controlling the stock of money solely and focusing on interest rates, credit availability, and a number of credit flows can therefore make a difference. This choice should be based on a judgment—supported insofar as possible by empirical and analytical evidence—as to whether it is money holdings alone that influence the decisions of various categories of spending units.

Money and Asset Portfolios • The Federal Reserve conducts monetary policy primarily by expanding and contracting the supply of cash reserves available to the banking system. Such actions seek to induce an expansion or contraction in loans and investments at financial institutions, with corresponding changes in the public's holdings of currency and deposits of various kinds. The proportions in which the public chooses to hold alternative types of financial assets depend upon a complex set of preferences, which, in turn, depend upon interest-rate relationships.

The process of expansion and contraction of money and credit stemming from Federal Reserve actions is fairly complex. But one aspect of it should be clearly understood: The money so created is not something given to the public for nothing as if it fell from heaven—that is, it is not a net addition to the public's wealth or net worth. There can be an immediate change in public wealth, but only to the extent that changes in interest rates generate capital gains or losses on existing assets.

Any change in the money stock is associated with a change in the composition of the public's balance sheet, as people and institutions are induced to exchange—at a price—one asset for another or to increase (or decrease) both their assets and their liabilities by equal amounts. Since all the items in the public's balance sheet might be changed as a result of these compositional shifts, the change in the public's liquidity is not likely to be summarized adequately in terms of any single category of financial assets.

It is, of course, possible that decisions to spend on goods and services are affected more by the presence of one type of financial asset than another in a spending unit's portfolio. But there is only scattered evidence of such behavior in various sectoral studies that have been undertaken to analyze the factors affecting the spending decisions of consumers, business, or state and local governments. Indeed, to the extent these studies do find spending decisions systematically affected by financial variables, it is often through changes in interest rates and availability of credit.

Money and Income and a Monetary Rule · One problem with the money supply as a guide to monetary policy is that there is no agreement concerning the appropriate definition of "money." One definition includes the total of currency outside commercial banks plus privately held demand deposits. A second also includes time deposits at commercial banks, and even more inclusive alternatives are sometimes used. On the other hand, there is a more limited definition, sometimes called "high-powered money" or "monetary base," which includes currency in circulation and member-bank reserve balances at the Federal Reserve banks.

These different concepts of money do not always move in parallel with one another—even over fairly extended periods. Thus assertions that the money supply is expanding rapidly or slowly often depend critically on which definition is employed. In the first half of 1968, for example, there was a sharp acceleration in the growth of currency plus demand deposits, but growth of this total plus time deposits slowed considerably.

On the other hand, relationships between movements in GNP and any of the money concepts have been close enough on the average—especially when processed through complex lags and other sophisticated statistical techniques—to be difficult to pass off lightly.

There is, of course, good reason to expect some fairly close relationship between money and income. This would be true even in a completely abstract situation in which it was assumed that the money supply per se had no direct influence on GNP and that monetary policy worked entirely through interest rates. Since interest rates and the money supply are inversely related, any rise in GNP produced by a reduction in interest rates and increased credit availability would be accompanied by at least some increase in the money supply.

The relationship also exists in a sort of "reverse causation" form— that is, as income goes up so does the demand for money, which the Federal Reserve then accommodates by allowing an increase in the actual money stock. This is precisely what happened during the 1961–65 period of accommodative policy, and it is always present to some extent as the Federal Reserve acts to meet the economy's changing credit needs. The problem of sorting out the extent of causation in the two directions still challenges economic researchers.

A one-sided interpretation of these relationships is sometimes used to support the suggestion that the Federal Reserve conduct policy on the basis of some fixed, predetermined guideline for growth of the money supply (however defined). Given the complex role of interest rates in affecting various demand categories and the likely variations in so many other factors, any such simple policy guide could prove to be quite unreliable.

The experience of the past several years illustrates the kind of difficulties that might be encountered in using the money supply (defined here as currency plus demand deposits) as the exclusive guide for monetary policy. As described previously, high interest rates in 1966 began affecting the nonbank thrift institutions, the mortgage market, and the homebuilding industry soon after the start of the year. But during the first four months of that year, the money supply grew at an annual rate of nearly 6½ percent, well above the long-term trend. Later that year, the financial situation of major mortgage lenders improved somewhat and housing eventually rebounded despite the fact that growth of money supply plus bank time deposits was proceeding at only a snail's pace.

Growth of the money supply in the second quarter of 1968 was at an annual rate of 9 percent. The reasons for this acceleration—to a rate almost double the growth in the preceding quarter—are not fully apparent. The Federal Reserve could have resisted this sizable increase in the demand for money more than it did, but interest rates in the open market would then have risen well above the peaks that were in fact reached in May. Whether still higher rates would have been desirable is another issue, which cannot be settled merely by citing the rapid growth of the money supply.

These illustrations suggest that any simple rigid rule related to the growth of the money supply (however defined) can unduly confine Federal Reserve policy. In formulating monetary policy, the Federal Reserve must be able to take account of all types of financial relationships currently prevailing and in prospect and be able to respond flexibly as changing economic needs arise. In deciding on such responses, careful consideration must be given to likely changes in interest rates and credit availability, in view of the effects of these factors on particular sectors of the economy—especially the homebuilding industry.

A Letter to His Critics: Money Supply in the Conduct of Monetary Policy

ARTHUR F. BURNS

The monetarist view is that a stable and low rate of growth of the money supply should be adhered to in order both to stabilize real output and employment and to reduce or eliminate inflation. The private sector is basically stable, monetarists argue, and erratic and excessive growth of the money supply are the cause of inflation and instability.

When Arthur Burns became chairman of the Federal Reserve Board (Fed) in 1970 he espoused many monetarist precepts. But rather quickly, monetarists began to criticize his handling of monetary policy. In particular, it was argued that rapid expansion of the money supply 1971– 73 had contributed to inflationary pressure which had been held back artificially by controls in 1971–72 and had then surged in 1973.

In September 1973, he was asked by Senator William Proxmire, then chairman of the Joint Economic Committee, to respond to these criticisms. The next selection is drawn from his response.

I AM WRITING IN further response to your letter of September 17, 1973, which requested comments on certain criticisms of monetary policy over the past year.

As stated in your letter, the criticisms are: (1) "that there was too much variation from time to time in the rate of increase in the money supply, that monetary policy was too erratic, too much characterized by stops and starts"; and (2) "that the money supply had increased much too much last year, in fact that the increase would have been too much even if we had been in the depths of a recession instead of enjoying a fairly vigorous economic expansion."

These criticisms involve basic issues with regard to the role of money in the economy and the role that the money supply should play in the formulation and execution of monetary policy. These issues, along with the specific points you raise, require careful examination.

CRITICISM OF OUR PUBLIC POLICIES

During the past two years the American economy has experienced a substantial measure of prosperity. Real output has increased sharply, jobs have been created for millions of additional workers, and total personal income—both in dollars and in terms of real purchasing power—has risen to the highest levels ever reached.

Yet the prosperity has been a troubled one. Price increases have been large and widespread. For a time, the unemployment rate remained unduly high. Interest rates have risen sharply since the spring of 1972. Mortgage money has recently become difficult to obtain in many communities. And confidence in the dollar at home and abroad has at times wavered.

Many observers have blamed these difficulties on the management of public economic policies. Certainly, the federal budget—despite vigorous efforts to hold expenditures down—continued in substantial deficit. There has also been an enormous growth in the activities of federally sponsored agencies, which, although technically outside the budget, must still be financed. The results of efforts to control wages and prices during the past year have been disappointing. Partial decontrol in early 1973 and the subsequent freeze failed to bring the results that had been hoped for.

Monetary policy has been criticized on somewhat contradictory counts—for being inflationary, or for permitting too high a level of interest rates, or for failing to bring the economy back to full employment, or for permitting excessive short-term variations in the growth of the money supply, and so on.

Needless to say, monetary policy is—and has long been—a controversial subject. Even the monetarists do not speak with one voice on monetary policy. Some influential monetarists believe that monetary policy should aim strictly at maintaining a constant rate of growth of the money supply. However, what that constant should be, or how broadly the money supply should be defined, are matters on which monetarists still differ. And there are also monetarists who would allow some—but infrequent—changes in the rate of growth of the money supply, in accordance with changing economic conditions.

It seems self-evident that adherence to a rigid growth-rate rule, or even one that is changed infrequently, would practically prevent monetary policy from playing an active role in economic stabilization. Monetarists recognize this. They believe that most economic disturbances tend to be self-correcting, and they therefore argue that a constant or nearly constant rate of growth of the money supply would result in reasonably satisfactory economic performance.

But neither historical evidence nor the thrust of explorations in business-cycle theory over a long century gives support to the notion that our economy is inherently stable. On the contrary, experience has demonstrated repeatedly that blind reliance on the self-correcting properties of our economic system can lead to serious trouble. Discretionary economic policy, while it has at times led to mistakes, has more often proved reasonably successful. The disappearance of business depressions, which in earlier times spelled mass unemployment for workers and mass bankruptcies for businessmen, is largely attributable to the stabilization policies of the last thirty years.

The fact is that the internal workings of a market economy tend of themselves to generate business fluctuations, and most modern economists recognize this. For example, improved prospects for profits often spur unsustainable bursts of investment spending. The flow of personal income in an age of affluence allows ample latitude for changes in discretionary expenditures and in savings rates. During a business-cycle expansion various imbalances tend to develop within the economy—between aggregate inventories and sales, or between aggregate business investment in fixed capital and consumer outlays, or between average unit costs of production and prices. Such imbalances give rise to cyclical movements in the economy. Flexible fiscal and monetary policies, therefore, are often needed to cope with undesirable economic developments, and this need is not diminished by the fact that our available tools of economic stabilization leave something to be desired.

Changes in the rate of turnover of money have historically played a large role in economic fluctuations, and they continue to do so. For example, the narrowly defined money stock—that is, demand deposits plus currency in public circulation—grew by 5.7 percent between the fourth quarter of 1969 and the fourth quarter of 1970. But the turnover of money declined during that year, and the dollar value of gross national product rose only 4.5 percent. I the following year, the growth rate of the money supply increased to 6.9 percent, but the turnover of money picked up briskly and the dollar value of GNP accelerated to 9.3 percent. The movement out of recession in 1970 into recovery in 1971 was thus closely related to the greater intensity in the use of money. Occurrences such as this are very common because the willingness to use the existing stock of money, expressed in its rate of turnover, is a highly dynamic force in economic life.

For this as well as other reasons, the Federal Reserve uses a blend of forecasting techniques. The behavior of the money supply and other financial variables is accorded careful attention. So also are the results of the most recent surveys on plant and equipment spending, consumer attitudes, and inventory plans. Recent trends in key producing and spending sectors are analyzed. The opinions of businessmen and outside economic analysts are canvassed, in part through the nationwide contacts of Federal Reserve Banks. And an assessment is made of the probable course of fiscal policy and also of labor-market and agricultural policies, and their effects on the economy.

In recent years, the Federal Reserve has placed somewhat more emphasis on achieving desired growth rates of the monetary aggregates, including the narrowly-defined money supply, in its conduct of monetary policy. But we have continued to give careful attention to other financial indicators, among them the level of interest rates on mortgages and other loans and the liquidity position of financial institutions and the general public. This is necessary because the economic implications of any given monetary growth rate depend on the state of liquidity, the attitudes of businessmen, investors, and consumers toward liquidity, the cost and availability of borrowed funds, and other factors. Also, as the nation's central bank, the Federal Reserve can never lose sight of its role as a lender of last resort, so that financial crises and panics will be averted.

VARIABILITY OF MONEY SUPPLY GROWTH

In the short run, the rate of change in the observed money supply is quite erratic and cannot be trusted as an indicator of the course of monetary policy. This would be so even if there were no errors of measurement.

The record of hearings held by the Joint Economic Committee on June 27, 1973, includes a memorandum that I submitted on problems encountered in controlling the money supply. As indicated there, week-to-week, month-to-month, and even quarter-to-quarter fluctuations in the rate of change of money balances are frequently influenced by international flows of funds, changes in the level of United States government deposits, and sudden changes in the public's attitude toward liquidity. Some of these variations appear to be essentially random—a product of the enormous ebb and flow of funds in our modern economy.

Because the demands of the public for money are subject to rather wide short-term variations, efforts by the Federal Reserve to maintain a constant growth rate of the money supply could lead to sharp short-run swings in interest rates and could risk damage to financial markets and the economy. Uncertainties about financing cost could reduce the fluidity of markets and could increase the costs of financing to borrowers. In addition, wide and erratic movements of interest rates and financial conditions could have undersirable effects on business and consumer spending. These adverse effects may not be of major dimensions, but it is better to avoid them.

In any event, for a variety of reasons explained in the memorandum for the Joint Economic Committee, to which I have previously referred, the Federal Reserve does not have precise control over the money supply. To give one example, a significant part of the money supply consists of deposits lodged in nonmember banks that are not subject to the reserve requirements set by the Federal Reserve. As a result, there is some slippage in monetary control. Furthermore, since deposits at nonmember banks have been reported for only two to four days in a year, in contrast to daily statistics for member banks, the data on the money supply—which we regularly present on a weekly, monthly, and quarterly basis— are estimates rather than precise measurements. When the infrequent reports from nonmember banks become available, they often necessitate considerable revisions of the money supply figures. In the past two years, the revisions were upward, and this may happen again this year.

Some indication of the extent of short-term variations in the recorded money supply is provided below. Table 1 shows the average and maximum deviations (without regard to sign) of M_1 from its average annual growth rate over a 3½-year period. As would be expected, the degree of variation diminishes as the time unit length-

TABLE 1. *Deviations in* M_1 *From*
Its Average Rate of Growth,
1970 Through Mid–1973
(Percentage change at annual rates)

Form of data	Average deviation	Maximum deviation
Monthly	3.8	8.8
Quarterly	2.4	5.5
Semiannually	1.8	4.1

ens; it is much larger for monthly than for quarterly data and is also larger for quarterly than for semiannual data.

In our judgment, there is little reason for concern about the short-run variations that occur in the rate of change in the money stock. Such variations have minimal effects on the real economy. For one thing, the outstanding supply of money is very large. It is also quite stable, even when the short-run rate of change is unstable. This October, the average outstanding supply of M_1, seasonally adjusted, was about $264 billion. On this base, a monthly rise or fall in the money stock of even 2½ billion would amount to only a 1 percent change. But when such a temporary change is expressed as an annual rate, as is now commonly done, it comes out as about 12 percent and attracts attention far beyond its real significance.

The Federal Reserve research staff has investigated carefully the economic implications of variability in the growth of M_1. The experience of the past two decades suggests that even an abnormally large or abnormally small rate of growth of the money stock over a period of up to six months or so has a negligible influence on the course of the economy—provided it is subsequently offset. Such short-run variations in the rate of change in the money supply may not at all reflect Federal Reserve policy, and they do not justify the attention they often receive from financial analysts.

The thrust of monetary policy and its probable effects on economic activity can only be determined by observing the course of the money supply and of other monetary aggregates over periods lasting six months or so. Even then, care must be taken to measure the growth of money balances in ways that temper the influence of short-term variations. For example, the growth of money balances over a quarter can be measures from the amount outstanding in the

TABLE 2. *Growth Rates of Money Supply
on Two Bases (Percentage change at
annual rates)*

Quarter	M	Q
1972— I	9.2	5.3
II	6.1	8.4
III	8.2	8.0
IV	8.6	7.1
1973— I	1.7	4.7
II	10.3	6.9
III	.3	5.1

last month of the preceding quarter to the last month of the current quarter, or from the average amount outstanding during the preceding quarter to the average in the current quarter. The first measure captures the latest tendencies in the money supply but may be distorted by random changes that have no lasting significance. The second measure tends to average out temporary fluctuations and is comparable to the data provided on a wide range of nonmonetary economic variables, such as GNP and related measures.

A comparison of these two ways of measuring the rate of growth in M_1 is shown in Table 2 for successive quarters in 1972 and 1973. The column labeled M shows annual rates calculated from end-months of quarters; the column labeled Q shows annual rates calculated from quarterly averages.

As may be seen, the quarterly averages disclose much more clearly the developing trend of monetary restraint—which, in fact, began in the second quarter of 1972. Also, the growth of M_1, which on a month-end basis appears very erratic in the first three quarters of 1973, is much more stable on a quarterly-average basis. For example, while the level of M_1 did not expand significantly between June and September, the quarterly-average figures indicate further sizable growth in the third quarter. For purposes of economic analysis, it is an advantage to recognize that the money available for use was appreciably larger in the third quarter than in the second quarter.

EXPERIENCE OF 1972–73

During 1972, it was the responsibility of the Federal Reserve to encourage a rate of economic expansion adequate to reduce unem-

ployment to acceptable levels. At the same time, despite the damp-
ening effects of the wage-price control program, inflationary
pressures were gathering. Monetary policy, therefore, had to balance the twin objectives of containing inflationary pressures and
encouraging economic growth. These objectives were to some extent
conflicting, and monetary policy alone could not be expected to cope
with both problems. Continuation of an effective wage-price program and a firmer policy of fiscal restraint were urgently needed.

The narrowly defined money stock increased 7.4 percent during
1972—measured from the fourth quarter of 1971 to the fourth quarter
of 1972. Between the third quarter of 1972 and the third quarter of
1973, the growth rate was 6.1 percent. By the first half of 1973, the
annual growth rate had declined to 5.8 percent, and a further slowing occurred in the third quarter.

Table 3 compares the growth of M_1 in the United States with that
of other industrial countries in 1972 and the first half of 1973. The
definitions of M_1 differ somewhat from country to country, but are
as nearly comparable as statistical sources permit. It goes without
saying that each country faced its own set of economic conditions
and problems. Yet it is useful to note that monetary growth in the
United States was much lower than in other major industrial countries and that it also was steadier than in other countries.

Table 4 shows, in summary fashion, the rates of change in the
money supply of the United States, in its total production, and in
the consumer price level during 1972 and 1973. The table is based
on the latest data. It may be noted in passing that, according to data
available as late as January 1973, the rate of growth of M_1 during
1972 was 7.2 percent, not 7.4 percent; and that the rate of increase
in real GNP was 7.7 percent, not 7.0 percent. In other words, on
the basis of the data available during 1972, the rate of growth of M_1

TABLE 3. *Growth in Money Suply*
(Percentage change at annual rates)

Country	1971 Q4 to 1972 Q4	1972 Q4 to 1973 Q2
United States	7.4	5.8
United Kingdom	14.1	10.0
Germany	14.3	4.2
France	15.4	8.7
Japan	23.1	28.2

was below the rate of growth of the physical volume of overall production.

Table 4 indicates that growth in M_1 during 1972 and 1973 approximately matched the growth of real output but was far below the expansion in the dollar value of the nation's output. Although monetary policy limited the availability of money relative to the growth of transactions demands, it still encouraged a substantial expansion in economic activity; real output rose by about 7 percent in 1972. Even so, unemployment remained unsatisfactorily high throughout the greater part of the year. It was not until November that the unemployment rate dropped below 5½ percent. For the year as a whole, the unemployment rate averaged 5.6 percent. It may be of interest to recall that unemployment averaged 5.5 percent in 1954 and 1960, which are commonly regarded as recession years.

Since the expansion of M_1 in 1972 was low relative to the demands for money and credit, it was accompanied by rising short-term interest rates. Long-term interest rates showed little net change last year, as credit demands were satisfied mainly in the short-term markets.

In 1973, the growth of M_1 moderated while the transactions demands for cash and the turnover of money accelerated. GNP in current dollars rose at a 12 percent annual rate as prices rose more rapidly. In credit markets, short-term interest rates rose sharply further, while long-term interest rates also moved up, though by substantially less than short-term rates.

The extraordinary upsurge of the price level this year reflects a variety of special influences. First, there has been a worldwide eco-

TABLE 4. *Money Supply, GNP, and Prices in the United States (Percentage change at annual rates)*

Item	1971 Q4 to 1972 Q4	1972 Q4 to—	
		1973 Q2	1973 Q3
Money supply (M_1)	7.4	5.8	5.6
Gross national product			
Current dollars	10.6	12.1	11.7
Constant dollars	7.0	5.4	4.8
Prices			
Consumer price index (CPI)	3.4	7.1	7.8
CPI excluding food	3.0	4.0	4.1

nomic boom superimposed on the boom in the United States. Second, we have encountered critical shortages of basic materials. The expansion in industrial capacity needed to produce these materials had not been put in place earlier because of the abnormally low level of profits between 1966 and 1971 and also because of numerous impediments to new investment on ecological grounds. Third, farm product prices escalated sharply as a result of crop failures in many countries last year. Fourth, fuel prices spurted upward, reflecting the developing shortages in the energy field. And fifth, the depreciation of the dollar in foreign exchange markets has served to boost prices of imported goods and to add to the demands pressing on our productive resources.

In view of these powerful special factors and the cyclical expansion of our economy, a sharp advance in our price level would have been practically inevitable in 1973. The upsurge of the price level this year hardly represents either the basic trend of prices or the response of prices to previous monetary or fiscal policies—whatever their shortcomings may have been. In particular, as Table 4 shows, the explosion of food prices that occurred this year is in large part responsible for the accelerated rise in the overall consumer price level.

The severe rate of inflation that we have experienced in 1973 cannot responsibly be attributed to monetary management or to public policies more generally. In retrospect, it may well be that monetary policy should have been a little less expansive in 1972. But a markedly more restrictive policy would have led to a still sharper rise in interest rates and risked a premature ending of the business expansion, without limiting to any significant degree this year's upsurge of the price level.

A Response to Burns

MILTON FRIEDMAN

Milton Friedman was one of the Fed's critics in 1973 (as he had been at other times). After Arthur Burns had defended the Fed's actions, Friedman commented on that defense in a letter to Senator Proximire dated February 20, 1974. The following is drawn from that letter.

ON SEPTEMBER 17, 1973, you asked the chairman of the Board of Governors of the Federal Reserve System to comment on certain published criticisms of monetary policy. On November 6, 1973, the chairman replied on behalf of the System.

The Reply makes many valid points. Yet, taken as a whole, it evades rather than answers the criticisms. It appears to exonerate the Federal Reserve System from any appreciable responsibility for the current inflation, yet a close reading reveals that it does not do so, and other evidence, to which the Reply does not refer, establishes a strong case that the Fed has contributed to inflation. The Reply appears to attribute admitted errors in monetary policy to forces outside the Fed, yet the difficulties in controlling and measuring the money supply are largely of the Fed's own making.

The essence of the System's answer to the criticisms is contained in three sentences, one dealing with the Fed's responsibility for the 1973 inflation; the other two, with the problem of controlling and measuring the money supply. I shall discuss each in turn.

RESPONSIBILITY FOR INFLATION

"The severe rate of inflation that we have experienced in 1973 cannot responsibly be attributed to monetary management." (italics added)

As written, this sentence is unexceptionable. Delete the word "severe," and the sentence is indefensible.

The Reply correctly cites a number of special factors that made the inflation in 1973 more severe than could have been expected from prior monetary growth alone—the worldwide economic boom, ecological impediments to investment, escalating farm prices, energy shortages. These factors may well explain why consumer prices rose by 8 percent in 1973 (fourth quarter 1972 to fourth quarter 1973) instead of, say, by 6 percent. But they do not explain why inflation in 1973 would have been as high as 6 percent in their absence. They do not explain why consumer prices rose more than 25 percent in the five years from 1968 to 1973.

The Reply recognizes that "the effects of stabilization policies occur gradually over time" and that "it is never safe to rely on just one concept of money." Yet, the Reply presents statistical data on the growth of money or income or prices for only 1972 and 1973, and for only one of the three monetary concepts it refers to, namely, M_1 (currency plus demand deposits), the one that had the lowest rate of growth. On the basis of the evidence in the Reply, there is no way to evaluate the longer-term policies of the Fed, or to compare current monetary policy with earlier policy, or one concept of money with another.

From calendar year 1970 to calendar year 1973, M_1 grew at the annual rate of 6.9 percent; in the preceding decade, from 1960 to 1970, at 4.2 percent. More striking yet, the rate of growth from 1970 to 1973 was higher than for any other three-year period since the end of the World War II.

The other monetary concepts tell the same story. From 1970 to 1973, M_2 (M_1 plus commercial bank time deposits other than large C.D.'s) grew at the annual rate of 10.5 percent; from 1960 to 1970, at 6.7 percent. From 1970 to 1973, M_3 (M_2 plus deposits at nonbank thrift institutions) grew at the annual rate of 12.0 percent; from 1960 to 1970, at 7.2 percent. For both M_2 and M_3, the rates of growth from 1970 to 1973 are higher than for any other three-year period since World War II.

As the accompanying chart demonstrates, prices show the same pattern as monetary growth except for the Korean War inflation. In the early 1960s, consumer prices rose at a rate of 1 to 2 percent per year; from 1970 to 1973, at an average rate of 4.6 percent; currently, they are rising at a rate of not far from 10 percent. The accelerated rise in the quantity of money has clearly been reflected, after some delay, in a similar accelerated rise in prices.

However limited may be the Fed's ability to control monetary aggregates from quarter to quarter or even year to year, the monetary acceleration depicted in the chart, which extended over more than a decade, could not have occurred without the Fed's acquiescence—to put it mildly. And however loose may be the year-to-year relation between monetary growth and inflation, the acceleration in the rate of inflation over the past decade could not have occurred without the prior monetary acceleration.

Whatever therefore may be the verdict on the short-run relations to which the Reply restricts itself, the Fed's long-run policies have played a major role in producing our present inflation.

There is much evidence on the shorter-term as well as the longer-term relations. Studies for the United States and many other countries reveal highly consistent patterns. A substantial change in the rate of monetary growth which is sustained for more than a few months tends to be followed some 6 or 9 months later by a change in the same direction in the rate of growth of total dollar spending. To begin with, most of the change in spending is reflected in output and employment. Typically, though not always, it takes another year to 18 months before the change in monetary growth is reflected in prices. On the average, therefore, it takes something like two years for a higher or lower rate of monetary growth to be reflected in a higher or lower rate of inflation.

Table 1 illustrates this relation between monetary growth and prices. It shows rates of change for three monetary aggregates and for consumer prices over two-year spans measured from the first quarter of the corresponding years. The average delay in the effect

TABLE 1. *Money and Prices*

Dates for M_1, M_2, M_3	Annual percent rates of growth from first quarter to first quarter of indicated years for				Dates for consumer prices
	M_1	M_2	M_3	Consumer prices	
1959 to 1961	0.8	2.5	4.6	1.1	1961 to 1963
1961 to 1963	2.4	5.9	7.6	1.3	1963 to 1965
1963 to 1965	4.1	6.9	8.3	2.7	1965 to 1967
1965 to 1967	3.7	7.2	6.7	4.2	1967 to 1969
1967 to 1969	7.3	9.4	8.8	5.5	1969 to 1971
1969 to 1971	4.8	6.3	6.4	3.9	1971 to 1973
1971 to 1973	7.2	10.4	12.6	[9.1][a]	1973 to

[a] First quarter 1973 to fourth quarter 1973.

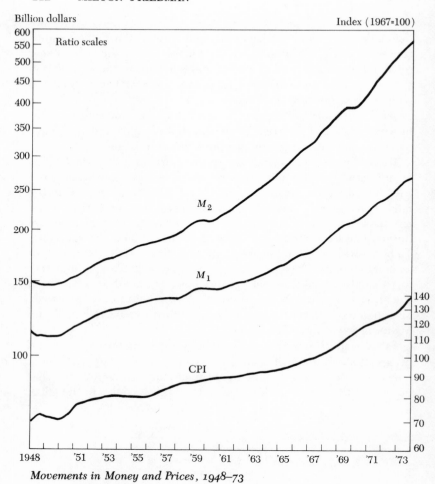

Movements in Money and Prices, 1948–73

of monetary change in prices is allowed for by matching each biennium for prices with the prior biennium for money. Clearly, on the
average, prices reflect the behavior of money two years earlier.

To avoid misunderstanding, let me stress that, as the table illustrates, this is an *average* relationship, not a precise relationship that
can be expected to hold in exactly the same way in every month or
year or even decade. As the Reply properly stresses, many factors

TABLE 2. *Recent Monetary Growth Rates*

Calendar Year	Annual percent rate of growth of		
	M_1	M_2	M_3
1970–71	7.0	11.8	12.8
1971–72	6.4	10.2	12.5
1972–73	7.4	9.5	10.6

affect the course of prices other than changes in the quantity of money. Over short periods, they may sometimes be more important. But the Federal Reserve and the Federal Reserve alone has the responsibility for the quantity of money; it does not have the responsibility, and certainly not sole responsibility, for the other factors that affect inflation. And the record is unmistakably clear that, over the past three years taken as a whole, the Federal Reserve System has exercised that responsibility in a way that has exacerbated inflation.

This conclusion holds not only for the three years as a whole but also for each year separately, as Table 2 shows. The one encouraging feature is the slightly lower rate of growth of M_2 and M_3 from 1972 to 1973 than in the earlier two years. But the tapering off is mild and it is not clear that it is continuing. More important, even these lower rates are far too high. Steady growth of M_2 at 9 or 10 percent would lead to an inflation of about 6 or 7 percent per year. To bring inflation down to 3 percent, let alone to zero, the rate of growth of M_2 must be reduced to something like 5 to 7 percent.

CONTROLLING AND MEASURING THE MONEY SUPPLY

"The conduct of monetary policy could be improved if steps were taken to increase the precision with which the money supply can be controlled by the Federal Reserve. Part of the present control problem stems from statistical inadequacies." (italics added)

Again these sentences from the Reply are literally correct, but they give not the slightest indication that the difficulties of controlling and measuring the money supply are predominantly of the Fed's own making. The only specific problems that the Reply mentions are the "paucity of data on deposits at nonmember banks" and the fact that "nonmember banks are not subject to the same reserve requirements as are Federal Reserve Members."

Nonmember deposits do raise problems in measuring and controlling the money supply, but they are minor compared to other factors. The Reply's emphasis on them is understandable on other grounds. Almost since it was established in 1914, the Fed has been anxious to bring all commercial banks into the System and has been worried about the defection of banks from member to nonmember status. It has therefore seized every occasion, such as the Reply provides, to stress the desirability of requiring all banks to be members of the System or at least subject to the same reserve requirements as member banks.

Control • Nonmember banks raise a minor problem with respect to control. Their reserve ratios do differ from those of member banks. But nonmember banks hold only one-quarter of all deposits, this fraction tends to change rather predictably, and changes in it can be monitored and offset by open market operations.

A far more important problem with respect to control is the lagged reserve requirement that was introduced by the Fed in 1968. This change has not worked as it was expected to. Instead, by introducing additional delay between Federal Reserve open market operations and the money supply, it has appreciably reduced "the precision with which the money supply can be controlled by the Federal Reserve." Other measures taken by the Fed have had the same effect. In an article on this subject published recently, George Kaufman, long an economist with the Federal Reserve System, concluded, "by increasing the complexity of the money multiplier, proliferating rate ceilings on different types of deposits, and encouraging banks, albeit unintentionally, to search out nondeposit sources of funds, the Federal Reserve has increased its own difficulty in controlling the stock of money. . . . To the extent the increased difficulty supports the long voiced contention of some Federal Reserve officials that they are unable to control the stock of money even if they so wished, the actions truly represent a self-fulfilling prophecy."

Even more basic is the procedure used by the Open Market Desk of the New York Federal Reserve Bank in carrying out the directives of the Open Market Committee. These directives have increasingly been stated in terms of desired changes in monetary aggregates rather than in money-market conditions. However, the Desk has not adapted its procedure to the new objective. Instead, it tries to use money-market conditions (that is, interest rates) as an indirect device to control monetary aggregates. Many students of the subject believe that this technique is inefficient. Money-market conditions are affected by many forces other than the Fed's operations. As a result, the Desk cannot control money-market conditions very accurately and cannot predict accurately what changes in money-market conditions are required to produce the desired change in monetary aggregates.

An alternative procedure would be to operate directly on high-powered money, which the Fed can control to a high degree of precision. Many of us believe that the changes in high-powered money required to produce the desired change in monetary aggregates can be estimated tolerably closely even now. They could be estimated with still greater precision if the Fed were to rationalize the structure of reserve requirements.

Measurement · Repeatedly, in the past few years, the Fed's statisticians have retrospectively revised estimates of monetary aggregates, sometimes, as in December 1972, by very substantial amounts.

The one source of measurement error mentioned in the Reply is the unavailability of data on nonmember banks. This is a source of error because nonmember banks report deposit data on only two, or sometimes four, dates a year. The resulting error in estimates for intervening or subsequent dates has sometimes been sizable, but mostly it has accounted for a minor part of the statistical revisions. In any event, this source of error can be reduced drastically by sampling and other devices which the Fed could undertake on its own without additional legislation.

More important sources of error are seasonal adjustment procedures and the estimation and treatment of cash items, nondeposit liabilities, and foreign held deposits.

It has long seemed to me little short of scandalous that the money supply figures should require such substantial and frequent revision. The Fed is itself the primary source of data required to measure the money supply; it can get additional data it may need; it has a large and highly qualified research staff. Yet for years it has failed to undertake the research effort necessary to correct known defects in its money supply series.[1]

CONCLUSION

For more than a decade, monetary growth has been accelerating. It has been higher in the past three years than in any other three-year period since the end of World War II. Inflation has also accelerated over the past decade. It too has been higher in the past three years than in any other three-year period sincce 1947. Economic theory and empirical evidence combine to establish a strong presumption that the acceleration in monetary growth is largely responsible for the acceleration in inflation. Nothing in the Reply of the chairman of the Federal Reserve System to your letter contradicts or even questions that conclusion. And nothing in that Reply denies that the Federal Reserve System had the power to prevent the sharp acceleration in monetary growth.

I recognize, of course, that there are now, and have been in the past, strong political pressures on the Fed to continue rapid monetary growth. Once inflation has proceeded as far as it already has, it will, as the Reply says, take some time to eliminate it. Moreover, there is literally no way to end inflation that will not involve a temporary, though perhaps fairly protracted, period of low economic growth and relatively high unemployment. Avoidance of the earlier excessive monetary growth would have had far less costly consequences for the community than cutting monetary growth down to an appropriate level will now have. But the damage has been done. The longer we wait, the harder it will be. And there is no other way to stop inflation.

The only justification for the Fed's vaunted independence is to enable it to take measures that are wise for the long-run even if not popular in the short-run. That is why it is so discouraging to have the Reply consist almost entirely of a denial of responsibility for inflation and an attempt to place the blame elsewhere.

1. On January 31, 1974, after this comment had been drafted, the Board of Governors of the Federal Reserve System announced "the formation of a special committee of prominent academic experts to review concepts, procedures and methodology involved in estimating the money supply and other monetary aggregates." I have agreed to serve as a member of this committee.

If the Fed does not explain to the public the nature of our problem and the costs involved in ending inflation; if it does not take the lead in imposing the temporarily unpopular measures required, who will?

Tax Rules and Monetary Policy

Paul Volcker succeeded Arthur Burns as chairman of the Federal Reserve Board in 1978. In 1978–79, output grew strongly but the inflation problem grew also. In the fall of 1979, the Fed announced that it was changing the way policy was made. There had been targets set for the rates of growth of the main monetary aggregates for some years. But now the Fed expressed a determination to keep to these targets. In the past the Fed had tried to use open market operations to achieve the money growth targets, but also to avoid sharp fluctuations in the federal funds rate (the interest rate that prevails when member banks lend reserves to each other). In the future, they said, this rate could move up or down to whatever extent was necessary in order to achieve the quantity targets for the money base and the money supply.

The result of this change of strategy has indeed been much greater volatility of interest rates and somewhat (but only somewhat) better success at achieving the money growth targets. In the next selection, written in June 1980, Martin Feldstein argues that the Fed's new determination to stick to its targets and fight inflation is generally to be applauded. Feldstein points out that the high interest rates that resulted from tight policy really are not as high as they look. Because of inflation, the real (or inflation-adjusted) interest rate, is less than the nominal rate. And the fact that interest payments are a deduction for income-tax purposes for both individuals and corporations lowers the effective interest rate even further.

THE CURRENT ECONOMIC slowdown is about to put the Fed's monetary policy to a severe test.

For the past eight months, the Fed has been able to pursue an appropriate policy of slowing the growth of the money supply. The public's overriding concern with inflation prevented or at least muted any criticism of the resulting sharp rise in interest rates. But as the economy now slides into recession, there will almost certainly be growing opposition to anything that appears to be a tight monetary policy.

For the moment, there is widespread relief that interest rates have dropped from the peaks of the past two months and that the Fed has cut the discount rate to 12 percent. But standards of comparison change quickly. It will no doubt soon be argued that a Treasury bill rate well above the 6½ percent average of the last five years is "too high" for an economy in recession. And when the recovery begins, it will bring with it rising interest rates and the familiar call for monetary accommodation. The Fed will be under substantial pressure to drop its plan for steady deceleration of the money growth rate.

TAX RULES AND INTEREST RATES

If the past is any guide, all of this upcoming debate about "high interest rates" and accommodation is likely to ignore the effects of tax rules and therefore to regard monetary policy as much tighter than it actually is. Over the past 15 years, the failure to recognize the interaction of tax rules and interest rates has confused the evaluation of monetary policy and spurred an inflationary growth of the money supply. The time has come to correct that error before it causes another round of excess monetary expansion.

From 1950 through the early 1960s, the interest rate on Baa bonds varied only in the narrow range between 3½ percent and 5 percent. In contrast, the past 15 years have seen the Baa rate rise from less than 5 percent in 1964 to more than 12 percent at the end of 1979. It is perhaps not surprising therefore that the monetary authorities and many private economists worried throughout this period that interest rates might be getting "too high." Critics of what was perceived as "tight money" argued that such high interest rates would reduce investment and therefore depress aggregate demand.

Against all this it could be argued, and was argued, that the *real* interest rate had obviously gone up much less. The correct measure of the real interest rate is, of course, the difference between the nominal interest rate and the rate of inflation that is expected over the life of the bond. A common rule-of-thumb approximates the expected future inflation by the average inflation rate experienced during the preceding three years. In 1964, when the Baa rate was 4.8 percent, this three-year rise in the GNP deflator averaged 1.6 percent; the implied real interest rate was thus 3.2 percent. By the end of 1979, when the Baa rate was 12.0 percent, the rise in the GNP deflator for the previous three years had increased to 7.8 percent, implying a real interest rate of 4.2 percent. Judged in this way, the cost of credit had also increased significantly over the 15-year period.

All of this ignores the role of taxes. Since interest expenses can be deducted by individuals and businesses in calculating taxable income, the net-of-tax interest cost is very much less than the interest rate itself. Indeed, since the nominal interest expense can be deducted, the real net-of-tax interest has actually varied inversely with the nominal rate of interest. *What appears to have been a rising interest rate over the past 25 years was actually a sharply falling real after-tax cost of funds.* The failure to recognize the role of taxes prevented the monetary authorities from seeing just how expansionary monetary policy had become.

The implication of tax deductibility is seen most easily in the case of owner-occupied housing. A married couple with a $30,000 taxable income now has a marginal federal income-tax rate of 37 percent. The 11.4 percent mortgage rate in effect in the last quarter of 1979 implied a net-of-tax cost of funds of 7.2 percent. Subtracting a 7.8 percent estimate of the rate of inflation (based on a three-year average increase in the GNP deflator) leaves a real net-of-tax cost of funds of minus 0.6 percent. By comparison, the 4.8 percent interest rate for 1964 translates into a 3.0 percent net-of-tax rate and a 1.4 percent real net-of-tax cost of funds. Thus, although the nominal interest rate had more than doubled and the real interest rate had also increased substantially, the relevant net-of-tax real cost of funds had actually fallen from 1.4 percent to a negative 0.6 percent.

Although home-buyers implicitly made this type of calculation, economists and the monetary authorities generally didn't. Monetary policy in the last decade was overly expansionary because the monetary authorities and their expansionist critics believed that the cost of funds was rising or steady when in fact it was actually falling significantly.

The fall in the real after-tax interest rate caused a rapid change in the price of houses relative to the general price level and sustained a high rate of new residential construction. There were, of course, times when the ceilings on the interest rates that financial institutions could pay caused disintermediation and limited the funds available for housing. To that extent, the high level of nominal interest rates restricted the supply of funds at the same time that the corresponding low real after-tax interest cost increased the demand for funds. In the past few years, the raising of certain interest-rate ceilings and the development of mortgage-backed bonds that can short-circuit the disintermediation process have made the supply restrictions much less important and have therefore made any interest level more expansionary than it otherwise would have been.

The low real after-tax rate of interest also encouraged the growth of consumer credit and the purchase of consumer durables. More generally, even households that do not itemize their tax deductions are affected by the net return that is available on savings. Because individuals pay tax on nominal interest income, the real after-tax rate of return on saving has become negative. It seems very likely that this substantial fall in the real return on savings has contributed to the fall in the personal saving rate and the rise in consumer demand.

For corporate borrowers, the analysis is more complex because inflation changes the effective tax rate on investments as well as the real net-of-tax interest rate. More specifically, historic cost depreciation and inventory accounting rules reduce substantially the real after-tax return on corporate investments. An easy-money policy raises the demand for corporate investment only if the real net cost of funds falls by more than the return that firms can afford to pay. This balance between the lower real net interest cost and the lower real net return on investment depends on the corporation's debt-equity ratio and on the relation between the real yields that must be paid on debt and on equity funds.

Although it is difficult to say just what has happened on balance, my current view is that expansionary monetary policy reduced the demand for business investment at the same time that it increased the demand for residential investment and for consumption goods.

It is useful to contrast these conclusions with the conventional Keynesian wisdom. According to the traditional view, monetary expansion lowers interest rates which reduces the cost of funds to investors and therefore encourages the accumulation of plant and equipment. In the context of the U.S. economy in recent years, this statement is wrong in three ways.

First, a sustained monetary expansion raises nominal interest rates. Second, although the interest rate is higher, the real net-of-tax cost of funds is lower. And, third, the lower cost of funds produced in this way encourages investment in housing and consumer durables (as well as greater consumption in general) rather than more invest-ment in plant and equipment. Indeed, because of the interaction of tax rules and inflation, a monetary expansion tends to discourage savings and reduce investment in plant and equipment. The low real net-of-tax rate of interest on mortgages and consumer credit is an indication of this misallocation of capital.

FOCUS ON THE MONEY SUPPLY

Perhaps the problems of misinterpretation and mismanagement might have been avoided completely if the monetary authorities and others in the financial community, as well as the Congress and the economics profession, had ignored interest rates completely and focused their attention on the money supply and the credit aggre-gates. Presumably, since the Fed's October 6 announcement, there will be more of a tendency to do just that.

But since the temptation to look at rates as well is very powerful, it is important to interpret the rates correctly. What matters for the household borrower or saver is the real net-of-tax interest rate. A very low or negative real net-of-tax rate is a clear signal of an incen-tive to overspend on housing and on other forms of consumption. What matters for the business firm is the difference between the real net-of-tax cost of funds and the maximum return that, with existing tax laws, it can afford to pay. The difficulty of measuring this difference should be a warning against relying on any observed rates to judge the ease and tightness of credit for business invest-ment.

Inflation will only be tamed by a consistent policy of tight money. The record so far this year has been encouraging. The Fed seems prepared to let interest rates adjust freely while it pursues a policy of gradual monetary deceleration. Congress and the administration did not rebel in response to the sharp rise in rates.

The major test of everyone's steadfastness will be faced as the recession becomes more clearly established. There will be pressure from some to ease money now in order to shorten the recession. An even more important test will come when the recovery begins and interest rates are carried up. The Fed will then be called upon to accelerate monetary growth and keep interest rates from rising. Both types of pressure must be resisted. What is needed is a long-term commitment by the Fed to pursue the current policy until inflation is eliminated, and enough political courage in the Congress and the administration to let the Fed do it.

America's New Financial Structure

Business Week

In the opening selection of this part on monetary policy, it was argued that credit rationing had played an important role in the impact of monetary policy. The next selection describes the Monetary Control Act of 1980 and predicts some of its effects. Business Week argues that monetary policy will be easier to operate as a result of the Act, but others are not so sure. Variations in the money supply may have larger or smaller effects on spending after regulation 2 is lifted. The results are uncertain. It is certain that greater volubility of interest rates is one result of the changes in financial structure.

THE FACE OF United States finance is changing at breakneck speed, turning topsy-turvy the timeworn precepts about what constitutes a bank and a thrift institution, the financial services each can offer, and where each can do business. In a matter of a few years, there will be far fewer financial institutions operating in the United States than the 40,000 existing today, and those remaining will deliver services to consumers and corporations more efficiently. The credit markets will operate more smoothly in feeding capital to the economy, and the Federal Reserve Board's job of monetary control will be made easier. Innovation will be the hallmark of success, and the small bank could well become as endangered a species as the family farm.

And if this prediction has been made often in recent years, the revolution in finance is now finally under way, helped along by the most sweeping piece of financial legislation in United States history, the Depository Institutions Deregulation and Monetary Control Act of 1980, which Congress passed last March.

WHAT THE MONETARY CONTROL ACT DOES

• The Federal Reserve will set new—and lower—reserve requirements for all commercial banks, savings banks, and savings and loan associations, instead of just for Fed member banks. These will be phased in over three years for member banks, seven years for other institutions. The Fed also becomes lender of last resort for all 40,000 depository institutions.

• All depository institutions can offer interest-bearing checking accounts, or negotiable order of withdrawal (NOW) accounts, after January 1, 1981, with an initial maximum interest rate of 5¼ percent. Such accounts are now available only in New England, New York, and New Jersey, and the maximum rate is 5 percent.

• All deposit interest ceilings, including the Fed's Regulation Q, will be phased out over six years.

• Federally chartered savings and loan associations and savings banks gain new lending and investing powers after January 1, 1981, enabling them to make more consumer loans, offer credit cards, and invest in commercial paper and corporate debt.

• State usury laws governing certain loans are wiped out for three years—by which time states are supposed to raise outdated borrowing rate ceilings.

A WIDER, BUT LOOSER NET

Major elements of the law are already beginning to fall into place, and by the mid-1980s, most of the law's effects will have been felt. The Monetary Control Act sets a gradual elimination of controls on prices—interest rates—in the banking industry, and gives traditional mortgage lenders new powers, including limited powers to lend to business. In addition, it brings all financial institutions under a wider, but looser supervisory net, with vast new regulatory powers for the Federal Reserve. Paralleling deregulation in most transportation and energy industries, the legislation guarantees a ferociously competitive environment by lifting price controls for all financial institutions. But the effect of financial deregulation on the United States economy will be more pervasive because it is certain to touch the change purses and cash drawers of every individual and corporation in the land.

The upheaval facing financial institutions, emanating mostly, not not totally, from the 1980 law, will bring:

• "True cost" banking requiring consumers and corporations to pay higher borrowing costs, but a more efficient way of providing money to borrowers.

• Higher mortgage rates, but a wider selection of mortgage instruments from which to choose.

• Higher rates paid on checking and savings deposits of consumers, with all institutions free to pay what they wish by 1986 at the latest, when all interest-rate ceilings die.

• Less differentiation between commercial banks and thrift institutions.

• "One-stop" banking for consumers and, ultimately, for corporations.

• Less market segmentation in types of services offered, although some institutions may be forced to "specialize" in order to survive.

• Less geographic segmentation as electronic funds transfer makes money move across today's arbitrary barriers. Eventually, the reality of the marketplace and the tendency toward "federalization" of regulatory oversight will hasten the adoption of some form of interstate banking in the United States.

• More conflict among depository institutions and such nonbanking interlopers as Merrill Lynch, Sears Roebuck, and American Express, with depository institutions struggling to retain market share.

When all this falls into place—in a decade or so—the nation's financial system not only will look vastly different than it does today but also will work better in terms of collecting and distributing capital. And because it will work better and more efficiently, the United States economy will be easier to manage. Today's system embraces 40,000 depository institutions—commercial banks, savings banks, savings and loan associations, and credit unions—all operating under rules that are at best archaic and at worst punitive. The system features $100 billion banks and $100,000 credit unions, sometimes competing for the same customers. It is not only an inefficient system, but a dangerous one. It includes so many weak fish that a sustained and aggressive anti-inflation policy by the Federal Reserve could bring hundreds of institutions to their knees.

A decade from now, the 40,000 institutions may be winnowed to half that number, or fewer, and only a few hundred will really count. Yet, because the coming changes will be so sweeping, the decade ahead figures to produce turmoil in the financial system on a monumental scale—a rough time to live through before the good times come.

SLUGGING IT OUT FIRST

In terms of casualties, the next decade could be the bloodiest period experienced by financial institutions since the Great Depression, with banks and thrifts slugging it out among themselves and against nonbank giants. Financial institutions will be operating by a whole new set of rules on a "level playing field," but interpretation of the rules will vary so widely that even the umpires—the regulators—will have a difficult time keeping the peace. The aggressive pursuit of new territory and new business by the most innovative institutions is certain to prompt court challenges, while financially strained institutions will be begging for protection from the regulators. By the time the decade is out, a final showdown over the prohibition on interstate banking will occur. Only then will it be possible to have a homogeneous banking system, rather than a fragmented and inefficient collection of financial institutions. But because it will tear at a basic tenet of states' rights, the fight over interstate banking could be the roughest of all.

The coming struggle will further precipitate "more interest-rate volatility than stability," says Henry Kaufman, partner and member of the executive committee of Salomon Brothers. Local regional pockets of savings will disappear, as all financial institutions are drawn into a "national competition for the pool of funds," Kaufman says. On the other hand, all forms of credit will be available in a more homogeneous, national market, in much the same way as a national securities market developed for housing. "We will have national financial institutions," says Kaufman. Virtually all observers agree that the ability of the new financial system to generate credit and meet credit demands will be enhanced, because the system will consist of big, nationwide, all-purpose institutions.

Commercial banks, savings and loan associations, savings banks, and credit unions all are affected by the law. When they begin to feel the pain of competing in a deregulated environment, some of the smaller institutions, by choice or necessity, will be swallowed up by the larger and stronger ones.

SEVERE STRAINS LED TO DECONTROL

Banks and thrifts for so long have operated under a crazy quilt of regulations and have been subjected to the conflicting jurisdiction of state and federal regulators that market segmentation and eccentric institutions are now endemic to the system. Severe pressures on financial institutions, emanating from high inflation and high interest rates, hastened the adoption of decontrol. By last March, when the legislation was passed and signed into law, the Federal Reserve Board's anti-inflation fight had been complicated by its weakened control over financial institutions, small savers had seen market rates of interest rocket past the meager rates they were receiving on passbook accounts, and the prime lending rate was headed for 20 percent. If these circumstances had not prevailed, says Thomas I. Storrs, chairman of North Carolina National Bank and NCNB Corporation, "I question whether the act would have passed."

High interest rates in the money markets bleed the thrifts—savings and loan associations and savings banks—which borrow short and lend long to an even greater extent than do commercial banks. Hobbled by the Fed's Regulation Q, which set interest-rate ceilings well below market rates on savings deposits, banks and thrifts have been unable to compete with the likes of Merrill Lynch Ready Assets Trust Fund and other money-market mutual funds. Although regulators had begun to chip away at these constraints prior to the law's passage, they failed to stanch the outflow of deposits. To compound the problem, nonbanking institutions came up with innovations that stole away business from the banking system, and ever-rapacious foreign banks continued to offer cut-rate loans to United States corporations and to move into areas off limits to United States banks by branching across state lines while domestic banks could not.

The Monetary Control Act has endorsed deregulation, and industry sources say it is only a matter of time before geographic and other remaining constraints are lifted, paving the way for legitimate national banking. Indeed, the actions of institutions like Citicorp, whose geographic reach exceeds its legal grasp, may force regulators and legislators to play catch-up once again with reality.

While the panoply of deregulation will not hit financial institutions in one fell swoop, some elements will be felt more keenly than others at the start. Of immediate significance to financial institutions and their customers will be the nationwide adoption of NOW accounts and the new commercial-bank-type consumer-lending powers allowed the thrifts, both occurring at the start of 1981. It is in these areas that "cost shock" will be felt soonest and hardest—obliging the smaller fish either to match what giant institutions pay for those deposits or to risk seeing their deposits drain away.

FAR-REACHING EFFECTS—BY 1985

The ultimate elimination of interest-rate ceilings will not be felt by the credit markets until the middle of the decade, but then it could have far reaching effects—making competition for funds that much more intense. And compete for deposits these institutions will—wherever the law will allow it.

Consumer deposits have traditionally been a cheap and stable source of funds for the banking business. But the grab that money-market mutual funds are making for some of that money has put the banks on notice, and giant bank holding companies such as Citicorp are already looking beyond their home markets to build a deposit base. In October, Citicorp's effort to tap consumer savings away from its home base of New York, through a Maryland credit-card subsidiary, was put on hold by the Federal Reserve Board. Citicorp has said it will seek a reversal of the Fed's ruling, which was based on a strict interpretation of what are permissible activities for bank holding companies. But the drive by large banking organizations to move into new areas—in search of deposits and of customers—through the use of electronic banking or credit cards is well recognized by regulators. Says Fed Vice-Chairman Frederick H. Schultz: "Citicorp is telling you something when you see the emphasis they're putting on this area."

By law, NOW accounts can be offered as of January 1, 1981—but only to individuals and nonprofit corporations. Business still will be left out by the rule against paying interest on demand deposits, and corporations will have to rely even more heavily on putting funds into money markets both here and in the Euromarkets overseas to get a fair return. But the shortest-term deposits on which banks can pay interest. That still will not match the Eurodollar market, where even overnight deposits earn interest, but it could attract more corporate deposits to the banks.

Once-cheap consumer deposits are going to become more expensive and precious for depository institutions to maintain as the bidding war for such deposits heats up. To compensate institutions will have to price NOWs sufficiently high to avoid losing money on the product. Most will require minimum balances and impose usage or per-check charges. All institutions that hope to survive will have to slug it out for these deposits. Corporate funds can go abroad, but consumer funds will stay home, and the only question is, who gets them.

At stake is control of nearly $1 trillion dollars in consumer deposits—both demand and time deposits. Kenneth J. Thygerson, chief economist for the United States League of Savings Associations, expects thrifts to price NOW accounts more aggressively than banks will. The banks, he argues, "only have to retain an existing deposit and consumer base." But the thrifts are hoping to attract new deposits, and so "can afford to be more aggressive in their pricing," Thygerson says.

BLURRING DISTINCTIONS

Indeed, some of the major California savings and loan associations have already announced their pricing schemes, and a few are willing to treat NOW accounts as loss leaders, at least initially. In September, Allstate Savings and Loan, a subsidiary of Sears, Roebuck & Company announced a charge-free account with a $500 minimum balance or $3,000 in savings, and it has already signed up 3,000 NOW accounts. After attracting new checking customers, Allstate hopes to hold onto these customers by offering some of the new consumer loans that customers would ordinarily get from a commercial bank.

Under the 1980 law, thrifts can offer credit cards and make more—and more varied—consumer loans. "I'm going to give you a little lower rate on a car loan and get you out of Bank of America," says one California savings and loan association official. "And once I get you, I'm going to keep you—I'm going to get everything you have away from Bank of America," he adds.

But George M. Salem, analyst at Bache Halsey Stuart Shields Inc., notes that in the aggregate, consumer time and demand deposits at the thrifts exceed those at commercial banks. "One of the largest competitive battles in the history of consumer banking is about to begin," Salem argues. "The entire customer relationship is at stake."

For the majority of commercial banks, thrift challenges to steal away their retail lending business are going to be worrisome. More than 12,000 of the nation's commercial banks have deposits of $100 million or less, and many are located in states where thrifts have muscle and will be able to branch more readily as of next year. Says one banking industry source: "There's going to be significant pressure on the commercial banks to rethink the attractiveness of home mortgage lending."

Actually, all the distinctions between commercial banks and thrifts will become increasingly muddied as a result of the 1980 legislation. Jonathan E. Gray, savings and loan industry analyst at Sanford C. Bernstein & Company, calls the banks and thrifts of the future "thanks and brifts."

One banking source says he wouldn't be surprised if, within a couple of years, "savings and loan associations will be clamoring to become members of the American Bankers Association and become known as full-service banks."

With savings and loan associations enjoying more commercial bank lending powers, as legislated by the Monetary Control Act, the fate of housing—an industry that has been financed largely by the thrifts—may be called into question. Housing money, says Thygerson, "will be available, but on terms quite a bit different from the past. Rates will be generally higher, but more than that, as an outgrowth of the new liabilities, we will see changes in the mortgage contract that make it a better hedge." A slew of new mortgage instruments are now being introduced to home buyers.

The gradual elimination of Regulation Q ceilings altogether, combined with the nationwide adoption of NOW accounts, is certain to raise operational costs for all institutions. "But it was time to do away with artificial rate limitations," says Richard K. Yowell, president of Second National Bank in Culpeper, Virginia. After years of "subsidizing home-buyers at the expense of savers," says Yowell, lending institutions will have to compensate by "subsidizing savers at the expense of home buyers." Because of this, mortgage rates are destined to remain high, Yowell warns.

In a world without Regulation Q ceilings, says Jerry L. Jordan, dean of the Anderson Schools of Management at the University of New Mexico, the planning process at financial institutions will have to undergo radical change. Bankers will have to realize that "no one is designing their deposits for them," Jordan says. Small commercial banks and thrifts around the country will be faced with the tough task of managing interest-rate-sensitive assets, or loans, and liabilities, or deposits, just as the large money-center banks have been doing for some time, with varying degrees of success.

PART FIVE   Stabilization Policy:
Its Record and Effectiveness

Anti-Recession Policies

GEORGE L. PERRY

The set of readings in this Part Five considers the record of macro-economic policy since World War II and whether or not active attempts to stabilize economic activity are warranted. George Perry thinks that policy does have an important role to play, especially in counteracting recessions. In the next selection, he reviews the record of fiscal and monetary policy over the post-World War II period. Perhaps the most important instrument of fiscal stabilization has been the automatic stabilizers, and Perry starts by reviewing their role. But his main emphasis is on the active policy measures taken to fight recession. He finds that policy was generally contractionary in the year leading up to a business-cycle peak, neutral in the peak to trough period, and expansionary after the trough. If the goal is stabilization—levelling off the peaks and aiding recovery in the troughs—this record looks pretty good. Perry faults policy, however, for curbing the rapid growth experienced in the run-up and for acting slowly to reduce unemployment as recessions developed.

THE RECORD OF FISCAL POLICY

FISCAL POLICY REFERS TO changes in taxes and expenditures as they affect the level of total demand in the economy. To examine historical experience with fiscal policy, a quantitative characterization of it is needed. It has long been recognized that changes in taxes and expenditures, and thus in the surplus or deficit,[1] come about from two causes: first, deliberate changes in tax rates and expenditure policies made by Congress and the president; and sec-

---

1. From here on, the term surplus will be used with the understanding that it can be negative and hence a deficit.

ond, the "automatic" changes in taxes and expenditures brought about, under unchanged policies, by variations in the level of economic activity. During recession, personal income and corporate profits are depressed, lowering the tax base and reducing revenues from their normal levels. At the same time, unemployment compensation and other transfer payments are enlarged, raising the level of expenditures above normal.

These induced changes in the budget are called automatic stabilizers and help level off swings in economic activity. Because the federal budget shares in the ups and downs of private incomes, the swings in private demand for goods and services are moderated, thus automatically restraining the swings in economic activity. The importance of automatic stabilizers can be seen from their operation in the recent recession. In the first quarter of 1975, before the antirecessionary tax rebates and tax cuts took effect, the budget deficit was $57 billion larger than it would have been with unemployment rates, incomes, and profits at pre-recession levels. If private incomes and profits had instead been depressed by this $57 billion, private demand would have been weaker and the recession much worse.

THE HIGH EMPLOYMENT SURPLUS

The induced changes are passive changes, responding to economic conditions, rather than active changes that cause movements in the economy. To get an indicator of fiscal policy that measures the active influence of the budget on the economy, revenues, expenditures, and the surplus in the budget calculated at some standardized level of economic activity are estimated. The most widely used indicator is the high employment surplus in the budget—the surplus that would prevail with the economy operating with a 4 percent unemployment rate. The choice of 4 percent is historical convention. A surplus calculated at any other constant level would do just as well.

To directly compare policies in different periods, the ratio of the high employment surplus to high employment gross national product is used and will be referred to as the potential surplus ratio. At any one time, this potential surplus ratio conveys the same information as the high employment surplus itself, and it keeps comparisons among different periods from being distorted by the growth of GNP.

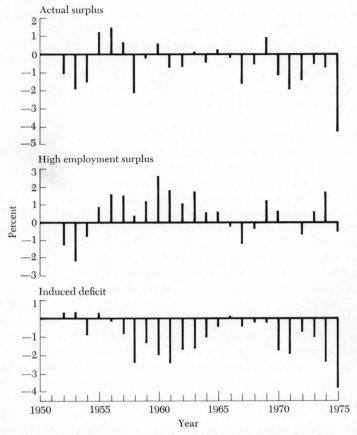

Actual and High Employment Budget Surplus and Induced Deficit as Percentages of Potential GNP, Fiscal Years 1952–75
SOURCES: Actual surplus, COMETS data bank; other data, Council of Economic Advisers.

The figure depicts the potential surplus ratio and the ratio of the actual surplus to potential GNP for fiscal years 1952–75. The difference between the two in any year, which is shown in the bottom part of the figure, measures the relative size of the surplus or deficit that is induced by deviations in actual economic activity from the high-employment path. As the figure shows, recessions generate large deficits. In 1975, that part of the deficit induced by recession was nearly 4 percent of potential GNP.

No level of the potential surplus ratio is "correct" for all time. The whole object of stabilization policy is to offset variations in total demand that would move the economy from the desired level of activity. As for fiscal policy alone, if total demand threatens to be too strong for whatever reason, stabilizing the economy calls for increasing the high employment surplus; if total demand prospects look too weak, stabilization calls for reducing the high employment surplus.

The case having been made for using the high employment surplus as an indicator of fiscal policy, its limitations should be noted as well. As a measure of economic impact, it is imprecise in at least two important respects. The first is that it implicitly assigns the same weight to all forms of revenue and all forms of expenditure. A dollar reduction in personal or corporate income taxes moves the full employment surplus as much as a dollar increase in defense purchases, personal transfers, or increased grants to state and local governments. A precise analysis would distinguish among the economic impacts in these different cases. Standardized surpluses assigning individual economic impact weights to different types of revenues and expenditures have been calculated by Oakland and Gramlich, among others. These adjustments characteristically assign a full weight of 1.0 to federal purchases, with weights of about 0.9 for personal taxes and personal transfers. There is less agreement about the weighing appropriate to other expenditures and revenue categories. The second imprecision arises because the timing as well as the size of the economic impact will differ for various spending and revenue categories. In general, purchases have an immediate impact whereas other expenditure or revenue changes may have their full impact only after some delay. In the case of defense procurement, economic activity can even precede purchases in the budget, as contracts are let and suppliers start hiring, ordering, and producing before the receipt of payments from the government.

Finally, during periods of rapid inflation, the interpretation of increases in the potential surplus ratio as deliberate fiscal policy actions differs slightly from that in noninflationary times. Inflation raises federal revenues more rapidly than expenditures. The consequent increase in the potential surplus ratio comes about not because of deliberate budget changes but because of rising prices and incomes. Interpreting this as a restrictive move in fiscal policy does make sense. Permitting the potential surplus ratio to rise from zero in the first quarter of 1973 to 2.1 percent in the third quarter of 1974 clearly reflected the administration's belief that fiscal restriction was desirable.

FISCAL POLICY IN RECESSION

Anti-recession action has been a widely accepted priority in stabilization policy. This meant trying to avoid recessions, limiting their severity if they occurred, and promoting recovery from recession so as to restore high employment levels. This commitment to avoiding or minimizing the downward swings of the business cycle makes periods of recession and recovery a natural center for an analysis of fiscal policy.

The three columns in Table 1 give changes in the surplus ratio for three intervals: in the four quarters leading up to the cyclical peak, between the peak and the trough of the recession, and in the first four quarters of recovery from the trough. As the signs on the changes have been reversed, a restrictive policy is shown as a negative change. The values shown are averages of the ratio over the four quarters ending in the quarter shown; this averaging blurs the effect of current policy changes, but also reduces the possibility of erratic

TABLE 1. *Fiscal Policy as Measured by Full-Employment Surplus Ratios, Five Recessions, 1953–75*

		Quarters from peak (P) or trough (T)		
		$P-4$ to P	P to T	T to T$+4$
Peak	Trough	Changes in full-employment surplus ratios (percentage points, sign reversed)[a]		
1953:Q2	1954:Q2	0.8[b]	−0.4	−2.0
1957:Q3	1958:Q1	0.0	0.0	1.2
1960:Q1	1960:Q4	−1.5	−0.9	0.8
1969:Q3	1970:Q4	−1.8	0.4	0.6
1973:Q4	1975:Q1	−1.2	−1.1	1.5[c]

SOURCE: Calculated from full-employment GNP and full-employment surplus series provided by the Council of Economic Advisers.

[a] A positive change is stimulative, a negative change restrictive; thus a change to a higher potential surplus ratio is shown as a minus.

[b] Change from quarter $P-2$.

[c] Change through quarter $T+2$.

quarterly movements distorting the true ongoing thrust of policy. Because the four-quarter average builds in a lag and there is some lag in the response of the economy to fiscal changes, it should also come closer to measuring the economic impact of the budget in the quarter shown.

In interpreting the magnitude of the changes shown a reduction of 1 percent in the surplus ratio—which would be a positive change of 1.0 in the table—can be thought of as roughly equivalent to a $17 billion tax reduction in today's economy. To give an idea of which changes are "significant" compared to the normal variability in the potential surplus ratios, changes greater than one standard deviation are shown in bold type.[2] Over the 1953–75 period, one standard deviation was 1.2 percent of potential GNP for the changes in the top half of the table and 0.9 percent for the changes in the bottom half. A restrictive change this large or larger occurs in about one-sixth of all quarters.

The most striking finding from Table 1 is that fiscal policy has contributed to the last three recessions. In each case, the surplus ratio grew substantially in the four quarters leading up to the downturn in business activity, using either the current or moving average measure of fiscal policy. Only in the quarters leading up to the 1953–54 recession was policy moving in a stimulative direction. And that was fortuitous, resulting entirely from the boom in Korean War spending. On that occasion, the decline from the spending crest coincided with the onset of recession. The drop in defense orders preceded it and helped bring on the economic downturn.

Policy was only a little more timely once the economy actually headed into recession. The current-quarter surplus ratios in the top half of the table show fiscal policy growing quite restrictive between the peak and trough of the 1953–54 recession, doing nothing in 1973–75, and becoming slightly more expansionary in the other three cases. Only in the 1969–70 downturn had policy become even moderately more supportive between the peak and trough of business activity. In the recessions of both 1960–61 and 1973–75, this averaged mea-

2. One standard deviation is a number that statistically measures the variability in a series. If their signs are ignored, approximately two-thirds of all quarterly changes in the 1953–75 period will be smaller than that number and one-third will be larger. The third that is larger will in turn be approximately divided into half restrictive and half stimulative changes.

sure of fiscal policy grew markedly more restrictive right through the worst of the economic downturn.

Policy usually got going the right way by the end of the recession. Only in 1954 did the surplus ratio grow in the four quarters following the trough in business activity. Here the conclusion is much the same with either the current-quarter or moving-average measure of fiscal action.

Before the recessions in 1957, 1969, and 1973, inflation complicated fiscal policymaking. Indeed, in 1969, taxes had only recently been increased to cool off an economy overheated by the Vietnam War. And in both 1969 and 1953, the aim of policy was probably a modest increase in unemployment from the very low levels that had been reached in the two wars. Only in 1960 did policymakers muff the stabilization job completely, bringing on a downturn when no conflict of goals complicated the outlook. But the other recessions give warning that, so long as policy must rely on restricting aggregate demand to slow inflation, it seems likely to push the economy toward recession in the process.

THE RECORD OF MONETARY POLICY

Monetary policy is the second major instrument for influencing total demand in the economy. Fiscal and monetary policy affect GNP independently and can either complement or substitute for each other. If differences in timing, which point to somewhat prompter effects from most fiscal policy changes, are ignored, the same overall economic impact could be achieved with either a combination of tight fiscal policy and easy monetary policy or one of easy fiscal policy and tight monetary policy. The former would involve relatively large high employment surpluses and would require lower interest rates and, for a time, more rapid money supply growth on the part of monetary policy; the latter would involve relatively small high employment surpluses and would require higher interest rates and slower money-supply growth. In other words, to achieve any given GNP target, a tight fiscal policy would require an easy monetary policy, which would include both lower interest rates at the target GNP level and faster money supply growth until the target was achieved.

Important as it is, monetary policy is a surprisingly elusive subject. The trouble begins when a simple way is sought to characterize it. The layman, people in the financial community, and many economists would characterize it by the level of interest rates. Many other economists, a group including but by no means limited to those loosely thought of as monetarists, would characterize it by the growth rate in the money supply.[3] The trouble arises because money, interest rates, and GNP are interrelated. The less money is supplied for a given GNP, the higher interest rates will be. The higher GNP is for a given interest rate, the more money will be demanded. And the higher GNP is with a given money supply, the higher interest rates will be.

The level of interest rates affects total private demand and thus the level of GNP. Higher interest rates especially discourage demand that depends directly on borrowing, such as the demand for consumer durable goods, business investment, and housing. The effect on housing is particularly severe because high interest rates drain funds from the primary source of mortgage loans—the thrift institutions—which cannot raise the rates they pay depositors to competitive levels. High interest rates may also influence demand less directly by reducing the net value of private wealth.

Because the impact of monetary policy on economic activity works primarily through interest rates and their effect on total spending, it may seem natural to use interest rates to characterize policy. For all practical purposes, the Federal Reserve can directly affect some rates and through them influence others. It pegged rates at low levels through World War II and the immediate postwar years. Then, in 1951, it reached an accord with the Treasury to stop doing so to allow freedom for countercyclical action. However, because interest rates are so sensitive to economic activity, it is not very useful to label all of their rise and fall over the business cycle as discretionary monetary policy, even if the movements are, in principle, controllable by the Federal Reserve. By analogy with the high employment surplus, one might estimate a high employment interest rate to

3. The money supply is defined as the sum of currency and demand deposits. When the discussion starts getting technical, interest-bearing time deposits are sometimes added to this to provide an alternative version of "money." Some would go further, adding savings and loan shares and so on, each addition to the total representing a close substitute for the one before it. Others would back up and analyze bank reserves since they are directly controllable by the Federal Reserve and come close to defining how large the money supply will be.

characterize monetary policy (that is, the interest rate that would be generated by the actual money supply and a high employment GNP). Actual movements in the interest rate above and below its high employment level could then be treated as an automatic stabilizer. But the monetary relationships among the money supply, GNP, and interest rates necessary for such a calculation are not very reliable, and it has not been pursued.

Many economists opt for characterizing monetary policy by the rate of growth of the money supply on the grounds that this ulti- mately will determine the growth rate of GNP. Since the demand for money is related to GNP, if GNP is "too high," money demand will run ahead of supply and interest rates will rise, bringing GNP down to where the demand for money equals the supply. But there is a good deal of professional controversy over the stability of this ultimate link of GNP to the money supply, and even more contro- versy over the strength of this link in the short run.

A further difficulty in characterizing policy arises from inflation. As the demand for money grows with the price level, the rate of money growth must be discounted by the inflation rate to get the growth rate in the real money supply, the measure that is relevant to real economic activity. Four percent money growth might be expansionary with a stable price level. But if prices are rising at 6 percent a year and if that price increase is not very sensitive to short-run variations in the level of economic activity, a 4 percent money growth unavoidably leads to a decline in the real money sup- ply of 2 percent a year. Simply characterizing policy by the real money supply, however, leads to the definition that policy is neutral when it is providing for normal real growth in the economy plus fully accommodating whatever ongoing rate of inflation exists. This is correct if real output is the only object of policy. But the definition is arguable if slowing inflation is a policy objective as well, especially if the inflation arises from excess demand. With no totally accept- able answer to all these questions, both real and nominal money growth rates will be examined in viewing the performance of mon- etary policy.[4]

A final complication arises because of the lags between monetary

4. In the paper from which this extract is drawn, Perry also considers interest rate movements. Because of the difficulty of interpretation we have omitted this material. (Editors)

TABLE 2. *Monetary Policy as Measured by Money Supply and Treasury Bill Rates for Five Recessions, 1953–75*

| | | Quarters from peak (P) or trough (T) | | |
| | | P − 4 to P | P to T | T to T + 4 |
Peak	Trough	Change in nominal money supply growth (annual percentage points)		
1953:Q2	1954:Q2	−2.1	−2.4	3.0
1957:Q3	1958:Q1	−0.1	−1.3	5.3
1960:Q1	1960:Q4	−4.4	0.1	2.4
1969:Q3	1970:Q4	−1.2[a]	−0.8	1.7
1973:Q4	1975:Q1	−2.1	−2.4	1.2
		Changes in real money supply growth		
1953:Q2	1954:Q2	−3.3	−1.8	2.8
1957:Q3	1958:Q1	0.0	0.0	5.4
1960:Q1	1960:Q4	−4.8	0.9	2.8
1969:Q3	1970:Q4	−1.9[a]	−0.5	2.0
1973:Q4	1975:Q1	−5.1	−5.8	6.4

SOURCES: Calculated from data on money supply and Treasury bill rates from Federal Reserve Bulletin, various issues, and the official gross domestic product deflator from COMETS data bank.

[a] In the paper from which extract is drawn, Perry explains that some slowdown in the growth rate of money should be associated simply with the slowdown in potential GNP growth. The $P − 4$ to P figures for the 1969–70 recession are adjusted on this account (0.2 has been added to both values). (*Editor*)

policy and its effects on economic activity and because brief variations in money growth rates are of little importance. For the present purpose, policy in a given quarter will be characterized by money growth rates in the four quarters ending with the given quarter, which both allows for some lags and smooths erratic movements.

MONETARY POLICY IN RECESSION

In Table 2 monetary policy around the last five post-Korean recessions is characterized in two ways. The table shows measures based on the nominal and the real money supply. The three columns give changes in the money growth rate for different intervals around recessions.[5] These changes are most relevant if one believes that accelerations or decelerations in money are what matter, as

5. The following example illustrates how the data in the table were computed. In 1952:.2 (a P - 4 quarter), the nominal money supply was 5.2 percent above its value in the same quarter of 1951. In 1953:Q2 (a P quarter) the money supply was only 3.1 percent above the level of 1952:.2. Thus, the slowdown in money growth was 5.2 − 3.1 = 2.1 percentage points. This is the figure at the top of column one.

opposed to departures from some fixed norm for money growth.

As with the earlier analysis of fiscal policy, it is useful to have some idea of variability in the monetary measures against which to 4b1judge their movements around recessions. For the changes shown, the standard deviations are 2.2 and 3.0 for money and real money, respectively.[6] Changes larger than these standard deviations are shown in bold type in the table. Of these, changes larger than one standard deviation can be expected in about one-sixth of all the post-war quarters. They can be thought of as "significantly" large movements in monetary policy.

The slowdowns in growth rates of the real money supply (lower half of table) show a clear, if imperfect, relation to recessions. The growth rate had slowed noticeably at all peaks except 1957, with only the 1969 slowdown smaller than one standard deviation in this measure.

Policy did not usually move decisively against recession even after it started. In three recessions, real money growth slowed between the peak and trough (P to T).

Around the 1957, 1969, and 1973 recessions, monetary policy was faced with the same conflict between goals for unemployment and price stability as faced fiscal policy. Monetary policy has no special power to control inflation other than by affecting aggregate demand. It thus runs the same risks of causing recession when it becomes restrictive and of worsening inflation should it become stimulative when demand is already too strong.

Slowdowns in nominal money growth (upper half of Table 2) are related to recessions, though not as strongly as the corresponding slowdowns in real money growth already discussed.

CONCLUSION

Most postwar recessions have been associated with a restrictive fiscal policy, a tight or tightening monetary policy, or both. These restrictive moves usually reflected the desire of policymakers to slow inflation. Today, stabilization policy is more difficult because of the persistence of inflation accompanied by excess unemployment and underutilized capacity.

6. See footnote 2 for a reminder of the meaning of standard deviation.

Rational Expectations

BENNETT T. MC CALLUM

The monetarist views of Milton Friedman follow two lines. The first is that monetary rather than fiscal policy is of primary importance in determining the stability of the real economy in the short run and inflation in the longer run. Second, because the private economy is basically stable and because policymakers are inept or overly concerned with the next election, it is better to stick to a constant growth rate of money and not to try and stabilize output and employment.

A new critique of active stabilization policy, that is sympathetic to Friedman but goes far beyond his view, has been developed by rational expectations theorists. They argue that even monetary policy is powerless to alter real output and employment if that policy is anticipated. To the extent that the private sector forsees policy actions it will offset them. The following selection by Bennett McCallum describes the new ideas.

EVER SINCE THE "Keynesian Revolution" in the 1930s and 1940s, it has been widely agreed that a major responsibility of any national government is to utilize monetary and fiscal policy actively in an effort "to promote maximum employment, production, and purchasing power," as stated in the United States Employment Act of 1946. Most economists, in other words, have accepted what Franco Modigliani terms "the fundamental message of [Keynes's] *General Theory:* that a private enterprise economy using an intangible money *needs* to be stabilized, *can* be stabilized, and therefore *should* be stabilized by appropriate monetary and fiscal policies."

There have been recent developments in macroeconomic theory, however, that suggest that the activist stabilization policies favored by Keynesians will be unsuccessful—not because of inept behavior on the part of policymakers, but for more fundamental reasons.

These developments have resulted from a revised conception of the way in which individual economic agents—consumers, workers, and firms—form their expectations about future values of economic variables relevant for current behavior. The revised conception is usually referred to as the hypothesis of rational expectations.

EXPECTATIONAL BEHAVIOR

It is perhaps obvious that individual agents' expectations of future economic conditions are important determinants of their current choices. Thus, for example, firms may base the current month's employment decisions partly on product demand conditions expected to prevail next month (and/or in months following), while labor union leaders and firms are influenced at wage-negotiation time by the amount of inflation expected for the next year or two. Similarly, consumers will be more willing to borrow funds at a given rate of interest (say, 15 percent) in order to purchase durable goods if they expect 10 percent inflation over the next year, than they would be if they anticipated no inflation.

Furthermore, agents' expectations change from month to month and year to year as business conditions change. So for an economist's model—i.e., his view of the economy—not to be misleading, it must incorporate a representation of expectational behavior that is itself not flagrantly incorrect. This is, of course, as true for large quantitative models embodying sophisticated econometric research as it is for other types of models, formal or informal.

At present, however, virtually all econometric models used for macroeconomic forecasting and for governmental policymaking rely, often implicitly, on representations of expectational behavior that are naive in the extreme. In these models, expected future values of any given variable are usually taken to depend only on the past behavior of that single variable, and with a relationship that is assumed to be unchanging over time and unrelated either to market conditions or to policy stimuli. For example, the value of the consumer price index expected to prevail a month or a year hence is represented in such models as a particular weighted average or extrapolation of values of this index actually observed in recent months or years. The models ignore the fact that the government has recently taken policy actions which will certainly affect next month's value of this index. More generally, the type of expectational behavior assumed for agents in these models neglects various factors that (according to the models themselves) would be useful in forming expectations. So, within the models, agents' expectational *errors*—discrepancies between expected and actual values—are apt to be systematically related to past values of other variables or even the expectational variable itself.

Moreover, the same sort of extrapolative expectational relation is also present in most noneconometric models, formal or informal. Consequently, naive expectational behavior is implicitly assumed in most macroeconomic analyses and forecasts.

A drastically different view of expectational behavior is, however, rapidly winning support in the economics profession. This view, expressed as the hypothesis of *rational expectations*, presumes that individual economic agents use all available and relevant information in forming expectations and that they process this information in an intelligent fashion. It is important to recognize that this does not imply that consumers or firms have "perfect foresight" or that their expectations are always "correct." What it does suggest is that agents reflect upon past errors and, if necessary, revise their expectational behavior so as to eliminate regularities in these errors. Indeed, the hypothesis suggests that agents *succeed* in eliminating regularities involving expectational errors, so that the errors will on average be unrelated to available information. In statistical terms, the errors are assumed to be uncorrelated with known values of all relevant variables. Thus, according to the hypothesis, expectational errors may often be large, but will not be systematically related to variables observable at the time of expectation formation.

Although the rational expectations hypothesis (or more briefly, REH) has become rather widely accepted among leading economic theorists, many economists have failed to embrace the notion. The two most common objections voiced by critics of REH are: (1) it is unrealistic to assume that people or firms process information as intelligently as the hypothesis presumes; (2) it is also unrealistic to assume that agents use information on all relevant variables in forming expectations. The point of the second objection is that information collection is difficult and costly, so it must be unprofitable to obtain data on *every* relevant variable, since some will be of negligible value to the forming of expectations. But this point is not actually an objection to REH but rather to applications in which informational costs are neglected for the sake of simplicity. In fact, the point is entirely consistent with the basic idea behind REH: that expectations are formed optimally, that is, so as to equate marginal costs and benefits of expectational activities. The first point, however, is a genuine objection to the rationality hypothesis, not merely a misunderstanding. But it is an objection that seems poorly founded. All theories or models are "unrealistic" in the sense of being extremely simplified descriptions of reality; they must be simple to serve their purpose. Like a map, a useful theory reflects only the aspects of reality that are important for the purposes at hand. So the true issue is: of all the simple expectational assumptions conceivable, which one should be embodied in a macroeconomic model to be used for stabilization analysis? REH advocates contend that the assumption should avoid the implication that there are unexploited possibilities in the economy for huge speculative profits (this would be the implication if expectations were formed by naive extrapolations), since the actions of thousands of entrepreneurs seeking such profits should guarantee that sizable opportunities will soon be exploited. But the REH, by assuming that *all* possibilities are exploited, accomplishes precisely this in a reasonably simple way.

EVALUATING POLICY ALTERNATIVES

Let us now consider an implication of the rational expectations theory for the usefulness of macroeconomic models of the type mentioned above—i.e., models that embody the presumption that expectations are not rational. It is obvious that, if expectational behavior is incorrectly represented, these models will provide inaccurate forecasts of future business conditions that are not as accurate as they might be. But this criticism is mild in comparison to one, eloquently put forth by Lucas, which concerns the models' usefulness in formulating policy.

In order to choose among different policy rules—in other words, patterns of monetary and fiscal behavior to be followed for a number of periods—a policymaking body first uses its preferred model in simulation exercises that predict what outcomes would result from the adoption of the contending rules. Then, given the various hypothetical outcomes, the authority selects the rule that yields the outcome considered most desirable (or least undesirable) in terms of its implied values of GNP, unemployment, inflation, and so on, over the near future. This procedure, which may be extremely complex, was highly regarded by the economics profession only a few years ago. But if the rational expectations hypothesis is correct, the procedure cannot be fruitfully applied with existing models. For the REH asserts that consumers, workers, and firms will perceive what sort of policy is being followed and take the effects of this policy into account when forming expectations. Thus, for example, agents will expect more inflation in the near future, and consequently will *act* differently, if the policymakers are in fact pursuing an "expansionary" policy, than they would under a regime of austerity. But that implies that the types of models being discussed—in which agents' expectations are explicitly or implicitly treated as naive extrapolations of past actual values—will systematically fail to take proper account of policy rule changes. Accordingly, the models' predictions will be incorrect and the policymakers' choice among contending policy rules will be based on erroneous presumptions about the consequences of the various policies.

This point seems simple enough, but its implications for the econometric modeling "industry" are tremendous. To a large and increasing extent, macroeconomic forecasting in business and government as well as academic institutions, is based on large-scale formal econometric models that fail to take policy changes into account. Thus, as Lucas stressed, their usefulness in policymaking is entirely undermined. Despite resistance from proprietors and users of these models, existing models will almost certainly be revised or supplanted in policymaking and policy-evaluating organizations. This will probably bring about substantial changes in forecasting models as well, since most of the large-scale models are intended by their proprietors to serve as tools for both forecasting and policy simulation.

And the point is, as our previous discussion was designed to suggest, relevant not only for policymaking based on formal econometric models, but for policymaking based on *any* model—formal or informal—that treats expectations as being formed in an extrapolative, nonrational manner. Thus it is probably quite relevant to actual policy decisions of the fiscal and monetary authorities of the United States and other industrial countries. Indeed, this new view may play an important role in helping us to understand why recent macroeconomic policy has been so distressingly unsuccessful. In any event, its basic validity has been accepted even by economists who are unpersuaded by other applications of the rational expectations hypothesis.

POLICY IMPLICATIONS

The implications of the REH for the way in which models are used to formulate policy are important, but its implications for policy itself are even more dramatic. It is this area that many commentators have in mind when they speak of the "rational expectations revolution" in macroeconomics, and it derives essentially from combining the REH with a second, older hypothesis—the "natural rate hypothesis" (NRH)—that had been widely accepted before the notion of expectational rationality gained prominence.

NRH concerns the relation between unemployment (or deviations of real aggregate output from capacity levels) and inflation rates—the famous "Phillips curve." In his oft-cited 1967 presidential address to the American Economic Association, Milton Friedman argued convincingly that any stable Phillips-type equation for the labor market should relate unemployment not to the rate of change of nominal wages, but to the rate of change of real or price-deflated wages. To suppose otherwise would be to assume a form of "money illusion" that is inconsistent with traditional economic theory. Friedman's hypothesis, which was independently put forth by Edmund Phelps, seemed startling at the time but subsequent studies provided enough empirical support that by the mid-1970s the economics profession had been almost universally converted to the NRH.

In this context, the importance of expectations behavior results from the fact that most wage agreements are made in nominal, not real, terms. Since it is real wages that are of concern to employers and workers, they respond by evaluating contemplated increases in nominal wages in relation to *expected* increases in prices. Thus the basic relationship posited by Friedman and Phelps is between the level of unemployment—a measure of excess supply in the labor market—and the proportionate change in the nominal wage rate less the proportionate change in the price level expected for the upcoming period (in other words, the expected inflation rate). The relationship is, of course, negative: for a given expected inflation rate, the greater the rate of unemployment, the smaller the increase in the nominal wage. Since the unemployment rate is itself negatively related to the excess demand for labor, the Friedman-Phelps relation is simply a specific case of the venerable law of supply and demand, which states that the (real) price of a commodity will tend to rise when demand exceeds supply at the prevailing price.

To describe the role of the Friedman-Phelps equation in a macroeconomic model, it will be useful to combine it with two additional equations. For a given level of capacity, the first relates the unemployment (negatively) to the level of real output, and the other relates output, via the production function and the demand for labor, to the real wage rate (again, negatively). Together, these two equations imply that the real wage will be positively related to the unemployment rate and, consequently, that the (proportionate) change in the real wage will be positively related to the change in the unemployment rate. Then by eliminating the proportionate change in the nominal wage from this last relation and the Friedman-Phelps equation, we obtain a relationship involving the current and most recent values of the unemployment rate, and the difference between the actual and expected rates of inflation. Solving for the current unemployment rate, we find that its value in any period (say, a month) is partly determined by its own most recent value—a feature that will be mentioned again—and partly by the *difference between the actual and expected rates of inflation*, i.e., the expectational error for the inflation rate. The effect of the previous unemployment rate is positive and that of the expectational error is negative. The equation we have developed represents one version of the NRH. Its crucial characteristic, which macroeconomists have accepted with near unanimity, is that it relates unemployment only to the *unexpected* portion of the inflation rate. In a steady, expected inflation, unemployment would tend to its "natural" level.

There are other ways of deriving basically similar NRH relations. Indeed, the most influential papers in the rational expectations literature have taken an approach in which expectational errors refer to misperceptions by individuals of current macroeconomic variables (caused by incomplete information) rather than mistakes in anticipating future values. The approach used in this paper was chosen primarily for its comparative simplicity.

We now come to the most dramatic implication of the rational expectations hypothesis for macroeconomic policy. Clearly, our NRH equation says that monetary and fiscal policies can affect the evolution of the unemployment rate only if they affect the expectational error for the inflation rate. According to the REH, however, such policies can have no *systematic* effects on the latter: with expectational rationality this expectational error, like all others, is random and uncorrelated with past values of all relevant macroeconomic variables. But policies, to the extent that they are systematic, are simply rules relating current values of variables controllable by policymakers to observed (hence, past) values of relevant variables. Thus the REH implies that expectational errors must be uncorrelated with the systematic portion of all control variables, which eliminates the only available route for influencing unemployment. In short, since the Federal Reserve and the Treasury cannot induce systematic expectational errors, they cannot exert any systematic influence on the evolution of the unemployment rate.

It should be emphasized that the foregoing does not imply that the policymakers' *actions* have no influence; unsystematic or erratic behavior on their part will induce expectational errors and fluctuations in the unemployment rate. But macroeconomic *policies*—sustained patterns of action or reaction—will have no influence because they are perceived and taken into account by private decision-making agents. Thus the adoption of a policy to maintain "full employment" will not, according to the present argument, result in values of the unemployment rate that are smaller (or less variable) *on average* than those that would be experienced in the absence of such a policy.

It should also be said that the result refers only to macroeconomic policies; it does not claim that minimum wage laws, conscription, or other microeconomic arrangements fail to affect unemployment. But it is nevertheless a stunning result, one that provides theoretical support for the view that the monetary and fiscal policymakers should not attempt to engage in activist countercyclical policies of the type associated with the term "fine tuning." Instead, it suggests that the Federal Reserve and the Treasury should strive to eliminate unsystematic fluctuations in variables under their control, such as the money stock and the level of government spending, since such fluctuations induce expectational errors and thereby increase the variability of unemployment.

FOCUS ON INFLATION

I have described recent developments in macroeconomic theory which suggest that activist monetary and fiscal policies will tend to be unsuccessful in stabilizing employment. The suggestion is not only that current understanding of the economy is inadequate for effective design of such policies but, more basically, that the behavior over time of unemployment, output, and other "real" variables will be virtually independent of the authorities' policy-rule choices. Thus, the main systematic effects of these choices will be on "monetary" variables—in particular, the general price level and its rate of change, the inflation rate. The clear implication is that, if the rational expectations and natural rate hypotheses are correct, monetary and fiscal policies should be designed to yield the sequence of price levels (or inflation rates) that is regarded as most desirable. In other words, the Federal Reserve and the Treasury should concentrate their attention on the prevention or reduction (if such is desired) of inflation, not of unemployment. There is no point in focusing policy choices upon variables, no matter how great their intrinsic importance, that cannot be systematically affected by these choices.

The Effectiveness of Anticipated Policy

MARTIN NEIL BAILY

Rational expectations theorists argue that private economic decisions are altered when the decision-makers anticipate monetary and fiscal policy actions. Martin Baily agrees with this view, but suggests that the implication of it is not necessarily to offset systematic policy. He argues first that the economy has become much more stable since the advent of active stabilization policies. He then describes some changes in the response of the private sector to business-cycle fluctuations. These changes may actually assist the goals of policy by making the private economy itself more stable.

WILL THE INITIATION OF active macroeconomic stabilization policies change the behavior of the private sector? If so, what will these changes be? And what are their implications for the design and effectiveness of stabilization policy?

Whether people anticipate policy and whether this matters are widely debated questions at present. The underlying issue is whether the sum of individual actions serves to maximize welfare in the absence of coordinating actions from a central authority. If the only cause of the business cycle is surprise events and if the private economy can itself act quickly to restore full-employment equilibrium following any initial shock, then policy actions are probably at best unnecessary and at worst undesirable. In such a context, it is natural to think of the private sector acting to minimize the impact of policy, to counteract its intent, just as most people minimize their liability for income taxes.

Post-Keynesian models often cite random shocks as the initiators of the business cycle, but stress the inability of the private economy to restore full employment in the short run. In this context it is more natural to think of the private sector welcoming the impact of policy and perhaps even reinforcing its effects. Since the view of the business cycle taken here is in the post-Keynesian tradition, the conclusions, not surprisingly, differ from those derived from more classical assumptions.

The rationality of expectations is the aspect of recent classical models that has received the most attention. But other assumptions are more crucial to the findings about policy, and they are much harder to accept. In particular, flexibility of prices is required in order that equilibrium be restored quickly after some disturbance.[1] To the extent that stickiness of wages or prices is caused by illusion or arbitrariness, rational expectations should rule it out. However, recent theories of wage and price setting and long-standing theories of imperfect markets have provided at least the beginnings of a reconciliation of rationality and stickiness. The persistence of wage and price inflation through recessionary periods is a fact to which theory must adapt.

THE CLIMATE OF GREATER STABILITY

The Federal Deposit Insurance Corporation is a remarkable institution. Prior to its existence, bank failures and runs on banks were very common. Since it came into being it has rarely had to pay out. Other things have not been equal, of course, but the fact that deposits are insured changes the behavior of depositors in a way that induces greater stability in the banking system. Fears of a run on the bank can become self-fulfilling as depositors scramble to withdraw funds. Even if an individual knows for a fact that a bank is basically sound, he is not being irrational to hurry to the teller's window for his money once the rush starts.

The analogy to the existence of stabilization policy is not exact, but it has some validity. If everyone believes that major depression and runaway inflation can be controlled, these events become less likely. A recession will not induce the same panicky cutbacks in investment or employemnt; an inflation will not induce the same flight from money and financial assets.

Deposit insurance aims at averting bank failures, but stabilization policy attempts to go beyond this—to smooth output fluctuations. The more stable the economic environment the fewer the economic resources that have to be devoted to contingency planning, to

1. The concept of price flexibility has to be defined relative to some time period. It is asserted here that the price level (or the rate of inflation) responds so sluggishly when there is deficient aggregate demand that it would take several years for the economy to restore equilibrium on its own (even assuming there is a stable adjustment). This is a period long enough for policy to be effective.

adjusting schedules, and to designing for flexibility. For example, a production process that may be the least-cost one when operations are near capacity may be a very high-cost one when capacity is underutilized. Greater stability of demand then permits the use of the least-cost process. Furthermore, when private individuals are risk averse, stabilization yields a tremendous gain. If the overall economic environment can be made less uncertain, a general gain in welfare will result.

Is there any sign that stabilization policy has actually produced greater stability? The Employment Act of 1946 marked an important turning point. It expressed the political will to avoid recession or depression, and the Keynesian revolution in macroeconomic theory held that stabilization policy could be the instrument of that will. The figure simply plots the rate of growth of real gross national product for the period 1901–76 while Table 1 gives some means and standard deviations for the GNP gap, unemployment, and inflation. The broad outlines of the story are familiar. But the change in the

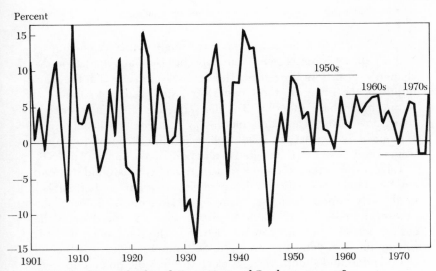

The Rate of Growth of Real Gross National Product, 1901–76
SOURCES: U.S. Bureau of the Census, *Historical Statistics of the United States: Colonial Times to 1970*, Pt. 1 (Government Printing Office, 1975), Series F3; *Economic Report of the President*, January 1977, p. 188; *Survey of Current Business*, vol. 57(July 1977), Table 1.2.

TABLE 1. *Variability of GNP, the Rate of Unemployment, and the Rate of Inflation, Selected Periods before and after 1946*

Period	GNP gap,[a] standard deviation	Unemployment rate		Inflation rate[b]	
		Mean	Standard deviation	Mean	Standard deviation
Before 1946					
1900–16, 1920–29	6.21	4.95	2.23	1.06	4.56
1920–41	12.99	11.52	7.59	−0.57	5.74
1900–45	13.58	7.77	6.51	1.86	6.11
After 1946					
1948–61	3.38	4.79	1.29	2.14	2.68
1962–73	2.46	4.74	0.88	3.37	1.84
1966–76	2.26	5.25	1.66	5.54	2.56
1946–76	3.56	4.95	1.34	3.84	3.60

SOURCE: U.S. Bureau of the Census, *Historical Statistics of the United States: Colonial Times to 1970*, Pt. 1 (Government Printing Office, 1975), Series F3, D9, D87, E135; *Economic Report of the President, January 1977*, pp. 188, 221, 242; *Survey of Current Business*, vol. 57 (July 1977), p. S-8 and Table 1.2.

[a] The GNP gap is defined as (GNP—trend GNP) / trend GNP, where trend GNP is computed from fitting a logarithmic time trend to GNP over the specific subperiod. Values are for real GNP.

[b] The inflation rate is measured by the consumer price index.

amplitude of cyclical fluctuations is surprisingly dramatic. The impact of the 1946 act is not seen immediately, but from about 1948 on the change is clear from the figure. The figure also reveals that the magnitude of the swings in the Great Depression were not so unusual as one might have thought. It is the sequence of three successive sharp downturns that marks off this period. Serious instability is evidenced even as late as 1946 itself, when the abrupt reduction in war-related expenditure resulted in a 12 percent decline in real GNP.

Table 1 shows that the standard deviation of GNP around its trend and the standard deviation of the unemployment rate are both higher in all early periods than they were in all later ones.[2] Some of the difference may be attributable to greater errors in the data for the earlier periods, but the general picture is the same even without relying on such data. For example, Schumpeter gives evidence of sharp booms and slumps going back all through the nineteenth century.[3] These swings appeared to last for several years and were not

2. The "standard deviation" is a measure of variability. The larger it is the more the particular series has fluctuated.

3. Joseph A. Schumpeter, *Business Cycles: A Theoretical, Historical, and Statistical Analysis of the Capitalist Process*, vols. 1 and 2 (McGraw-Hill, 1939).

perceived as uncorrelated movements around a full-employment equilibrium.

The rate of inflation, as measured by the consumer price index, has also varied less in the postwar period. But the average rate of inflation has been higher, especially in the years 1966–76. Price stability has not been achieved.

Table 1 and the figure give only crude evidence. But for what it is worth, it is consistent with the view that the Keynesian revolution taught us how to stabilize the real variables of output and unemployment but not how to combine low and stable unemployment with price stability. The same figures present a challenge to anyone trying to make the case that policy can and should control the price level, but has no influence on real variables.

It is important to make a full accounting of the changes that took place in the way economic policy is made. Before World War II it was thought that raising taxes to balance the budget in a recession and allowing "unsound" banks to fail were both neutral or laissez-faire policies. Understanding how to avoid destabilizing the economy and enacting social programs that automatically stabilized it were both at least as important as was learning how to use discretionary policy.

Finally, two qualifications are in order. First, the postwar period has not been uniformly stable. The erosion of confidence during 1973–75 was an important reversal of trend. Second, cyclical instability is by no means the only form of serious uncertainty for firms; shifts in comparative advantage are another. The point remains that one major source of instability has been ameliorated.

HOW HAS THE BUSINESS COMMUNITY REACTED TO THE CHANGED CLIMATE?

A review of the business press from 1946 to the present was undertaken.[4] The aim was to assess the evolving attitudes of the business community to the overall climate of greater stability and to the economic problems of the 1970s. Three phases will be distinguished. The first is from 1948 until the beginning of the 1960s

4. Two Yale undergraduates, Jon Friedman and Kathy Sheehan, surveyed *Business Week* and the *Commercial and Financial Chronicle* for me. Their reports were supplemented by some reviewing of my own.

(leaving aside the immediate postwar years); the second from the beginning of the 1960s through 1971; the third since 1971.

Even as early as 1946, the business community showed considerable awareness of the aims of stabilization policy and the mechanisms by which it might work. In 1946, *Business Week* discussed in detail the Employment Act and the formation of the Council of Economic Advisers. However, the general tone throughout this period was very cautious. There was great fear of budget deficits, a mistrust of government intervention of any kind, a fear of letting inflation get out of hand, and a general skepticism about whether policy really could do anything to help smooth the cycle. The independence of the Federal Reserve was viewed as extremely desirable, largely because its governors were trusted to resist the inflationary printing press more than was the Treasury, which was viewed as too political.

The second phase of the postwar period covered the activist and generally expansionist policies followed during the 1960s. In its March 17, 1962, issue, *Business Week* commented: "John F. Kennedy is beginning to show what kind of President he intends to be. . . . He will be a president who intervenes overtly and systematically in areas of the United States economy that, in theory at least, always operated on their own. . . . All modern presidents have intervened in the economy to some extent. The distinctive thing about the Kennedy brand of intervention is that it has been accepted as a conscious and consistent policy." The rapid growth with low inflation in the mid-1960s was to a considerable extent attributed to the activist policy measures. Even the skeptics, who had been given to frequent complaints about the "Keynesian nonsense," began to speak of a consensus concerning the benefits of using fiscal and monetary policies to control the economy.

The third phase, beginning in 1971, is the hardest one to characterize. Clearly, there has been a change in the climate since the 1960s in terms of both policymaking itself and the reactions to it. Policymakers have displayed much more concern with inflation, and the confidence of businessmen in the desirability of policy has waned. But expectations have not returned to what they were in the old days. In the 1970s, there remains a view that the path of the economy is governed by an interaction between the endogenous economy and policy actions and that policy has tremendous importance.

"The fundamental cause of recession and high unemployment is not . . . history, but inflation. Inflation can cause recession in two basic ways. *The first (and most common) has to do with government actions,* while the second . . . [is that] if inflation is virulent enough, it will cause recession directly, by draining purchasing power enough to retard consumption significantly."[5]

The current decade is a complex time for policymaking, and a simple story will not suffice to explain it. The main theme has been the fight against inflation, by mild recession, by controls, and by tolerating a very high level of unemployment. The business press reveals an almost obsessive concern with predicting policy. Nevertheless, they made some wrong guesses. When sales began to fall in 1973–74, the business community did not quite believe policymakers would sit on their hands and allow a deep recession. Once it became clear that they would, however, the consensus developed (correctly) that the recovery would be slow. The fear of inflation would (and did) restrain any powerful measures toward stimulus.

Any review of this kind is necessarily subjective. But the division into three reasonably distinct phases seems justified. The 1940s and 1950s were a period of learning about what policy can do—for both the private sector and the policymakers. During the 1960s, people had considerable confidence in stabilization policy and a belief that it was a major factor in determining output. Policy shifted emphasis in the 1970s, and a good deal of enthusiasm was lost, but it was still seen as a major factor in determining output.

THE EFFECT OF CHANGING ATTITUDES ON BUSINESS decisions

Evidence confirms that the changes in business attitudes described above were reflected in shifts in business behavior.[6] A given fluctuation in output or sales has induced different responses in three important decisions variables of firms—employment, inventories, and investment—depending upon the postwar phase in which it occurred.

5. Irwin L. Kellner, "Quarterly Business Conditions Analysis," *Business Report* (Manufacturers Hanover Trust, June 1977). (Emphasis added.)

6. In the paper from which this extract is drawn, the evidence presented is econometric. Only a summary of the findings is given here.

What signs of the changes in the expectational environment would be expected? If policy has smoothed cyclical fluctuations, increased the probability of a return to full employment, and reduced the probability of extreme outcomes, firms will view a given short-run change in output as less likely to persist or intensify. The adjustment of employment and investment to short-run movements in output will, therefore, be less complete. Firms will be more willing to take a long view. Despite a downturn, they will continue to invest; and they will tend more to hold onto their workers. Similarly, they will react less to upturns. Output changes will still have an impact, but it will become less pronounced.

THE RESPONSE OF EMPLOYMENT

When an individual firm is struck by a downturn or an upturn in demand, the way it reacts depends importantly on whether the change is expected to continue, intensify, or be reversed in the near future. The firm can react with some combination of three actions: laying off or hiring workers, varying hours of work per worker, and increasing or decreasing inventories. Each element of the decision costs something. Hiring, firing, and training costs are incurred directly by firms when employment is varied. Income uncertainty and the disutility of overtime are costs faced by workers when either employment or hours are varied. They become costs for the firm to the extent that firms must compensate workers for them with higher base wage rates or overtime premiums.

Holding inventories allows a gap between production and sales, but at the cost of interest expenses and storage charges. Firms may also hold excess labor rather than piling up unsold inventories. This labor hoarding may take the form of payment for more hours than employees actually provide or of requiring less intense effort from employees during downturns.

Quarterly data on output and employment for the private non-farm economy were examined over various periods between 1948 and 1976. The response of employment to output is strikingly different during the period 1948–61 than it is in later periods. The size of the response is different and, to a lesser extent, so is the speed. In the 1948–61 period, employment changed roughly one for one with output, allowing for a year to adjust. Most of the adjustment of employment occurs in the current and the following quarter. The results after 1961 look very different. The adjustment of employment to output changes is significantly less than equi-proportional. The response of employment in the same and the following quarter, in particular, is dramatically reduced.

These findings are, therefore, consistent with the view that once firms had learned of the amelioration of the business cycle (i.e., after 1961), they were more willing to retain employees in the face of an output decline. They expected that business would pick up again fairly quickly and the workers would be needed again.

It was noted earlier that the 1970s marked a shift in policy toward fighting inflation. In 1975, firms expected an extended recession. Retaining employees other than those required for current production needs looked less desireable in 1975 than in the 1960s. The findings for the period including the 1975 recession do show a return to a somewhat more complete adjustment of employment to output.

THE RESPONSE OF INVENTORIES

An efficient firm compares the costs of varying employment with the cost of using inventories to adjust the gap between sales and production in the short run. If firms after 1961 are varying employment less in response to a given output variation compared with earlier years, as the preceding section suggested, then they are changing behavior at the employment-output margin, and consistent change at the inventory-sales margin can be expected.

Furthermore, any change since 1948 in the relation between a distributed lag of past sales and firms' expectations of future sales also should show up. Specifically, a short-run increase in sales will raise expected sales by a smaller amount after 1961. Similarly, a fall in sales will lower expected sales by less.

To examine this, the relation between business inventories and final sales is considered. Again, there are substantial differences between the 1948–61 period and the later periods.

The descriptive picture does look consistent with the changes described above. After 1961, firms take a longer view when incorporating information about current and past sales into an expected sales estimate. And they are more willing to meet increases or decreases in sales by inventory adjustment (thereby reducing the extent of employment changes following a change in product demand).

THE RESPONSE OF ORDERS FOR PRODUCERS DURABLES

The accelerated resonse of investment to changes in output has been seen as a major determinant of the business cycle and as a potentially important source of dynamic instability in the economy. The simple accelerator says that the level of investment depends upon the change in real output. Growth in output then stimulates a high rate of investment demand, which feeds back to induce further growth in output. In most econometric work the simple accelerator is assumed to be softened in its effects by lags and by the impact of changes in the cost of capital. If producers' expectations have altered because of the existence of stabilization policy, then the parameters of the accelerator will alter. Producers will not change their desired stock of capital as much in response to short-run fluctuations in output.

The MIT-Penn-SSRC Quarterly Econometric Model estimates new orders for producers' durable equipment using a flexible accelerator equation. The way in which the parameters of this equation have changed over time was examined. After 1961, the amount of "acceleration" was markedly lower than in earlier years. That is to say, a given change in business output induced a smaller and slower response in orders for new equipment after 1961. As was true for employment, the period including the 1975 recession does show some erosion of confidence.

CONCLUSION

Two main strands run through recent thinking concerning the interactions between stabilization policy and private economic behavior. The first is that private economic behavior will be altered by the existence of active policy. The second is that policy will become ineffective if it is anticipated. This paper has offered support for the first of these ideas and has disagreed with the second. The results generally indicate that the shortrun response of the economy has become more stable. When the private sector anticipates stabilizing policies, the task of those policies is made easier, not harder. Rather than abandoning the use of monetary and fiscal policy to keep the economy on an even keel, we urgently need to find ways of combining a stable GNP with price stability.

Equilibrium Business-Cycle Theory
ROBERT LUCAS AND THOMAS SARGENT

In the next selection Robert Lucas and Thomas Sargent argue force-fully that Keynesian analysis is "fundamentally flawed." They offer instead an outline of "equilibrium business-cycle theory" that they feel should replace Keynesian analysis. In their model individuals do have rational expectations and stabilization policy is, at best, ineffective. Their piece differs in emphasis from the selection by McCallum, how-ever. It is not enough to attack Keynes. It is necessary also to put for-ward an alternative theory—one that is both consistent with observed business cycles and in which stabilization policy is ineffective. The key points of the Lucas-Sargent approach are that (1) prices and wages are flexible and all markets clear (hence the name equilibrium business-cycle theory) and (2) private decision-makers have rational expecta-tions, so that they are correct on average, but in the short run they do make mistakes or suffer misperceptions. These short-run mispercep-tions are crucial to the Lucas-Sargent explanation of fluctuations in output and employment.

Some fluctuations in business activity are caused by exogenous events—wars or crop failures. But most cycles, they argue, are actually the result of erratic and unpredictable policy actions. For example, the government causes an unexpected decrease in the money supply. A par-ticular firm and its workers find that the market price of the product they produce has fallen. They do not realize that this decline in their own product price is simply part of a general decline in prices. For if they did, then they could simply lower their own wage rates and selling prices with no real reduction in wages or profit margins. Instead, they erroneously believe that it is the price of their own product relative to other prices that has fallen. So, workers decide to leave the firm to find alternative jobs or to work less for a while until conditions improve for their firm's product.

The importance of the assumptions of market clearing and rational expectations are that the recession will be self-correcting. In the long run, people will correctly perceive the overall economic situation and full employment will be restored. Persistent price and wage stickiness will not impede the adjustment.

INTRODUCTION

FOR THE APPLIED ECONOMIST, the confident and apparently suc-cessful application of Keynesian principles to economic policy which

164

occurred in the United States in the 1960s was an event of incomparable significance and satisfaction. These principles led to a set of simple, quantitative relationships between fiscal policy and economic activity generally, the basic logic of which could be (and was) explained to the general public, and which could be applied to yield improvements in economic performance benefiting *everyone*. It seemed an economics as free of ideological difficulties as, say, applied chemistry or physics, promising a straightforward expansion in economic possibilities. One might argue about how this windfall should be distributed, but it seemed a simple lapse of logic to oppose the windfall itself. Understandably and correctly, this promise was met at first with skepticism by noneconomists; the smoothly growing prosperity of the Kennedy-Johnson years did much to diminish these doubts.

We dwell on these halcyon days of Keynesian economics because, without conscious effort, they are difficult to recall today. In the present decade, the United States economy has undergone its first major depression since the 1930s, to the accompaniment of inflation rates in excess of 10 percent per annum. These events have been transmitted (by consent of the governments involved) to other advanced countries and in many cases have been amplified. These events did not arise from a reactionary reversion to outmoded, "classical" principles of tight money and balance budgets. On the contrary, they were accompanied by massive governmental budget deficits and high rates of monetary expansion: policies which, although bearing an admitted risk of inflation, promised according to modern Keynesian doctrine rapid real growth and low rates of unemployment.

That these predictions were wildly incorrect and that the doctrine on which they were based is fundamentally flawed are now simple matters of fact, involving no novelties in economic theory. The task which faces contemporary students of the business cycle is that of sorting through the wreckage, determining which features of that remarkable intellectual event called the Keynesian Revolution can be salvaged and put to good use, and which others must be discarded. Though it is far from clear what the outcome of this process will be, it is already evident that it will necessarily involve the reopening of basic issues in monetary economics which have been viewed since the 1930s as "closed," and the reevaluation of every aspect of the institutional framework within which monetary and fiscal policy is formulated in the advanced countries. This paper is in the nature of an early progress report on this process of reevaluation and reconstruction.

EQUILIBRIUM BUSINESS-CYCLE THEORY

Economists prior to the 1930s did not recognize a need for a special branch of economics, with its own special postulates, designed to explain the business cycle. Keynes founded that subdiscipline, called *macroeconomics*, because he thought that it was impossible to explain the characteristics of business cycles within the discipline imposed by classical economic theory, a discipline imposed by its insistence on adherence to the two postulates (a) that markets be assumed to clear, and (b) that agents be assumed to act in their own self-interest. The outstanding fact that seemed impossible to reconcile with these two postulates was the length and severity of business depressions and the large scale unemployment which they entailed. A related observation is that measures of aggregate demand and prices are positively correlated with measures of real output and employment, in apparent contradiction to the classical result that changes in a purely nominal magnitude like the general price level were pure "unit changes" which should not alter real behavior. After freeing himself of the straight-jacket (or discipline) imposed by the classical postulates, Keynes described a model in which rules of thumb, such as the consumption function and liquidity preference schedule, took the place of decision functions that a classical economist would insist be derived from the theory of choice. And rather than require that wages and prices be determined by the postulate that markets clear—which for the labor market seemed patently contradicted by the severity of business depressions—Keynes took as an unexamined postulate that money wages are "sticky," meaning that they are set at a level or by a process that could be taken as uninfluenced by the macroeconomic forces he proposed to analyze.

When Keynes wrote, the terms "equilibrium" and "classical" carried certain positive and normative connotations which seemed to rule out either modifier being applied to business-cycle theory. The term "equilibrium" was thought to refer to a system "at rest," and both "equilibrium" and "classical" were used interchangeably, by some, with "ideal." Thus an economy in classical equilibrium would be both unchanging and unimprovable by policy interventions. Using terms in this way, it is no wonder that few economists regarded equilibrium theory as a promising starting point for the understanding of business cycles and for the design of policies to mitigate or eliminate them.

In recent years, the meaning of the term "equilibrium" has undergone such dramatic development that a theorist of the 1930s would not recognize it. It is now routine to describe an economy following a fluctuating path with some random movements as being "in equilibrium," by which is meant nothing more than that at each point in time, postulates (a) and (b) above are satisfied. This development, which stemmed mainly from work by K. J. Arrow and G. Debreu, implies that simply to look at any economic time series and conclude that it is a "disequilibrium phenomenon" is a meaningless observation.

The research line being pursued by a number of us involves the attempt to discover a particular, econometrically testable equilibrium theory of the business cycle, one that can serve as the foundation for quantitative analysis of macroeconomic policy. There is no denying that this approach is "counter-revolutionary," for it presupposes that Keynes and his followers were wrong to give up on the possibility that an equilibrium theory could account for the business cycle. As of now, no successful equilibrium macroeconometric model with the same level of detail as the large Keynesian econometric models has been constructed. But small theoretical models have been constructed that show potential for explaining some key features of the business cycle long thought to be inexplicable within the confines of classical postulates. The equilibrium models also provide reasons for understanding why estimated Keynesian models fail to hold up outside of the sample over which they have been estimated. We now turn to describing some of the key facts about business cycles and the way the new classical models confront them.

For a long time, most of the economics profession has, with some reason, followed Keynes in rejecting classical macroeconomic models because they seemed incapable of explaining some important characteristics of time series measuring important economic aggregates. Perhaps the most important failure of the classical model seemed to be its inability to explain the positive correlation in the time series between prices and / or wages, on the one hand, and measures of aggregate output or employment, on the other hand. A second and related failure was its inability to explain the positive correlations between measures of aggregate demand, like the money stock, and aggregate output or employment.

We now have rigorous theoretical models which illustrate how these correlations can emerge while retaining the classical postulates that markets clear and agents optimize. The key step in obtaining such models has been to relax the ancillary postulate used in much classical economic analysis that agents have perfect information. The new classical models continue to assume that markets always clear and that agents optimize. The postulate that agents optimize means that their supply and demand decisions must be functions of real variables, including perceived relative prices. Each agent is assumed to have limited information and to receive information about some prices more often than other prices. On the basis of their limited information—the lists that they have of current and past absolute prices of various goods—agents are assumed to make the best possible estimate of all of the *relative* prices that influence their supply and demand decisions. Because they do not have all of the information that would enable them to compute perfectly the relative prices they care about, agents make errors in estimating the pertinent relative prices, errors that are unavoidable given their limited information. In particular, under certain conditions, agents will tend temporarily to mistake a general increase in the price level as an increase in the *relative* price of the good that they are selling, leading them to increase their supply of that good over what they had previously planned. Since everyone is, on average, making the same mistake, aggregate output will rise above what it would have been, whenever this period's average economy-wide price level is unexpectedly high. Symmetrically, average output will be decreased whenever the aggregate price turns out to be lower than agents had expected. The hypothesis of "rational expectations" is imposed here because agents are supposed to make the best possible use of the limited information they have. It is assumed that they make errors of expectation in the short run but do not systematically over- or underestimate the price level (or other variables) over any prolonged period.

It is an easy step to show that this theory implies correlations between revisions to aggregate output and unexpected changes in any variables that help determine aggregate demand. In most macroeconomic models, the money supply is one determinant of aggregate demand. Thus, the theory easily can account for a tendency for output to rise following an unexpected increase in the money supply.

While such a theory predicts positive correlations between the inflation rate or money supply, on the one hand, and the level of output on the other, it also asserts that those correlations do not depict "trade-offs" that can be exploited by a policy authority. That is, the theory predicts that there is no way that the monetary authority can follow a systematic activist policy and achieve a rate of output that is on average higher over the business cycle than that achieved if it simply adopted a fixed-growth-rate-of-the-money-supply rule of the kind Friedman and Simons recommended. For the theory predicts that aggregate output is a function of current and past unexpected changes in the money supply. Output will be high only when the money supply is and has been higher than it had been expected to be, i.e., higher than average. There is simply no way that on average over the whole business cycle the money supply can be higher than average. Thus, while the preceding theory is capable of explaining some of the correlations long thought to invalidate classical macroeconomic theory, the theory is classical both in its adherence to the classical theoretical postulates and in the "nonactivist" flavor of its implications for monetary policy.

A Critique of Equilibrium Business-Cycle Theory

ARTHUR M. OKUN

Arthur Okun disagreed with the Lucas-Sargent criticism of Keynesian analysis and disagreed with their alternative view of the business cycle. In Okun's view the stickiness of wages and prices, that is an important part of the Keynesian model, derives from contractual relationships between buyers and sellers. These relationships are developed by the individual economic agents for sensible and rational reasons but have the side-effect of making real aggregate output and employment susceptible to fluctuations in nominal aggregate demand.

In the next selection, however, Okun presents his criticisms of the Lucas-Sargent equilibrium business-cycle model. Do short-run misperceptions provide a plausible basis for the kind of business cycles that are observed?

IN MY JUDGMENT, the theory of rational-expectations-with-misperceptions provides an explanation of the business cycle that: represents a constructive effort to deal with questions that sorely needed to be asked, is logically impeccable and theoretically satisfying in its response to those questions, does not identify in operational terms the specific nature of the cyclical process, and fails to account for the duration and many key features of the actual cycle.

THE MICRO-MACRO BRIDGE

The centerpiece of microeconomics is the purely competitive auction market in which buyers and sellers participate atomistically as price-takers and where supply and demand are equated continuously by variations in price. These individual markets aggregate into a Walrsian general equilibrium model in which aggregate output is supply-determined, changing only when production functions shift, or when stocks of capital and natural resources change, or when the flow of labor offered at a given real wage changes (because of either changes in population or changes in tastes concerning work activity). In that aggregation of perfect markets, shifts in nominal aggregate demand affect only prices and never quantities.

Macroeconomics contrasts sharply with these implications of aggregated microeconomics. It begins with the observation that output (real GNP) and employment display significant deviations around their supply-determined trends that are (a) persistent and (b) usually associated with movements in nominal GNP in the same direction. These fluctuations around the trend of real activity are the "business cycle" (a term that is not meant to imply strong periodicity). Clearly, the business cycle could not happen in aggregated classical microeconomics. Thus any macroeconomics that is connected to microeconomics by a solid bridge must explain how it departs from the classical micro model in its conception of the operation of markets.

In fact, Keynes was explicit about the nature of his amendment. He departed from classical microeconomics *only* by modifying the labor supply function to include a wage floor. And, he offered many (indeed too many) explanations for the wage floor. But his bridge was defective; none of the explanations flowed directly from the implications of optimization by economic agents or from a specific institutional constraint. Many of the followers of Keynes operated with no bridge to microeconomics. Instead, they adopted the "fixprice method" (in Hick's terms), explicitly assuming away variations in prices and wages. And then, necessarily, nominal disturbances were found to have—purely and solely—real effects. (Indeed, this tradition began in the pre-Keynesian era, as illustrated by the accelerator theory of investment.)

The fixprice finesse may have helped economists develop a sharper focus and a better understanding of real relationships, like the consumption function, inventory and fixed investment functions, cyclical productivity relationships, and multiplier-accelerator interactions. But it had important costs. One of these was a professionally disturbing gap between macroeconomics and microeconomics. In effect, at the beginning of the macroeconomics semester, students were required to forget what they had learned in microeconomics about the equilibrating function of prices and wages. More seriously, by operating with models that took prices and wages as given for pedagogical purposes, economists tended to think of them as given for general purposes. Thus, the finesse contributed to the long lags in professional progress toward a satisfactory theory of the causes and consequences of inflation.

When the Phillips curve supplanted fixprice in the Keynesian model, it emerged as "an empirical generalization in search of a theory," as Tobin aptly put it. And the entire structure was seriously undermined when that empirical generalization collapsed.

In the last dozen years or so since that collapse, serious professional efforts have been made to construct that sorely needed macro-micro bridge. Those efforts, including the particular ones conducted by the "rational expectations school," are asking the right questions and working to provide illuminating answers.

THE MISPERCEPTIONS VIEW

The particular bridge supplied by the rational expectations school amends the classical model simply and solely by assuming that buyers and sellers in any particular market may have imperfect information about prices in *other* markets. Then, even if each market passes all the standard tests of continuous clearing, complete atomism, and costless transactions, the imperfect information about other markets creates the possibility of a business cycle—of real effects from disturbances in nominal aggregate demand. And there are persuasive reasons why rational agents may have imperfect information about developments in markets in which they are not operating. Some pieces of information have costs that exceed their value. Thus, the theory is firmly grounded in the assumption of rational behavior and optimization.

In response to a generally unexpected jump in nominal aggregate demand, the aggregated classical microeconomics would predict a proportionate rise in all product and factor prices with no changes in quantities. In contrast, the rational expectations theory would envision some initial expansion of quantities resulting from misperception. A seller finding a surprisingly high price in the market for his product may respond by producing and selling a larger volume of output, because he may well not fully recognize the higher replacement costs of his inputs or the higher revenues available from alternative outputs. Some sellers in product markets may be focusing their attention on the markets in which they are operating and thus not become aware of similar price movements in factor markets and other product markets. They may then respond to a higher price for their product as though it was a higher relative price when in fact it may merely parallel the rise in the general price level.

Similarly, following the rise in nominal aggregate demand, workers encountering unexpectedly higher wages in their particular labor market may offer more work. They may respond that way for either or both of two reasons: (1) because they have a positive elasticity of supply of work effort with respect to real wages and fail to recognize the increase in consumer prices occurring in product markets; or (2) because they do not recognize that nominal wages are higher in other labor markets as well, thus raising the return from selling their labor elsewhere.

This model abandons explicitly the assumption (often implicit) of the competitive market-clearing model that all information has zero costs. Information costs to participants in any one market about prices in *other* markets are the grains of sand thrown on the frictionless classical machinery to destroy its conclusion that nominal disturbances have only nominal effects. With that small exception this model preserves the entire apparatus of classical microeconomics. It constructs a logically and theoretically satisfactory bridge. Misperceptions about prices in other markets can account for *some* cycle in real activity.

THE NATURE OF THE MISSING INFORMATION

To begin my critique of the theory, I see no way to assess the role of misperceptions about relative prices in the actually observed cycle until the rational expectations theorists give these misperceptions much more operational content than they have thus far. In general, the proponents stress the rational expectations *despite which* the cycle takes place; I wish they would focus more sharply on the misperceptions or the missing information, which are allegedly the *cause* of the cycle. In the spirit of Howard Baker, I wish to be told what the decision-makers don't know, for how long they don't know it, and why they don't find out. Is there any direct empirical evidence that sellers lack timely information about other prices that are relevant to their "true" marginal costs? Are there persuasive *a priori* reasons why sellers are likely to lack such information in important ways for prolonged periods?

Operating on my own intuition, I find it implausible that important information is sufficiently costly to outweigh its value to rational agents on a timely basis. For one thing, by reading the newspapers, market participants obtain a virtually costless flow of information from the reporting on the monthly indices of consumer and producer prices. Even more significantly, firms and households operate in both product and factor markets at essentially the same time. How much of a communication gap or lag can rationally be maintained between the personnel manager and the sales manager of a given firm? How much of an effort is required within the family to ensure communications between the workers and the shoppers?

How long can a rational agent collect wage offers in various labor markets and still maintain a serious misperception in the face of his actual experience? If he samples twenty labor markets and obtains twenty wage offers which all lie below his initial mean expectation of wages, he must revise that expectation downward, sharply and quickly—even if he is unable to calculate that the probability of drawing such a sample is slightly less than one in a million. Is it really plausible, as econometric labor-supply functions based on this model imply, that the deviation of "anticipated wages" from actual wages narrows at a rate of only 15 to 36 percent a year?

Let me raise a different question about the nature of the misperceptions and missing information. Any theory that attributes decision-making errors by private agents to missing information implies that there exists, in principle, some set of correct, timely information that would eliminate these errors. That information needs to be identified specifically. Indeed that task may have important implications for public policy. The model seems to point directly to the potential benefit from filling the critical gap of missing information that accounts for decision errors. Clearly, the production of information is subject to huge economies of scale; and, because of laws on disclosure, the government is likely to be the most efficient collector of proprietary information from businesses and households. Within the framework of this model, one must ask whether the Bureau of Labor Statistics holds the key to eliminating the cycle.

THE DURATION OF THE CYCLE

More evidence about the nature of the missing information might quell my doubts and refute my tentative hypotheses. But if my suspicions are well-founded, misperceptions about relative prices are only a small first step toward accounting for a cycle of the duration and amplitude that are actually observed. And they barely begin to explain prolonged periods, like 1958–63 and 1975–77, when output and employment remained below their equilibrium values (by anyone's measure). How much of the basic profile of such periods should be attributed to consistent, repetitive overestimates by sellers of general inflation (relative to their known selling prices)? Survey data from households and business executives in those periods display no consistent pattern of overestimating inflation, so far as I am aware. Inflation forecasts made by professional economists were remarkably accurate in the early 1960s and in 1976–77 as well.

Indeed, the forecasts of real activity made by economists in 1958 and 1975 (and every other recession year) accurately implied that the economy would remain in slack territory for a considerable period of time. Even an unintelligent autocorrelation equation could have rendered that verdict with a high degree of reliability in March 1958 or March 1975. What is going on at such times? When economists predict that rational decision-makers will continue to restrict output below a full macroequilibrium, are we really predicting that they will continue to operate with erroneous perceptions of relative prices? And when rational private decision-makers hear our voices, how can they keep ignoring valuable free information that identifies their mistake? Because private decision-makers are too intelligent to make repetitive, serially correlated errors, misperceptions about relative prices can be only a small part of the story of long slack periods (and equally long boom periods like 1966–69).

When rational expectations theorists explicitly recognize the problem of persistence, they agree—and indeed insist, as an implication of their model—that the private decision-makers should not make repetitive errors in the same direction in their forecasts of relative prices. But then, to account for the persistence of slack and booms, they must graft onto their cycle models lags or adjustment costs that maintain persistent movements in output and employment after the initiating relative-price misperception has disappeared. I view this search for a hybrid model as a productive and promising line of inquiry that requires and deserves much further work. It points toward a business-cycle theory based on rational expectations with misperceptions and with something else. So far, that something else has been specified much more clearly in terms of the properties of difference and differential equations than in terms of economic behavior. And, in the process, the solid macro-micro bridge of the simple model gets shaky (or at least obscured from my vision). Once misperceptions about relative prices are eliminated, what prevents that prompt restoration of a full-blown competitive equilibrium consistent with accurate relative-price information? Is a second type of sand being thrown on the classical machinery in such hybrid models? I look forward to further modeling in this area that should help to answer my questions.

SALIENT FEATURES OF THE CYCLE

I have raised questions and expressed doubts about the ability of the rational-expectations-with-misperceptions model to account for the duration of the cycle and especially of prolonged periods of slack that are actually observed. I would argue further that many other salient characteristics of the cycle cannot be satisfactorily explained by that model. Obviously, any tractable theory is simplified and cannot explain or predict every feature or characteristic of experience. But it ought to have a fair degree of verisimilitude. In particular, the implications of any model for fiscal and monetary policy can be taken seriously only if its implications for other key features of the cycle stand up under empirical observation. Let me state some stylized cyclical facts which do not seem to be explicable by rational-expectations-with-misperceptions.

Inventory disequilibria · The hallmark of United States postwar recessions has been inventory liquidation, following a major build-up of inventories at the peak of the expansion. Standard models that assume price-taking and continuous market clearing do not suggest that a disappointment about relative prices will lead traders to liquidate inventories. For example, a sudden drop in the demand for, and hence the price of, wheat that leads farmers to decrease production in the future will generally lead traders to increase stocks initially. (The price tends to fall enough currently relative to its new future expected value to provide traders with that incentive.) Why then, in the business cycle, is the aggregate cutback in production accompanied by a cutback in stocks?

Cyclical productivity patterns · Output per hour worked fluctuates in a procyclical pattern. Extant efforts to explain that phenomenon rest on disequilibria or on transactions and adjustment costs that are non-Walrasian. Can it be explained within the framework of a model that views labor markets and product markets as Walrasian?

Quits and layoffs · Quits have a procyclical pattern and are a coincident indicator at turning points. In other words, the quit rate is highest at the top of the business cycle boom. But if workers lack information about wages in *other* labor markets, then they should be less likely to quit when their wages accelerate unexpectedly. According to the equilibrium business-cycle model, should not quits be countercyclical or at least display long lags at turning points? Layoffs display a marked countercyclical pattern. Can that (or indeed the very existence of layoffs) be explained by the model? The frequency of help-wanted signs and the volume of help-wanted advertising display strong procyclical variations. Can these be explained in the framework of the classical microeconomics adopted by this model?

Wage differentials · Pay differentials between high-wage and low-wage industries vary countercyclically. And that is the case even though cyclical fluctuations in employment tend to be greatest in the high-wage industries. Can that be explained within the framework of this model?

General pay increases in recession · During recent periods of recession and slack, like 1975–77, many nonunion firms granted general pay increases to their workers when the firms were recruiting *no* new workers at all. Why would sensible employers raise wages under such conditions at those points in time, regardless of how they expected prices or wages to move in the future?

Profits in boom years · Corporate profits (in real terms) are especially high in years of emerging excess demand. If corporations are committing decision-making errors that lead to unduly large output under such circumstances, why do their income statements look so good?

Auction markets · Prices of industrial commodities traded in organized auction markets have fallen in postwar recessions (including 1974–75); most other prices have not fallen (and rose strongly in

1974–75). Can this special behavior of auction markets be explained within the framework of a model that views all markets as auction markets?

OPEC · The record of 1974–79 makes clear that increases in the price of oil add to the price level for a given path of nominal GNP. Should that be viewed as a relative-price misperception? (Some economists invoked rational-expectations arguments to predict erroneously that oil prices could not raise the price level, given nominal GNP.)

Despite the methodological contributions made by the model of rational-expectations-with-misperceptions, the assumption of universal auction markets has put it into a straitjacket. It offers a logical explanation of how an economy consisting entirely of markets like those observed for soybeans and silver could nonetheless experience some business cycle. The implications of that model strengthen my conviction that a soybean-silver economy would not display a business cycle with the duration or key characteristics actually observed. And I am equally convinced that the resulting guide to macro policymaking in a soybean-silver economy is fundamentally inapplicable to the actual United States economy.

PART SIX New Approaches to Macroeconomic Policy

An Efficient Strategy to Combat Inflation
ARTHUR M. OKUN

Macroeconomists of differing views agree that an entrenched pattern of wage and price increases, monetary growth, and aggregate demand growth has to be broken if inflation is to end. In principle, this should be possible without suffering a major recession. If only the momentum of inflation or inflationary expectations could be broken. This tantalizing prospect of disinflation without excess unemployment has motivated a variety of suggested strategies for solving the problem. First, Arthur Okun suggests a diversified attack. The economy needs a "big push" to get back to reasonable price stability. His proposals were written in 1979 when the Carter administration was in power, an he comments on that administrations' anti-inflation strategy.

CHRONIC INFLATION has been the outstanding feature of the American economy in the 1970s, and it is our foremost economic ill as we approach the decade of the 1980s. The chronic inflation of the 1970s is a new and different phenomenon that cannot be diagnosed correctly with old theories or treated effectively with old prescriptions. If left untreated, the syndrome of chronic inflation is likely to become more severe and to impose even greater economic and social costs in the 1980s. An efficient anti-inflationary program must be diversified. It needs three major elements: enough fiscal-monetary discipline to provide a safety margin against excess demand; a coordinated federal initiative to reduce private costs; and constructive measures to obtain wage-price restraint.

A DIVERSIFIED ATTACK ON INFLATION

Inflation must be reduced substantially over the years ahead. That task can be accomplished only gradually; and it can be accomplished effeciently only through the concerted use of a variety of anti-inflationary policies, including fiscal-monetary restraint, federal cost-reducing initiatives, and wage and price restraint.

Fiscal-Monetary Restraint • In battling against inflation, we must accept some downside risks on output and employment in the short run to clear the way for sustained growth in the long run. In retrospect, we did not balance these risks prudently enough in setting fiscal-momentary policy during 1977–78. We must do better in the future to establish a safety margin against overly strong markets.

On the other hand, we must recognize the ill effects of overdoses of fiscal and monetary restraint. Those effects are clear in the sad experience of 1974–75, when we crusaded against inflation by relying solely on tight budgets and tight money. During fiscal year 1974, the federal budget was nearly balanced in the face of a recession; during calender year 1974, the growth of money (currency and demand deposits) was held to 4.5 percent. The beneficial impact on inflation was disappointingly small, while the unfavorable impact on employment, production, and capital formation was enormous.

Using that approach, the nation squanders about $200 billion of real production and roughly 5 million worker-years of jobs for every point that it reduces the inflation rate. The evidence of recent years suggests that, through its fiscal and monetary policies, the federal government can control—within a reasonable margin—the total growth of the GNP measured in dollars. But it cannot control the division of that growth between increases in output and increases in the price level. When the government pushed the economy into deep recession and prolonged slack, each dollar trimmed from GNP meant a loss of roughly $0.90 of output and a saving of about $0.10 on the price level. Any anti-inflationary proposal that relies solely on balancing the budget and tightening money is, in reality, a proposal for an encore of that experience. It should carry a truth-in-packaging label revealing that its probable contents are 90 percent production losses and job losses and only about 10 percent inflation saving.

Undoubtedly, inflation could be eliminated by fiscal-monetary restraint alone, but the consequences of such a strategy for production, employment, capital formation, and our social fabric would be horrendous. Average citizens cannot reasonably be expected to recognize those consequences fully, and it is understandable that some of them grasp at the straw of budget balancing in the hope of a rescue from inflation. But our political leaders ought to know better, or to learn better.

Federal Cost-Reducing Initiatives • Federal policies have pervasive impacts on costs and prices in many sectors of the economy. The federal government adds to the price level when it imposes cost-raising taxes, like excises on products or payroll taxes on employers. Its regulations affecting safety, health, and the environment are a source of higher costs and prices—necessary in part, but unnecessary to some degree. Its economic regulation of industries with public utility characteristics influences their prices and costs. In pursuing certain equity objectives, the government sets floors on some prices (as in the dairy and sugar programs) and on pay (as in the minimum wage). It affects the output of various private industries through such provisions as acreage controls and restrictions on timber cutting and oil leasing. It also influences prices and costs through tariffs and other restrictions on imports.

Because most individual government actions and policy changes in these areas have relatively small effects, they often go unnoticed; yet they add up to a great deal. In my judgment, the most serious inflationary stimulus in recent years came from a series of such self-inflicted wounds incurred during 1977: a major increase in payroll taxes on employers, a large rise in the minimum wage, reinstituted acreage controls on farmers, added regulatory burdens on business, and new barriers to imports.

Proposals that would reduce costs have been frequently rejected. Hospital cost containment was not enacted by the last Congress; presidential proposals to cut certain federal excise taxes were ignored. Indeed, some congressional leaders now advocate a new value-added tax that would surely add to our inflationary woes.

Enormous anti-inflationary benefits could be reaped in this area. We could cut federal payroll taxes on employers; we could use grant formulas to encourage states and cities to lower their price-raising and cost-raising taxes. We could reform regulation to reduce its cost burdens. This is the most efficient strategy for curbing the price level. It does not put people out of work, and it need not constrain private price and wage decisions.

As a first step into this area, I have suggested a procedural reform; the development of a system of inflation scorekeeping. The

Congressional Budget Office (or General Accounting Office) should be asked to issue a quarterly report that identifies all actions and proposals by the president and by the Congress that would either raise or lower the price level and estimates their dollar impact. Nobody has yet told me why this idea is defective, but nobody has acted to implement it.

Wage-Price Restraint · During recent years, the wage-price spiral has been the fundamental source of rapid inflation in the United States. An efficient cure for inflation must get directly at that source. At the present time, the administration's program of wage-price standards deserves our full support.

Any plea for voluntary cooperation in our society implies a threat of focusing the spotlight of public opinion on flagrant violators. Beyond that, the present program carries a threat of sanctions associated with the privileged relations that many business firms have with the federal government. These provisions strengthen the credibility of the program, though they invoke an unlegislated bureaucratic power that is not ideal. All in all, I can accept them. It would also be useful for the president to have clearly legislated authority to delay major wage or price decisions that could threaten the entire program. But the very discussion of such legislation would intensify the widespread fears of business that we are on the road to controls. In fact, I do not expect the president to seek control authority, and I would emphatically oppose mandatory controls over prices and wages.

As originally proposed by the president, the program was reasonably equitable as between business firms and workers. But its fairness depended heavily on the provision for real wage insurance.[1] Without that provision, the standards impose on workers a heavier burden of restraint and much more potential risk than they do on businessmen.

America's workers are being asked to ante up for the deal. Thus far most are doing so. Despite a few collective bargaining settlements that exceeded the wage standard, the behavior of pay since last October has accorded remarkably well with the standard. On the other hand, the behavior of industrial prices suggests significant violations of the price standard. But the identification of violators is

---

1. Workers were to be given tax relief if prices rose by more than wages. (*Editor*)

apparently a complex and difficult task. All in all, I expect this program to contribute to the deceleration of inflation as wage restraint passes into price restraint, and as businesses are made more conscious of the urgent need for their cooperation.

Our historical experience and that of many other countries suggests that informal, "semivoluntary" policies of wage and price restraint can help significantly over some periods of time. But such programs have crumbled as economic conditions have changed and resistance has mounted. Eventually they are phased out, then reshaped and reinstituted. Keeping an incomes policy in the antiinflationary arena is not easy. P. T. Barnum once noted that keeping a lamb in a cage with a lion requires a large reserve supply of lambs. Similarly, society may need a reserve supply of incomes policies. We will need some program of wage-price restraint for years to come.

Along with other economists, I have been advocating the development of a tax-based incomes policy that would reward compliance or penalize noncompliance with the guidelines. The social interest in wage and price restraint can be better pursued by providing marketlike incentives through the tax system than by relying on voluntary appeals or rigid mandatory rules. The tax approach would allow people to make choices in light of the rewards or penalties provided, making it worthwhile for most firms and workers to practice the restraint that benefits the entire society. Undoubtedly such a program would add to the burdens on the tax system, but so do the rules governing capital gains, the residential energy credit, and the targeted jobs credit.

In combination with fiscal-monetary restraint, a federal cost-reducing program and a tax-based incomes policy are essential parts of an efficient strategy to combat inflation. Some of these proposals are untried and unproved; some pose administrative problems and meet political opposition from major interest groups. But I am convinced that these proposals are realistic, not "imaginative" as some have labeled them.

Two popular doctrines are imaginative indeed. One is that inflation will either simmer down naturally or become tolerable to the American people. The other proclaims that fiscal and monetary restraint can cure inflation without deep and prolonged recession. These strategies have been tried and proved false. It is time to face the realities of the new disease of chronic inflation and to use the prescriptions that are appropriate for curing it.

The Tax-Based Incomes Policy

HENRY WALLICH

In the next selection Henry Wallich discusses in more detail the idea of a tax-based incomes policy. Whereas Okun preferred the incentive (or carrot) of a conditional tax break, Wallich advocates the penalty (or stick) of a conditional surtax. In other ways the two proposals are the same.

AMONG THE SEVERAL VERSIONS of tax-based incomes policies (TIP) that have been under discussion, this paper focuses on the approach colloquially referred to as the "stick approach," on which Professor Sidney Weintraub of the University of Pennsylvania and I have collaborated since 1971. The stick version of TIP seeks to restrain inflation by imposing a tax on employers granting excessive wage increases. There is no interference with the forces of the market: employers who, for some reason, wish to raise wages substantially, can do so. TIP, therefore, in no way involves wage and price controls.

If other well-functioning weapons against inflation were readily available, there would be no need to discuss TIP. It is because the orthodox methods work slowly that leads me to believe that a device such as TIP, despite its obvious inconveniences, deserves consideration at this time.

Fiscal and monetary policy, the orthodox weapons against inflation, so far have not been successful in winding it down. This does not mean that they would be without effect in the long run. Nor do I believe that the cost of applying them, measured against realistic alternatives, would be as high as is sometimes believed. The alternative to successfully combating inflation is not a constant rate of inflation. We do not have the choice between doing something about inflation and leaving it alone. Left alone, it will accelerate. This tendency results from the fact that inflation increases the degree of uncertainty with which all participants in the market must cope. Thus business, labor, borrowers, lenders will all tend to inject mounting insurance premia into their wage, price, and interest rate behavior to guard against the contingency of higher inflation. Inflation itself tends to generate accelerating inflation unless effectively restrained. Accelerating inflation, however, means sure recession sooner or later. The cost of letting inflation run, therefore, is higher than even a costly form of restraining it.

TIP, moreover, should not be viewed as an outright alternative to monetary and fiscal restraint. In 1971, wage and price controls were viewed as such an alternative, and fiscal and monetary policy accordingly turned expansive. I do not believe that TIP could offset the consequences of excessively expansive monetary and fiscal policies. Some restraint by use of these traditional tools will continue to be needed.

Nevertheless, an appropriate combination of TIP and the standard tools of fiscal and monetary policy offers great promise for the longer run, once the present inflation has been wound down. TIP, continuously employed, would exert continuous restraint on wages and prices. This means that fiscal and monetary policies could be somewhat more expansionary once reasonable price stability has been restored. TIP would tend to reduce the "noninflationary rate of unemployment." Whatever the level of unemployment consistent with reasonable price stability (or a constant rate of inflation), the restraints imposed by TIP would tend to make it somewhat lower. Fuller utilization of resources and larger output would thus become possible. The payoff to a successful effort to wind down inflation would thus become very large over time.

The approach rests on the well-documented fact that prices follow wages. Numerous researchers have arrived at that conclusion. At the same time, of course, prices influence wages, although the relationship is less close. There are other cost factors that often are claimed to be responsible for inflation—high profits, high interest rates, monopolistic practices, high prices of food, of oil, and the depreciation of the dollar. While at times each of these does exert an effect, the main factor governing prices nevertheless is wages. With about 75 percent of national income representing compensation of labor, it could not be otherwise. All other elements, although at times possibly significant, are bound to be small by comparison. Therefore, restraint of wages means restraint of prices. Labor does not lose from wage restraint. Whatever it gives up in the form of higher wage increases, it can expect to get back in the form of lower price increases.

FORM OF TAX

A penalty in the form of an increase in the corporate income-tax rate, equal to some multiple of the excess of a wage increase over a guideline, is one of several options. It would have the advantage of relative difficulty of shifting the burden to consumers. It would have the disadvantage, on the other hand, of uneven impact as between capital-intensive and labor-intensive firms. Also, it would not be applicable to firms with losses, although such firms are perhaps less likely to grant excessive wage increases. The difficulty of applying an income-tax penalty to unincorporated business, nonprofit institutions, and governments, would not weigh heavily if TIP is applied only to a limited group of large corporations.

THE GUIDELINE

The setting of a guideline for nonexcessive wage increases is not as critical a decision within the TIP framework as is sometimes argued. The consequences of a relatively high guideline can be compensated by more severe penalties for overshooting. The likelihood that a relatively low guideline will be frequently overshot can be compensated by a more moderate penalty. The concern that a guideline will become the minimum rather than the maximum should be largely allayed by the favorable effects of a guideline on wage-setting in smaller firms, unincorporated businesses, and other employers that probably would not be covered. The guideline should embody the well-known principle that nationwide rather than industry or firm-wide productivity gains are the proper standard for wage increases. The guideline would be the sum of this long-term nationwide productivity trend and an amount, such as perhaps one-half of the going rate of inflation, that would allow for the fact that inflation must be wound down gradually rather than overnight. At the present time, this sum might be 5.5 percent, reflecting 2 percent for productivity and 3.5 percent for inflation. The guideline would have to be reset periodically, perhaps annually, at lower levels ideally, until wage increases equal productivity gains.

If prices follow wages, as can be expected, labor would not suffer from accepting a moderate guideline even if, at the original rate of inflation, this guideline seemed to leave no room for real wage increases. As inflation decelerates, real wage gains will be restored to their normal level, i.e., on average equal to average productivity gains.

COSTING THE WAGE INCREASES

To establish the tax consequences of overshooting the wage guideline, exact costing of a bargaining agreement including all types of fringes, is necessary. This requires measuring the total increase in compensation, including pensions, medical benefits, cost-of-living adjustments, improvement in working conditions, and others. It also becomes necessary to determine the increase per employee, or per hour worked, or per hour worked in each differently paid employee category. In all probability, the best approach would be an index of increases covering all employee categories, weighted by hours worked.

COVERAGE

Conceptually, TIP can be applied to all employers, including unincorporated business, nonprofit institutions, and governments. Penalties other than the corporate income tax would, of course, have to be employed for some of these. In practice, limiting applicability to the largest thousand or two thousand firms seems preferable from an administrative point of view. The largest one thousand firms alone cover about 26 percent of all nongovernmental payroll employees. These firms also are the pattern setters for wages so long as the economy is not overheating. The existence of a guideline should help uncovered employers restrain the demands confronting them.

RESTRAINING AN INCREASE IN PROFITS

In terms of nationwide averages, prices move with wages. Under some circumstances, the link may loosen. Some of these instances are not capable of being remedied. For instance, a decline in productivity, a rise in oil prices, and the consequences of a drop in the dollar, are "real" phenomena which affect the availability of goods. They are bound to affect real wages. This is not the case, however, of a loosening of the linkage of wages and prices that is reflected in a change in profit margins. In the unlikely event that deceleration of wages should fail to be followed by deceleration of prices without any of the above noted factors being present, profit margins would widen. The share of profits in GNP, in that event, would rise as a consequence of wage restraint.

This contingency could be guarded against by changing the corporate profits tax rate in such a way as to restore the after-tax share of profits to its previous level. Given the close historical link between wages and prices, this "corporate sector excess profits tax" probably would rarely, if ever, be triggered. But its existence would serve as a protection against an adverse shift in the distribution of income.

Towards a Reconstruction of Macroeconomics
WILLIAM FELLNER

Some rational expectations theorists claim that inflation can be controlled without inducing any significant excess unemployment. William Fellner does not take such an extreme position, but he does argue that a policy of tough demand restraint need not create a major recession. The key, he says, is credibility. If workers and firms really believed that inflation would never be accommodated by expanding the supply of money, then they would adjust their own wage- and price-setting. There would be a period of recession, but it would be short.

The anti-inflation strategy of the incoming Reagan administration is very much in sympathy with Fellner's views. It is intended that a deceleration of money growth will, in turn, decelerate nominal GNP growth and bring down inflation. Influence expectations, they argue, and wage and price increases will diminish without serious recession.

SKETCHING THE CONTENT OF THE CREDIBILITY HYPOTHESIS

MACROECONOMIC THEORY, which owes a huge debt to Keynes's work of 1936, has a deficiency from which it should be freed to be useful for more than an analysis of the policy requirements of a past period with very special characteristics—the 1930s. Macroeconomic theories describing the determination of output in single periods can be developed into theories of sustainable long-run growth paths, but only if it is clearly recognized that in the neighborhood of such a growth path there cannot occur significant and lasting deviations of actual movements of the price level from expected movements. The employment policy results and other economic and social consequences of major unexpected movements of the price level are exceedingly damaging, even if it takes a short while for the damage to be clearly observable. Keynes and Keynesians have paid little attention to what this implies for economic theory as well as for policy. Their monetarist critics, who have shown awareness of the problem, have not placed it in the center of the debate on the fundamentals of macroeconomics and have not worked it out or clarified it sufficiently. The fact that the world has recently suffered the consequences of significant inflationary disturbances has much to do with the influence of a macroeconomic theory that has not been adequately reconstructed.

If demand management policies will not succeed in conditioning market expectations to a reasonably predictable behavior of the price level—that is, if the public's expectations will not be formed according to credible price-level targets of the authorities—then we shall be heading for comprehensively controlled societies, administered with reliance on significantly enlarged police power. The issue has by now become a dramatic one, and it is wrong to talk around such a crucial issue by using evasive terminology on controls. Implied in the conditioning effort that is required for avoiding a transition into such a state is the need to recognize that the relation of the authorities to the public has an essential game-of-strategy aspect. The authorities must act on assumptions about the public's responses, and members of the public must act on their assumptions about the responses of other members of the public and on assumptions about the reactions of the authorities to these. This is why credibility is of utmost importance—a fact that has gradually become clearer to at least some policymakers but that has not been recognized as an essential element of a usable macroeconomic theory.

In their behavior in such a strategy situation, the authorities must be aware that no demand management policy can be successful in trying to validate an expectational system such as develops in markets without regard to the price-level objectives of the policymakers. To try to validate an internally inconsistent and unstable expectational system is a hopeless effort. Nor will the effort to condition the markets to sustainable price-level expectations be successful if the determination of the authorities lacks sufficient credibility, because in that case the effort will lead to protracted "stagflation" that, in turn, is apt to lead the authorities to give up. Lack of credibility is self-justifying.

This position involves rejecting recent policy procedures based on the idea that we should take for granted money-wage and price-setting practices that developed in view of the public's past price experience during an inflationary period, and that we should aim for the money GNP that corresponds to an acceptable real GNP and to an acceptable employment level, given such pricing behavior by the public. Except for a short-term payoff to policymakers which is provided by the temporary fooling effect of unanticipated inflation, such an "accommodating" policy has proved self-defeating. It is self-defeating because it renders the expectational system that is so accommodated unstable upward, thereby destabilizing the economy and giving rise subsequently to the high costs of suppressing an accelerating inflationary process. The so-called Phillips trade-off between inflation and unemployment is a purely short-run phenomenon that must not be allowed to serve as a basis for demand management policy.

Demand management through monetary and fiscal policy can prove successful only if it succeeds in conditioning the public's price-level expectations by creating an environment of appropriate restraint to which decision-makers in the markets must adjust to avoid heavy losses. To imply that markets will continue for long to be guided by the past price behavior observed during a period of lax policies, and will do so regardless of how firmly convinced the public is that there has been a change in policy, means building on assumptions that are not borne out by historical experience; these are the assumptions that provide excuses for postponing again and again the changeover from lax to sustainable policies. It is, of course, inevitable that the transition from a period in which the expectational system was allowed to "run wild" to a period of conditioned price-level expectations should involve uncomfortable adjustments; but the more the adjustments are postponed, the costlier they become. Only if this adjustment has not been postponed too long, can its discomfort be reduced by a policy of gradualism in restoring price stability.

Macro-equilibrium requires that the output decisions in the markets should be guided by price-level expectations to which the decision-makers have become conditioned by those in charge of demand management policies (monetary and fiscal policies) and it requires that the behavior of the price level to which expectations have become geared should be a sustainable behavior that can in fact be validated by the appropriate policies. These conditions require the restoration of a practically stable price level.

UNCONVINCING OBJECTIONS

I am unconvinced by two objections frequently encountered in discussions with my professional colleagues.

In the first place, it is often said there is little hope that wage and price behavior will adjust to demand policy objectives. This would suggest that the blocking of a reasonable policy effort would last long enough to make adoption of effective direct controls inevitable. But if this diagnosis should prove realistic, the reason would be the lack of consistency and credibility of the demand-management policy declaring its determination to persist in creating no more aggregate demand than is called for by price-level objectives and by the output movements compatible with these. It is essential to keep in mind that after all major inflationary interludes in economic history it is precisely the consistency and credibility of demand management efforts that made stabilization possible. It is equally essential to keep in mind that in the postwar United States until the second half of the 1960s, the dismal view that the markets could and would keep sabotaging a price-level oriented demand-management policy would have been regarded as pure phantasy.

Try to visualize an environment in which it would again be fully believed that upward deviations from the known price-level targets of the authorities would impose a heavy penalty on all employers and a significant deterioration in the job outlook for workers. Each individual employer and worker or workers' representative would then have to tell himself: If in my small area I behave inconsistently with the general policy objective and many other individuals do the same in their areas, then business conditions will deteriorate greatly, and I will then regret my behavior; my main goal should then have been to avoid commitments that would make me share the exceedingly poor sales or employment outlook of the rest of the community. Alternatively, if while behaving inconsistently with the general policy objectives, I keep the possibility in mind that the others will not behave in the same way, then, too, I will regret my behavior because it will have led to a restriction of my sales volume beyond any degree that might (in some cases) reflect my increased market power. This latter consideration derives its justification from the fact that shifts in market power would come through even if the price-level targets of the authorities were observed. To deny that the market environment can be shaped along these lines means to assert that the now relevant part of American economic history began in 1965. Yet, what changed demonstrably about 1965 was the behavior of the policymakers—with no consistent or sufficiently pronounced signs of disillusionment on their part until very recently—and market behavior changed in response to policy changes. This will become clear as we go along.

Needless to say, one must be prepared to encounter hurdles on the way back from an accelerating inflation to a sustainable behavior of the price level. Hurdles are encountered because at the start of the transition back to normalcy the determination of the authorities to persist may not yet be credible, but this is not the only reason. The other reason is that, at the beginning of the transition process past, commitments create for the sellers of goods and services a problem of trade-offs between (1) charging the costs developing from the past commitments and therefore losing sales volume and (2) not charging these costs in full for the sake of maintaining their sales volume at a more satisfactory level. Either choice is uncomfortable, and in some circumstances an economy on the way back to normalcy will indeed have to go through a period in which continued steep price increases are temporarily combined with a cyclical contraction of output. But if the policy effort is consistent, tomorrow's "past commitments" will cause the sellers smaller difficulties than today's and the transition period will not last long.

Some economists deny the validity of considerations such as these because they maintain that expectations depend on the lagged past behavior of variables without regard to the credibility of future policy action. But this view disregards the fact that the past behavior of all variables was also significantly influenced by expectations about the behavior of policymakers and thus by the credibility of the authorities' avowed objective. For some time now the credibility of the authorities' anti-inflationary assertions has been extremely low in the United States as in the rest of the world and this is reflected in the recent resistance of inflationary cost and price trends to occasional policy restraint. In 1973 and 1974, inflationary expectations and the corresponding pricing practices were further strengthened by the widely held belief that by additional demand creation the authorities would and should "accommodate" inevitable burdens arising from partly natural and partly man-made supply limitations. Thereby the authorities would and should ease a "pass-through" of specific price changes with inflationary consequences for the general price level—as if such monetary accommodation could improve the position of those sectors on which the burden was imposed by a binding constraint. The obstinacy of inflationary money-wage and price-setting practices had a great deal to do with the lack of obstinacy of the authorities in their pursuit of anti-inflationary objectives.

Another frequently heard objection to the position I take is that it overdramatizes the difference between a system that does and one that does not reply on direct wage and price controls. Between the comprehensive controls of the police state and abstention from the use of direct wage and price controls, it is argued, there is a large intermediate area. There does indeed exist a large intermediate area, but it is practically certain to prove an area of demoralization and low performance. It is possible to threaten with wage and price controls and not to adopt them them, or to adopt them in form but not to enforce them; it is possible to enforce them haphazardly on rare occasions more or less at random; last, but not least, it is possible to enforce them against those who are unpopular with the average voter or with the press, but not against others. But if demoralization of the society is to be avoided, one should surely be careful about when and how the penal system is used and against whom and how its use is threatened. The intermediate area between comprehensive wage and price controls and reliance on demand-management policies without direct controls is highly objectionable, even if not objectionable in precisely the same sense as a well-organized and thoroughly policed system of political and economic control. It is remarkable how many euphemisms—ranging from "jawboning" to "social consensus"—have cropped up in recent years for hiding the true character of that large intermediate area. We have here the latest version of George Orwell's "Newspeak" for describing spotty and haphazard interferences by which uncertainty can be raised to an exceedingly high level throughout the economy.

THE FUTURE OF MACROECONOMICS

It does seem clear that in some essential respects the macro-theoretical systems of the future will have to possess different properties from those in which our students have been trained. When we try to visualize future developments in the area of economic theory, it is advisable not to take into account the possibility that the United States (or any other major Western country) will for a long time be lost and demoralized in an area of haphazard and ineffectual interferences under partial government controls administered with a view to the next election. If that possibility should turn out to be the case, its intellectual counterpart is likely to be represented by bizarre and basically uninteresting variants of Keynesianism. The possibility cannot, of course, be entirely disregarded, but for our present purposes we may leave it aside.

A rigorously controlled economic and political system which is a genuine alternative, needs a demand-management theory whose role is much less central in the general analytical structure than has been the role of our demand theories in recent decades. In such a system demand management becomes a handmaiden of comprehensive administrative planning, probably with subsidies as well as rigorous price controls included in the planning operations, and thus with inflation and deflation much less a problem. In these systems, the difficulties to which the population is exposed develop mainly from a very high degree of dependence of the individual on those in charge politically. It is this power structure that, in the specific area of economic affairs, reflects itself in a low level of innovating activity and in a lack of adjustability of the product mix to the desires of the public.

If we are to succeed in avoiding unpalatable political and economic alternatives, we shall need a macro-theory assigning the proper role to the problems I have addressed. Expressed differently: Unless we develop our analysis in a framework recognizing the significance of these problems, we shall before long witness basic changes in our economic and political environment, and these changes will have become acceptable only because we shall by then have moved into an area of low performance and demoralization.

The Productivity Growth Slowdown

MARTIN NEIL BAILY

This book of readings has emphasized aggregate demand and the impact of government policy on demand. One of the most important of the economic difficulties of the past ten years, however, has been the slow growth of aggregate supply. Real GNP and output per worker-hour have grown very slowly. In this next selection, Martin Baily describes the problem and some of its possible causes.

INTRODUCTION

THE CONVENTIONAL MEASURE of productivity is called average labor productivity and is measured by total real output (i.e., inflation-adjusted) per hour of labor input. This measure of productivity in the private business sector of the United States economy grew at an average annual rate of 3.1 percent a year[1] from 1948–1968. This rate fell to 2.2 percent from 1968–73 and fell again to 0.78 percent from 1973–79. Adjusting for the impact of the business cycle, the level of average labor productivity in 1979 was 16.5 percent below where it would have been if the 1948–68 trend had continued unchanged.

Average labor productivity does not just tell you how productive are workers themselves. This measure of productivity will rise if each hour of work is combined with more capital or more advanced capital or if the work-place is more efficiently organized. But it does measure the total available output generated by the private sector, for a given level of work input, and is thus closely linked to the average level of living standards. In practice too, the marginal product of labor, and hence the average real wage per hour of work, has tended to rise at about the same pace as average labor productivity. Based upon twenty years of experience, wage and salary workers had come to expect real wage increases on average of about 3 percent a year. Since 1968, these gains have not been achieved. Dis-

1. All growth rates are computed using average changes in natural logarithms, this gives slightly different answers to those from conventional calculations.

appointment over real wage gains may well have pushed up wage demands in collective bargaining and worsened the inflation problem.

THE APPARENT ROLE OF CAPITAL

Economic thinking for at least a century has regarded the amount of capital combined with each hour of labor input as the principal determinant of average labor productivity. Thus it was natural that the blame for the slowing down of labor productivity growth would be fixed first on capital. The amount of capital per worker-hour, or the capital-labor ratio, grew at 3.6 percent a year from 1948–68. This growth rate fell to 2.9 percent a year from 1968–73 and to 1.3 percent a year from 1973–79. All figures refer to capital defined as equipment and structures in the private business sector of the economy. Thus, it is true that the United States economy was not adding to the amount of capital per worker at the same rate after 1968. And undoubtedly this slowing of capital accumulation contributed to the slowdown in labor productivity growth.

But the importance of capital to the slowdown story has been questioned on two main grounds. First, the decline in labor productivity growth seems more dramatic than is explicable by capital, even in the private business sector. Economic theory predicts that a decline in the rate of growth of the capital-labor ratio should cause a decline in labor productivity growth by an amount dependent on the share of profit in total income. If profits represent about 30 percent of income, then a decline in the growth rate of the capital-labor ratio from 3.6 percent to 1.3 percent will result in a decline in labor productivity growth by 0.3 (3.6–1.3) or roughly 0.7 percentage points. In fact, the decline in labor productivity growth has been much greater.

Second, if particular parts of the private business sector are considered separately, the role of capital seems to go the wrong way. For example, the manufacturing sector of the economy has experienced a slowdown in labor productivity growth that is less dramatic than that of the private business sector as a whole but is still quite pronounced. Yet in the manufacturing sector, the capital-labor ratio actually grew more rapidly from 1973–79 than in earlier periods!

Thus, many writers concluded that capital could play only a secondary role in the story of the slowdown and that the primary role must be a decline in the rate of total factor productivity growth or TFP growth. TFP is really just a catch-all. A calculation is made of how much output growth can be attributed to an increase in labor input and how much to an increase in capital input. Whatever is left is attributed to TFP growth. From 1948 to 1968, it was found that a lot of output growth was left unexplained by capital and labor inputs. This was attributed to TFP growth and considered to be the result of technical change. After 1968, there was less to attribute to TFP growth and after 1973 it seemed that TFP was actually falling. The economy was using its resources of capital and labor less effectively.

ALTERNATIVE EXPLANATIONS OF THE SLOWDOWN

What could cause the decrease in the effectiveness with which the factor inputs are used to produce output? Many, indeed too many, alternatives have been proposed.

1. Energy and other raw materials prices rose sharply in 1973. The conventional calculation of TFP is made without the explicit recognition that energy is a separate factor of production. If producers have changed their production methods in order to save energy on other materials, this could show up as decline in measured productivity.

2. If the baby boom introduced an influx of inexperienced workers, or if workers in general are taking more vacations or working less hard on the job, this would lower productivity. Some have argued that high taxes have discouraged work effort.

3. Government regulation of industry has increased. Firms are now required to show increased concern for the safety of their workers and to minimize their pollution of the environment. Whether or not these regulations are worthwhile or are applied efficiently is not an issue for this paper. Whatever one's views, it remains true that output as conventionally measured takes no account of the safety of workers or the pollution of the environment. Thus measured productivity has probably been adversely affected by the increase in regulation. This reminds you that productivity, while it is important, is not our only concern.

4. There may have been a decline in the opportunities for tech-

nological advancement. And there has been some decline in expenditures on research and development.

5. The high and variable rates of inflation and the periodic bouts of recession of the past ten years may have created a climate of uncertainty that discouraged investment and innovation and reduced efficiency.

It is not possible here to review and critique all the arguments for and against these alternative explanations for the slowdown. It has proven very hard to quantify their effects and really test their relative importance. Probably several of them have contributed to some degree.

THE ROLE OF CAPITAL ONCE AGAIN

It was stated earlier that the conclusion of conventional analysis is that capital does have some role in the story of the slowdown, but that it is not center stage. In one sense this conclusion is irrefutable. The United States economy did not suddenly and dramatically stop saving and investing in the 1970s. But in my own research I have suggested that a correct understanding of the slowdown involves capital in a very central and important way.

TFP was described as a measure of the effectiveness with which the factors of capital and labor are used to produce output. My argument is that TFP has declined principally because of a decline in "capital effectiveness." The standard analyses of the importance of capital are based on an estimate of the *stock* of capital in the economy. This estimate is based, in turn, on the past history of investment, i.e., on how many capital goods have been accumulated. An assumption is made about how long capital goods last before being scrapped. But the crucial question for productivity is not the stock of capital but the effective flow of capital services that is actually combined with labor-hours to produce output. And it is not at all hard for substantial changes to take place in the flow of services for some given estimated stock of capital. A plant can operate three shifts seven days a week. It can operate one shift for five days. It can be on short-time or closed temporarily. It could be scrapped because of obsolescence even though it had not worn out. Obsolescence is the key word. There has been a decline in the effective capital input, I argue, not because of a collapse in investment, but because capital in place has become obsolete.

Why has the problem of obsolescence become so severe in the past ten or fifteen years? Two of the most important answers have already been given. The rise in energy and raw materials prices and the increase in regulation have had major effects on the capital stock. Old energy-using capital has been modified to save energy or has been scrapped or used less intensively. An additional cause of obsolescence is that the nature of the products produced has been changed. In part this too is due to energy and regulation. The auto industry has had to make huge new investments and scrap large chunks of old capital in order to produce the smaller but safer cars demanded by government and the market. Foreign trade has also been important. The United States now imports *and* exports much more than was true fifteen years ago. Exports of aircraft and soybeans now pay for imports of steel, oil, autos, and television sets. But uneconomic steel plants cannot be used to produce aircraft. The big expansion of trade has brought benefits but it has also imposed adjustment costs on the economy.

The clearest signal of a decrease in capital effectiveness comes from financial markets. The market value of all corporate stocks and bonds can be added up and compared to the estimated replacement cost of the capital owned by corporations. In 1965, the market valued the corporate capital stock at $1.14 for every dollar of replacement cost. By 1978, this had fallen to $0.58 for every dollar. There may be several reasons for this, but it seems very likely that one important reason is that the capital stock in 1978 was regarded as obsolete.

CONCLUSION

As in other areas, economists disagree about the causes of the slowdown in productivity growth. My own view of the importance of capital obsolescence is regarded as speculative by others. But nevertheless there is fairly broad agreement among economists that whatever the cause of the problem, measures should be taken to stimulate investment as part of the solution. Tax incentives are the obvious way to do this. If I am right and capital obsolescence is important, then the case for investment stimulus is even stronger.

A Guide to Supply-Side Economics
Business Week

Tight monetary restraint is an orthodox conservative prescription to fight inflation. But the Reagan administration has also embraced the much more controversial new approach called supply-side economics. Supply-siders argue that high taxes and high levels of government spending have caused tremendous distortions in the economy. These in turn have caused or exacerbated the problems of inflation and low productivity growth. Cuts in taxes even without cuts in expenditure, they argue, will increase supply more than they increase demand and will therefore raise productivity and reduce inflation.

One supply sider is Arthur Laffer, author of the Laffer curve. Laffer argues correctly that tax revenue is zero when tax rates are zero, but is also zero when tax rates are 100 percent (because none will work or invest). Thus, tax revenue rises for a while as tax rates are increased, but then reaches a maximum and starts to decline as rates are raised further. This is because work and investment are discouraged, and hence income is reduced by so much at very high tax rates that tax revenues falls when tax rates are increased. Laffer's controversial assertion is that in the current United States economy rates are so high that we are actually beyond the peak of the tax-revenue or Laffer curve. He suggests that a cut in tax rates would move the economy towards the peak and hence raise tax revenue.

Keynesians have long admitted the possibility that a tax cut enacted when an economy was in deep recession could possibly stimulate demand enough to raise income and output enough that tax revenue would actually increase. But Laffer is proposing an alternative scenario that depends upon the incentive to work and could be applied in a full-employment economy.

IN AN ASTONISHINGLY few years, supply-side economics has captured the public imagination, eliciting nods of approval from politicians of both parties and acknowledgement from economists of almost every theoretical stripe. This phenomenon has been sparked by the obvious failure of the traditional Keynesian policies of demand management to extricate the economy from chronic double-digit rates of inflation, lagging productivity, and sluggish real growth.

But while supply-side economics has turned into a buzzword, it has come to mean different things to different people. To most econ-omists—including such a long-standing Keynesian as 1980 Nobel laureate Lawrence R. Klein of the University of Pennsylvania as well as conservative Martin S. Feldstein of the National Bureau of Economic Research—it means shifting resources from consumption to investment. The primary way to do that is to tilt tax cuts away from stimulating consumption toward stimulating investment.

The ideas underlying President-elect Ronald Reagan's economic program, however, go far beyond this concept. Reagan's ideas embrace the theories associated with economist Arthur Laffer of the University of Southern California. In Laffer's view, tax rates have grown so high that they have weakened the incentives to work, save, and invest, with the result that both economic activity and govern-ment tax revenues have suffered. Laffer thus argues that personal tax cuts such as those in the Kemp-Roth bill—30 percent spread over three years—will spur growth without being inflationary because they would swiftly produce higher tax revenues and increased savings to offset the initial drop in the government's tax take.

ADAM SMITH'S HEIRS

This idea is hardly new. Back in the eighteenth century, Adam Smith warned that "high taxes, sometimes diminishing the con-sumption of the taxed commodities and sometimes by encouraging smuggling, afford a smaller revenue to government than what might be drawn from more moderate taxes." And in the late 1940s the Australian econometrician Colin Clark said a tax burden in excess of 25 percent could discourage savings and work.

Such ideas, however, were overshadowed in the postwar period by the apparent success of Keynesian demand management. It is only recently that they have been resurrected and elaborated by a loose triumvirate consisting of Laffer, Paul Craig Roberts of George-town University, and Washington (D.C.) economic consultant Nor-man Ture, drawing on the supply-side insights of Columbia University economist Robert Mundell. These three have developed the foundation of a more elaborate theory that harks back to classical economics. While many economists find it hard to swallow the sup-ply-side theories entirely, the trio's policy prescriptions have attracted a small but growing following at such conservative think tanks as San Francisco's Institute for Contemporary Studies and the Hoover Institution at Stanford University.

The prescriptions are:

• Large and sustained cuts in personal tax rates and business taxes to induce increased work effort and capital investment.

• Relatively restrained monetary management, with the aim of bringing monetary growth in line with the long-run growth potential of the economy. This may require moving to some form of a gold standard.

• An end to fiscal and monetary fine-tuning and greater reliance on the internal dynamics of a free-market economy.

• A slowing of the growth of government spending, to halt the continuing rise in the nation's tax burden relative to gross national product and also to free financial resources for private investment.

The basis of the pure supply-side approach is a rejection of Keynesian demand management and a resurrection of Say's Law of Markets, the famous notion of the classical eighteenth-century French economist Jean Baptiste Say that "supply creates its own demand." This theory holds that there can never be a serious and continuing shortage of purchasing power in an economy because production automatically returns to producers the wherewithal to buy the goods that are produced. If goods are left unsold, the classical economists argued, prices would fall to the level where all the items would eventually be sold. Moreover, the presence of unsold goods means that consumption is falling and savings are rising. The increase in savings, in turn, will force interest rates down and push investment up. Thus, any slack in consumption is automatically offset by investment. In classical theory, therefore, the cyclical ups and downs of an economy are phases in the process of adjustment that always tends toward full employment. Serious economic crises can result only from governmental or private interferences with the free market.

As Keynes saw it, the Depression of the 1930s demonstrated the falseness of Say's law. Because prices did not fall very rapidly and savings failed to generate offsetting investment, Keynes argued that a shortage of purchasing power could grow progressively worse as

consumers cut back expenditures and business responded by curtailing production and investment. Indeed, the economy could settle at exceedingly depressed levels of economic activity and high
unemployment. Keynes's solution: use of government spending to
stimulate demand. In short, Keynes's reply to Say was that "demand
creates its own supply."

THE GOVERNMENT'S FAILURE

The classical supply-siders are convinced that Keynes was wrong.
They argue that it was not the inherent instability of the economy
that caused the Depression but rather, as Ture explains, "an ill-
conceived series of government actions both precipitated the downturn and impeded the recovery: the tariff wars of the 1930s, a series
of punitive tax hikes, a huge drop in the money supply, and antisup-
ply measures such as the deliberate destruction of agricultural products."

Say's law, says Laffer, is important not only because it encapsu-
lates classical theory but also because it asserts the primacy of supply as the only sustainable source of real demand—"the idea that
people produce in order to consume." Insists Ture: "Higher government spending or a tax cut cannot directly increase total demand
and output. If the government borrows money to finance its
increased spending or replace its lost revenues, it merely shifts the
use of disposable income from those who buy its bonds to those
benefiting from spending programs or tax cuts, but total spending
and income remain the same. Similarly, if it monetizes its added
debt by simply printing money, prices will rise but not total output."

While classical supply-siders claim that Keynesian policies have
been ineffectual in boosting aggregate real output—although Mundell disagrees with his three colleagues on this point—they argue
that the policies have been very effective in laying the groundwork
for the nation's twin problems of high inflation and slow growth.

Ideally, demand management calls for symmetrical offsetting policies at different stages of the business cycle: monetary ease, higher
spending, and tax cuts during a recession; tight money, spending
cuts, and tax increases during a boom. In practice, however, the
government—while quickly increasing spending, cutting taxes, and

easing money in a downturn—has failed to reverse course sufficiently on the upside.

Changes in tax rates lie at the heart of the supply-side economics," says Roberts, "is to regard tax-rate changes as relative price
changes affecting the supply and form of labor, savings, investment,
and visible economic activity. Until recently, this aspect of fiscal
policy was totally ignored by macroeconomic models."

WHAT TAX CUTS MEAN

Roberts and his supply-side colleagues argue that cutting marginal tax rates—that is, the additional tax a person pays, often as
high as 70 percent on unearned income, when income increases—
will have a number of positive effects on the economy. They claim
it will boost net wages and encourage work through such means as
increased overtime, less absenteeism, more part-time work, later
retirement, and shorter periods of unemployment. It will also leave
more money to be spent and—more critically—to be saved, they
say, and the availability of more savings and the incentive of higher
returns will encourage investment. "We think these effects are pervasive," says Laffer.

Mundell further argues that rising taxes have had so large an inflationary impact on the cost of many goods and services that they have
led many people to forgo purchases and perform services themselves that could be more efficiently handled by others. "This hurts
productivity and reduces the level of economic activity," he says.

Tax avoidance itself has become a thriving industry, misallocating
vast amounts of capital and effort into unproductive tax shelters and
"subterranean" activities. According to some estimates, under-
ground economic activity makes as much as 20 percent of true gross
national product. "Such activity," says Laffer, "not only reduces
investment but, by failing to shoulder its share of the tax burden,
results in higher taxes and lower incentives for the visible economy."

GOLD STANDARD

Can tax cuts turn the economy around and rescue it from the
quagmire of stagflation? The supply-siders are convinced it can, and
they point to the 1964 Kennedy tax cut as a prime example of the

successful application of their fiscal therapy. "The Kennedy tax cut worked," says Roberts, "but not for the reasons that the Keynesians who devised it thought. Marginal tax rates were cut across the board from 91 percent to 70 percent at the top and 20 percent to 14 percent at the bottom, and business taxes were also cut. The total package came to $12 billion in 1964 dollars. Yet the economy took off without a significant stepup in inflation."

To critics who point out that inflation was quiescent then and is raging at double-digit levels now, the supply-siders reply that unwavering monetary restraint is an essential part of their strategy. Indeed, to enforce discipline on the monetary authorities, they advocate moving toward reestablishment of a gold standard. Says Mundell: "Monetary restraint is difficult to maintain in a world of shifting exchange rates, huge international flows of stateless money, and continual disagreement about what constitutes money itself." A gold standard, the supply-siders say, would remove discretion from monetary authorities, shield them from political pressure, and establish new credibility in the markets regarding monetary policy—a development that would lead to lower inflationary expectations and interest rates.

Most economists, however—from liberal-leaning Nobel Laureate Paul Samuelson to arch-conservative Nobelist Friedrich von Hayek—remain highly skeptical. While acknowledging that the incentive effects of tax policy have received too little attention in the past, they believe that the impact of such policies is being grossly exaggerated by the supply-siders. More important, they see little evidence that large tax cuts combined with monetary restraint can produce a rapid increase in real output and productivity. Rather, they see big tax cuts as a risky program that could lead to still higher interest rates, accelerate measured inflation, abort capital spending, and ultimately put irresistible pressure on the Fed to monetize the exploding federal deficit.

Still, there is no denying that the Keynesian prescriptions of the past are inapplicable to the present. And the idea of a virtually painless therapy that would simultaneously put more money in everyone's pockets, vanquish inflation, and accelerate real growth is a compelling political vision. Given the degree of public frustration over the economy and the president-elect's own supply-side predilections, the theory may well receive a testing.

Some Supply-Side Propositions

HERBERT STEIN

Many conservative economists disagree with the supply-siders. As conservatives they applaud the desire to cut the size of government, but they think it vital to control aggregate demand. Cuts in tax rates without corresponding expenditure cuts will on balance be inflationary. Many economists of differing viewpoints also question the wisdom of cuts in personal taxes when they see a need to stimulate business capital formation.

Herbert Stein is a conservative economist. He was chairman of the Council of Economic Advisers under Presidents Nixon and Ford. In the final selection he roundly criticizes the supply-siders.

THERE IS A rising tide of literature and talk about supply-side economics. For the benefit of noneconomists who may be wondering what this is all about, I will put down here my view of what are and are not "supply-side" propositions and what the current state of the evidence is.

The following are *not*, in my opinion, "supply-side" propositions. Although they all have to do with supply, they were common currency long before the new school of thought emerged, about five years ago.

1. "Supply" is an important element in economic analysis. The first parrot who got a Ph.D. in economics for learning to say "supply and demand" knew that.

2. Increasing the supply of total output is important for individual welfare and national strength. That is what "The Wealth of Nations" (1776) is about.

3. The supply of output depends on the supply of resources, or inputs. The early economist who first said "land, labor and capital" knew that.

4. The supply of resources, and therefore total output, is affected by public policy. For example, economists 150 years ago argued against budget deficits on the ground that they diverted saving from productive investment. Moreover, the possibility of affecting output by policy remained an active element in public discussion. Thus, in

the 1950s there was an intense public debate about economic growth, with presidential candidates competing to see who could offer the largest growth target. This was a debate about ways to increase total inputs.

TAXES AND TAX REDUCTIONS

5. The supply of resources will be influenced by the tax system. I remember learning about this in my high-school course in economics, which goes back almost 50 years.

6. A tax reduction will make the national income higher than it would otherwise have been, and the revenue loss from the tax reduction will therefore be less than if the national income had not been induced to rise. This was one of the pillars of Andrew Mellon economics.

7. A tax reduction will raise the national income by more than the amount of tax reduction. This was the essence of "trickle-down" theory as actively espoused by the Republican Congress in 1948 and 1954. If a tax cut did not increase the national income by more than the tax cut, there would be nothing to trickle down from the immediate beneficiaries of the tax cut to the rest of the population. Whether this proposition was correct or not is unproved, but it is not a new idea.

8. A tax-rate reduction will increase the total revenue. At this point we come to an idea that looks like the new supply-side economics and we must make a fine but important distinction. The idea that a tax-rate reduction might increase the revenue has been a standard proposition in economics for many years—possibly 40—but it has heretofore been derived from "demand-side" or Keynesian reasoning. The argument has been that a cut of tax rates leaves more money in people's hands, as a result of which they spend more, and the total increase in spending exceeds the initial tax reduction, because the increased spending of one person raises the income of another person and induces him to spend more, and so on. Moreover, the increased demand thus created induces businesses to invest more. If these additional expenditures and investments are large enough, they will raise the national income enough to yield an increased amount of revenue, even with reduced tax rates.

In a primitive form this was the "pump-priming" argument of the

1930s. In slightly more sophisticated form it became a key item in the New Economics of the 1960s.

A basic assumption of this line of argument is that there is a large quantity of unutilized resources available to be brought into production without any increase in real wage rate or in the return to capital. This makes it possible for the increase of demand to be translated into an increase of real output and not simply to blow off in higher prices.

Valid or not, this proposition is old and surely not part of supply-side economics.

We may now turn from what, in my opinion, are not "supply-side" propositions to some that I believe do fit that category.

9. A tax reduction, not accompanied by a reduction of government expenditures, will raise the total revenue, and will do so by operating on the supply side of the economy. We visualize a state of affairs in which the total output is limited by the supply of resources—i.e., there are no unemployed resources—but there are more resources that would be supplied if the real rate of return to them was greater. A cut of tax rates will increase the after-tax return to productive resources, causing more of them to be supplied. That will increase the national income and the tax base. This increase in the tax base will yield more revenue at the reduced tax rate.

The basic point to note about this proposition is that it is not a proposition about ideology or even about economic theory but is a proposition about magnitudes. Theory does not even tell us whether a reduction of tax rates will increase or decrease the supply of labor or saving. But even if we bypass that argument, and stipulate that the effect is positive, the magnitude of the effect is all-important.

For example, suppose that we start with a tax system that takes 40 percent of the national income, leaving 60 percent as the after-tax return to the suppliers of productive resources. Then we cut the effective tax rate 10 percent, from 40 percent to 36 percent. That increases the after-tax return from 60 percent to 64 percent, or by 6⅔ percent. If the revenue is not to be reduced, the national income must rise by 11.11 percent, so that the 36 percent tax rate will yield as much as the 40 percent formerly did. That means that a 6⅔ percent increase in the return to resources must yield an increase of 11.11 percent in output, or 1⅔ times as much.

Whether the quantitative relationships will be such that a cut of tax rates not accompanied by a cut of expenditures will increase the revenue is a question that we cannot answer with certainty. The answer surely depends on the kinds of taxes involved and on other circumstances. But one can be fairly confident that the relationships are not such that an across-the-board income tax rate cut will increase the revenues within any relevant period of time.

This form of the supply-side proposition is of critical importance for political reasons. That is, the tax-cutting prescription would be much less attractive if it were universally understood to be a recommendation for enlarged budget deficits or reduced government spending. Moreover, the proposition loses its claim to intellectual originality if it only says that taxes and spending should both be reduced, or that a tax cut will reduce the revenue "less than some people think."

10. Less political and ambitious supply-siders might be willing to settle for the proposition that a tax-rate cut, not accompanied by an expenditure cut, will nonetheless increase real output, even if it also reduces total revenue.

But even this more modest proposition is not axiomatically true and depends on magnitudes whose size we don't know very well. Again, granting that a tax-rate cut would increase incentives to work and save, we must also recognize the effect of the tax cut in people's hands. If their increased demand for consumption exceeds their increased output, and government spending is not reduced, there must be less investment.

This point was made by Michael Evans, whose econometric studies are frequently cited as support for supply-side propositions: "To the extent that the increase in private sector saving generated by tax cuts is offset by a decrease in public sector saving, additional funds will not be available for investment." And if the increase in private sector saving is less than the decrease in public sector saving (the increase in the budget deficit resulting from the tax cut) private investment will be crowded out and there is no reason for counting on an increase in the long-run growth rate.

The conditions required for a tax cut to lead to some increase of output are less demanding than those required to get an increase in output sufficient to raise the revenue. But the evidence for the existence of even these less onerous conditions is not strong.

EXCESS OF DEMAND

11. An extreme, and currently very popular, version of supply-side economics is that the way to tackle the inflation problem is from the supply-side, especially by cutting taxes. The argument is simply that inflation results from an excess of demand over supply, and there is no sense in correcting that by the painful method of restricting demand when it could be done by the pleasant way of raising supply. The answer is of course equally simple. What we can do on the supply side is not big enough to solve the problem. We have demand growing by about 12 percent a year and supply growing by about 2 percent a year, which yields 10 percent inflation. To increase the rate of growth of supply by 50 percent from 2 percent a year to 3 percent a year, which is a difficult task, would still leave an enormous inflation, especially if the increase of supply is accomplished by means like cutting taxes which at the same time increase demand.

What I have said here is not an argument for or against cutting taxes, or for or against any other policy. It surely is not meant to deny that cutting taxes and expenditures, or restructuring the tax system, can be beneficial in many respects. I am only making a plea for modesty in recognizing the difference between what one knows and what one doesn't know.

Despite the tone of much of the current argument, the propositions of supply-side economics are not matters of ideology or principle. They are matters of arithmetic. So far one must say that the arithmetic of any of the "newer" propositions is highly doubtful. Supply-side economics may yet prove to be the irritant which, like the grain of sand in the oyster shell, produces a pearl of new economic wisdom. But up to this point the pearl has not appeared.